THE POLITICS AND
IR COMPANION

THE POLITICS AND IR COMPANION

SECOND EDITION

ROBERT LEACH AND
SIMON LIGHTFOOT

 macmillan international HIGHER EDUCATION   palgrave

First published 2018 by
PALGRAVE

Palgrave in the UK is an imprint of Macmillan Publishers Limited, registered in England, company number 785998, of 4 Crinan Street, London, N1 9XW.

Palgrave® and Macmillan® are registered trademarks in the United States, the United Kingdom, Europe and other countries.

ISBN 978–1–137–57339–1 paperback

This book is printed on paper suitable for recycling and made from fully managed and sustained forest sources. Logging, pulping and manufacturing processes are expected to conform to the environmental regulations of the country of origin.

A catalogue record for this book is available from the British Library.

A catalog record for this book is available from the Library of Congress.

Printed and bound in Great Britain by Bell and Bain Ltd, Glasgow

BRIEF CONTENTS

CONTENTS

BOXES

PREFACE

The Politics and International Relations Companion is the second edition of *The Politics Companion*, first published in 2008. That book was the eventual end product of a persuasive pitch by Steven Kennedy of Palgrave Macmillan over dinner with Robert Leach, its eventual author. At the time there was some discussion on whether there should be a separate volume on international relations. This did not materialise, so Robert Leach included some coverage on international relations. Robert later suggested that if and when a second edition was deemed necessary, an additional co-author should be involved who could provide both a fuller treatment of international relations and globalisation, as well as more up-to-date coverage of developments in pedagogy and student study skills, as Robert had by this time retired from teaching. Steven Kennedy once more used his considerable powers of persuasion to sign up Simon Lightfoot of Leeds University at a UACES Conference in Cork. Following Steven's retirement after a hugely successful career in publishing, the book was nudged towards completion in the capable hands of Lloyd Langman. Simon particularly wishes to thank Lloyd for his support and encouragement during what was a challenging period of his life. Caroline Domingo went beyond the role of copy editor suggesting some excellent additions to the manuscript and helping to bring the book to life. Chloe Osborne, Elizabeth Holmes, Ms. Soujanya Ganesh, Project Manager, Mr. Bagavathyperumal Thillainayagam and his composition team also deserve thanks for turning the draft into the finished manuscript. Any errors remain the responsibility of the authors.

Many other debts are almost too obvious, such as those to many authors, ancient and modern. In particular, Jack Holland and Laura Considine improved the sections on International Relations with supportive yet critical comments on earlier drafts. The inspiration for elements of 'researching your essay' came from a brilliant resource created by Alex Beresford, and Simon is extremely grateful to Alex for allowing the use of them here. Terry Hathaway and Mette Wiggen also suggested useful material for the study skills sections. The study skills examples were tried out on students at Leeds, and Simon thanks them for comments and feedback. Simon would also like to thank Robert, who remained supportive and encouraging throughout.

Simon wishes to record that Sam and Ben have been with him at every stage of this book. His love and thanks go out to them both. Robert once more would like to thank his loyal and supportive wife, Judith.

INTRODUCTION TO THE SECOND EDITION

Those familiar with the first edition of this book, published in 2008, will notice several significant changes in this new edition, including an additional author, Simon Lightfoot, working with Robert Leach; a change in title, to include International Relations specifically; major changes in structure; and expanded and updated content.

Additional author

The whole academic study of politics and International Relations has become so extensive and increasingly specialised that it is almost impossible for a single author to have the breadth and depth of knowledge to cover the entire discipline. In addition, Robert Leach, who is now retired from teaching, felt he needed a younger collaborator, in touch with current pedagogic developments in the delivery of the subject and with some different specialised interests within the disciplines of politics and International Relations, to help take the book forward into the future. The major contributions of Simon Lightfoot from the University of Leeds to this new edition, particularly on study skills, international relations and globalisation, should be obvious to those acquainted with the original book.

Politics and International Relations

Although the first edition was simply titled *The Politics Companion*, it included some material on international relations, as indeed any introduction to politics arguably must do. Yet it was not given extensive coverage, partly reflecting the development of International Relations as a substantially distinct discipline for much of the 20th century. Steven Kennedy, who commissioned the first edition of this book, has since written on the growth of the subject since his own time as an International Relations student in the early 1970s:

> when it was a tiny subject taught (in almost all cases in small separate departments) in a number of universities you could count on your fingers. Today, by comparison it has become a dominant or central element in the curriculum of politics departments with introductory courses on global politics often the most popular with students and an increasing presence right through degree programmes. (Kennedy 2013)

We have, perhaps belatedly, acknowledged the importance of international relations to the study of politics in the title and also with expanded coverage in the text. One alternative might have been a separate volume on international relations. Yet, as International Relations already occupies such a crucial role in university politics departments, this might be a mistake. Moreover, it has become increasing difficult to separate the politics and government of states from issues surrounding international relations, international political economy, and globalisation. Thus, there remains a strong case for studying politics and international relations together.

Changes in structure

The original structure of the book in large part reflected design and organisational constraints associated with the whole series of *Palgrave Student Companions*, which cover a diverse range of subjects, including both traditional university disciplines and more vocational courses. While the recommended framework sometimes seemed inappropriate for the study of politics, it was substantially followed in the first edition. Yet this involved an artificial separation of 'Theories and Approaches to the Study of Politics' (old Part II) and 'Key Research and Debates' (old Part V). Moreover, two essentially reference sections on key terms (old Part III) and key thinkers (old Part IV) divided the book in the middle. Both authors of the second edition argued successfully for a substantially revised (and hopefully more logical) structure. The new book is split into five parts, most of which are further subdivided into sections (as in the first edition), but the material has been significantly reordered.

The new structure

Part I 'What is Politics and What is International Relations?' is by far the shortest, although not necessarily the easiest. It discusses key issues about the nature of politics and of international relations and the interaction between them. It explores several definitions of the subject, and the continuing tension between facts and values (or positive political science and normative political theory), but concludes that politics is inherently controversial, which is part of its appeal.

Part II, entitled 'The Study of Politics and International Relations' is divided into four sections. Section 1 examines the evolution of Western political practices and ideas from the ancient Greeks to the early 20th century. Section 2 focuses on modern behavioural political science, including its implications for traditional studies of political philosophy, government and public administration. Section 3 explores the study of International Relations as an almost autonomous discipline for much of the 20th century. Section 4 discusses the impact of globalisation and international political economy both on the politics and government of states and on international relations.

Part III focuses on studying politics and international relations. Section 1 explores what students should expect from their course and the variety of programmes on offer. Section 2 provides practical advice on study skills, making the most of lectures and seminars, producing written assignments and dissertations, giving oral presentations, and revising for examinations. Section 3 concentrates on methodology. Section 4, entitled 'Research-led employability', advises on how the skills developed from studying politics and international relations can be used for employment or further study.

Part IV explores key political terms and concepts. This is a key reference source for the definition and further exploration of many of the concepts that have been highlighted in bold earlier in the text. Many of these concepts are 'essentially contested', their interpretation reflecting competing ideological perspectives, and it is important to appreciate alternative usages and shades of meaning.

Part V provides generally brief biographies, key works, and leading ideas of many of the political thinkers mentioned earlier (marked with an asterisk when first mentioned). Again, this is a key reference source. It is anticipated that students will often need to flick from earlier parts of the book to consult specific entries on both key terms and key thinkers.

Expanded and updated content

Together with the major changes outlined above in the authorship, title, and structure of the book, which have significant implications for content, every part and every section has been substantially revised and updated, to take account of more recent developments in politics and international relations and further advances in scholarship and research.

Referencing

Extensive cross-referencing is provided throughout the book. Key concepts that are defined in Part IV are highlighted in bold, and Part V provides generally brief biographies of some of the key thinkers mentioned earlier in the book (marked with an asterisk when first introduced). These include explanation of their main contribution to the study of politics, together with relevant details of their lives, work, and principal publications. There are also cross-references to other parts of the book (in brackets, with relevant page numbers) where particular theories or the ideas of key thinkers are discussed further.

References to other books and articles use the Harvard system, with brief reference to the author, date of publication, and page provided in the text and full details in the References [for an explanation of referencing systems see page 153]. We have sometimes departed slightly from the usual formula by proving the date of original publication in square brackets before the date of the edition used (and citing just this in the text where the date is significant). This is particularly important for older texts. For example, a reference only to the date of a modern translation of Rousseau or Tocqueville is unhelpful to students, who should be told when these works were actually written. Some less famous long-dead writers may even be mistaken by the unwary for modern authors.

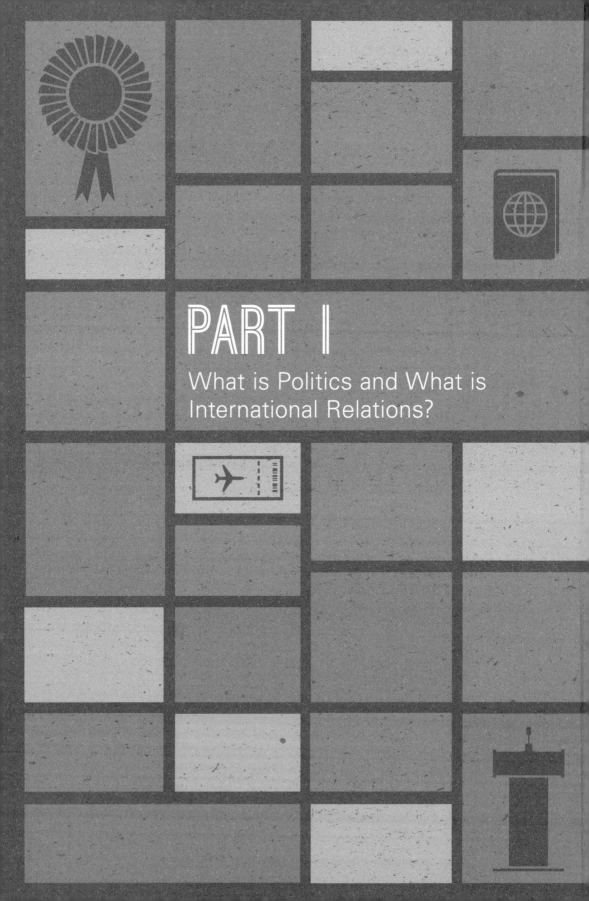

PART I

What is Politics and What is International Relations?

Contents

INTRODUCTION

Assuming that most readers of this book are either already committed to, or seriously considering, studying politics and/or international relations, it seems sensible to begin by trying to define and explore these terms. After all, those who are planning to spend part of their life in studying a subject need to know what it is they are studying. Yet introductory chapters exploring the nature of a subject or discipline are often among the most difficult (and one suspects, the least read). Defining politics turns out to be far from straightforward. There are brief, snappy one-liners that are eminently quotable but often raise more questions than they answer (see Box 1.1).

> **Box 1.1 What is politics?**
> 'Who gets what, when, how' (Harold Lasswell, American political scientist).
> 'The authoritative allocation of value' (David Easton, American political scientist).
> 'The art of the possible' (R. A. 'Rab' Butler, British Conservative politician).
> 'The personal is political' (Feminist slogan).

There are similar problems in defining international relations. Brown and Ainley (2009, 1) offer three. Firstly 'the *diplomatic-strategic* relations of *states*', secondly '*cross-border transactions* of all kinds, political, economic and social', and thirdly '*globalisation*...for example world communication, transport and financial systems, global business corporations and the putative emergence of a global society'.

Students commonly want to get to grips immediately with key issues, ideas, institutions, and processes that interest and concern them rather than abstruse debates over the nature of politics and international relations. In some respects such fundamental questions might be more easily answered at the end of a book or course than at the beginning. Certainly, they are questions to come back to and reconsider, again and again, in the light of further study. Yet they should not be ducked at the outset. None of us comes to study these subjects with a blank sheet. We all have preconceptions, notions of what politics and international relations are about, sometimes unconscious assumptions that we have not really explored. Each of us needs to confront these preconceptions, because they will shape how we approach the subject. We also need to question the assumptions of others about the nature of politics and international relations, because there are fundamentally conflicting views over what they are really about among some of the greatest thinkers who have analysed them. Different views on the nature of subjects inevitably influence what is studied and how it is studied.

POLITICS AND INTERNATIONAL RELATIONS: TWO SUBJECTS OR ONE?

One fundamental question is: are we talking here about two subjects or one? There are many courses and university departments entitled 'Politics and International Relations'. However, there are also many other courses and departments simply described as 'Politics' or 'Political Science', which do not specifically mention 'International Relations' in their title. Nevertheless, most of these may include, as compulsory elements or major options, aspects of international relations. In addition, there are other courses and departments simply entitled 'International Relations', often coexisting with quite separate courses and/or departments, described as 'Politics', 'Political Science', or sometimes 'Government', which may cover international relations only cursorily or not all.

Indeed, for much of the twentieth century International Relations developed as a largely autonomous discipline. Very few academics were involved in research into both the domestic politics of states and international relations. Although both disciplines clearly dealt with aspects of power and conflict, and both focused on states from different perspectives, political scientists studied political institutions and processes *within* states, while international relations specialists were concerned principally with the interrelationships *between* states. Even so, as Brown and Ainley argue, 'the international and the domestic interact and cannot easily be separated.' Increasingly, as we shall see below, the politics of states and international relations are becoming more closely interdependent. Here we treat both, as distinctive, but necessarily related, aspects of politics. It is customary to refer to 'international relations' to mean the object of study (and actual relations between states/global actors) and 'International Relations' to mean the discipline. We apply this convention throughout the book to avoid confusion.

POLITICS AS GOVERNMENT, GOVERNING, OR GOVERNANCE

The *Shorter Oxford English Dictionary* simply defines politics as 'The science and art of government'. Certainly the institutions and personnel of government feature strongly in the treatment of politics in the media, as well as in virtually all politics textbooks. Yet what is **government**? In the media and in common speech 'the government' is generally identified with those national leaders who are currently in supreme charge of a country's domestic and foreign policy, such as the Chinese President, the German Chancellor, the UK Prime Minister, aided by other ministers, advisers and officials. This 'government of the day', as it is sometimes described, is transient and only part of a country's whole system of government or **constitution**, which includes not only the governing or '**executive**' role, but also law-making (or **legislation**) and adjudicating on the law, the function of the **judiciary**. Additionally, those who are formally responsible for government are aided by an army of officials who advise on and subsequently implement (or sometimes fail to implement) government policy and decisions.

Even so, only the relatively few have been directly involved in government throughout recorded history. This remains true even in modern representative democracies. Abraham Lincoln's celebrated definition of **democracy** as 'government of the people, by the people, for the people' is misleading. The most that may be claimed is that the people have influence over government, but they are not, in any realistic sense, part of government. Thus, if politics is identified purely and simply with government, it effectively excludes the vast majority of ordinary people. If politics is for the many as well as the few, it must involve the governed as well as the governors. Thus government is part of politics, not the whole of it.

In so far as government is generally regarded as beneficial, or at least a necessary evil, it is because of the framework of peace, law and order that it provides within a political community or state, (although anarchists argue that we would be better off without any kind of government). Indeed, while both individual state governments and international institutions (such as the United Nations Organisation) are key players in **international relations**, the latter are still widely characterised in terms of **anarchy**, because there is no effective world government to maintain global peace, law and order. Thus if politics is simply equated with government, it hardly includes international relations.

B. Guy Peters (in Leftwich 2004, 23) argues that 'the ultimate and defining purpose of politics is governing and making public policy.' This focus on *governing*, rather than simply government, is rather broader and more inclusive. It shifts the focus from the institutions and personnel directly involved in government to the *process* of governing and to *public policy*. Many more people and organisations may be involved in the process of governing than 'the government'. Political parties, a huge range of interest groups, the media, private sector firms, and voluntary organisations of all kinds, as well as public opinion, may influence the making and implementation of public policy.

Yet governing, like government, still implies control, doing something to someone else. The few govern; the rest are governed. The fashionable term **governance** reduces this implication. Governance blurs the distinction between governors and governed and suggests we are all part of the process of governance. To quote a celebrated American book, 'Governance is the process by which we collectively solve our problems and meet our society's needs. Government is the instrument we use' (Osborne and Gaebler 1992, 24).

Within this broad process of governance the role of government itself is, arguably, changing. Modern government increasingly involves 'steering' rather than 'rowing', to employ the terminology of Osborne and Gaebler (1992, 25–48), or 'enabling' rather than 'providing'. Guy Peters (1997, 56–57) uses the term 'societal governance', while Rod Rhodes (1997, 46–60) even talks of 'governing without government'. An extreme example of the distinction is that Belgium, between the start of 2010 and the end of 2011, went 589 days without a government due to the complexity of the coalition negotiations following an election, yet the country kept functioning.

Politics is about the state

Another view is that politics is about the state. The state may be defined as a compulsory political and governmental unit that is sovereign over a particular territory. Much of the modern study of politics is clearly about the state, or states. It may sometimes focus on the government and politics of a specific state. It may involve a more systematic comparative approach, but this in practice normally consists of comparisons between states. The study of international relations may imply a broader approach but still focuses principally on the interaction of independent sovereign states, each using its power and resources to protect and promote its own interests. While 'supranational' government of various kinds (for example the United Nations, the European Union) may have growing influence, as well as nongovernmental organisations (NGOs) and, increasingly, transnational corporations (TNCs), many would argue that real power in international relations still rests largely with states.

Thus anyone studying politics will soon have to confront the concept of the state, which seems to involve much more than government but is difficult to define with any precision. According to some interpretations, the state appears rather sinister, something to fear (see Box 1.2). It is a compulsory association; you belong to it whether you want to or not. Moreover, both Max Weber* and Leon Trotsky* suggest that it ultimately rests on coercion or force. This matches some of our own experience and expectations. If we ignore the power of the state and flout its laws or refuse to pay its taxes, we can be punished by fines or imprisonment. Thus the state can deprive us of our property, our personal freedom, and even, in many countries, at many times, our lives. All this suggests that politics is inseparable from force and coercion (see for example Nicholson in Leftwich 2004, 41–52).

Box 1.2 The state

'The state is a human community that (successfully) claims the monopoly of the legitimate use of physical force within a given territory' (Max Weber, German sociologist).

'Every state is founded on force' (Leon Trotsky, Russian Communist revolutionary).

Yet while an element of compulsion and coercion is inseparable from the conception of the state, it is also simply a political community to which people belong and to which they often feel some sense of allegiance and identity (although we acknowledge that that statement in itself is controversial). Moreover, the state protects its members from external threats and internal disorder. It provides law and security to enable people to go about their own business peacefully and pursue their own lives. The framework of the state seems the precondition of economic growth and development, as illustrated in the emergence of new states in East Asia. Modern states, moreover, can provide other services that we want and need – such as education, health care, social security, culture and civilisation. The modern state can be a 'welfare state'.

Different conceptions of the state – the coercive and potentially oppressive state and the welfare state – underlie different views of the state and politics. Because the state has coercive power and may oppress its citizens, many have sought to limit its scope. Thus some liberals and conservatives would distinguish between the state and **civil society**, between a public sphere that is a legitimate field for state intervention and politics and a purely private sphere of home, family, and voluntary activities from which the state and politics should be firmly excluded. From some perspectives, the less the state does, the better. Economic liberals would distinguish between the state and the market and seek to exclude the state from most or all economic activity. This is a perspective that has been at the heart of the recent privatisation of many activities once run by the state.

Yet many conservatives have also emphasised the importance of maintaining the authority of the state to preserve order and protect property. Some **liberals** (sometimes called social liberals) and even some **conservatives** have sought to use the power of the state to provide opportunities to help individuals to realise their potential. Many **socialists** in the past sought to give the state much more power, to establish a political system in which the state owned the means of production and effectively controlled the economy. **Fascism** was associated with a **totalitarian** theory of the state, according to which the state was all-embracing and excluded from no sphere of activity.

All these perspectives stress the real or potential power of the state for good or evil. Yet states may not always appear so very powerful in practice. A focus on the formal institutions and processes of the state neglects the contribution to the political process of non-state organisations and interests, such as financial institutions, major manufacturers and retailers, trades unions, and other pressure groups. Some argue that it is such powerful interests that really determine key issues rather than states and their governments. Moreover, even very large and apparently powerful states may appear impotent in the grip of global economic forces they cannot control. Indeed, today large transnational corporations (TNCs) may have more effective power than many states. By contrast, we are also now familiar with the concept of failed or failing states, no longer capable of preserving law and order within their boundaries. One implication is that those who wish to study politics should focus on power rather than states or their governments.

POWER

The notion that politics and international relations are essentially about **power** implicitly or explicitly underpins many approaches to the study of the subject. Those who argue politics is about power do not necessarily accept that power rests where constitutions or laws claim. Indeed, some argue that effective political power may rest outside government and the formal apparatus of the state altogether, with, for example, the army, powerful economic interests, media moguls, religious leaders, and, in the international sphere, transnational corporations (TNCs). In such circumstances government ministers and state officials may appear mere puppets of others who control the real strings of power.

Box 1.3 What is power?

'Political power grows out of the barrel of a gun' (Mao Zedong*, Chinese Communist leader).

Power is 'the production of intended effects' (Bertrand Russell, British philosopher, 1938).

A has power over B to the extent that A can 'get B to do something that B would not otherwise do.' Robert Dahl*, American political scientist, 1957, 201).

'A exercises power over B when A affects B in a manner contrary to B's interest' (Steven Lukes 1974, 37).

'International politics, like all politics, is a struggle for power' (Hans Morgenthau* 1948, 25).

However, those who argue that politics is about power often disagree over what political power is, who has it, and how far power is narrowly concentrated in the hands of the few or more widely dispersed. This is not an argument that can easily be resolved by appeal to the evidence, as the evidence is contentious, not least because there are considerable problems in defining power and even greater difficulties in measuring it.

Some would equate power simply with physical force or coercion. This view has already been touched upon in the discussion of the state (above) and appears to match aspects of reality. There are many examples both in the recent and more distant past of military leaders using the power of the armed forces to seize control of government (Finer [1962] 1988). The exercise of physical force seems only too obvious an aspect of modern politics around the world today, and not just within states. Military power has long been a major or decisive factor in the conduct of international relations. History shows a focus on 'Great Powers' as defined by military power and a quest for a 'balance of power'. When it was suggested that the pope might be involved in peace negotiations at the end of the Second World War, Stalin* cynically asked 'How many divisions does the pope have?' The birth of the nuclear age, whereby nuclear powers cancel each other out in defence terms, and the debates around globalisation meant that other types of state power became important within international relations. Thus we see the discussion around hard and soft power.

Thus, political power can not rest for long entirely on physical force alone. Those who seize power violently commonly seek to maintain it by other means. It is noteworthy that the three most notorious 20th-century dictators, Hitler, Mussolini, and Stalin, owed neither their rise to power nor their exercise of power primarily on their control of the army and their readiness to use crude physical force, however ruthless they showed themselves to be. Instead their power rested, to a greater extent than is widely acknowledged, on the willing acceptance of their rule by many, and perhaps most, of those over whom it was exercised (although, of course, such compliance might significantly reflect government control of education and the media). The collapse of communism and the Arab Spring show that when the general population withdraw their consent for a regime, it can crumble very quickly.

Indeed, political power is more usually associated with other forms of influence than physical force. This has always been true, but it is particularly apparent in the modern world, where some form of **representative democracy** has become the most common form of government. Democracy implies that ultimately power rests with the people or at least with the majority of the people. Alexis de Tocqueville*, the generally sympathetic French observer of early 19th-century American democracy, concluded that the majority was 'all-powerful', to the extent that he was worried about the 'tyranny of the majority' (Tocqueville, [1835, 1840] tr. Bevan 2003, 287–322). Others since have talked (respectfully or critically) of the power of public opinion. Indeed, it is not difficult to find instances of governments altering course in response to a strong expression of public opinion. Yet others may point to the way public opinion may be influenced or manipulated, perhaps by government itself, perhaps by the media, perhaps by an influential minority. Indeed, the most subtle and sinister aspect of power, some would argue, is the power to shape how people think.

It is has been plausibly argued, particularly by Marx* and his followers, that the ruling ideas in every age are the ideas of the ruling class. For Marx, the wealthy few, who control the 'means of production', are the real ruling class. Political power reflects economic power. Thus under **capitalism** it is the **bourgeoisie**, who own and control capital, who really control the state and the international economy, whether they occupy a formal role in government or (more often) do not. It would be conceded, even by those American political scientists such as Dahl and Lindblom* (1953) who argue that political power is fairly widely dispersed, that business interests nevertheless wield an influence over government disproportionate to their numbers. However, although few would deny the importance of business power in modern politics, the extent of its influence and control over government is more contestable. Ultimately, the Marxist hypothesis can neither be proved nor disproved.

Others have different perspectives on who really exercises power (see Box 1.4). It has often appeared throughout history and across the modern world, that there is 'a power behind the throne'. Thus it may seem in some societies, both in the past and today, that some religious leaders have more extensive influence and real power than secular rulers and can tell them what they can or cannot do. It may be state officials, who are in theory mere functionaries only implementing government policy, who really exercise power behind the scenes. It may be simply men, who, from a radical feminist perspective, exercise power over women everywhere. It may be the rich who effectively 'call the shots', buying influence around the world without needing to exercise formal positions of power.

Box 1.4 Who has power? Various perspectives

Bureaucracy Rule of officials
Democracy Rule of the people
Oligarchy Rule of the few
Patriarchy Rule of men (literally, rule of the father)
Plutocracy Rule of the rich
Theocracy Literally rule of God; in practice rule of priests or religious leaders

Besides this question of who has power there is also the question, 'What is power for?' Is power simply an end in itself, or a means to an end? Admittedly, power itself seems to attract some people, and it has even been claimed that power is an aphrodisiac. Yet power is a capacity to do something, or 'produce intended effects' in Bertrand Russell's words (Box 1.3). Holding power is not necessarily the same as exercising it. Perhaps power should be judged in terms of outcomes. The failure to do much with power may reflect a cautious conservative political outlook or it may reflect a failure of will. However, it may also or alternatively have something to do with the constraints on power. Those who acquire prestigious political roles on the national or international stage often discover that they have less power to make real change than they expected.

Ultimately the long debate among political scientists over the nature and distribution of political power has been inconclusive. Some of the simpler definitions put forward by Dahl and others have been shown to be inadequate. However, broader and more subtle interpretations of power, including the power to set the political agenda or shape people's preferences, make it even more difficult to study its exercise. So, however power is defined, it is almost impossible to measure its distribution in the same way as, for example, the distribution of the population (by age, sex, occupation etc.) or the distribution of income and wealth. Thus Lincoln Allison (in McLean and McMillan 2009, 434) pessimistically concludes that 'the concept of power has not filled the central role in the study of politics which many pioneers hoped it would'.

CONFLICT, AND THE RESOLUTION OF CONFLICT

Some conceptions of politics and international relations make them sound rather too cosy and consensual, downplaying the inevitability of political conflict. Any decisions about who gets what, how, and when has the potential to bring different groups and organisations into conflict. In the making of public policy some win and others lose. The notion of a benign government 'steering' or 'enabling' rather ignores the point that governments often have to choose between unpalatable alternatives and take unpopular decisions. Government may also sometimes have to force its decisions on those who are strongly opposed. This is true not only of key domestic issues but of foreign policy, especially issues of peace and war, and the whole field of international relations, including defence policies and alliances with other states.

Indeed, in the conduct of international relations, while it is possible to talk of 'international governance' and the ways in which 'the international community' can work together to promote some agreed end, such as limiting climate change, or reducing global poverty, conflict has often appeared more evident than co-operation throughout much of recorded history.

A common perspective is that politics arises out of conflict. Indeed, much of the distaste that some people feel for politics seems to be related to the conflict it involves. It is sometimes imagined that much of this conflict is unnecessary, that it is artificially stimulated by politicians and political parties who feel bound to oppose whatever 'the other side' proposes or who appear to love conflict for the sake of it. Indeed, politics is often identified purely and simply with party politics and deplored for that reason. If only these partisan politicians could come together to form an all-party coalition to work for the interests of the whole country or if government could be put in the charge of some disinterested experts! Similarly, it is suggested that pressing global problems such as disarmament, third-world poverty, or climate change can be solved by international conferences of world leaders and experts. Behind such hopes there is an assumption that there is often a single 'right answer' to problems that men and women of good will, freed from partisan considerations, would discover.

Yet more commonly there is no such right answer but irreconcilable positions reflecting conflicting interests. If there were universal agreement on ends and means there would be no need for politics. Politics arises because humans disagree over issues where collective binding decisions on the whole political community are required. We have not just different but conflicting interests. States manifestly appear to have conflicting interests, which they pursue in their relations with other states.

For some, the essential conflict is between individual human beings. The English political thinker Thomas Hobbes* (1588–1679) graphically described the natural condition of humanity as a perpetual 'war of every man against every man', as they want the same things that they cannot all have, because of scarcity. This view of humanity as in ceaseless competition for scarce resources is the perspective of mainstream economics, from the classical economists such as Adam Smith* or David Ricardo down to modern neoliberal economists. Most economists assume that human beings are motivated by their own rational self-interest. It is competition between countless self-interested individual consumers and producers in the marketplace that it is the motor of economic activity. Indeed, modern **rational choice** economists (such as Buchanan*, Tullock*, Olson*, or Niskanen*) are particularly scornful and dismissive of the notion that humans can behave altruistically and prefer someone else's interest to their own. Thus they do not accept the protestations that politicians and public servants commonly make that they are serving the public or national interest. These economists make the (fairly common) assumption that politicians and bureaucrats are in the business of government for what they themselves can get out of it.

Yet humans also appear to be naturally sociable. They belong to families, tribes, gangs, faiths, and larger groups of all kinds. Thus the conflict may seem to be between not so much individuals but groups pursuing their own collective interests. Much of politics seems to involve conflict between many different groups each expressing (or 'articulating') their own rival views and wishes. The conflict can be deeply divisive, passionate, and sometimes violent. Within states there are often bitter conflicts over, for example, specific building developments (e.g. new roads or airports), nuclear power, abortion, animal rights, civil liberties, and war. Some of these reflect opposed economic interests, while others reflect conflicting values that may not easily reduce to individual self-interest. Moreover, the choice, when it is made, is not one from which individuals can easily opt out. A political ruling on, for example, whether or not to ban hunting, build a new airport, increase tax on alcohol, change speed limits on cars, or declare war involves a decision that is binding on the whole community. In such conflicts, some win and others lose. Where a group feels the quality of their lives is adversely affected by a political decision, or simply that it is morally wrong, the outcome is not easily accepted.

Some would argue that such specific conflicts mask more fundamental divisions within human society such as conflicts between social classes, or between different ethnic or religious communities, or between men and women.

It appears even more obvious that politics is about conflict when one considers not just politics within states, but between states. The hitherto dominant realist interpretation of **international relations** assumes states use their resources to pursue vigorously their own conflicting national interests in conditions of **anarchy**.

Other perspectives have assumed rather fearsome antagonisms that threaten the future of humanity. These include the ideological 'Cold War' between Soviet **communism** and Western **democracy** and **capitalism** (until its abrupt end in 1989) or between faiths, cultures, or 'civilisations' (the view of Samuel Huntington*), a contentious interpretation that some would say is illustrated by the continuing 'war on terror'.

POLITICS IS ABOUT CONFLICT AND CONSENSUS

Altogether the notion that politics is about conflict has plenty of evidence to support it. Yet if politics is only about conflict, the outlook for humanity is gloomy indeed. Some insist that politics is not just about conflict but about the reconciliation of conflict, the pursuit of compromise and **consensus** (or agreement). If politics is to succeed, it has to bring people together and not just reflect their conflicting interests.

The French political scientist Maurice Duverger* talks of the 'Janus face' of politics. (Janus was a Roman God with two faces, pointing in opposite directions.) Duverger argues that conflict and integration are two opposed but inseparable aspects of politics. He claims that 'politics involves a continual effort to eliminate physical violence.... Politics tends to replace fists, knives, clubs and rifles with other kinds of weapons', although, he sadly acknowledges that 'it is not always successful in doing so'. (Duverger, tr. Wagoner 1972, 221). This accords with the sense in which the words 'politics' and 'political' are commonly used. When people talk of a 'political solution' to a problem (for example, Northern Ireland or Syria) they mean a solution involving peaceful negotiation rather than violence and war. For Duverger, politics is about both conflict and the search for compromise and consensus.

This is often how politics seems to operate in democratic countries. Clearly, individual politicians and political parties represent conflicting interests. They do not, by and large, create political conflict but reflect real differences of interests and views in the wider community. In putting forward their own case and exposing the weaknesses of their opponents they are contributing to effective public debate and better evidence-based public policy. This is, or should be, many would argue, what the political process is all about (Crick [1962] 2000, and see also Crick in Leftwich 2004). Yet an engagement in debate almost presupposes a readiness to make concessions, to settle sometimes for half a loaf, echoing the aphorism of Conservative politician, Rab Butler that 'politics is the art of the possible' (see Box 1.1). On many issues politicians and parties must also be prepared to compromise, to accept an outcome that is, from their perspective, less than ideal, in order to secure some kind of agreement. Moreover, any political leader or party that hopes to win majority support cannot afford to articulate a single interest but must seek to represent and 'integrate' a range of interests, which means persuading others, including their own supporters, to understand different views and interests and make concessions. The same is true in international relations, when governments commonly seek to resolve conflict through negotiation and diplomacy rather than war. So politics is not just about conflict but also about resolving conflict.

Yet, while some object to the conflict involved in the political process, others criticise the search for compromise. Indeed compromise solutions are often denounced as a sell-out or betrayal, an abandonment of principle, a spineless appeasement of opponents. Thus the former British Prime Minister Margaret Thatcher boasted that she was a conviction politician who abhorred consensus: 'For me, consensus seems to be the process of abandoning all beliefs, principles, values and policies' (Thatcher speaking in 1981, quoted in Kavanagh 1990, 7), although Mrs Thatcher was sometimes a rather more pragmatic politician than her own rhetoric suggested. Perhaps the most celebrated instance of the dangers of the pursuit of compromise and consensus was the appeasement of the dictators in the 1930s, culminating in the Munich agreement with Hitler in 1938. A year later even the known horrors of war seemed preferable to further appeasement, which became a pejorative term.

POLITICS IS ABOUT CONVICTIONS, IDEAS, AND PRINCIPLES

Much of the writing on politics that has come down to us from the past has been unashamedly normative. In other words, it is concerned with how politics should be, rather than how it is. Political philosophers for two and a half thousand years have argued over how human beings should live together, over the best form of government, over the justification for private property and its distribution, over how far citizens should obey the state and what rights and freedoms they should enjoy. Indeed, many of these rights and freedoms are now proclaimed as international, unconstrained by state borders. These ideas have continued to inform political debate and influence political change down the ages and through to the present day.

Thus, the US Declaration of Independence (1776) proclaimed, 'We hold these truths to be self-evident, that all men are created equal, that they are endowed by their Creator with certain inalienable rights, that among these are life, liberty and the pursuit of happiness.' The French Declaration of the Rights of Man (1789) pronounced 'Men are born free and remain equal in rights.' These were bold, ambitious claims, and it is easy to point out how far reality fell short of the rhetoric. Yet there were substantially successful campaigns to apply some of these rights, to abolish the slave trade and the institution of slavery, to promote freedom of speech, to end religious and racial discrimination, to emancipate women, and much else. Many of these rights and freedoms have since been enshrined in state constitutions and in the United Nations Universal Declaration of Human Rights (1948) and the European Convention on Human Rights (1951). A commitment to international law and institutions, as well as to national self-determination, inspired the early liberal approach to international relations that emerged from the First World War and its immediate aftermath. There are also modern political creeds or ideologies, often linked with political parties, publicly committed to greater equality and social justice, or more freedom for the individual, or whatever. Thus, ideas, values, and principles seem central to much of modern political debate, yet they have been largely absent from this discussion over the nature of politics, so far at least.

There are reasons for the omission. As we have seen, at least one modern major theoretical approach to the study of politics assumes humans are motivated by rational self-interest and that any ideals they proclaim are just a form of protective colouring or simply self-delusion. Indeed there are abundant examples of political hypocrisy: politicians who extol the sanctity of marriage and family values while conducting extramarital affairs, or who accumulate wealth while preaching socialism, or who jet around the world promoting resource conservation. There are also sad reminders of how inspiring political ideals like freedom and equality can be perverted. As the French revolutionary Madame Roland mournfully observed as she passed the Statue of Liberty on the way to her own appointment with the guillotine in 1793, 'O Liberty! What crimes are committed in thy name' ('que de crimes on commet en ton nom'). One thinks of other political movements similarly inspired by high ideals that ended in tyranny, as portrayed in George Orwell's bitter satire on the 1917 Russian revolution, *Animal Farm* (1945), in which the animals' dream of equality ends in the cynical slogan, 'All animals are equal, but some are more equal than others.' Disillusion with the fruits of communism helped influence a wider rejection of political ideologies for the politics of **pragmatism** ('what matters is what works').

Yet it was not just because of the betrayal of such political ideals that traditional political philosophy and political ideologies fell from fashion. The emergence of logical positivism in the early 20th century revolutionised the study of philosophy and led to the rejection of 'metaphysics', under which title was included moral and political philosophy. This was among the influences on the development of a parallel revolution in the study of social sciences, including politics, which involved the rejection of **normative** political theory for the positive scientific analysis of political behaviour [see Part II, Section 2, below]. The **behavioural revolution** reached its climax in the 1950s, which also saw the announcement of the death of political philosophy (Laslett 1956) and, at the close of the decade, the end of ideology (D. Bell 1960).

Similarly, the early 20th-century liberal approach to international relations associated with US President Woodrow Wilson*, involving self-determination of peoples and the establishment of the League of Nations to peacefully resolve disputes, was undermined first by the determination of existing colonial states to protect their empires and later by the ruthless use of military force by dictators to secure territorial expansion. Thus liberal idealism was replaced by **realism**, and Morgenthau's ([1948] 1978) assumption that states pursue interests in terms of power.

It has since become clear that the obituaries on the study of political philosophy were premature. The study of political ideas is now very much alive. Even so, it remains marginalised in many accounts of the nature of politics, which continue to emphasise the political process over political aims and values. Yet politics without hopes, dreams, and values is ultimately a rather mean-spirited business. The growth of political apathy and alienation, particularly but not exclusively among the young, is often lamented, the reasons for it much discussed, and possible remedies put forward (Putnam 2000; Stoker 2017). Mainstream democratic politics faces growing apathy on one side and intolerant fanaticism on the other. It has to offer some ideals, inspiration, and hope that encourage people to engage with it.

Box 1.5 Normative political theory and positive political science

Normative political theory involves the prescription of norms of conduct and values and the study of what *ought to be* rather than what *is*.

Positive political science involves the 'positive' or 'objective' scientific analysis of political behaviour.

We are perhaps in danger of forgetting that politics can inspire as well as disappoint. There are those who have given their lives so that others can enjoy the rights and freedoms now largely taken for granted. They include Abraham Lincoln, who fought a war to abolish slavery and preserve democracy in the United States; Mahatma Gandhi*, whose inspired nonviolent campaigns of **civil disobedience** eventually secured the establishment of a free democratic India; and Martin Luther King*, the black American civil rights leaders who dreamed 'of a day when the sons of former slaves and of former slave owners will be able to sit down together at the table of brotherhood'. One might think also of the defiant speech of Nelson Mandela*, on trial for his life in the South Africa of apartheid in 1964: 'I have cherished the ideal of a democratic and free society in which all persons live together in harmony and with equal opportunities. It is an ideal which I hope to live for and achieve. But if needs be, it is an ideal for which I am prepared to die.' Unlike Lincoln, Gandhi, and King, who died in pursuit of their political ideals, Mandela survived, to become the first black president of the new post-apartheid South Africa.

There is, unhappily, abundant evidence that political ideals can be betrayed or sold short, and they can also be dogmatically and fanatically pursued. Yet ideals can inspire, even if they are often only imperfectly realised. Thus, although proclamations of human rights may sometimes be more honoured in their breach than their observance, they set a standard of conduct that has already materially influenced political behaviour for what many of us would consider the better. The same hopes continue to drive international efforts to secure peace between nations, alleviate poverty, especially in the developing world, and conserve the global environment.

SO WHAT IS POLITICS (AND WHAT IS INTERNATIONAL RELATIONS)?

'What is politics?' is the title of an excellent edited volume of essays in which a number of distinguished political scientists provide their own answers – and incidentally rubbish the views of some of their fellow contributors and their editor (Leftwich 2004). Their vehement disagreement may not inspire confidence. Some politics students may feel dismayed that so many leading experts cannot even agree on what their subject is about. The same is true of International Relations, which now covers far more than diplomacy, alliances, and wars.

Some of the answers discussed (both here and elsewhere) may seem more plausible than others, but none seems totally satisfactory. Some are perhaps more appealing than others, but that does not necessarily make them correct. There are, indeed, no incontrovertibly right answers. There are many key concepts in the study of politics and international relations that are 'essentially contested', including, as we have seen, the definitions of both 'politics' and 'international relations'. These essentially contested concepts reflect differing and competing interpretations of the world and human society. A student needs to understand these competing perspectives and different answers and weigh them against the available evidence. But on many key issues the evidence is inconclusive. Ultimately, you will have to make up your own mind on many aspects of the subject and on the very nature of politics and international relations. That should not be a source of anxiety. These subjects are inherently controversial. To many of us that is what makes them so fascinating.

GUIDE TO FURTHER READING

You may consult entries on 'politics' and 'international relations' in ordinary dictionaries and encyclopaedias, but more usefully in specialist politics dictionaries. Most standard politics textbooks provide an introduction to the question 'What is politics?' Particularly useful is the discussion provided in the first chapter of Andrew Heywood's *Politics* (2013). The same question is addressed more extensively by a range of authors in the excellent collection of essays edited by Adrian Leftwich (2004). You may also want to consult the widely recommended and provocative book by Bernard Crick, *In Defence of Politics* ([1962] 2000) as well as the same author's contribution to Leftwich (2004) above. (However, Crick's view of politics is a little idiosyncratic, effectively excluding the politics and government of authoritarian states). A stimulating and thoughtful introduction to the literature is Gerry Stoker's *Why Politics Matters* (2017). Specifically on international relations, there is an excellent introductory chapter in Chris Brown and Kirsten Ainley's *Understanding International Relations* (2009).

PART II

The Study of Politics and
International Relations

PART 2 SECTION 1

THE EVOLUTION OF THE STUDY AND PRACTICE OF POLITICS

Contents

INTRODUCTION

Politics has been studied and written about for at least two and a half thousand years. This section provides a very brief overview of the evolution of the theory and practice of politics in the West from the fifth century BCE to modern times. It discusses some of the major Western perspectives on politics of previous ages and their continuing importance for modern politics. Past political thinkers addressed big political questions of their day, many of which remain relevant. Where does power lie? What is the best form of government? What are the causes of political instability and change? How should scarce resources be distributed among individuals and communities? Why and how far should we obey the law? Why do states find it so difficult to live at peace with each other? How far can war ever be justified?

Past thinkers naturally focused on the key issues and problems of their time. Thus the ancient Greeks were familiar with a wide variety of political systems and frequent regime change, so it was natural that they should speculate on the best form of government and the causes of political stability and change. Similarly, from the late Roman Empire through to the end of the Middle Ages a key issue was the relationship between the temporal power of the state and the spiritual power of the church. Following the religious conflicts in Europe from the 16th century onwards, issues of political obligation and religious toleration loomed large, as they do again today.

Yet although people have speculated on politics for two and a half thousand years or more, it is only within the last century that it has become more systematically studied as a major discipline or social science in universities across the Western world. This is discussed in the following Section 2, which focuses on the important new theories and approaches that have transformed the modern study of politics, from the behavioural revolution onwards. Yet as new theories were exposed to criticism, older perspectives acquired a new lease of life, sometimes in fresh variants. Thus many of the theories and approaches discussed here in this section remain current and continue to shape the way politics is researched and studied today.

PAST AND PRESENT

Some writers from remote periods can seem startlingly modern, so much so that we can be in danger of forgetting the very different historical context in which they lived and worked. Today, most politics students read thinkers such as Plato*, Machiavelli*, or Rousseau* in modern translation. This of course makes them much easier to understand, but it can involve an element of distortion. There may be no exact modern language equivalent to the terms they use. Even apparently familiar concepts derived from ancient Greek or Latin, such as 'democracy', 'tyrant', 'republic', or 'dictator', which may bear some resemblance to the way in which they were originally employed by Greeks and Romans, also carry distinctive modern connotations.

There are similar problems even with less ancient texts written in our own language. Indeed, to an English-speaking student, 17th-century English texts by Hobbes* and Locke* can seem much more 'remote' and 'difficult' than modern English translations of Greek texts two thousand years older. One reason for this is that these 17th-century English writers use some expressions that are no longer common and employ other apparently more familiar terms, such as 'liberties' and 'rights', in distinctive ways. This is not to deny the continuing relevance of their ideas but simply to emphasise the importance of context. Some of the great political texts of the past may appear to have a timeless quality, and indeed are often written in abstract terms without reference to contemporary political institutions and events. Yet inevitably they were strongly influenced by contemporary political practice, even where this may not be immediately apparent. We need to understand the times the authors lived in, the specific historic situation in which they thought and wrote.

The various periods of history discussed here inevitably give a very abbreviated account of critical political developments. Some of the concerns of the past may seem to have little relevance to politics today. However, some ancient preoccupations that once appeared to belong to a vanished age (such as the conflict between religious and secular authority) have more recently been dramatically revived.

THE CONTRIBUTION OF GREECE AND ROME

(roughly from the 5th century BCE to the 5th century CE)

Why should anyone studying politics in the early 21st century be expected to pay serious attention to the political practices and ideas of some ancient Greeks and Romans who lived two to two and a half thousand years ago? One answer is that the Greeks virtually invented politics, both the term itself and its practice. Some of the key terms still employed in the study of politics today, particularly those used to describe systems of government, are derived from ancient Greek, while others are of Latin origin.

Yet however fascinating the politics of Greece and Rome, we would know little about them but for the quality of contemporary writing that has survived. It is the historian Thucydides* (460–404 BCE) who brings to vivid life the political debates within and between ancient Greek states and their very different systems of government, including the first known form of democracy in Athens of the 5th century BCE. Plato* (427–347 BCE) and Aristotle* (384–322 BCE) are widely regarded as two of the greatest philosophers and political theorists of all time. The speeches of Demosthenes are still studied as models of political oratory. While Roman political thought was rather less original, Roman political institutions and practices have been immensely influential. The term 'Republic' is derived from the Latin *Res Publica* ('public affairs' or 'the public sphere'). The republican ideal has had a long recurring impact on subsequent political history in the West. The letters and speeches of Cicero* (106–43 BCE) illuminate the politics of the last years of the Roman Republic, and we owe our knowledge of the late Republic and early Empire to a number of outstanding Roman historians. Roman law remains today the basis of the legal systems of much of continental Europe. Thus the ancient Roman world has an enduring legacy.

Athenian democracy

Whether or not the ancient Greeks invented politics, they certainly developed its systematic study. The ancient Greek world involved a virtual laboratory of different political systems. Although the Greeks shared a substantially common language and culture, and could on occasion sink their political differences to combine against a common enemy, they lived in a large number of small independent and often contending political communities, each with its own distinctive form of government. Some of these states involved government by a single ruler, a **monarchy** (rule of one) or tyranny (implying an illegitimate seizure of power). Others were ruled by a small minority, variously described as an **aristocracy** (literally, rule of the best), **oligarchy** (rule of the few), or plutocracy (rule of the rich).

Athens, followed by some other states, had developed a more broad-based system of government called **democracy**, meaning literally the rule of the people, although this did not in practice include all adult inhabitants but only full citizens (excluding women, slaves, and foreign residents). However, Athenian democracy, in marked contrast with modern **representative democracy**, did involve direct citizen participation in key decisions, including issues of taxation and spending, **justice**, defence, trade, diplomacy, and war.

The frequent wars between Greek states in the fifth and fourth centuries BCE arose not only from conflicts of interest but also from the states' contrasting political systems and values. Moreover, there were conflicting class interests within states, some of those living under tyrannies or oligarchies casting envious eyes in the direction of Athens, while a number of rich Athenians hankered after a system of government closer to that of Sparta, the great rival of Athens. Thus the long Peloponnesian War (431–404 BCE) between Athens and Sparta and their respective colonies and allies, described by the historian Thucydides, can be seen (like the recent Cold War between the West and Soviet communism) as an ideological struggle between rival political systems.

Some of the key participants were clearly conscious of this, as can be seen from the words Thucydides puts into the mouth of the Athenian leader Pericles* (c. 495–429 BCE) in a funeral oration near the beginning of the war. Although Thucydides himself was no friend of democracy, he sought to narrate the history of times he had lived through as accurately and dispassionately as possible. Whether he was recalling the words and arguments of Pericles himself, or simply reconstructing what he might have said, hardly matters. While the historian's own political sympathies were perhaps towards oligarchy, he supplies one of the most eloquent and powerful cases for democracy ever made. The speech continues to inspire modern democrats. Even though the institutions of Athenian democracy were very different from those of modern representative democracy, the values proclaimed by Pericles still resonate.

Thus, 'power is in the hands not of a minority but of the whole people' and 'everyone is equal before the law'. There is also toleration of the tastes and behaviour of others. 'We do not get into a state with our next-door neighbour if he enjoys himself in his own way, nor do we give him the kind of black looks which, though they do no harm, still do hurt people's feelings' (Thucydides 1972, 145). Yet Pericles assumes the need for active political participation. 'We do not say that a man who takes no interest in politics is a man who minds his own business; we say that he has no business here at all'. He emphasises the importance of rational public debate, maintaining that there is no incompatibility between words and deeds. 'The worst thing is to rush into action before the consequences have been properly debated...' (Thucydides 1972, 147).

For all its enduring eloquence, this speech of Pericles presents a rather rosy and idealistic picture of Athenian democracy, which was neither shared by all Athenians nor by many Greeks in other states. Athens, with its strong navy, was a great power in the Greek world and often pursued its interests aggressively and ruthlessly. Thucydides was clearly very interested in interstate politics (now explored in the semi-autonomous discipline of **International Relations**) as well as in the internal politics of particular states. One example is his account of the dialogue between the Athenians and the people of the island of Melos, which is expressed in terms that anticipate the modern argument between political realists and idealists in the field of International Relations (and is often cited in modern works).

The Athenians wanted to persuade the Melians, who wished to remain neutral, to join their alliance in the war against Sparta. The Melians pleaded for justice and fair play. The Athenians responded that such considerations were irrelevant, for they had the power to force compliance and the Melians should be sensible and recognise the fact and save their skins. The Athenians argued that it was 'a general and necessary law of nature to rule whatever one can....You or anybody else with the same power as ours would be acting in precisely the same way.' A protracted resistance by the Melians was eventually overcome. Men of military age were put to death, while the women and children were sold into slavery (Thucydides 1972, 400–408). The Athenians employed the political language of self-interest and naked force (sometimes later described by the German term *Realpolitik*), repeatedly used down the centuries. While the rule of law might apply within Greek states, anarchy still prevailed in relations between states, as it has done substantially since.

Plato and Aristotle

Thucydides sought to provide a faithful record of the political conflicts he had lived through. He articulates a wide range of political arguments, but although he had his own political preferences, he was not essentially in the business of recommending particular institutions or ideas. Others were concerned with the ideal or best practicable form of government. Leading Greek thinkers did not divide human knowledge into discrete disciplines but, rather, believed in its essential unity and inter-connection. Nor did they make the modern distinction between positive social science and normative political philosophy. They considered that the search for moral and political truths was essentially no different from the search to discover mathematical truths or knowledge of the physical universe. For both Plato and Aristotle moral philosophy, theorising about the life that people should lead, was intimately connected with political theory and speculation over the best form of government (Sinclair 1967).

Yet the contrasts between the two philosophers are perhaps more marked than the similarities. Plato's political philosophy was clearly influenced by his own political experience and observation, but his pungent criticism of democracy does not relate to particular institutions or events. Like his master Socrates* (who was sentenced to death by Athenian democracy) he believed that 'virtue is knowledge'. For Plato, democracy inevitably involved the rule of ignorance. He compares the people to a great beast. Political persuasion – oratory and other tricks of the politician's trade – has nothing to do with real moral and political wisdom, which only the true philosopher possesses. This leads to his rather impractical-sounding conclusion that philosophers should be rulers. However, this is not so far away from the frequently voiced view today that government should be taken out of the hands of politicians and given to experts of one sort or another – businessmen, or scientists or suitably qualified bureaucrats.

Aristotle, another great philosopher, took a different view from Plato's on key questions. His approach to the study of politics was rather more practical or scientific. Although, like Plato, Aristotle speculated over the ideal state, he seemed more interested in actual states and the best practicable form of government, which he considered could involve a mixed system. He was less hostile to democracy than Plato and assumed that a citizen of a free state would actively engage in public affairs, as man (but not woman!) was naturally a political animal.

Both Plato and Aristotle were, however, speculating about relatively small autonomous political communities, a form of state that was already on the way out in the face of the rise of empire, such as that of Aristotle's one-time pupil Alexander the Great and, later, that of Rome. The good life no longer self-evidently involved being a free citizen of an independent free state. There was thus some retreat from political engagement. Later Greek moral philosophy, such as the contending schools of the Stoics and Epicureans, had fewer immediate political implications. However, some Stoic thinkers such as Chrysippus developed notions of a universal **natural law** and universal **citizenship**, which almost seem to anticipate ideals of world government. Such ideas later struck a chord with some Romans, particularly when Rome's political dominion came to appear to its citizens almost coterminous with the civilised world. Moreover, citizenship was extended to many whose ethnic origins were far from Roman. Thus the Roman empire became multicultural (to use a modern term).

The Roman Republic

Yet the growth of Rome's political empire effectively destroyed the Roman **Republic**, a development that was not only feared and lamented by some of those who lived through the Republic's decline, such as Cicero, but also many since who have valued the republican ideal. The Roman Republic was supposedly established after the expulsion of Rome's last king, and to some today the term 'republic' signifies simply any state that is not a monarchy. For others, the notion of a republic remains bound up with political freedom and active citizenship. For the modern French and Americans, and many besides, the name 'republic' has become synonymous with democracy. Yet although the Roman Republic involved notions of public service and active citizenship, it was much less of a democracy than ancient Athens and was really more of a mixed system of government with subordinate democratic elements. (Indeed, this limited democratic element was a positive attraction of the republican model to some, such as the American 'founding father' Madison*, who feared an unrestrained populist democracy).

Recurring conflict between patricians (leading families who normally dominated government) and plebs (the people) in the Roman Republic foreshadowed similar conflicts in some Italian, Dutch, and Swiss cities from the 15th to the 18th centuries. The names of Roman institutions (e.g. Senate) and some Roman concepts have been freely adapted by later political systems, although it does not follow that these governments have necessarily much in common with that of ancient Rome. However, the more open attitude of the Romans to **citizenship** has been influential, and the framework of Roman **law** has perhaps been Rome's greatest political legacy.

The classical legacy

Thus the political institutions and ideas of ancient Greece and Rome have had an enduring impact on the political practice and theory of the Western world ever since. Latin was the *lingua franca* of the educated classes in western Europe for many centuries after the destruction of the Roman empire. The pagan philosophers Plato and Aristotle were incorporated first into medieval Christian theology (Aristotle originally through Muslim Arabs, such as Averroes*) before being regularly reinterpreted from the Renaissance onwards. In the 18th and 19th centuries educated Europeans commonly knew rather more about ancient Greek and Roman history, ideas, and institutions than those of their contemporary neighbours (and sometimes even their own states).

Interpretations (and sometimes misinterpretations) of Greek and Roman models informed much of the political reforms and revolutions of more modern times (e.g. the American and French revolutions, the 1848 Roman Republic, and constitutional changes over much of western Europe). In the 20th century the words of Pericles appeared on the sides of London buses in the midst of the First World War (1914–1918, fought, it was claimed 'to make the world safe for democracy'). A few years later the Italian dictator Mussolini drew heavily on Roman symbols and culture in the process of establishing a **fascist** state and a new 'Roman' empire. Because of all this, for good or ill (and perhaps largely for good), the classical legacy can hardly be ignored today (Fox 2006).

RELIGION AND POLITICS

(from roughly the late Roman Empire onwards)

From the later Roman Empire through to the 17th century some of the most potent political divisions and conflicts in the Western world were linked to religious differences. Religion continued to be an important factor in politics in the 18th and 19th centuries but appeared to be of diminishing political significance in the 20th, at least until, around the new millennium, the irruption of conflict and terrorism apparently inspired by religious convictions. A new wave of religious martyrs and calls for 'holy war' has demonstrated the survival of a mind-set lately seen as obsolete in the modern world.

The rise of Christianity and Islam

The immediate cause of the increased relevance of religion for political behaviour from the late Roman Empire onwards was the rise of new monotheist religious creeds that demanded full and exclusive allegiance. By and large, the polytheist religious beliefs of the ancients had not posed a significant threat to political authority. The gods were certainly worshipped, their divine aid sought, their apparent anger appeased through sacrifices. Particular states might have their own favoured divinities, their own shrines and temples dedicated to particular deities whose protection they sought. Yet this did not necessarily imply any divided loyalties. Religion was essentially an adjunct of the state. There was rarely conflict between civic and religious obligations, which were mutually reinforcing.

Judaism was unusual in being monotheist, and this caused some problems for the Romans in the government of Palestine but few beyond, as Jews were not evangelical in seeking converts to their faith. The new religions, Christianity and later Islam, which swept through the Mediterranean world and beyond, were both monotheist and evangelical. They had dramatic implications not only for personal conduct but for political allegiances. Battles between Christians and Muslims were a recurring feature of the medieval and early modern periods. Similarly, there were conflicts between religious leaders and secular rulers within states.

Empire and papacy, church and state

Although Christians were prepared to 'render unto Caesar the things that are Caesar's', ultimately they recognised a higher authority than the state. The more devoted adherents were prepared willingly to embrace martyrdom rather than deny their faith. The power of the Roman Empire was helpless in the face of such obstinate religious convictions.

Nor did the conversion of the emperor Constantine to Christianity solve the problem of divided loyalties, either for the Roman Empire or for the successor states that arose from its destruction. This was a problem that the Christian theologian Augustine* (354–430) wrestled with in the twilight of Roman Empire. Emperors and kings might embrace the faith, but this did not make them the highest authority worthy of obedience for devout Christians. In 800 Charlemagne created a new 'empire' in the west, which subsequently evolved into the (substantially German) Holy Roman Empire. This heralded a long-running conflict between the spiritual authority of the pope and the secular power of the emperor, replicated elsewhere in western Europe between church and state.

Later medieval philosophers and political theorists such as Aquinas* (c. 1225–1274) and Marsilius (c. 1275–c. 1342) were, for good reason, substantially preoccupied with the relationship between spiritual authority and temporal authority, papacy and empire, church and state. The prevailing assumption was that all power stemmed from God, and spiritual authority was higher than temporal authority. Moreover, the authority of kings and princes was limited to their own lands, while the pope claimed authority over the whole of Christendom (or at least Western Christendom), still seen as a unity, despite its political divisions.

For a period in the Middle Ages this spiritual power was manifest rather than theoretical. Religious authority could sanction a change of ruler. Popes excommunicated and deposed emperors and kings and authorised rebellions. They also instigated or endorsed wars, including the crusades launched against Islam, another faith apparently requiring the total allegiance of its followers. In some respects, the crusades could be seen initially as a reaction against the rapid spread of Islam, which had engulfed north Africa and Spain, as well as threatening what both faiths regarded as holy lands in the Middle East and the declining Orthodox Christian Byzantine empire. Some on both sides fought both for their fellow believers and for personal salvation. Of course, religion often provided a cloak for other, more material, interests. Princes sought the church's endorsement of their own ambitious designs. Some were simply after loot.

Later, in the early modern period of the 16th and 17th centuries, the conversion of the 'heathen' to Christianity provided convenient cover for aggressive wars of conquest and colonisation by European powers around the globe.

The impact of the Protestant Reformation

Yet if religious motives were commonly mixed with others, religious convictions still loomed large in daily life and patently influenced political behaviour. This became even more evident when the always fragile unity of Western Christendom was destroyed by the Protestant Reformation, begun when Martin Luther (1483–1546) nailed his theses on the church door of Wittenberg in 1517. Rival versions of Christianity provoked religious wars in Germany, France and the Netherlands, and political upheavals in England and Scotland. Numbers of Protestant and Catholic martyrs demonstrated that some were still prepared to die for their faith, as the early Christians had done. Others were prepared to risk horrific punishments as they plotted to assassinate apostate rulers. A climate of fear and terror led to the persecution, expulsion, and even sometimes extermination of religious minorities. Wars between states, particularly the Thirty Years War from 1618 to 1648, were substantially inspired by religious differences.

These religious upheavals had momentous political consequences. The old medieval debate on the relationship between the two powers was apparently ended by the subordination of spiritual to temporal authority. In England, Henry VIII declared himself the head of the church, and the religious faith of the English became subject to the changing tastes of successive rulers. Conflict over religion in Germany was for a time suspended with the Peace of Augsburg (1555), under which the religious faith of the peoples of German states was to be effectively determined by their rulers, a formula more widely adopted in Europe after the Treaty of Westphalia of 1648.

However, the challenge to the traditional authority of the church from some forms of Protestantism also had potentially damaging implications for secular authority. Thus, in Germany the princes had been given an early warning of the dangers posed by radical Lutheran ideas with the Peasants War (1524–1525), which Luther himself disowned. In Scotland John Knox's brand of Calvinism led to the rejection of bishops and the established religious hierarchy and, ultimately, the flight of the Catholic Mary Queen of Scots. Her son James VI of Scotland and subsequently James I of England was to sum up the danger of extreme Protestantism to royal authority in the terse formula 'No bishop, no king'. In the Netherlands the ultimately successful Protestants' revolt against their Catholic Spanish rulers established a flourishing Dutch Republic that provided a standing warning to kings of the potential dangers of religious freedom. In England extreme Protestants, or Puritans, formed the core of parliamentary opposition to the crown, which was to lead eventually to the English Civil War, the execution of Charles I (1649), and the temporary institution of a republic. Although this was reversed by the restoration of the monarchy in 1660, the limitations on royal power became clear when the Catholic James II was ousted in the so-called Glorious Revolution of 1688.

Early modern political theory

Despite the continued influence of religion on political behaviour, much of the political thought in the early modern period differed markedly in tone and substance from that of the Middle Ages. The moralising of Christian theologians was replaced by the cynical political realism of the Florentine Niccolo Machiavelli* (1469–1527), who, in his best-known work *The Prince*, advised rulers to break promises as the occasion demanded. Flouting conventional religion and morality, he argued that it was more important for rulers to appear good than to be good and safer to be feared than to be loved.

Later thinkers were less concerned with the old medieval debates over the relationship between spiritual and temporal power than with the consequences of the breakdown of political authority, as witnessed in France in the late 16th century and in England in the mid-17th century. The scope and limits of political obligation – why and how far should we obey the state – became a dominant theme in political theory. Bodin* (1530–1596), who experienced the French religious wars, and Hobbes* (1588–1679), who lived through the English Civil War, both argued in favour of obedience to a supreme and undivided sovereign power. In the case of Hobbes the argument was utilitarian, rather than moral or religious, and grounded in a pessimistic estimate of the capacity of self-interested and acquisitive humans to live together peaceably without a common power to keep them in order.

For others, such as Locke* (1632–1704), obedience to the state was conditional rather than absolute, grounded in a contract according to which both sovereign and subjects had obligations. Thus there was a limited right of rebellion if the sovereign failed to keep his side of the bargain. Locke, and subsequently Montesquieu* (1689–1755), also disagreed with Hobbes on sovereignty, championing a division of powers, between executive, legislative and judicial authority. This theoretical debate increasingly reflected the conflicting models of government, for example the absolute monarchy of the French King Louis XIV ('l'état, c'est moi', 'the state, that is me') and the limited parliamentary monarchy in Britain from the late 17th century onwards.

Yet religion remained a potential and sometimes actual basis for political conflict within and between states. Religious minorities still faced persecution, partly because they seemed to offer a very real threat to political stability. Some fled to the New World. Louis XIV expelled France's Protestant minority, the Huguenots, many of whom sought refuge in England. In the Netherlands and subsequently in England the case for toleration of different faiths was advanced by thinkers such as Spinoza* (1632–1677) and Locke. Over time these arguments became more influential, at least for varieties of Protestantism, although anti-Catholic riots remained a feature of British politics until at least the late 18th century. Yet although around Europe as a whole the church (whether Catholic or Protestant) remained rich and apparently powerful, by this time it no longer represented a substantial threat to the state.

The growth of secularism

With the spread of the ideas of the Enlightenment [see next section], the influence of established religion in the political sphere generally declined in the face of increased secularism. From the late 18th century onwards there was in some countries a deliberate severance of the state from the church. Thus the United States was established as a secular state from the beginning, the First Amendment to the Constitution proclaiming 'Congress shall make no law respecting an establishment of religion, or prohibiting the free exercise thereof.' In France, through various regime changes following the 1789 revolution, the Catholic Church was frequently in conflict with anticlerical radicals. Eventually, the Third French Republic was established as a secular state, with a wholly secular system of state education (and this remains true for today's Fifth Republic). Nor was Islam immune from the prevailing secularism. Mustafa Kemal Ataturk's modernisation of Turkey, for long the leading independent Islamic power, involved the establishment of a secular republic in 1923. The separation of the state from direct involvement with religion seemed particularly advisable for those countries with a diversity of faiths. Thus India, predominantly Hindu but with a substantial Muslim minority as well as Christians, Sikhs, and others, was established as a secular republic in 1947.

Not all nations have sought to separate church and state; some, like the United Kingdom, retain an established religion, while others make explicit reference to religion in their constitution. However, even in these countries, the political role and influence of the church has generally significantly declined compared with previous periods. Even many believers seem to feel that politics and religion do not, and should not, mix. Religious leaders are often wary of engaging in political controversy, perhaps conscious that they might upset some of their own flock.

With the obvious exception of the Jews, who continued to suffer discrimination generally and in some countries suffered state-sponsored persecution, culminating in the horror of the Holocaust, religious minorities have generally suffered less discrimination in most western states from the later 19th century onwards. Specific disabilities have been removed, and a right to freedom of conscience and religious observance has been widely recognised. Yet, if the grievances of religious minorities generally declined with their increased toleration (with Northern Ireland a significant exception), religious identities commonly had continuing implications for political attitudes and behaviour in many countries, notably for party affiliation and voting. **Christian Democrat** parties dominated Italy and Germany for decades following the Second World War and played a role in several other countries, where there remained a significant if declining link between religious allegiance and electoral choice.

Even so, religion was not perceived to have much significance for politics in the second half of the 20th century in the West. Few books on politics gave religion more than a cursory mention, if that. This has changed with the revival of religious fundamentalism, most obviously perhaps Islamic fundamentalism, but also Christian, Hindu, and Jewish fundamentalism. Fundamentalists of all stripes are convinced that they have 'the truth', based on the literal interpretation of sacred texts, about which they are not prepared to make any concessions or compromises. This alone has implications for what many consider the whole nature and process of politics. Some fundamentalists go on to justify and practice political assassinations, suicide attacks, terror, and war to further their objectives. This not only threatens stability and security within states but peace between states. The mass murder of entire communities simply because of their religious allegiance, a lamentable feature of some earlier periods, has returned. One modern American political scientist, Samuel P. Huntington* (1927–2008) concluded that the clash of (essentially religious) civilisations has replaced ideological conflict in the post–Cold War world (Huntington [1996] 2002).

ENLIGHTENMENT, PROGRESS AND MODERNITY

The term 'enlightenment' refers to the new climate of ideas which emerged principally in the 18th century, although it was substantially influenced by the scientific revolution and other new thinking in the 17th century (e.g. Descartes, Hobbes*, Newton, Pascal,

Spinoza*, Locke*). While the Enlightenment affected Europe as a whole, and subsequently North America (Franklin, Jefferson*, Madison*, Paine*), its main centre was France (e.g. Montesquieu*, Voltaire*, Diderot, Rousseau*), and there was also a significant flowering of ideas in Scotland (Hume*, Smith*) and, subsequently, Germany (Kant*, Hegel*). Moreover the impact of Enlightenment ideas continued into the 19th and 20th centuries.

The Enlightenment is linked with modernity, the key assumptions, values and principles of our modern world, although in the later years of the 20th century a movement described as **postmodernism** involved a substantial reaction against Enlightenment assumptions. The Enlightenment is associated with trust in science, reason, and human progress, rather than faith, **tradition**, and **authority**. Some of its leading figures were, if not anti-religious, at least sceptical of established religion and critical of the power of the church. Thus the Enlightenment encouraged secularism, the separation of the state and politics generally from the church and religion.

Revolution

The wider political impact of the Enlightenment is rather more contentious. The political sympathies of its leading thinkers were mixed. Some favoured benevolent despotism, others a more limited or mixed system of government; few could be described as radicals or democrats. Yet questioning authority and tradition was inherently subversive, and the debate the Enlightenment opened up gave currency to new political ideas that have helped to transform the language of politics. Key political concepts aired by the thinkers of the Enlightenment with potentially revolutionary implications included **freedom**, **equality**, **rights, government by consent**, the **separation of powers**, popular **sovereignty**, and **representative democracy**. It is, however, contentious how far the ideas of the Enlightenment can be said to have 'caused' the revolutions that may more plausibly be attributed to changes in material circumstances and in the balance of interests in society.

Even so, the Enlightenment was succeeded by a series of dramatic political **revolutions** in first North America, then France and elsewhere in Europe, and subsequently other continents. The extent and frequency of these political upheavals was relatively new. Regime change, though a marked feature of the ancient world of Greece and Rome, had become extremely rare in the Middle Ages and early modern period. **Monarchy** of one kind or another was the predominant form of government and substantially the only form in larger states. Disputed successions could lead to civil war or interstate war but rarely involved a fundamental transformation of the whole political system. The political upheavals in England in the 17th century were an exception, but they were originally inspired by religious rather than political differences, and the more radical ideas that briefly emerged were soon suppressed. In the 18th century Britain's constitutional monarchy remained exceptional in what is described by historians as the 'age of **absolutism**'.

The American Revolution

The first great political revolution of modern times, and for many years the only one that long endured, was that of Britain's former American colonies. The 1776 American Declaration of Independence was a document that was thoroughly imbued with the ideas of the Enlightenment, as were the later debates over the system of government for the new United States of America and the **constitution** that emerged. The American founding fathers did not necessarily wish to push the principles of liberty, equality and government by consent to their logical conclusion. Arguably, they were more interested in the protection of **property**. Slavery was maintained, and checks and balances in the new constitution were designed to limit the influence of the people on government. Yet America did become the first modern representative democracy, and slavery was eventually abolished following the American Civil War (1861–1865). It was on one of the battlefields of that war that Abraham Lincoln powerfully reaffirmed the values of the American revolution in the Gettysburg address (see Box 2.1).

Box 2.1 The American Revolution: Government of the people

From the American Declaration of Independence, 1776
We hold these truths to be self evident, that all men are created equal, that they are endowed by their creator with certain inalienable rights, that among these are life, liberty and the pursuit of happiness. That to secure these rights, governments are instituted among men, deriving their just powers from the consent of the governed. That whenever any form of government becomes destructive to these ends, it is the right of the people to alter or abolish it, and to institute new government, laying its foundation on such principles and organising its powers in such form, as to them shall seem most likely to effect their safety and happiness.

The preamble to the Constitution of the United States of America
We the people of the United States, in Order to form a more perfect Union, establish Justice, insure domestic Tranquillity, provide for the common defence, promote the general Welfare, and secure the Blessings of Liberty to ourselves and our Posterity, do ordain and establish this CONSTITUTION for the United States of America.

From Abraham Lincoln's Gettysburg Address, 1863
Four score and seven years ago our fathers brought forth on this continent a new nation, conceived in liberty and dedicated to the proposition that all men are created equal. Now we are engaged in a great civil war, testing whether that nation or any nation so conceived and so dedicated can long endure…

We here highly resolve that these dead shall not have died in vain, that this nation under God shall have a new birth of freedom, and that government of the people, by the people, for the people shall not perish from the earth.

The French Revolution

Revolution proved contagious, particularly for the French monarchy that had powerfully assisted the American rebellion, not because of any sympathy for the values of liberty, equality, and government by consent but to avenge earlier defeats by Britain in the Seven Years War. The radical ideas behind the French Revolution were expressed in the Declaration of the Rights of Man and Citizen of 1789 (see Box 2.2) and led to the establishment of a republic in 1792 and the execution of Louis XVI in 1793.

While the origin and course of the French Revolution were due primarily to specifically French circumstances, there was a two-way flow of ideas between America and France that helped inspire revolutionaries in both countries and elsewhere. Those directly involved included the American scientist and statesman Benjamin Franklin who became the first United States ambassador to France on the eve of revolution and the Frenchman Lafayette who fought in the American War of Independence and was influential in the early stages of the French Revolution. The English radical thinker Tom Paine* was actively engaged in both the American and French revolutions. Paine wrote *The Rights of Man* (1791–1792) and *The Age of Reason* (1794–1796), works thoroughly imbued with the spirit of the Enlightenment.

Box 2.2 Articles from the French Declaration of the Rights of Man and Citizen, 1789

1. Men are born free and remain free and equal in rights. Social distinctions may be founded only upon the general good.

2. The aim of all political association is the preservation of the natural and imprescriptible rights of man. These rights are liberty, property, security, and resistance to oppression.

3. The principle of all sovereignty resides essentially in the nation. No body nor individual may exercise any authority which does not proceed directly from the nation.

4. Liberty consists in the freedom to do everything which injures no one else; hence the exercise of the natural rights of each man has no limits except those which assure to other members of society the enjoyment of the same rights. These rights can only be determined by law.

5. Law can only prohibit such actions as are hurtful to society. Nothing may be prevented which is not forbidden by law, and no one may be forced to do anything not provided for by the law.

6. Law is the expression of the general will…

Whereas the American Revolution occurred on another continent and was not initially seen as for export, the French Revolution had obvious implications for other European states. In fighting a war of survival against hostile European powers, revolutionary France sought to spread its message of liberty, equality, and **national sovereignty** to countries such as Italy, Germany, and Poland. The revolutionary war was, like the Peloponnesian War between Athens and Sparta and the Cold War between the West and the Soviet Union, a war between rival political systems and values, an ideological war. Although the revolution that began in France in 1789 ultimately failed, the idea of revolution survived, particularly in France but also elsewhere in Europe, to inspire the revolutions of 1830 and 1848, the Paris Commune of 1870, and ultimately the Russian Revolution of 1917. The threat of revolution and counter-revolution has been a recurring feature of states across the globe over the last century. Regime change, rare before 1776, has become relatively common.

NATIONALISM AND THE NATION-STATE

The growth of **nationalism** and **nation-states** was a further legacy of both the American and French revolutions. **States** had previously been created principally by force of arms, and preserved and extended by the same means, as well as by the marriage alliances and procreation of their ruling dynasties. The state was closely identified with its ruler, who in theory had absolute power. As Louis XIV tersely observed, 'L'état, c'est moi' (the state, that's me). Those who were subjects of the state normally had no choice in the matter, unless (rarely) there was a disputed succession. Notice the change signified by this language in the preamble to the American constitution, 'We the people...do ordain and establish this constitution for the United States of America', or more explicitly in the French Declaration of the Rights of Man, 1789, 'The principle of all sovereignty resides in the nation.'

This new principle of national self-determination was revolutionary in its implications, dangerously so for multinational states such as the Austrian, Russian, and Turkish empires, with disaffected Hungarian, Polish, and Greek national minorities. Equally, it strengthened the aspirations of politically divided peoples, such as the Germans and Italians, to seek a single united state. Ultimately, but not immediately, self-determination was also to be demanded by the subject peoples of European colonial empires.

The principle of self-determination had further significant direct implications for international relations and especially wars between states. Before the late 18th century most wars had been dynastic or religious or a mixture of both. The American War of Independence was different. It came about because Britain's American colonies sought independence from the British crown and state. The French Revolution in turn encouraged nationalism elsewhere, initially in emulation of French revolutionary nationalism and later in reaction against it. Subsequent 19th-century wars, such as the War of Greek Independence, the wars of Italian unification, the Austro-Prussian War, and the Franco-Prussian War, were bound up with the cause of national liberation and national unity.

What is a nation? Most definitions suggest that a nation consists of a people bound together by some common characteristic, such as a language or religion or culture or ethnicity. However, there are no clear objective criteria. Instead, a nation exists in the minds of its members: it is 'an imagined community' (B. Anderson 1983). Yet how does national consciousness grow? Some writers (e.g. Kedourie 1993) suggest that this was sometimes the result of elite manipulation, rather than a spontaneous eruption of popular feeling. Others have linked the rise of nationalism with industrialisation and the development of modern communication (Deutsch 1966; Gellner 1983; Hobsbawm 1990).

Whatever the cause of the growth of nationalism, its consequences were extensive for states, assisting the unification of some and the disintegration of others. It also helped to transform relations between states. Although the Italian nationalist Mazzini* optimistically hoped that a new Europe organised around nations would promote international peace and harmony, later history suggests that it led instead to competition and conflict between rival nation-states.

While the US entry into the First World War in 1917 effectively enshrined the principle of national self-determination as a war aim, it proved difficult to implement fully in the subsequent peace treaties, because the victorious European states (the United Kingdom,

France, Italy) were more concerned to preserve their own security and extend their own empires, while the defeated states (Russia, Austria, Turkey, Germany) could not defend their old borders. In so far as many new independent states subsequently emerged after the Second World War, this was largely the result of victorious internal liberation movements, combined with the diminishing will and capability of Western colonial powers to retain their old empires. Many of the new states that emerged after both wars contained substantial disaffected minorities and were hardly coherent nations. Even so, it is difficult to deny that the huge growth in the number of independent sovereign states after both world wars did broadly reflect the growth of national self-determination.

The study of international relations in the 20th century revolved around the relations of sovereign *states*, which are commonly identified with coherent *nations*. Thus the international assemblies established after both world wars, the League of Nations and the United Nations, represented independent sovereign *states*, or units of government, rather than *nations*, or communities of peoples. In practice many of these states contain disaffected minorities, some of whom seek national independence (for example, many Catalans in Spain, French-speaking inhabitants of Quebec in Canada, and Scots in the United Kingdom). Yet whether existing states constitute coherent nations or not, they are still regarded as the main actors in international relations, despite the growth of international governmental organisations (IGOs), nongovernmental organisations (NGOs), and transnational corporations (TNCs).

LIBERALISM, CAPITALISM, AND DEMOCRACY

(from the late 18th century to the present)

Liberalism, **capitalism**, and **democracy** are three terms at the heart of the modern analysis of politics. Each term is distinct: liberalism is a political creed, capitalism is an economic system and democracy is a form of government. Yet all three had common roots in the Enlightenment and (to many) appeared compatible, as one might assume from their frequent use in combination, such as 'liberal capitalism' or 'liberal democracy', particularly to describe the modern Western world. At the same time these hybrid terms not only suggest at least the possibility of a different kind of capitalism or another variant of democracy but also hint at an element of tension between their constituent elements. Any student of politics has to consider the relationship between liberalism, capitalism, and democracy, although first it is important to explore the meaning of each term separately.

Liberalism

Liberalism is a term commonly employed to describe a broad political, economic or philosophic outlook that appears to be widely shared in the modern Western world, so much so that it is sometimes described as a dominant or 'hegemonic' **ideology**. Indeed the words 'liberal' and 'liberalism' have become used so broadly and variously as to require some interpretation or qualification as they are employed in different senses or in different contexts. Yet all these variants of liberalism are ultimately derived from their common origins in the 16th-century Reformation, the 17th-century Scientific Revolution, and the 18th-century Enlightenment. **Individualism** is the premise they share, the notion that all theorising about society, economics, and politics starts with individual men and women. Society is simply an aggregate of individuals, no more and no less than the sum of its parts. The classical liberal economic theory of Adam Smith* (1723–1790) and David Ricardo assumes that countless individual consumers and producers, acting independently and in their own rational self-interest (see **rational choice** theory), determine the price and output of goods and services as well as wages, profits, interest, and rent. The liberal political theory of James Mill (1773–1836) and Jeremy Bentham* (1748–1832) assumed individual citizens would, if free from external pressure, use the vote and other means of political influence in their own self-interest.

The key liberal value, **freedom**, was necessary if the individual was to be able to act in his or her rational self-interest. In the 18th century the most obvious obstacle to the free exercise of individual choice was government in some shape or form. The **state** often appeared to be the enemy of freedom. In the political sphere, autocratic governments limited freedom of expression and innovation. In the economic sphere, governments sought to control trade and industry, imposing all kind of restraints on market forces through direct intervention, duties, and taxes. The enhancement of the freedom of the individual seemed to require controls on government. The liberal political programme thus involved limited constitutional government rather than **absolutism**. Government by **consent** of the governed would provide a check on wilder state schemes and wars. The slogan 'no taxation without representation', used by the parliamentary opposition to the monarchy in Britain, was later adopted by the American rebels against the British government. It was of course assumed that this would put an effective brake on government taxation and expenditure. Thus there was, initially, no apparent contradiction between the liberal political programme and the liberal economic programme. Limited constitutional government would assist laissez-faire ('leave alone') policies and the free market.

Capitalism

Liberalism has been closely associated with industrial capitalism, an economic system that emerged over much the same period as liberalism, which indeed is sometimes represented as the ideology of the industrial bourgeoisie. Liberals had always emphasised the sanctity of private **property** and the freedom of individuals to use and dispose of their property as they saw fit. A key feature of capitalism is production for exchange and profit rather than immediate use by the producers. It assumes private ownership of resources used for production and capital accumulation and also assumes a largely free market for goods and resources. Capitalism further acknowledges that some have surplus wealth and income to invest in productive resources in pursuit of profit and thus further wealth, although of course there is an element of risk in such investment. Thus any profits reaped are deemed a reward for enterprise and risk-taking.

There can be little doubt that industrial capitalism, over time, facilitated an unprecedented cumulative expansion of productive capacity, national income, and living standards in industrialising countries (although some clearly benefited far more than others). The growth of capitalism inevitably also had important social and political consequences. Ownership of capital overtook the ownership of land as the most important route to wealth and influence in society. In all industrialising countries capitalists had increasing political influence, which they used to further their interests as they perceived them. Industrial capitalism also led to the increased concentration of a fast-growing population in expanding urban centres and the emergence of a spatially concentrated industrial working class with more potential for effective political organisation, initially through trades unions and various forms of voluntary bodies or **pressure groups** and subsequently through mass **political parties**. The political geography of industrialising states was transformed, with rapidly developing manufacturing cities acquiring more economic and political weight.

To an extent the content of politics changed also, partly from the increased political influence of these class interests but also in response to the needs and problems of an industrial society and economy. Thus, although there was a continuing presumption in orthodox economics against state intervention, in practice in almost all advanced industrial economies there was an increase in state regulation (e.g. in banking and transport) and in state provision of amenities and services, initially in public health and education and subsequently in old age pensions, sickness and unemployment insurance.

Business (that had earlier benefited from a relaxation of some state controls) was not necessarily opposed to this growth in state intervention. Thus business interests often favoured state services (particularly education, health, and family support), which both assisted the creation of a better trained, healthier work force and transferred some business costs to the taxpayer that might otherwise have had to be met out of profits. Even attitudes to free trade varied with changing circumstances. In the mid-19th century this was supported by British business but opposed by many French, German, and American business interests that wanted protection against lower-cost British manufactured goods. Later, in the early 20th century, faced with increased foreign competition from Germany, the United States, and Japan, British businessmen demanded 'fair trade' (effectively protection) rather than free trade.

Democracy

Industrial capitalism was to flourish under a variety of political regimes, although it appeared particularly compatible with liberal democracy. Today the terms 'liberal' and 'democracy' are commonly combined, but in the early 19th century liberalism did not necessarily entail democracy. Many liberals then desired little more than the end of **absolutism** and a greater say for the middle classes in government, through assemblies or parliaments with a rather wider franchise. They wanted reform not **revolution**. They did not seek to extend political power to those without property, whom they feared.

In the early 19th century only radical liberals advocated democracy, a political system virtually defunct from the time of the ancient Greeks, until resurrected in a rather different form in modern times. Direct democracy on the ancient Greek model hardly seemed feasible for the geographically extensive states that dominated 18th-century Europe. What changed this calculation was the notion of **representative democracy**, government controlled by, and accountable to, elected representatives of the whole people. The practice of electing representatives had been long familiar in some countries, but election was limited to the few, so that representatives were drawn from and served a small minority of the people and moreover commonly only exerted a partial and occasional influence over government. Advocates of representative (or liberal) democracy (such as James Mill and Jeremy Bentham) assumed that a government controlled by, and accountable to, a parliament elected by the whole people would have to pursue the interests of 'the greatest happiness of the greatest number'. Thus, representative government would be a true democracy.

Yet even the founding fathers of the American constitution, who freely invoked the name of the people and the notion of popular **sovereignty**, sought to put checks and balances in the way of unrestrained people power. James Madison* (1751–1836), in particular, distinguished between the representative principle that he associated with a **republic** and that of a full democracy. 'It may well happen that the public voice, pronounced by the representatives of the people, will be more consonant to the public good than if pronounced by the people themselves, convened for the purpose' (Madison and Jay [1787–1788] 1987, number X, 126). However, in practice some of the checks on popular sovereignty, such as the electoral college to choose the president, never operated as the founding fathers envisaged, and the American system of government did rapidly become the first functioning modern representative democracy.

American democracy in the early 19th century was an object of some curiosity and wonder in old Europe, largely still ruled by absolute monarchs. The account of this strange new world and novel system of government by a young French aristocrat, Alexis de Tocqueville* (1805–1859) whose own family had suffered executions and (temporary) dispossession in the French Revolution, became a best seller (*Democracy in America*, two volumes, 1835, 1840). Tocqueville was convinced that in America the sovereignty of the people was a reality. 'The people reign in the American political world like God over the universe' (Tocqueville [1835, 1840] 2003, 71). He admired some aspects of American society and politics, particularly the spirit of freedom and equality he discerned, although he was critical of others (especially the treatment of native Americans and black slaves). He also feared the threat to individual freedom from what he called the 'tyranny of the majority'. Yet whatever his personal reservations about American democracy, he was convinced that it represented the future. European states such as France, Britain, and Germany would be unable to resist the democratic tide. He plainly concluded that those liberals who sought limited political reform short of full democracy were doomed to disappointment. 'When a nation starts to tamper with electoral qualifications, we can anticipate, sooner or later, their complete abolition.... For after each concession, the strength of democracy increases...and the process can be stopped only when universal suffrage is achieved' (ibid., 70).

Tocqueville presciently predicted the outcome of the electoral reform process in countries such as Britain, where initially modest extensions of the franchise led to granting the vote first to working-class males and ultimately to women (a development Tocqueville had not foreseen and of which he would not have approved). Today, after successive waves of democratisation (Huntington 1991) liberal democracy has become the dominant system of government globally. Tocqueville was also well aware that democracy involved a fundamental transformation of politics, which went far beyond constitutions and formal institutions of government to include political parties and other forms of political association and a free press. 'A new political science is needed for a totally new world' (Tocqueville 2003, 17).

Democracy and liberalism

Democracy appeared in many ways the logical culmination of liberal political principles – government by consent, freedom, equality, the enlightenment ideas embodied in formal statements of human rights. The Enlightenment had been originally a Western world phenomenon. The values of the Enlightenment – **rights**, **national sovereignty**, **freedom**, and **equality** – were not initially for export to Asia, Africa, and South America. Those of other **races** and religions, who were commonly subject to Western colonial exploitation, were not felt to be the equals of white Europeans. The **toleration** of variants of Christianity was not extended to other 'heathen' religions.

Yet the rapid dismantling of the former European colonial empires in and after the Second World War was accompanied by the recognition of **human rights** unlimited by nationality, race, culture, or, crucially, gender. Here there was a marked switch from the earlier emphasis on the rights of *man* to *human* rights. Documents such as the United Nations Universal Declaration of Human Rights (1948) (Box 2.3) and the European Convention for the Protection of Human Rights and Fundamental Freedoms (1950) seemed to fulfil the promise of the Enlightenment, extending rights and freedoms beyond national frontiers and distinctions of race, religion, and gender to all humanity. (However, a theoretical commitment to equal rights for women, ethnic minorities and those of different faiths has not necessarily involved equal rights in practice.)

Box 2.3 From the United Nations Universal Declaration of Human Rights, 1948

Article 1 All human beings are born free and equal in dignity and worth. They are endowed with reason and conscience and should act towards each other in a spirit of brotherhood.

Article 2 Everyone is entitled to all the rights and freedoms set out in this Declaration, without distinction of any kind, such as race, colour, sex, language, religion, political or other opinion, national or social origin, property, birth or other status.

Further articles provided for a whole range of social and welfare rights beyond those envisaged in the 18th century, including 'the right to take part in the government of his country' (article 21), 'the right to social security' (22), 'the right to work', 'free choice of employment' and 'equal pay for equal work' (23), 'the right to rest and leisure' including 'periodic holidays with pay' (24), 'the right to a standard of living adequate for the health of himself and his family, including food, clothing, housing and medical care and necessary social services' (25), 'the right to education'(26).

Although representative democracy seemed to embody the liberal attachment to toleration, free speech, and human rights, it also seemed to some to threaten liberal economics, the principle of **free markets**, and **laissez-faire**. Newly enfranchised citizens, following their own rational self-interest, commonly demanded more interference with **free market** forces rather than less. Thus farmers sought duties on imported grain to keep prices up and maintain income derived from land. Businesses wanted protection from foreign competition. Workers commonly opposed a free market in labour that might depress wage rates. Many voters wanted more public services, such as state education, health care, or housing, subsidised or free at the point of use. These tensions led to a split among liberals. Some liberals (sometimes called 'social liberals' embraced social reform, justifying state intervention as an expansion of individual **freedom** and **rights**, involving a right to education, health care, work and a 'living wage.' Economic liberals continued to assert that the **free market** was the essence of their creed.

Democracy and capitalism

There was a more obvious potential conflict between democracy and capitalism. Democracy assumed political equality. Capitalism involved massive economic inequality. Conservatives and liberals feared, and **socialists** hoped, that the political equality implicit in democracy would lead to much greater economic equality. They assumed that the many who were relatively poor would use their increased political power to secure a massive redistribution of income and wealth (involving extensive interference with another liberal value, the freedom to acquire, use, and bequeath private property without state interference). Democracy thus appeared a potential threat not only to old landed wealth but the new wealth of the industrial capitalists.

All socialists in the 19th and early 20th centuries assumed that full democracy was incompatible with capitalism and looked forward to the latter's replacement by a new economic system. Those socialists committed to representative democracy saw it as the first step towards this goal, while others, such as Marx* and his successors, denied that what they called 'bourgeois democracy' was real democracy or a threat to capitalism. To many Marxists the failure of parliamentary socialism to transform the economic system and create a more equal society simply confirmed that representative government did not really involve the rule of the people [see subheading on Marxism, below]. Others who were not Marxists were also sceptical about popular sovereignty, arguing that behind the façade of parliamentary democracy, elite rule continued [see subheading on elitism, below].

Threats to liberalism, capitalism, and democracy

In the course of the 20th century, liberalism, capitalism, and democracy all appeared under serious threat at one time or other. **Liberalism** for a long time seemed a political creed of declining appeal and relevance, and political parties that retained the name 'liberal' commonly found themselves squeezed between the mass parties of the **left** and **right**. **Capitalism** experienced a serious crisis following the slump precipitated in 1929 and periodic scares since (e.g. the 2008 banking crisis) that have seemed for a time to confirm predictions of its inevitable collapse. Moreover, from the Russian revolution in 1917 to the fall of the Berlin wall in 1989, capitalism faced what appeared to be a viable alternative economic system in the centralised command economies of the Soviet Union and its allies. Following the First World War (fought 'to make the world safe for democracy'), liberal democracy also appeared to be under threat from the **right** in the form of both traditional authoritarian **dictatorships** and a new creed, **fascism**, as well as from the **left** in the shape of Soviet **communism**. Fascist dictators partially legitimated their rule by recourse to the apparently democratic device of the **plebiscite**, while the 'peoples democracies' of the Soviet Union and, later, Eastern Europe maintained an electoral façade for single-party dictatorships.

THE RISE AND DECLINE OF THE MARXIST CHALLENGE

(from the mid-19th century onwards)

Until 1989 and the fall of the Berlin wall, the contrast between the liberal democracies of the capitalist West (the 'first world') and the Marxist-Leninist regimes of the former Soviet Union, its allies and satellites (the 'second world') was naturally a major focus for the study of comparative politics. Moreover, the 'Cold War' between these opposed systems was a key theme in the study of **international relations** from 1945 to 1989. Communism no longer represents a realistic challenge to liberal democracy, but modern students of politics still need to know something of Marx* and Marxism, as for much of the 20th century a significant proportion of the world's peoples were subject to regimes inspired by particular interpretations of Marxism. Moreover, Marxist theory and analysis has long been a significant strand in modern social science and has made (and continues to make) a major contribution to the study of politics.

Marx and Engels

Karl Marx (1818–1883) and his collaborator Friedrich Engels* (1820–1895) saw conflicting economic **class** interests at the heart of politics and historical change. As they wrote at the beginning of the *Communist Manifesto* (1848), 'The history of all hitherto existing society is the history of class struggle.' Broadly speaking, Marxists argue that political power reflects economic power. Real political power is in the hands of those who own and control the means of production in any society, regardless of whether it is formally an absolute monarchy, a constitutional monarchy or some kind of republic. Thus, in the modern industrial capitalist economies that were emerging in the West in the 19th century, effective power was in the hands of the **bourgeoisie** or capitalists rather than hereditary rulers or the old landed aristocracy on the one hand or the mass of the people on the other.

In assuming the primacy of economic factors, Marx implicitly denied or at least significantly constrained the autonomy of politics. This debate over the role of economic factors in shaping political activities and outcomes continues, and not just among Marxists. It relates back to old arguments in philosophy about free will and determinism and continuing discussion over the relative importance of **structure** and **agency** among social scientists and historians. It is an issue that any student of politics has to consider, because it has to do with the nature and scope of the subject.

Yet Marx himself was never a wholehearted economic determinist. He famously argued, 'Philosophers have only interpreted the world in various ways; the point is to change it' (Marx, *Theses on Feuerbach*). Elsewhere he wrote that men make their own history but not in circumstances of their own choosing.

Marx assumed that capitalism would ultimately be destroyed by its own internal contradictions. Competition among capitalists would lead to falling rates of profit, and capitalists would be forced to increase the exploitation of their workers to stay in business. The poverty and hardship (or 'immiseration') of the workers would intensify until they rose in revolution. Then capitalism would be replaced by socialism, although Marx said very little about what this revolution would entail or about the socialist society that would succeed it. He did indicate that there would have to be a temporary 'dictatorship of the proletariat' to prevent counter-revolution, before the institution of a classless society to be organised on the principle 'from each according to his abilities, to each according to his needs'. In the absence of class conflict the state would 'wither away'. Coercive government of the old kind would no longer be necessary.

Marxism and democracy

In assuming a preponderant if not necessarily determining role for economic forces in politics, Marx denied that true democracy was compatible with capitalism, for how could political power be in the hands of the people when economic power remained heavily concentrated? Alternatively, if democracy was a reality and the people did have effective power, they would surely use it to improve their lot and establish a more equal socialist society rather than preserve the existing capitalist society. As capitalism, with its accompanying gross inequality, continued to thrive, democracy was not a reality. Thus although Marx certainly considered himself a democrat, he scornfully dismissed the parliaments of his day as 'committees for discussing the common affairs of the bourgeoisie'. In other words they served the interests of industrial capitalism rather than the people as a whole.

One explanation for this in Marx's lifetime was that the British Parliament and most other representative bodies were not elected by anything near a universal franchise. Subsequently, following the extension of the vote, some followers of Marx in Germany and elsewhere hoped that **socialism** could be achieved peacefully, through the ballot box. Eduard Bernstein* (1850–1932) was the most prominent of these 'revisionists'. Yet while socialist parties later won elections and formed governments, either innate caution or the constraints of the capitalist economy and the parliamentary political system inhibited their actions, so that they failed to use their control of government to establish a socialist economy and society. The British Marxist Ralph Miliband* (1924–1994) gloomily concluded in *Parliamentary Socialism* (1972) that the British Labour Party had consistently sacrificed socialism for what he called 'parliamentarism'.

Other Marxists rejected revisionism and continued to deny that what they still called 'bourgeois democracy' was real democracy, even with a universal adult franchise. The argument in part revolves around the ability of voters to perceive their own real interests. It had been a key assumption of early advocates of representative democracy that individuals perceive and act on their own rational self-interest. Thus a government elected by and accountable to the people would be constrained to act in the interests of the majority. But Marx and his followers did not assume that individuals would necessarily be guided by their own rational self-interest. Marx had asserted that 'It is not the consciousness of men that determine their being, but on the contrary, their social being that determines their consciousness' (Marx, tr. McLellan, *A Contribution to the Critique of Political Economy*, 1859). In other words, it is our upbringing and our economic and social circumstances that shape what we think. Elsewhere he wrote, 'the ruling ideas of every age are the ideas of the ruling class (Marx The German Ideology, 1846).' Thus, in a capitalist society the workers would share the economic and political outlook of the capitalists.

Lenin and Marxism-Leninism

Other Marxists argued that the workers in advanced industrialised Western states had been effectively seduced from revolutionary socialism by improved living standards and imperialism. One of Marx's key predictions, the increasing impoverishment of the working class, had failed to come to pass. The Russian revolutionary Marxist leader Lenin* (1870–1924) gave one plausible explanation: **imperialism**, the 'highest stage of capitalism', involved the transfer of exploitation from the Western working class to the subject peoples of European colonies.

When Lenin seized power in the Bolshevik Revolution of November 1917 he promptly dissolved the newly elected Russian Parliament. He proclaimed instead 'All power to the soviets' (workers' councils). Lenin scornfully dismissed what he called 'bourgeois democracy' that only offered a *formal* equality and effectively excluded workers from power. He argued that the Soviet government he had established in Russia was a genuine 'proletarian democracy'. In reality, the 'people's democracies' established in the Soviet Union and subsequently in Eastern Europe and elsewhere involved rejection of some of the fundamental principles of liberal representative democracy. They established centralised one-party dictatorships with no effective competition for power and with only very limited toleration of dissent and free expression. Under Lenin's successor, Stalin* (1879–1953), even this limited toleration of dissent was extinguished, as millions perished in a series of purges that included most of Lenin's leading Bolshevik colleagues. The governments of the Soviet Union and its satellites in the post–Second World War era did not indulge in such wholesale murder but did remain ruthless oppressive dictatorships.

However, the Soviet Union still seemed to offer a radical alternative to capitalism in managing the economy. From 1917 until 1989 there were two competing economic models, the communist command economy and Western capitalism. For a time it appeared that the ruthless forced industrialisation of the previously backward Russian economy by a succession of centrally imposed five-year plans had enabled the Soviet Union almost to catch up with the West. Jobs of some kind for all contrasted favourably with the rising unemployment and poverty in the West in the 1930s.

After the Second World War the world was dominated by two superpowers, the USA and the USSR. In specific fields such as armaments and space exploration the USSR appeared to be competing successfully. Yet in the economic sphere as in the political sphere choice was absent or constricted, and the rapid development of heavy industry and arms-related products was at the expense of consumer goods and living standards. Even so it appeared that the Soviet economic model was a viable alternative to capitalism. Thus some Marxists in the West swallowed any of the reservations they felt about restrictions on political freedom and continued to support 'actually existing socialism' against the capitalist alternative. Others condemned it as a betrayal of socialism.

It should be emphasised that other variants of Marxism continued to have some influence in the West. These include the revisionist Marxism of Bernstein and others, still influential within social democratic and socialist parties that were prepared to work within the framework of parliamentary democracy. There were also various forms of Trotskyism, Titoism (in former Yugoslavia), and the distinctive Eurocommunism of the once strong Italian Communist Party, influenced by the important Italian theorist Antonio Gramsci* (1891–1937). The 'Critical Theory' of the Frankfurt school, the existential Marxism of Sartre* (1905–1980), and the structural Marxism of Althusser* (1918–1990) and Poulantzas* (1936–1979) were all influential in the academic study of politics, as well as having a (generally much more limited) impact on political practice (McLellan 1979).

The continuing relevance of Marx and Marxism

The subsequent implosion of the Soviet empire has substantially destroyed the credibility of the hitherto dominant interpretation of Marx's thought, Marxism-Leninism. Most of those who lived under it have no desire to return to it. Some students might conclude that there is no longer much point in bothering too much with Marx and Marxism. Yet Marx remains a hugely important thinker whose ideas cannot be dismissed because one interpretation of Marxism has been apparently discredited. Marxist theory has to be addressed by any serious student of politics, and indeed any social scientist, including those with no sympathy for any kind of socialism. In some ways the end of Soviet-style communism makes it easier to tackle Marxist thought without too many preconceptions.

Why does Marxism remain relevant? First of all, Marx (and Marxists) still offer a cogent analysis of **capitalism**. While Marx was aware of the tremendous potential for increased production and wealth that industrialisation offered, he and Engels were also only too aware of the downside of capitalism. This included both massive inequality and the debilitating effect on the conditions of labour for many industrial workers (the important Marxist concept of 'alienation'). Marx was also prescient on the development of capitalism, anticipating the impact of monopoly and even global capitalism. However he clearly under-estimated the resilience and adaptability of capitalism and, **social democrats** would argue, the scope to manage capitalism so as to reduce its destructive capacity through a 'mixed economy'.

Secondly, Marx emphasised the continuing importance of economic and other external constraints on political action. He, and certainly some of his followers, may have exaggerated the importance of '**structure**' over human '**agency**'. The influence of Marx himself and the political career of Lenin certainly suggest that individuals can change history. Yet we are also only too aware of the constraints under which political leaders and governments operate, particularly perhaps the increased economic and environment impacts of **globalisation**.

Thirdly, the Marxist critique still has important implications for the now dominant liberal democratic systems under which many in the world currently live. There are all kinds of important criticisms of particular democracies, relating to electoral systems, the funding of parties and electoral competition, media bias, and so on. However it is the Marxist critique that gets to the heart of matter. Do the people, or can the people, really have effective power in a system where productive resources are controlled by the few? Can political **equality** be a reality without much greater economic equality? Alternatively, if political equality is a reality, why has it not led to significantly greater equality of wealth and income? Indeed, modern research indicates that inequality, both between states and within states, continues to grow significantly (Piketty 2014).

THE ELITIST CHALLENGE – PARETO, MOSCA, AND MICHELS

Another challenge to liberal democracy was advanced by a group of thinkers, now described as classical elitists, who flourished in the late 19th and early 20th centuries: Vilfredo Pareto* (1848–1923), Gaetano Mosca* (1858–1941) and Robert Michels* (1875–1936). Mosca ([1896] 1939) briefly summarised the elitist perspective. 'In all societies… two classes of people appear – a class that rules and a class that is ruled. The first class, always the less numerous, performs all political functions, monopolises power and enjoys the advantages that power brings, whereas the second, the more numerous class, is directed and controlled by the first.'

Once this would have appeared a simple truism, hardly worth asserting, but the growth of **representative democracy** and the notion of government by the people provoked these thinkers to obstinately insist that power was still effectively in the hands of the few, even in states that were nominally democratic. Thus the classical elitists, like Marx, considered the parliamentary democracies of their day to be shams, concealing the continued concentration of power in the hands of a small ruling class or elite.

However, there are crucial differences between Marx's underlying assumptions and those of the classical elitists. For Marx political power reflected economic power, and thus under capitalism, where real wealth and control of the means of production remained in the hands of few, real democracy was impossible. Yet Marx believed that after a revolution the masses would take power, while the classical elitists considered elite rule inevitable, a fact of life. This did not mean that any particular elite was permanent. Indeed, as Pareto observed, history was a 'graveyard of elites'. Yet although elites are repeatedly overthrown, they can only be replaced by new elites, never by the rule of the people. Elite rule, rule by the few, is permanent.

Indeed, classical elitism had at least as many damaging implications for socialism as for democracy. According to Michels ([1911] 1962) there was an 'iron law of **oligarchy**' that operated in all organisations, even in those ostensibly committed to democracy, including political parties like the social democrats, which could never be effectively controlled by the mass of ordinary party members or the working class as a whole. Thus socialism was an impossibility. Michels himself had been an active member of the German Social Democrats as a young man but later left, disillusioned. He declared that 'The socialists might conquer but not socialism, which would perish in the moment of its adherents' triumph.' Thus socialist parties and politicians could not create an egalitarian socialist society. Some would argue that this judgement was confirmed by the course of the Bolshevik revolution; others by the failure of the leaders of social democratic parties to introduce socialism after victories at the polls.

Elitism, fascism, and democracy

Pareto's elitism was to be one of various influences on Italian fascists, who seized power in 1922 after Mussolini's so-called march on Rome. While Pareto himself appeared to support fascism, Mosca, who had earlier opposed representative government, moved in the opposite direction to defend it and condemn fascism. His later theory allowed for competition between rival elites who might be relatively open and responsive to pressure from the masses (Bottomore 1966). These ideas were compatible with an elite theory of democracy, such as that advanced by Joseph Schumpeter* (1883–1950), involving limited competition between political parties, where all the policy initiatives come from the party leadership rather than ordinary members. Yet this is a conception of intraparty democracy far more constrained and limited than democratic socialists had envisaged.

Fascism, like Stalinist communism, appeared for a time to provide another ideological alternative to liberal democracy, although it never had much intellectual substance. Indeed, it is easier to describe fascism in terms of what it was against than what it was for. Fascism involved a reaction against the **rationalism**, **individualism**, **liberalism**, and parliamentarism that constituted the mainstream post-Enlightenment Western tradition from the early 19th century onwards. Fascism stood for the state and nation rather than the individual, action rather than intellectual debate, leadership, order, and discipline rather than the liberal democratic values of bargaining and compromise. Following the rise of Hitler and Nazism, all this became marginal to the virulent anti-Semitism and extreme racism that led to the horrors of the Holocaust. The defeat of the Axis powers in 1945 virtually destroyed fascism and Nazism, although they have had a flickering afterlife in parts of Latin America and in some European far right parties.

The triumph of liberalism, capitalism, and democracy

Despite these ideological challenges from the left and the right, liberalism, capitalism, and democracy have all apparently survived and thrived in the modern world. Progressive or social liberalism was essentially the dominant element in what came to be called the social democratic or Keynesian consensus in the decades after the Second World War. The capitalist economies of the West flourished in 'les trente glorieuses' (the 30 glorious years) after the war, to the extent that even socialist political parties now talked of channelling or transforming capitalism rather than abolishing it. Economic liberalism subsequently made a remarkable comeback in the last quarter of the century, so much so that the **free market** is now widely endorsed across the political spectrum. Following the implosion of Soviet **communism** and the transformation of Chinese communism, capitalism appears now global and apparently unchallengeable.

Democracy too has become almost universally approved (although not necessarily so universally practised). The surviving **dictatorships** in Europe have been transformed into parliamentary democracies. Former European colonies, now independent sovereign states, have largely maintained democratic forms. India remains the largest functioning democratic system in the world. Many of the former **communist** one-party states have been transformed into competitive multiparty representative democracies. Successive waves of democratisation (Huntington 1991), particularly after the collapse of Soviet communism, have firmly established representative democracy as the main form of government in the world and the only one generally regarded as legitimate. Thus, by the early 21st century, liberalism, capitalism, and democracy seemed to have merged into a global value system, a dominant or hegemonic ideology to which, following the end of the Cold War, there appeared to be no alternative, apart from the political nihilism of **terrorism** inspired by religious fundamentalism.

Continuing tensions

Yet although liberalism, capitalism, and democracy have survived and flourished to hold sway over much of the world, there are still significant continuing tensions among the three. The huge disparities in wealth and income under capitalism, even more apparent between nations than within nations now capitalism is global, continue to call into question the assumption of political equality that remains central to democracy. Economic liberals assert that one cannot 'buck the market'. The helplessness of individuals and whole communities in the face of global market forces seems to limit the scope for real democratic change through popularly elected politicians and parties. This is one of the factors that has perhaps contributed to a growing mood of popular frustration, disillusion, and apathy towards democratic politics, evident in declining voting figures and party membership. Such disillusion and apathy threaten the active citizen participation that remains at the heart of the democratic ideal.

GUIDE TO FURTHER READING

It is difficult to recommend books covering the whole time span of this section. Heywood (2015a) and Morrow (2005) provide a thematic guide to political theories, while Sabine (1951), although old, is still perhaps the most comprehensive history of Western political theory. Boucher and Kelly (2017) have edited a book on political thinkers, and Rosen and Wolff (1999) have provided a handy collection of readings. On particular periods there is Sinclair (1967) on Greek political thought, Lloyd-Jones's (1965) broader survey of the Greek world, and Fox (2006) on the history of ancient Greece and Rome. Leff (1958) is useful on medieval political thought and Hampsher Monk (1992) on modern political thought. Yet most of the key thinkers are best read by students for themselves. There are many good modern translations of key political thinkers described here.

A legitimate criticism of much of the analysis in this section is the Eurocentric and Western bias that still dominates much of the academic study of politics today. This will only change when its study becomes truly global. However, Frankopan (2015) provides a compelling alternative perspective on political, economic, and social history.

Time chart of key political developments, concepts, and thinkers

Period	Events/institutions	Concepts	Thinkers
Ancient Greece (down to 4th century BCE)	Persian wars	Law	Pericles
	Peloponnesian War	Justice	Thucydides
	Death of Socrates	'Polis' ('city state')	Socrates
	Rise of Macedon	Ideal state	Plato
		Democracy	Aristotle
		Natural Law	Stoics

Roman Republic and Roman Empire (down to 5th century CE)	Growth of Rome Carthaginian wars Civil war Roman Empire Rise of Christianity Decline of Rome	Republic Citizenship Roman law Universal empire	Cicero Augustine
Dark Ages and Middle Ages (down to 15th century CE)	Barbarian invasions Schism between Rome and Byzantium Rise of Islam Crusades Church versus state	Feudalism Hereditary monarchy Christendom Papal supremacy Spiritual and temporal power	Averroes Aquinas
Early modern period (late 15th, 16th, and 17th centuries)	Renaissance Invention of printing Discovery and colonisation of the 'New World' Reformation Inquisition Religious wars Dutch Republic Scientific Revolution	Protestantism Sovereignty Absolutism Political obligation State of Nature Contract Religious toleration	Machiavelli Bodin Grotius Hobbes Spinoza Locke
18th century 'Age of Enlightenment'	Slave trade Beginnings of industrialisation and capitalism Dynastic wars American War of Independence French Revolution	Absolute monarchy Separation of powers Enlightenment Rationalism Popular sovereignty Revolution Citizen rights Liberty, equality, fraternity Federalism	Montesquieu Hume Rousseau Smith Kant Paine Jefferson Madison Burke Godwin Wollstonecraft
19th century	Napoleonic empire (partial restoration of old regimes) Industrial Revolution Urbanisation 1830 and 1848 revolutions Rise of nation-states American Civil War Growth of colonial empires	Nationalism Constitutional reform Liberalism Capitalism Conservatism Representative democracy Class Socialism Collectivism Race Imperialism	Bentham Hegel Maistre Owen Tocqueville Marx and Engels Proudhon Mill Green Comte Pareto Nietzsche

(Continued)

Period	Events/institutions	Concepts	Thinkers
20th century	First World War	Militarism	Michels
	Bolshevik Revolution	Pacifism	Lenin
	Votes for women	Elitism	Weber
	Rise of dictators	Pluralism	Trotsky
	Economic depression	Self-determination	Gramsci
	Second World War	Fascism and Nazism	Gandhi
	Cold War	Racism	Popper
	Decolonisation	Balance of power	Mao Zedong
	European Community	Genocide	Keynes
	Fall of Berlin Wall	Behaviouralism	Hayek
	Terrorism	Feminism	De Beauvoir
	Globalisation	Constructivism	Friedan
	Rise of the BRICS	Political Economy	Dahl
		Women's rights	Rawls
		Patriarchy	Nozick
		Neoliberalism	Buchanan
		Public choice	Foucault
		Neo-conservatism	Lyotard
		Postmodernism	
		Environmentalism	

PART 2 SECTION 2

MODERN POLITICAL SCIENCE AND POLITICAL IDEAS

Contents

INTRODUCTION

The last section involved a very broad survey of the interaction of political practice and theory over two and a half thousand years. This section concentrates on the development of the modern political science coupled with the decline and subsequent revival of interest in political ideas.

THE EXPLOSION IN THE STUDY OF POLITICS

Although politics has been analysed and written about for over two and a half thousand years, it was only in the 20th century that its systematic study in universities really took off. Degree courses and scholarly research into **politics** exploded initially in the United States. By the 1920s, politics was on the curriculum of over a hundred American universities. There were similar, if generally later and less extensive, developments around the Western world. The systematic study of **international relations** grew rather later and more slowly. A significant catalyst was the First World War and the need to avoid a similar catastrophe in the future, but international relations were only more systematically studied after the Second World War and ensuing Cold War [see Section 3, below].

Not only were far more people studying politics; the content and methodology of the subject was transformed. Partly this reflected a substantial increase in the number of **states**, and a widening range of systems of **government** and styles of politics, as a consequence of the disintegration of old empires and the emergence of many new politically independent **sovereign** states, making **comparative politics** far more extensive and complex. Yet the sheer scope of government and politics within modern industrialising countries also expanded rapidly, with significant increases in state functions, public spending and taxation, as well as generally (but not invariably) more popular involvement in the political process. Significant, if uneven, progress towards **representative democracy** shifted much of the focus of study from the relative few directly involved in government to the political culture and behaviour of the masses, including studies of voting, **political parties**, and **pressure groups**.

Yet the biggest changes were in how politics was studied. Politics was now increasingly regarded as a science, one of the fast growing social sciences (such as economics, psychology, and sociology), and aspiring to the same rigorous methodology as the physical sciences. Significantly, when American politics specialists came together to form a national umbrella organisation for their fast-expanding discipline in 1903, they called it the American Political Science Association (APSA). The London School of Economics and Political Science had been established in 1895, although few British universities initially followed its example. Indeed, some British politics academics were reluctant to call their subject a science. When they formed a national organisation for their discipline in 1950, half a century after the founding of the APSA, it was called the Political Studies Association (Grant 2010).

THE BEHAVIOURAL REVOLUTION

Modern political science is closely associated with the behavioural revolution that dominated the study of politics in the United States in the mid-20th century and became increasingly influential elsewhere. The term 'revolution' is hardly too strong to describe the impact of **behaviouralism**, which not only involved the introduction of a new rigorous scientific research methodology but the rejection or marginalisation of much of the traditional study of politics, including constitutional law and political theory. Thus, in an often quoted pronouncement, Peter Laslett (1956) declared the death of political philosophy. What mattered was not what political philosophers argued *should* happen but what actually *did* happen, political behaviour, dispassionately measured and analysed. Behaviouralists sought to frame hypotheses or theories that could be tested against the evidence, through the collection and analysis of relevant data, in the manner of other sciences. This required mastery of advanced statistical methods to substantiate or reject tentative hypotheses. The methodology was inductive, deriving a general law or principle from a number of observed particular instances, although it was acknowledged that some initial hunch might guide the search for data.

Thus, for example, a researcher might guess that those who are most educated are more likely to vote. To test this tentative hypothesis the research would seek to correlate electoral turnout with levels of education. If a positive link was apparently established, suggesting that the most educated are indeed more likely to vote, this would seem to support the original hypothesis. Others might seek to replicate the research to confirm or refute the findings, perhaps for another time period or in another country. If this new research led to contrary conclusions, perhaps suggesting that the least educated were more likely to vote, this would invalidate any general link between turnout and education levels (although it might be possible to refine the original hypothesis to suggest a link in specified circumstances).

The points about replication and possible refutation are crucial. Any scientific research should be capable of being replicated in this way. Karl Popper* (1902–1994) argued that falsifiability rather than verifiability should be the criteria for a scientific hypothesis ([1934] 1959). Countless sightings of white swans cannot prove the hypothesis that all swans are white, but the hypothesis can be disproved by the discovery of a single black swan. A scientific hypothesis should be framed in such a way that it could be falsified by the discovery of evidence to the contrary. Popper held that theories are unscientific if they are expressed in such broad general terms that it is impossible to test them by seeking empirical evidence that might refute them.

There can be little question that the discipline of politics benefited considerably from the new rigour brought about by the behavioural revolution. There were particularly significant advances in the study of voting, political parties, pressure group activity, and political culture and the whole field of comparative politics [see below].

POLITICAL SCIENCE

Not all those who studied and taught politics in the mid-20th century were entirely comfortable with the label 'political science', which marginalised or even totally rejected traditional moral and political theory. Thus a leading British academic, Bernard Crick (1920–2008), reasserted what he called the normative and ultimately moral dimensions of the study of politics (Crick 1959). One example is the long and continuing debate over human rights, from Locke* onwards, later embodied in state constitutions and international charters. Arguably, the study of politics would be impoverished if such questions of value were excluded.

Moreover, it may be questioned whether a value-free political science is even possible (Grant 2010). Crick argued that American behaviouralism was far from being value free, but 'culture-bound and shot through with liberal American values' (Kavanagh 2007, 115), implicitly assuming the superiority of US democratic institutions and processes.

Indeed, it was hardly an accident that modern political science developed initially in the first modern liberal democracy and soon spread largely to other liberal democracies. Although there was a strong commitment to the study of comparative politics, including military dictatorships, traditional monarchies, communist one-party states, and what came to be described as 'illiberal democracies', there was a tacit and sometimes explicit assumption that liberal democracy was preferable to the alternatives. Huntington (1991) later divided democratisation into three main periods or 'waves', from the mid-19th century onwards, culminating in the late 20th century, when democratic regimes replaced dictatorships in Latin America and southern Europe and one-party communist regimes in Eastern Europe. The clear underlying assumption was that this meant progress.

Perhaps it is a mistake to be too hung up over the word 'science', which in its original sense, derived from Latin, meant simply 'knowledge'. Students of politics may aspire to scientific rigour and objective judgement, but we are hardly neutral observers, as we are investigating ourselves, our own society and political system, along with others. Moreover, our knowledge of politics is inevitably provisional and incomplete, always liable to be questioned and even refuted by new theories, methodologies, and empirical research.

The comparative approach

Those at the forefront of the behavioural revolution fully appreciated that political science must be comparative. This was hardly new. Political thinkers from Aristotle* onwards had shown an interest in comparative government, and more recent writers such as Montesquieu* and Tocqueville* were fascinated by political systems other than their own. Yet one problem in comparing politics in different countries is that each appears to have its own specific institutions and processes and its own particular political terminology. Even institutions and processes with similar names may have a very different role in other political systems, so that we may not be comparing like with like. Thus those described as 'presidents' do not share the same functions and powers across states. 'Legislatures' are not all chosen in the same way and may operate very differently. The role of 'political parties' may vary in important respects between political systems.

Moreover, merely studying other political systems besides our own is insufficient. The more systematic study of comparative politics requires a comparative framework and methodology, focusing on a wide range of different political systems. Only then is it possible to develop plausible general hypotheses and test them against the evidence of political practice in many countries. Thus the study of comparative politics moved beyond limited comparisons of a few Western political systems to a global approach, taking in communist political systems and the politics of developing nations.

The systems model

One early proposed solution to the complex diversity of comparative politics around the world was to adopt a simple model that might be applied to politics anywhere, the systems model. Systems theory was used in various fields (such as biology) to describe any self-regulating system. It was adapted by Talcott Parsons* for the study of sociology and by David Easton* and Gabriel Almond* for politics. One of the great merits of the systems approach was that it focused on the interrelationship of parts of the political process with each other and the wider economic, social, and natural environment. Moreover, its terminology and analysis could, in theory, be applied to any political system.

The basic systems model is very simple (see Figure 2.1). Inputs are fed into the system from the wider environment, converted by the system into outputs that in turn affect the environment and, through a feedback process, lead to new inputs. Applied to politics, the inputs are the 'demands' made by people, for example, for jobs, higher living standards, and better public services, backed by 'supports' in the shape of taxes, compliance, participation, and so on. These demands and supports are processed by government to produce 'outputs' in the form of laws, policies, and decisions that in turn affect people and feed back into fresh demands and supports. Some versions of the model suggest that such institutions as **pressure groups** ('articulating' demands) and **political parties** ('aggregating' demands) act as key intermediary 'gatekeepers' between people and government. Others distinguish between the formal 'outputs' of government (laws, decisions on taxes and spending, etc.), and the actual 'outcomes' as they affect people in practice. This is a useful distinction, as decisions may have unintended consequences and the final outcome of a particular policy may vary from, and sometimes even contradict, the stated intention of government.

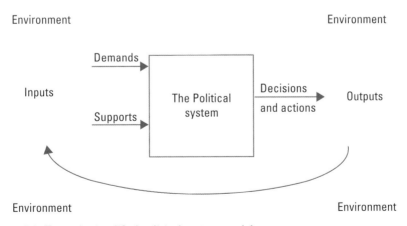

Figure 2.1 Easton's simplified political system models

Source: Easton (1965).

While systems theory had a substantial impact on the way politics was studied and explained, it was also subjected to some criticism. One objection was that it essentially involved little more than a new description of the political process and new terminology (or jargon). As a theory it was effectively unfalsifiable [see arguments of Popper, above]. Moreover, although the systems model purported to provide a framework for the analysis of any political system, some detected an implicit American or Western bias. Others argued that it focused on the maintenance of political stability and failed to explain system breakdown, crises, and **revolutions**.

In focusing on inputs into and outputs from the whole political system, the systems model also substantially downplayed the role of **government** and the **state**, viewed almost as a mere conversion mechanism (converting inputs into outputs) or as a mysterious 'black box'. In practice, American political science in the mid-20th century focused largely on the inputs of people into the political process, through voting, through membership and support of political parties, and participation in pressure group activity, and the underlying political culture, shaped by socialisation and political communication. Government and the 'outputs' of government, such as laws, policies, and specific decisions, were relatively neglected. Partly as a consequence of such criticism, the full systems model has been largely abandoned, although some of its key terms are still routinely used and its emphasis on politics as an interactive and interdependent process remains.

Problems with the study of comparative politics

Sidney Verba, one of the standard bearers of the new comparative politics, confessed in 1985 that it 'has been disappointing to some' especially, he suggests 'in comparison to past aspirations and hopes' (quoted by Peter Mair in Goodin and Klingemann et al. 1996, 314). One obvious problem with a comprehensive approach was the increasing number of states and the wide range of political systems. In 1945 there were just 50 members of the United Nations. By 2011 there were 193. Most of these states differ massively in size, in social structure, in the level of economic and political development, in the formal structure of government, and in their longevity and stability. Even basic statistical comparisons for key indicators (e.g. population, national income and growth, unemployment levels, literacy, electoral turnout) are not always reliable. In such circumstances meaningful comparison is often difficult. Indeed, many comparative specialists no longer try to be comprehensive, instead choosing to concentrate on narrower area studies, such as African politics or Scandinavian politics, or specialising in particular types of regimes, such as parliamentary democracies or military dictatorships. Others prefer to focus on key institutions or processes in modern Western parliamentary democracies, examining elections, voting, political parties, and pressure group activity.

One obvious way to bring some order into an increasingly crowded field is through the classification of political systems. Under the influence of the Cold War, regimes were commonly classified under three headings, depending on whether they were part of the 'first world' (the liberal democratic and capitalist West), the 'second world' (the alternative communist bloc), or the 'third' or 'developing' world (effectively, the rest of the globe). Needless to say, each 'world' contained a wide range of political and economic systems, particularly the third or residual category. This classification, which was always flawed, became effectively redundant with the end of the Cold War in 1989. Some comparative politics specialists were so disoriented by the virtual implosion of the 'second world' that they talked of a 'death in the family'. Others attempted to design new typologies more suited to an altered reality (e.g. including such categories as 'Islamic states'), without establishing any general consensus. Indeed, the collapse of the Soviet bloc has further increased both the number and variety of states, magnifying the problems of effective and meaningful comparison and of developing new 'grand theories' covering the whole range of very varied political systems.

Others object that this whole approach is too state-centred. Although the behavioural revolution involved a shift in comparative studies from government to politics and from elite to mass behaviour, it remained essentially focused on sovereign states. Yet any student of politics today soon becomes aware of the growing importance of **international organisations** (both governmental and nongovernmental) and **transnational corporations**. These, together with the growth of cross-national political identities, attitudes, and behaviour, suggest that the framework of independent sovereign nation-states may no longer be entirely adequate for the study of comparative politics in the modern world [see Sections 3 and 4, below].

Here we focus on some of the main developments in political science in the 20th century and key areas of study

VOTING AND ELECTORAL CHOICE

Hague, Harrop, and McCormick (2016) note that voting behaviour is the most intensively studied question in all political science. It was hardly a key issue at all until the 19th century. Before then, in almost all countries, few if any voted with (generally) only a marginal impact on politics and government. Yet voting became central to the theory and practice of modern liberal democracies where the study of political science was expanding rapidly. Moreover, detailed election results, along with official census returns, other public records, and commercial opinion surveys, supplied a mass of data for a rigorous scientific analysis of voting behaviour, using the latest advanced statistical techniques. In the 1940s and 1950s analysis of data still depended on the time-consuming use of punched cards, limiting the scope for examining correlations. Subsequently the introduction of computers enabled complex analyses of an ever-expanding quantity of data.

Much of the early ground-breaking work in elections and voting was carried out in the United States. Pioneering studies included *The People's Choice* (Lazarsfeld, Berelson, and Gaudet 1944) and *The American Voter* (Campbell et al. 1960). This work was soon imitated in the United Kingdom (e.g. Butler and Stokes, *Political Change in Britain*, 1969) and other Western states. One early finding, rather disquieting to those committed to representative democracy, was that most voting, both in the USA and elsewhere, appeared to be habitual. Instead of individual voters dispassionately weighing up the programmes and policies of rival parties and the merits or demerits of individual candidates, most seemed to cast their votes for the same party from one election to the next. Moreover, some research indicated that the minority of 'floating voters' who changed their vote between elections were not the most discriminating and knowledgeable but often among the most politically apathetic and ignorant.

Of course, habitual support for one party is not necessarily thoughtless and irrational, as that party might consistently represent the interests and concerns of a particular section of the electorate (such as trade union members or home owners). Yet it might also reflect the process of political socialisation: the cumulative influence of family, schooling, local community, religion, and workplace on political loyalties. Where all these social pressures were in the same direction, they might prove difficult to resist. Where an individual received very different political messages from parents, teachers, neighbours, local church leaders, and fellow workers, political allegiances might be less predictable. Even so, studies in the mid-20th century indicated that most voters decided their political allegiance early, perhaps at the first election in which they were eligible to vote, and many stayed with this early party preference over time.

The first major survey of voting in the USA, Lazarsfeld et al. (1944), concluded that 'social characteristics determine political preference'. Thus if you knew the occupation, education, religion, ethnicity, and local community of a voter, you could predict his or her electoral choice with tolerable accuracy. Later research at Michigan University produced a rather more complex and subtle explanation of the social pressures leading to a choice of party identification, which did not necessarily involve always voting for that same party (Campbell et al. 1960). Surveys of UK general elections were undertaken by Nuffield College, Oxford, from 1964 onwards, while a succession of books explored the factors influencing voting (e.g. Pulzer 1967; Butler and Stokes 1969). These largely mirrored the correlation of social factors with electoral choice found in US surveys. Pulzer (1967, 98) boldly declared, 'Class is the basis of British party politics; all else is embellishment and detail.'

Indeed, other factors, such as gender, age, or religion, appeared less important than occupational class in Britain. Women appeared slightly more inclined to vote Conservative than men in early postwar elections, perhaps because most women then were not subject to the same workplace and trade unions pressures, as well as having longer life expectancy – older voters were less likely to favour Labour. This correlation between age and party preference was not necessarily confirmation of the common assumption that as people grow older they grow more conservative (with a small 'c') and resistant to change. Butler and Stokes (1969) concluded that the long-term political allegiance of most voters was shaped by the prevailing political climate when they came of age. Older voters in early interwar elections first voted when Labour was relatively weak. By contrast, many of those who first voted in 1945, when the tide was flowing Labour's way, retained their Labour identity subsequently.

These early studies of voting behaviour by American and British political scientists focused on single countries – 'The *American* Voter', 'Political Change in *Britain*' – and were thus not comparative. Moreover, some of the analysis of electoral choice and party preference in the USA and the United Kingdom reflected assumptions around particular political cultures and specific electoral and party systems that were not typical of other countries. Thus the vast majority of modern democracies do not employ the simple plurality (or 'first past the post') electoral system still used in the USA and for Westminster parliamentary elections in the United Kingdom. Nor do other representative democracies have only two major parties competing for power, as in the USA and (substantially, until recently) in the United Kingdom. Additionally, in many Western countries there were cross-cutting religious and ethnic cleavages on top of social or occupational class differences. Thus political identities were more complex, with Catholicism attracting support for Christian democratic parties in Italy, Germany, France, and some Latin American countries. Even so, in most continental European democracies, voters showed a strong party identity in early postwar elections, as they did in the United Kingdom and the United States.

Yet, from the latter part of the 20th century onwards there has been a general trend towards 'party dealignment', or the weakening of older party identities and increasing electoral volatility across the Western world, coupled with a marked general decline in previously high electoral turnout. Figure 2.2 shows the fall in the votes for the two main parties in the United Kingdom since 1945, although interestingly the 2017 election showed an upswing in votes for the Labour and Conservative parties. All this may perhaps reflect some disillusion with party politics in general and, more specifically, with party convergence ('they're all the same'), as well as a progressive weakening of old class and religious divisions. Thus in Italy there has been a collapse in support for the Christian Democrats and Communists, who had dominated postwar Italian politics, and the rise of quite new parties. Elsewhere in Europe older parties did not suffer such total eclipse but faced increased competition from new populist parties. Only in the United States has the dominance of the two old parties, Democrats and Republicans, remained substantially intact.

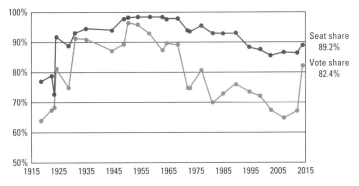

Figure 2.2 Two-party % share of the vote 1918–2017 (the United Kingdom)

Source: Institute for Government analysis of the House of Commons Library Election Statistics and the 2017 general election result.

POLITICAL PARTIES

If voting is central to the modern study of liberal democracies, so also are political parties. Electors do not generally vote for the individual candidate but for the party he or she represents. Indeed, it is party that gives the voter an effective choice between different policies and programmes. While independents without a party label can and do stand for election, they are rarely elected and often attract only a derisory vote. Parliaments and legislatures largely or wholly consist of members attached to parties. Governments, both in presidential and parliamentary systems, are essentially party governments, although in a parliamentary system the government may consist of either a single party or a coalition of parties. Party commonly plays a crucial role at other levels of government, in local and regional government and now also in some supranational bodies such as elections for the European Parliament. So political parties are crucial elements in the politics and government of liberal democracies today, as well as looming large in some other regimes, such as one-party states and illiberal democracies.

Yet if parties are omnipresent in modern politics and government today, it was not always so. In Britain, it was only in the course of the 19th century, with the growth of the franchise, that the Liberals and Conservatives became disciplined parliamentary parties with an extra-parliamentary organised membership. By that time parties with a mass following were already a feature of US, French, and German politics. While some old parliamentary parties subsequently built up a nationwide membership to support electioneering and funding, some newer parties were founded outside parliament to seek parliamentary representation (e.g. Labour in the United Kingdom). Both old and new parties felt obliged to cede some influence to this wider membership, over the selection of party candidates, over policy, and even over the choice of leader.

An early academic analysis of political parties was undertaken by Ostrogorski*, a Russian who had studied in France and visited both Britain and America. His book, *Democracy and the Organization of Political Parties* (1902), focused on the British and US party systems. Ostrogorski feared that the radical and unrepresentative extra-parliamentary mass membership of parties might effectively control the more moderate parliamentary leadership. Some politicians expressed similar fears.

A strongly contrasting analysis of political parties was published in 1911 by a German sociologist Robert Michels* (1876–1936) who studied in England and France as well as Germany, where he had once been an active socialist and member of the Social Democratic Party. Michels is linked with Pareto* and Mosca* as a classical elitist [see above, Section 1], who argued that power is inevitably concentrated in the hands of the few. He argued in his book *Political Parties* (1911) that real power remained with the party leadership rather than ordinary members, because of what he called 'the iron law of oligarchy'. The party elite was organised, cohesive, full-time, and relatively expert, and enjoyed the support of a professional centralised bureaucracy, while the mass membership was relatively disorganised, part-time, and amateur. Thus the central party machine continued to dominate, even where power was theoretically controlled by ordinary members. This analysis soon seemed uncomfortably prophetic, particularly to some disillusioned members of left-wing parties, dismayed by the compromises of their leaders. Even so, arguments over power and influence within modern political parties continue down to the present day.

Party systems

The number of parties significantly involved in the struggle to secure representation and a role in government can vary considerably among countries. The main variants are one-party, two-party, and multiparty systems.

One-party systems can result from deliberate limits on party competition, for example simply banning other parties as in some former communist states or in right-wing dictatorships. Alternatively, even where other parties are free to fight elections, one party may remain overwhelmingly dominant. This was sometimes the case in newly established states, where one party or movement was identified with the successful drive for independence or majority rule (e.g. the Congress Party in the first decades of India's independence or the African National Congress in South Africa).

In a pure two-party system, two major parties dominate elections and representation in assemblies and, between them, monopolise control of government. The long duopoly of the Republicans and Democrats in US politics is the clearest example of a two-party system, although for periods the United Kingdom had a two-party system by most, if not all, criteria, and some other states in the English-speaking world have also for a time had substantially two-party systems.

Multiparty systems feature several significant competing parties and commonly involve coalition government. They are the norm rather than the exception in modern representative democracies. A distinction is sometimes drawn between stable multiparty systems and unstable multiparty systems. In the former it seems relatively easy to form and maintain a coalition government, perhaps because ideological differences are not wide or deep (e.g. the Netherlands, Germany, or Sweden until more recently). In the latter, perhaps because of the existence of substantial extremist or anti-system parties, it is difficult to form any kind of government with prospects of an enduring majority. Examples include the Fourth French Republic (1946–1958) and postwar Italy, where governments were often fragile and short-lived with frequent political crises.

Why do some countries have two-party systems and others multiparty systems? The French political scientist Maurice Duverger* (1917–2014) plausibly connected two-party systems to the first-past-the-post electoral system (sometimes termed 'Duverger's law'). Certainly, the most conspicuous examples of a two-party system (the United States and until recently the United Kingdom) have both long used the first-past-the-post method of election (more accurately described as the 'single member, simple plurality system'). Under such a system there is no close relationship between the proportion of votes cast and parliamentary seats won. Third and minor parties whose support is geographically widely dispersed (e.g. Liberal Democrats, Greens, and UKIP in the United Kingdom) are seriously underrepresented in such a system, although parties whose support is geographically concentrated (e.g. Scottish or Welsh nationalists) can do relatively well. In the United Kingdom the introduction of more proportional representation in elections for Scotland's Parliament, the Welsh Assembly, the Northern Irish Assembly, London, and the European Parliament have all led to a wider range of parties being represented.

Altogether, there is plenty of evidence that electoral systems can have a significant impact on the range of parties involved in representative assemblies and in government. Even so, there is no simple correlation between electoral systems and party systems. In British politics there has sometimes been a three- or four-party system at Westminster despite the first-past-the-post electoral system. Moreover, multiparty systems elsewhere often appear to reflect multiple and cross-cutting social or ideological cleavages. Duverger himself acknowledged that the French Fourth Republic's multiparty system reflected three such cross-cutting divisions (planning versus the free market, religious convictions versus anticlericalism, and support for and opposition to the Soviet Union). More recent changes in the electoral system in the Fifth French Republic, some designed in part to polarise choice, have led to two leading parties ('Gaullists' under various official names and socialists) dominating most presidential and national assembly elections. Yet although the communists have been relatively marginalised, the far right National Front has made an increasing impact on French elections.

Types of party

Organised political parties of some kind or other now feature in every continent and in most countries, including virtually all representative democracies, as well as quite a few states whose democratic credentials appear more questionable. Some classification is important to provide a framework for analysis of what has become a very crowded field, although it is not easy for find a useful typology. Parties differ considerably in their size, longevity, and general importance. Many parties that feature in elections are tiny and ephemeral, yet some others have played an important role in the politics of their country for a century or more. Clearly, parties may also differ radically in their aims, principles, and policies. They are frequently categorised according to their apparent location on the **left–right** political spectrum [see key concepts]. Thus parties are often described as left, centre, or right, with gradations within each category ('extreme left', 'centre-left', 'far right', etc.). Such a typology relates principally to ideas, with planning, public services, and social justice favoured by the left while the free market, property, law and order are stressed by the right, although it also reflects associated interests, particularly class interests. Yet in many countries, particularly on the European continent, there have long been other social cleavages (religious, urban/rural, linguistic, and ethnic) that cut across economic class divisions and may considerably complicate both ideological conflict and the party system (Lane and Ersson 1999)

One simple distinction, still commonly cited in textbooks, is that between ideological and pragmatic parties. In practice, parties of the left were rather more likely to endorse formally their political values and aims, sometimes in the party's constitution. Although some parties of the right, influenced by neoliberal ideas, proclaimed their free market principles with as much ideological fervour as their socialist opponents, the traditional conservative line was to abhor **ideology**. Thus they boasted instead of their flexible, pragmatic, and 'common-sense' approach to the problems of government. Yet such parties often showed considerable ideological consistency in practice, while left-wing parties commonly displayed some flexibility in interpreting their core principles. This is hardly surprising. A party that shows no consistency loses credibility, while one that has no capacity to adapt to altered circumstances dooms itself to irrelevance. Thus the distinction between ideological and pragmatic parties was always relative rather than fundamental.

Duverger (1954) provided an early typology of parties, based on their organisational features. Yet at least two of his four categories are now of more historical than contemporary importance. One, the 'cell party', based on Lenin's organisation of the Russian Bolsheviks around the principles of an elite 'vanguard' party and 'democratic centralism' (later imitated by communist parties in other countries), is today of sharply diminished significance. Similarly, the militia party, organised as a fighting force on military lines, was a feature of fascist and some other right-wing parties, particularly in the interwar period, although it might still be an appropriate description for some parties in the Middle East.

Duverger's other two categories were the 'caucus' (or 'cadre') party and the 'branch' (or 'mass') party. Yet by the time he was writing, the older caucus or cadre parties (like the then still surviving French radical party), formed by loose groupings of politicians in national parliaments or assemblies, already found it difficult to compete effectively with modern mass parties with a strong extra-parliamentary organisation. Such mass parties had a formal democratic constitution and a clearly identified leadership, accountable (in theory at least) to millions of paid-up members recruited in a comprehensive system of local branches, and were supported by a central national organisation with salaried professional staff. This model, developed by left-wing parties such as the German Social Democrats, was increasingly imitated by parties of the right and centre, and soon became the norm. However, it is increasingly questionable how far leading political parties today are still 'mass' parties in any meaningful sense [see below].

The party leadership, party members, and voters

There was always some potential for tension or conflict between the parliamentary leadership of mass parties and their 'grassroots' membership. Beer (1982) quotes Lowell to suggest that Ostrogorski's fears of grassroots member dominance [see above] were exaggerated in British parties then. He cites Robert McKenzie (1963) to reaffirm that they were still exaggerated in the 1950s and 1960s. Yet Ostrogorski drew attention to an enduring problem still faced by parties today. Effectively they have to satisfy two overlapping but distinctive markets, the mass of voters and party members.

This mattered less when many of a party's voters were also party members or at least identified strongly with a party, as was arguably the case when truly mass parties flourished, in the middle of the 20th century. The problem has been intensified by more recent developments. Almost everywhere party membership has declined sharply, and the active membership even more so. Effectively, most modern political parties retain the organisational trappings of the mass party without the mass membership that is its justification. Only a tiny minority of voters are now active paid-up members of political parties. This is bad news for parties that depend substantially on their members, to some extent for money but to a much greater extent for unpaid work in maintaining a grassroots organisation and fighting elections. Yet parties that do not listen to their dwindling active supporters risk alienating this still important resource. Indeed, party members retain some significant powers, including the selection of party candidates locally, often a role in electing the party leader, and some scope for influencing policy.

Such powers seem the minimum criteria for any party to be considered internally democratic. Yet such internal party democracy can saddle parties, in extreme cases, with an unelectable leader and programme, if party activists are markedly out of line with voters. Moreover, leaders seeking to broaden and modernise the party's image by, for example, selecting more women and ethnic minority candidates, can be effectively frustrated by unrepresentative elderly, male, white, local party activists.

Some analysts suggest that the more electorally successful modern parties seek to avoid this problem by radically transforming themselves, marginalising their members, and pursuing a pragmatic and consensual approach designed to appeal to as many voters as possible. Such parties are described as 'catch-all' parties, a term introduced by Kircheimer (1966) and developed by others (Panebianco 1988; Katz and Mair 1995). The 'catch-all' party unashamedly seeks power rather than the representation of any social group (such as the working class or Catholics). Instead it seeks support wherever it can be obtained, using modern marketing techniques. Such catch-all parties may be dominated by charismatic leaders who reach out directly to voters through the mass media rather than through the party organisation. To this extent, party members may seem to matter less. It is sometimes argued that the party leadership also deliberately changes party procedures to bypass grassroots party activists or reduce their influence.

This trend towards elite domination of parties was identified by Katz and Mair (1995) in their seminal work on cartel parties. This model characterises party members as the 'cheerleaders for the elite (20). The 'cartel party' model also shows how parties have become increasingly reliant upon the state for finance [see below]. Table 2.1 shows the development of party organisation over time.

Table 2.1 Party organisation models

Party Type	Time Period
Elite Party	19th Century
Mass Party	1880–1960
Catch-all Party	1945–
Cartel Party	1970–

Source: Katz and Mair (1995).

A party's strategy will always be strongly influenced by the competition it faces and the party system to which it belongs. Thus Downs* (1957) argued that the rational party strategy to maximise electoral support was to appeal to the median voter and the middle ground, particularly in a two-party system (see Figure 2.3). However, such a strategy may be less successful in countries with a multiparty system, particularly where this reflects continuing deep class, ethnic, regional, and religious divisions in the electorate.

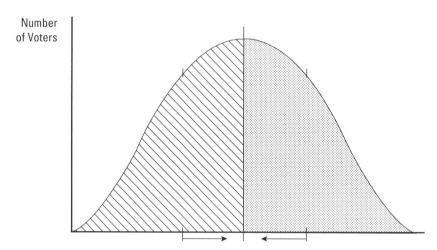

Figure 2.3 Median voter

More recently, the weakening of party identities and loyalties and increasing electoral volatility has introduced much more unpredictability into party systems. Parties with long strong traditions can suddenly face melt-down, as the Italian Christian Democrats have found. New major parties such as Berlusconi's Forza Italia, have come from nowhere into government (and sometimes have subsequently declined as fast). Political circumstances have precipitated major shifts. Thus the fall of the Berlin Wall, and the ensuing collapse of communism in the former Soviet Union and Eastern Europe, had major consequences for Western communist parties. Most of the former Italian Communist Party (that had long pursued its own version of Eurocommunism) reinvented itself as the Democratic Party of the Left and briefly formed part of a left-of-centre coalition. The less flexible French Communists have continued to decline. In the new successor democratic or quasi-democratic regimes in Eastern Europe, Asia, and the former Soviet Union a range of new parties have flourished briefly in a shifting constellation of political forces.

More recently, central and south America and Europe have seen the rise of new populist parties, mainly of the right but including some on the left. A common element of this new populism is a rejection of the old parliamentary elites and, in Europe, opposition to immigration (both from within the EU and outside) (see Kaltwasser et al. 2017). It remains to be seen how far these new parties and movements will prove ephemeral, yet it certainly appears that most of the older mass membership parties of both the left and right are suffering decline, with a far smaller proportion of voters remaining actively involved. Whether this reflects a decline in political engagement or perhaps new forms of engagement (through for example the internet and social media) remains to be seen.

The finance of parties

One reason why parliamentary parties initially sought members was because they needed money for organisational support, campaigning, and research, although fees were generally kept low to attract a broad membership base. The steep decline in party membership almost everywhere has led to a similar reduction in party funds. This matters, because it can make parties over-dependent on a few rich individuals and organisations, who may be seen to be buying influence over policy. In most parliamentary democracies laws have been passed to enforce disclosure of party funding, but transparency does not remove the problem, and it certainly fails to ensure a level playing field in party competition. Thus many countries have introduced some measure of state funding for political parties, as well as limitations on party spending, particularly on elections.

PRESSURE GROUPS, INFLUENCE AND POWER

While membership of, and active participation in, political parties seems to be in steep decline almost everywhere, involvement in other organisations and groups remains as strong as ever. Political scientists commonly use the umbrella term **'pressure groups'** to describe all this. It is not an ideal term. Many groups hardly appear to be exercising political pressure much of the time, although even the most apparently apolitical of organisations can be drawn into politics on occasion. Thus a local allotment association or tennis club whose members hold a diversity of political views and party affiliations may unite to protest at a new planned road over their grounds. Yet many other organisations are continually involved in the political process. These include major businesses and bodies looking after key industries and business interests generally, as well as trade unions, consumer groups, and a whole range of specialist groups promoting specific causes or interests.

It is difficult to assess with any accuracy the success of such groups in influencing the political process. The success of parties can be measured in terms of the proportion of votes and seats won and control of government. It is much more difficult to measure the influence of individual pressure groups or the cumulative effect of pressure group activity. However, the power of some groups is legendary. Thus the National Rifle Association (NRA) has been successful in frustrating almost any effective gun control legislation in the United States, despite recurrent mass shooting tragedies. Those who manufacture and sell firearms in European states and recreational shooting groups also seek to influence their own governments on gun sales and gun use, but with far less success. The power of the NRA in the United States may be down to their greater resources and organisational skills or it may simply reflect the prevailing US political culture (expressed in the Second Amendment to the US constitution, the right to bear arms).

Clearly the power of groups can also change over time. In the United Kingdom Ted Heath took on the National Union of Miners (NUM) and lost both his own job as prime minister and his party's control of government. Margaret Thatcher took on the same union a decade later and won, cementing her own and her party's power. It was not necessarily a consequence of Thatcher's greater determination or skill, but perhaps a reflection of the long-term decline of the coal industry and a matching decline in the miners' capacity to threaten power supplies and the national economy.

PLURALIST AND ELITIST PERSPECTIVES ON POWER

Despite all the obvious problems in assessing the cumulative effect of pressure group activity, some political scientists have tried hard to assess how far **power** appears to be fairly widely diffused, in accordance with pluralist assumptions and democratic values, or how far it seems to be concentrated in the hands of a relatively small elite or elites.

Pluralism is closely linked with mainstream American political science. It grew out of the pioneering group theory of Arthur Bentley* (1870–1957) who argued: 'All phenomena of government are phenomena of groups pressing one another.' Group competition he saw as the essence of the political process and the science of politics: 'when the groups are adequately stated, everything is stated' (Bentley 1908). Pressure group theory was developed by a succession of leading American political scientists, including David Truman, Nelson Polsby, Charles Lindblom* and, above all, Robert Dahl*. They and others carried out extensive research into the activities of countless groups and found evidence of their influence on specific public policies or decisions. There was always a significant normative element to this apparently dispassionate social science. The United States was claimed as the cradle of modern democracy, which assumes that power is widely dispersed. Many American political scientists were intent (perhaps largely unconsciously) on demonstrating that power was in fact dispersed, as evidenced by the countless competing groups all pressing on government.

Thus American pluralists approved of pressure group activity. They maintained that the cumulative result of such activity aided and improved the democratic process rather than subverting it (as some early critics of pressure groups had argued). In an open democratic society there were ample opportunities for anyone who wanted to defend an interest or promote a cause to organise with others to influence decision-makers and the wider public. This, pluralists argued, commonly encouraged those who took a different view to establish opposed groups, leading to a balance of interests (sometimes described as countervailing power). The information and arguments provided by conflicting interests and causes put more relevant knowledge in the public domain, thus improving the quality of debate and aiding decision-making. Pluralists saw this competition for influence among countless groups as the essence of democracy. Governments needed to be responsive to these pressures if they wanted to maintain their popularity and power.

Some pluralists implied that governments passively responded to the sum of group pressures, acting as neutral arbiters among conflicting interests in society. Others suggested that the pluralists had a rather rosy view of the prospects for ordinary people to have effective political influence. Radical **elite** theorists argued that effective power was far more concentrated than the pluralists maintained. Briefly, critics of pluralism argued that there were massive inequalities in resources and influence between some groups and others, and that the **state** was far from neutral but encouraged some interests while effectively excluding others.

The old European classical elitists were antidemocratic in outlook [see Section 1, above]. Many US elite theorists were radical political sociologists. They lamented what they perceived as the concentration of power in what was supposed to be a democracy. C. Wright Mills*, in his classic study of American government and politics *The Power Elite* (1956), argued that there were close interrelationships and a shared outlook among the US political, military, and business elites. There was an essentially similar analysis of the role of the influential role of interlocking elites within Western states generally (and the United Kingdom particularly) by the British Marxist Ralph Miliband*, who dedicated his own book *The State in Capitalist Society* (1969) to the memory of C. Wright Mills.

However, much of the argument between elitists and pluralists focused not on power at the level of the **nation-state** but on detailed case studies of power and decision-making in specific urban **communities**, both in the United States and elsewhere. These studies were suggestive rather than conclusive on the distribution of urban power and often seemed to do no more than confirm the initial assumptions of theorists on both sides. Floyd Hunter (1953) showed that decision-making in Atlanta, Georgia, was substantially dominated by business interests, while the wider community, and blacks especially, had little influence. In marked contrast Robert Dahl* (1961) concluded that there was no single elite dominating decision-making in New Haven, Connecticut. Instead different groups were influential in different policy arenas and political influence was relatively widely dispersed, as the pluralist model suggested. Similar studies of urban power in the United Kingdom and France were no more conclusive. Thus some concluded that case studies can only be illustrative; they do not prove anything.

Critics of research by Dahl and other pluralists suggested they focused too much upon influence on overt decision-making. Bachrach and Baratz (1962, 1970) argued that there were two faces of power: the power to influence and make decisions on issues that have arisen for public debate, and the power to deflect potentially dangerous issues from being brought forward for decision. Steven Lukes (1974) suggested there is a third dimension to power. Power can be exercised more subtly in such a way that issues do not even arise. Lukes cites in support a comparison of the air pollution policies of two apparently similar US steel cities, one of which introduced clean air policies while the other avoided the issue (Crenson 1971). In the latter, the steel company that provided the main employment in the town successfully kept pollution off the agenda 'without acting or entering into the political arena'. Its reputation alone, Crenson argued, was sufficient to prevent the issue coming up for decision.

Some pluralists, dubbed neo-pluralists, including Charles Lindblom, the economist J. K. Galbraith*, and even Robert Dahl himself in his later work, have made concessions to their critics. Thus neo-pluralists accepted that the state is not a neutral referee but an active (and often partisan) participant in the game. While continuing to maintain that power and influence is fairly widely dispersed, they acknowledged that some interests, particularly business interests, have considerable practical influence while others may be virtually excluded from the political process.

This neo-pluralism can be compared with another theory of power and decision-making, **corporatism**, fashionable in Western Europe (but not in the United States) particularly in the 1970s. Both pluralism and corporatism saw groups as important in the political decision-making process. Yet whereas pluralism implies countless groups in competition to influence government, corporatism suggested a much more constrained policy process in which a few peak or umbrella groups representing the key interests of capital and labour were closely involved with government in a relationship of mutual dependence. To critics, this highly limited form of interest representation involved a bypassing of both parliament and people. (Dunleavy and O'Leary 1987 discuss corporatism under the general heading of **elitism**.) However, while modern **Marxists** assumed corporatism involved sacrificing the interests of labour to the needs of **capitalism**, **neoliberals** considered that corporatism involved far too many concessions to producer interests in general, and labour interests in particular. Some neoliberals indeed criticised not just corporatism but the wider pluralist influence of groups on the policy process. They argued that an alliance of client groups dependent on public services and producer groups (including both business interests and trade unions) have contributed to a malign growth in postwar government spending and taxation.

POWER AND DEMOCRACY

Thus the long-running debate over the effective distribution of power in Western political systems was ultimately inconclusive, although it generated much important research and extended and deepened our understanding of the political process. It also illustrated some of the difficulties in separating **positive** social science from **normative** political theory. Behind the on-going debate on how power is *actually* distributed in modern Western political systems, seemingly a question of fact, there were issues around how it *should* be distributed, a question of value. Despite the insistence of early **behaviouralists** that the two issues should be kept separate, they have been almost inextricably linked in practice. The (largely unspoken) premise behind the radical elitist critique of modern Western democracy from those such as C. Wright Mills and Ralph Miliband is that power should be more widely dispersed than it is. On the other side of the debate Robert Dahl, a major figure in the behavioural revolution, has never been solely concerned with demonstrating that power is fairly widely dispersed in practice. He effectively developed a new theory of democracy, which he preferred to call 'polyarchy', based on group politics to which he clearly attached positive value.

Yet in some respects this work was untypical of modern political science, as the study of pressure group behaviour and influence was rather less susceptible to methods involving the collection and analysis of statistical data. The examination of the influence of particular individuals and groups on key decisions (or sometimes non-decisions) inevitably involved some essentially subjective judgements. While case studies of decision-making in particular communities were certainly suggestive, they could hardly *prove* that power was relatively dispersed or effectively concentrated. Moreover, it was difficult to *generalise* from the findings in the specific communities. Even if it was true that political influence in New Haven, Connecticut (the focus of Robert Dahl's *Who Governs?* 1961), was dispersed rather than concentrated, this did not necessarily mean that it was similarly dispersed in other American cities, still less elsewhere.

POLITICAL CULTURE, POLITICAL SOCIALISATION AND POLITICAL COMMUNICATION

So far the emphasis here as been on observable political behaviour, voting (or sometimes not voting) joining parties, engaging in pressure groups or political movements. Yet this behaviour clearly reflects underlying beliefs and assumptions. Thus political scientists have also sought to explore the political ideas that communities and nations hold, their **political culture**. The beliefs people hold about politics may crucially affect the whole functioning of government and the political system, particularly in states claiming to be democratic. Thus democracy may hardly seem viable if the majority have no knowledge of, or interest in, politics and government and have little or no confidence in their ability to have any influence on decisions that affect them.

How people acquire their political culture is also highly relevant. Much of what is called political socialisation involves the cumulative early influence of family background, schooling, local community, local faith groups, leisure interests, and early employment experiences. On top of these family and community influences, individuals are also exposed to the messages of the mass media and national political leaders, a much more top-down form of political communication. While pluralists assume that, in a liberal democracy, individual citizens are exposed to a sufficiently wide range of ideas and interests to enable them to form their own judgement on key political issues, elitists perceive a strong and persistent bias in the whole process of political communication.

Leading American political scientists, fully committed to a comparative approach, sought to measure and analyse political knowledge and attitudes across countries. In a pioneering study Almond* and Verba (1963) supervised in-depth opinion surveys in five countries, the United States, the United Kingdom, Mexico, West Germany, and Italy, and discovered considerable differences in their national political cultures. West Germany, they found, had a 'subject' political culture, in which people neither expected nor wanted to have much influence on government. Italy had a more 'parochial' political culture in which people identified with their own area rather than the country as a whole, with negative implications for participation in national politics. Survey evidence suggested the United States had a more 'participant' political culture, in which citizens both wanted and expected to have political influence, although the downside of this active citizenship was that Americans had less respect for the law and authority generally. Almond and Verba concluded that the United Kingdom (whose political culture was then characterised in terms of 'homogeneity, consensus and deference') came closest to what they regarded as an ideal 'civic' culture that blended elements of a subject and participant culture. Thus the British combined respect for the law and legitimate authority with confidence in their ability to influence the political process.

Almond and Verba assumed that political culture had major implications for political behaviour and, more specifically, for a flourishing democracy. Thus one might conclude that some nations are more suited to democracy than others. Yet of course changes in political practice and political behaviour may lead to changes in political attitudes. The apparently successful operation of democracy over a period may transform political attitudes. Recognising that political cultures can evolve over time, Almond and Verba later sought to repeat their research and found some significant changes over time (Almond and Verba 1980). Germans now took political participation and civic responsibility more seriously, while national confidence had declined in both the United Kingdom and the United States. These changes might be seen as the consequence on the one hand of Germany's 'economic miracle' and continued political stability and on the other of worsening economic and political problems in the United Kingdom and the United States.

Although Almond and Verba's research and analysis was impressive in breadth and depth, not everyone was convinced by their conclusions. One criticism was that in seeking to characterise national political cultures, they had downplayed or ignored evidence of significant subcultures, based (for example) on region, ethnicity, class, or gender. Thus some observers in the postwar period perceived a marked contrast between elite and mass culture and identified a distinctive working-class political subculture in Western countries such as the United Kingdom, Italy, and Germany, (Parkin 1971). In the United States there are distinctive subcultures associated with the south and with particular ethnic minorities (such as blacks and Hispanics). Feminists have often claimed that women's political attitudes and behaviour are significantly different from men's. The whole concept of a national political culture thus may obscure substantial political divisions within a nation, derived from people's very different experiences of life and work.

Political consensus

Yet others would still perceive a shared national political consensus that transcends such divisions. Such a consensus may simply reflect real political homogeneity, the absence of deep social and economic divisions. Alternatively it may reflect a willing compromise and sharing of power between different interests and subcultures in what Lijphart* (1977) has termed a consociational democracy. However, not everyone would accept that such a political consensus either exists in practice or should exist. For Marxists the consensus was always a phony or imposed consensus that did not reflect the real interests of the poor. People were effectively conditioned what to think by their upbringing, their education, the media, and the whole economic and social system they experienced, so that they could not conceive of any realistic alternative. The Italian Marxist Antonio Gramsci* used the term '**hegemony**' to describe the dominance of bourgeois ideas under capitalism. Steven Lukes (1974) suggested that the most subtle and effective use of power is the power to shape, in effect, how people think. It is a point made in a rather different way by Foucault* and leading postmodernist thinkers [see below], who argue that knowledge, and the language used to express knowledge, reflects power, an argument taken up by some feminists.

Post-material culture

For all kinds of reasons the study of political culture and even the term itself rather fell from academic favour. Yet some political scientists continued to examine the impact of people's attitudes and values on their political behaviour. Thus Ronald Inglehart* (1977) has found evidence for a change to '**post-material**' values in advanced Western states. The hypothesis suggests that a new political generation who take for granted levels of material prosperity and security are inclined to value post-material goals, including quality of life and self-fulfilment. This may be exemplified by the emergence of new social movements (such as the women's movement, the peace movement, the green movement) and new forms of political participation (the politics of protest rather than more formal electoral and parliamentary procedures). Some of this might be regarded as healthy for democracy, although not perhaps traditional representative democracy.

Yet it has also been noted that the evidence for such 'post-material' values is more sparse in Eastern Europe and other parts of the globe, where living standards are rather lower and there is an understandable continuing attachment to 'material' values. Indeed, much of the early enthusiasm of former communist societies in Eastern Europe for democracy and the EU was perhaps bound up with the hope and even expectation of the enjoyment of Western living standards. One cynical observation was 'democracy comes on four wheels', implying that these former communist peoples desired the same consumer goods widely enjoyed in advanced Western democracies. Certainly there seems to be less enthusiasm for green ideas, green pressure groups, and green parties in some of the newer European democracies.

Social capital

Despite the recent rapid spread of regimes formally endorsing democracy around the world, the long-term future of this system of government is hardly assured, even in apparently mature stable democracies. More than any other political system, democracy depends on the willing political support and participation of ordinary people. In long-established democracies the general decline in voter turnout, the sharp fall in membership and active involvement in political parties, and survey data indicating growing distrust of elected politicians and the whole political process all suggest a growing crisis of confidence in democracy. Some argue that there is a marked decline in engagement with the public sphere, a retreat into the private world of work, leisure, and family that bodes ill for the health of democracy. This is reflected in the rise of so-called post-truth politics where a loss of trust in political institutions and greater personalisation of how we acquire our political knowledge through the internet produces the situation whereby some politicians are able to present reality through a very distorted lens. Prominent post-truth campaigns were seen during the Brexit referendum campaign in the United Kingdom, during Donald Trump's presidential campaign, in the public statements of President Putin, and in certain debates in India (see Rose 2017).

The work of Robert Putnam* on **social capital** is sometimes cited in this connection. Putnam has long had a interest in the influence of political attitudes on the functioning of democracy. An early book *The Beliefs of Politicians* (1973) concentrated on the views of political elites, comparing the attitudes of politicians and party activists in the United Kingdom and Italy. His later work has focused on wider social attitudes and behaviour. Thus in his comparative study of regional governments in Italy, *Making Democracy Work: Civic Traditions in Modern Italy* (1993), he first identified the importance of what he called social capital (essentially the extent of social networks and community engagement) for a healthy functioning democratic system. In a seminal article published in 1995 he went on to argue that social capital was declining in modern America. He proceeded to document this thesis with extensive research into levels of social and communal interaction in the United States, published in *Bowling Alone: The Collapse and Revival of American Community* (2000). 'Bowling alone' was a metaphor for the solitary leisure activities of Americans, apparently increasing at the expense of more social, interactive pursuits. Putnam argued that the decrease of even such apparently apolitical activities as social dining and bridge clubs involved a decline in social capital, with damaging implications for civic engagement and democracy.

Putnam's work is substantially in the tradition of research into political culture established by Almond and Verba. Over time he has directed his interest to three of the five countries studied by them (the United Kingdom, Italy, and the USA), although the focus of his work is distinctive. His social capital thesis has been influential and provoked an extensive debate. Some have questioned whether the apparent decline in social capital found in the USA is replicated in other Western societies, pointing to increased participation in some forms of pressure groups and social movements (e.g. Hall 1999). However, another line of criticism is directed at Putnam's assumptions. Thus it is arguable that some 'solitary' activities that do not involve physical social interaction, such as communication via the internet, may not be damaging for democracy but may even assist more direct participation in politics (e.g. Margetts 2002, 201). Others again are critical of the whole concept of social capital and its underlying implications. Thus Theda Skocpol* (1996, 20–25) complained that Putnam's approach assumed that 'spontaneous social association is primary and government and politics are derivative'.

GOVERNMENT

The **behaviouralist** approach, perhaps inevitably, focused substantially on aspects of mass politics that were most easily observed and measured – although not necessarily the most important – such as voting, parties, and pressure groups, all seen as inputs to the political system. Behaviouralism impacted less on the study of government and its outputs, where critical aspects of the conduct of leading politicians and public servants were less open to the observations of political scientists.

Thus studies of British and US government substantially relied on traditional analysis of published sources rather than the new social scientific research. One focus was on the heads of government in leading Western countries. There was a long-running controversy over the power of the prime minister in the United Kingdom, with some arguing that this had grown at the expense of the cabinet (Mackintosh 1962; Crossman 1963) and others (Jones 1965) responding that the prime minister lacked clear executive powers and was only as powerful as his or her colleagues allowed him or her to be. The office and its holders continues to fascinate (e.g. King 1985; Hennessy 2000), but current wisdom suggests that much depends on the personality and style of individual prime ministers and leading colleagues and on changing political circumstances.

There have been similar arguments over the power of US presidents (Rossiter 1957; Neustadt 1960, 1991; Schlesinger 1973; Rose 1988). While presidents have clearer executive powers, as well as the additional prestige of head of state, they face further constraints, commonly including a hostile Congress, on top of a constitutional limit to their term of office that often appears to make them perceived 'lame ducks' well before the end of their occupancy of the White House. The German chancellor and French president both similarly have their own distinctive sources of power and constraints over its exercise. In all cases, much seems to depend on the personality of the holder and differences over time in political circumstances, which does not tell us much about the essence of government and public service.

Democracy and bureaucracy

Whatever the form of their governments or political executives, all modern states require an extensive staff of permanent salaried officials to implement their policies and manage their services, a public **bureaucracy**. The term 'bureaucracy' has acquired some negative connotations of inertia, time-wasting, and inefficiency, although Max Weber*, its key early theorist, considered bureaucracy the most rational and efficient way of running any large organisation in the private or public sector. For Weber, key features of bureaucracy included written rules, open competitive recruitment, promotion on merit and qualifications rather than patronage, and a clear chain of responsibility and accountability in hierarchically structured organisations.

In representative democracies there is an assumption that the leading state officials at the head of the state bureaucracy are ultimately accountable to politicians elected by the people. The relationship between elected ministers and senior appointed officials has become the focus of some scrutiny by political scientists and others. Thus it is sometimes suggested that it is appointed officials rather than elected politicians who shape key decisions and wield effective power.

There are plausible explanations for bureaucratic power. Politicians are temporary, their tenure of office limited by the whims of voters, while leading government officials are more permanent. Although politicians need communication skills to win elections, they do not necessarily have any knowledge or expertise in the services they are asked to run nor do they normally last long enough to acquire the skills they lack, while the officials (who nominally serve them) have been appointed on merit and qualifications and may have spent much of their working lives within the organisation. They are professionals, while ministers are amateurs. Moreover it is the hierarchy of officials who are responsible for implementing policy, often over a long period of time. Perhaps as a consequence, there may be a pronounced difference between announced policy decisions and eventual policy outcomes. Thus (it can be plausibly argued) bureaucracy effectively trumps democracy.

However, the relationship between elected politicians and senior appointed officials varies from country to country, depending on all kinds of factors relating to the durability of governments and the length of tenure of ministers on the one hand and the recruitment, organisation, and culture of the state bureaucracy on the other. Thus France is sometimes held to illustrate government by appointed officials rather than elected ministers. This seemed particularly the case during the Fourth French Republic (1946–1958), where elected governments were often short-lived and weak, while French communications, energy supply, and finances were effectively modernised by elite state technocrats, recruited from the prestigious *grandes écoles*, such as the École Polytechnique, the École Nationale d'Administration (ENA), and the Inspection des Finances (IF). The dominance of technocrats to some extent survived the transition to the Fifth Republic. Thus President De Gaulle despised the old professional politicians and preferred to appoint qualified technocrats as ministers. President Giscard d'Estaing was himself a graduate of all three of the *grandes écoles* (above) and appointed other ministers from a technocratic background. 'Giscard's regime was seen in France as the apotheosis of the gradual takeover of political power since 1958 by the new civil service mandarins and technocrats with their tight old boy networks' (Ardagh 1982, 84). Since then, there has been rather more criticism of the rigidity and exclusiveness of the French bureaucracy, although its merits still seem to outweigh its problems.

The British civil service remains very different. Although following the Northcote-Trevelyan reforms of the 19th century it aspired to recruit the best brains by open competition, it did not seek to train its recruits in specialised skills like the French *grandes écoles* but rather assumed that those who had excelled in traditional academic disciplines would be able to transfer their superior brain power to the business of any government department. Leading British civil servants were thus generalists rather than specialists, often moved from department to department to gain breadth of experience. Nor was there much in-service training to remedy any deficiencies in their knowledge and skills. (The establishment of a Civil Service College has only partially rectified this deficiency.) Thus while the Permanent Secretaries who head government departments normally have far longer and more varied experience of government than the ministers they serve, they may not have any greater specialist technical expertise. Even so, its is often argued that they, rather than ministers, shape departmental priorities and key decisions, as implied in the long-running BBC TV comedy series *Yes Minister* and *Yes Prime Minister*. (The sales of these series to many other countries and their apparent popularity suggest that their central message resonates elsewhere.)

However, the evidence is inconclusive. Clearly, changes in government do often lead to changes in policy, and individual ministers who are sufficiently determined can make a difference. Nor is the relationship between elected politicians and leading civil servants necessarily adversarial. Indeed in the United Kingdom they often seem to share the same educational and social background and move in similar circles. The introduction of

Special Advisers with a party political background into government, some of whom go on to become members of parliament (MPs) and ministers, has blurred the distinction between politician and bureaucrat still further.

MANAGING THE PUBLIC SECTOR

It was long assumed in the United Kingdom that what was then called 'public administration' was quite different from management in the private sector. Indeed the Royal Institute of Public Administration (RIPA) was founded before the Political Studies Association. Sceptics suggested that the British study of public administration was too uncritical, not entirely fairly, as the case for reform and reorganisation of the civil service and both central and local government was vigorously made. Yet there were tacit assumptions that managing the public sector was quite different from business management and that leading officials could be trusted to serve the wider public interest, assumptions that were to be vigorously challenged by rational or public choice theory [see below].

One problem that all those researching public bureaucracies face is government secrecy, particularly in the United Kingdom where access to recent cabinet and other documents is restricted by Official Secrets Acts. Even so, two leading American political scientists Heclo and Wildavsky showed what could be done in a path-breaking analysis of decision-making at the centre of British government, *The Private Government of Public Money* (1974), based on thousands of interviews of leading civil servants and ministers, who were quoted extensively with ranks but not names supplied, an anonymity necessary for respondents to speak freely. Their conclusions rather reinforced the view that British ministers and civil servants inhabited a similar social environment and shared similar views. Even so, the authors were perhaps over-impressed with this insiders' view of the British government's control of public expenditure, which later in the 1970s came badly unstuck, leading to a second edition (1981) exploring what had gone wrong.

Compared to the largely centralised bureaucracies of France and the United Kingdom, the US bureaucracy is characterised by extensive decentralisation, partly but not wholly a consequence of federalism, and the numerous 'checks and balances' within the American constitution. Thus 'the United States is blessed with many hundreds of different forms and layers of public administration, which might collectively be described as a national bureaucracy, but which are characterised by extreme fragmentation and decentralisation' (Hames and Rae 1996, 161). Control of this complex multilayered bureaucracy is subject to on-going political power struggles, particularly between the presidency and Congress, for many US public agencies do not have a clear chain of command, and accountability. A succession of US presidents have struggled to control the bureaucracy and promote greater efficiency through changing management techniques, which have included planned, programmed budgeting systems (PPBS), management by objectives (MBO), and Zero-Based Budgeting (ZBB), most of which were subsequently exported abroad to the United Kingdom and elsewhere. Yet over and above all these fashionable systems was a pervasive mistrust of public bureaucracy and public spending, particularly as exemplified by the growing influence of public choice theory.

THE INFLUENCE OF ECONOMICS: RATIONAL CHOICE (OR PUBLIC CHOICE) THEORY

Politicians and leading public bureaucrats had long been perceived, ideally at least, as servants of the people. Politicians in a parliamentary democracy are elected by the people, and they can be subsequently removed by those who chose them if they disapprove of their performance in office. Elected ministers determine policy, which is implemented by officials. That at least is the expectation, although it often appears that leading public servants have more practical influence over policy and (particularly) implementation. Even so, both ministers and officials claim to serve the wider public interest rather than themselves, in marked contrast with the private sector, where some assume that the economy prospers when individual producers and consumers pursue their own self-interest. The assumption that different ethical assumptions operated in the public sector compared to the private was vigorously challenged by what is variously described as rational, or public, choice theory.

The US analysis of public bureaucracies did not seek to replicate the research methodology that Heclo and Wildavsky sought to apply to the United Kingdom [see above] but instead borrowed the essentially deductive assumptions of classical and neoclassical economics. Economists did not trouble to interview leading politicians or public officials to discover what they thought they were doing and why, because they already knew (or thought they knew) what motivated them: the pursuit of their own rational self-interest. Rational or public choice theory refused to accept that those who worked in the public sector were concerned to promote the public interest. Instead it was simply assumed that they pursued their own interests in the same way as those who worked in the private sector.

While rational choice by business firms and individual producers and consumers has long been a key assumption in classical and neoclassical economic theory, public choice theory extends this assumption to political behaviour and the public sector. A pioneering study by Anthony Downs* applied economic assumptions of rationality to voting and party competition (*An Economic Theory of Democracy,* 1957). James Buchanan* and Gordon Tullock* in *The Calculus of Consent* (1962) applied similar assumptions of the pursuit of rational self-interest to government and the public sector. Downs (*Inside Bureaucracy*, 1967) and William Niskanen* (*Bureaucracy and Representative Government*, 1971) used the same kind of approach to analyse the behaviour of those working in public sector **bureaucracies**. Largely immune from the discipline of the market and from the assumed goal of private sector firms to maximise profits, public sector bureaucrats, they argued, would pursue their own self-interest by maximising the size of their own 'bureau' (office, agency, or department). They would do this by increasing the size and scope of its responsibilities, its workforce, and its budget. This would boost the status, income, career prospects, and job interest of key bureaucrats. Another American social scientist, Mancur Olson* (*The Logic of Collective* Action, 1978) used rational choice theory to explain why special interest groups favouring protection or subsidies against the wider public interest were often effective in influencing policy makers. Their activities commonly led to an alliance between public sector bureaucrats and client groups to increase state spending and taxation.

RATIONAL CHOICE, POLITICS AND GOVERNMENT

Public choice theory challenged the assumption that public administration was quite distinct from the private sector and that it operated under very different principles from business firms. Instead, rational choice theorists argued, the pursuit of rational self-interest governed human behaviour in government organisations as it did in private firms, with the only crucial difference being that the state had monopoly powers and most state organisations were not subject to competition and market discipline. In so far as the public have become more cynical about professions from politicians and state officials that they serve the public interest, it is partly in response to popularised versions of neoliberal and public choice economics (Hindmoor in Hay, Lister, and Marsh 2006, 93).

Public choice theory was enthusiastically taken up by New Right politicians (for example Margaret Thatcher and Keith Joseph in the United Kingdom and those around Ronald Reagan in the USA) who were critical of the growth of the state and public sector employment and expenditure. Public choice theory provided both an explanation for state growth and some practical remedies. These remedies included cutting back on government generally, downsizing, privatising and 'contracting out' some state activities, and exposing others to competition both from the private and voluntary sectors and from within the public sector. Private sector techniques and principles were introduced into public sector management. The development of internal markets or 'quasi-markets' into the delivery of public services would, it was anticipated, introduce the discipline of competition into the public sector.

Those who found public choice theory unpalatable could resort to various different lines of criticism. One obvious response is to deny its basic assumptions about human motivation and behaviour. Thus examples can be found of human beings not pursuing their own rational self-interest, sacrificing their lives for others or undergoing life-threatening surgery to donate a kidney to help a relative. One obvious issue here is how far such altruistic behaviour is exceptional rather than typical. Moreover, some apparently altruistic activities (donations to charities or other 'good causes') may have a more self-interested motive (public recognition, honours, influence over others). Yet there is still a problem with the core premise of rational or public choice theory. It rests on an admittedly plausible assumption, but one that cannot be proved.

Another line of argument is to stress the influence of social conditioning on human behaviour. Thus most people vote, despite the suggestion of Downs* that voting is irrational because the minimal chance of an individual vote materially affecting the outcome cannot compensate for the 'costs' (in time and effort). **New institutionalists** [see next section] stress the importance of institutional cultures in influencing attitudes and behaviour. It is certainly plausible that employees can be socialised into accepting norms of service to others in the armed forces, hospitals, and schools, for example, and it is even in their self-interest to comply with such established norms of behaviour.

One distinctive argument (from the British political scientist Patrick Dunleavy, 1991) largely accepts the assumptions of the public choice school on human motivation and behaviour but questions the conclusions they derive from these assumptions.

Thus Dunleavy argues that self-interested public bureaucrats will not necessarily pursue what Niskanen* described as bureau maximisation but instead 'bureau-shaping'. Senior public sector bureaucrats have often substantially co-operated with and largely accepted major cutbacks, as well as privatisation and contracting out. Dunleavy suggests reasons for this. Thus senior bureaucrats are rarely directly affected by budget cuts, which commonly involve fringe agencies and activities, and junior staff. Cuts in the departments' total workforce more often affect unskilled workers and outlying activities rather than senior managers and professionals. While contracting out some services previously provided in-house, such as cleaning and catering, may significantly affect the pay and conditions of manual workers, it can provide increased work and promotion opportunities for accountants and administrators specialising in contract specification and regulation. There may even be the chance of a profitable management buy-out. Moreover, some senior managers may prefer to lose direct responsibility for managing awkward unionised manual workers. The same goes for activities that may be so troublesome to manage that senior bureaucrats are only too happy to 'outsource' or transfer them to others.

Some argue that increased competition within the public sector has been counterproductive, involving additional costs in managing internal markets and contracts with contentious implications for service levels. At the same time, competition has also arguably reduced the scope for co-operation within and between public services. Why should successful institutions (e.g. schools, hospitals) want to share the secrets of their success with leading competitors? Thus critics suggest that the reorganised public sector has lost some of the traditional values of the public sector, including co-ordination and co-operation between agencies. At the same time the public sector may not always benefit from the presumed discipline of the market, as some institutions simply cannot be allowed to fail.

Yet it seems clear that public choice theory is here to stay. The work of Downs, Buchanan, Niskanen, and Olson in particular has transformed ways of thinking about politics and government. No one embarking on the study of politics can afford to ignore the implications of their analysis of political attitudes and behaviour. It has stimulated new thinking throughout the discipline. One consequence has been to re-focus on the core activities of government, which had been relatively neglected by behaviouralists, partly because the interaction of leading politicians and public sector bureaucrats was less susceptible to systematic statistical analysis. Public choice theory has restored government and the state to centre stage.

From old to new institutionalism

More recently, some academics have sought to bring the state and state institutions back in to the study of politics, as part of what has been termed a 'new institutionalism'. Theda Skocpol* (1979) re-emphasised the importance of the state and political institutions generally in her study of revolutions. She went on to become one of the editors of an influential collection of essays under the title *Bringing the State Back In* (Evans, Rueschmeyer, and Skocpol 1985). One of the pioneers of the new American political science Gabriel Almond (1988) noted 'the return of the state' (which from a European perspective had never gone away). Yet it was James March and Johan Olsen in a seminal article (1984) and then a book (1989) who re-established the important of institutions, both state institutions and institutions more generally, and who coined the term 'new institutionalism'.

Thus March and Olsen (1984, 734) argued that 'the organisation of political life makes a difference'. It cannot all be reduced to individual motivation and behaviour. Political institutions influence the behaviour of individuals by shaping their 'values, norms, interests, identities and beliefs' (March and Olsen 1989, 17). There are institutional rules of behaviour, 'standard operating procedures and structures that define and defend interests'. Institutions 'are political actors in their own right' (March and Olsen 1984, 738). Thus the new institutionalism re-emphasised the importance of the institutional context in which politics takes place.

What exactly was new about the new institutionalism? It was more analytical and theoretical and less descriptive than the old institutionalism or public administration studies. However, it also involved a partial reappraisal of the old institutionalism, which was never as purely descriptive and atheoretical as some of its critics suggested. Thus Rhodes (1997, 63–83) has mounted a vigorous defence of older institutional approaches. He praises particularly the study of comparative government by the American Herman Finer (1932) and the work of British writers on public administration, such as William Robson (1928, 1948, 1960), though Rhodes admits that Robson displayed 'two of the institutional approach's defects: a mistrust of theory and a reformism bordering on the polemic'.

The new institutionalism recognised the importance of theory and sought to explain rather than reform institutions. Vivian Lowndes (in Lowndes, Marsh, and Stoker 2018) suggests that the new institutionalism involved a shift from a focus on organisational structures to the institutional rules or norms that guide and constrain the behaviour of individuals. There was also, she argues, a more informal conception of institutions, a focus on 'informal conventions as well as formal rules'. There was a more dynamic view of institutions that might evolve incrementally over time. There was also a concern to analyse the interplay of societal and institutional values. Finally, the new institutionalists addressed the relationship between specific political institutions and the political and social system as a whole of which they are a part. Thus institutions are 'differentiated' rather than simply integral parts of the state or political system, but they are not independent entities, in that they are inevitably embedded in a specific locality and a specific historical time. As another commentator has observed:

> Institutionalism is characterised, unremarkably perhaps, by its emphasis upon the institutional context in which political events occur and for the outcomes and effects they generate. In contrast to…behaviouralist and rational choice orthodoxies it emphasises the extent to which political conduct is shaped by the institutional landscape in which it occurs, the importance of the historical legacies bequeathed from the past to the present…. (Schmidt in Hay, Lister, and Marsh 2006, 98)

The new institutionalism covers a wider range of distinctive strands or strains. Guy Peters (in Goodin and Klingemann 1996, 207–213) distinguishes among five types of institutionalism (normative, rational choice, historical, social, and structural), expanded to seven by the same writer in 1998. Vivien Schmidt (in Hay, Lister, and Marsh 2006, 102–114) distinguishes four distinctive strands to the new institutionalism: rational choice institutionalism, historical institutionalism, sociological institutionalism, and discursive institutionalism, which overlaps with Guy Peters's typology. However, in illustrating these distinctive strands she acknowledges that there are extensive mutual influences among the tendencies and differences of emphasis within them.

Rational choice institutionalism is perhaps the most surprising and interesting among these different types or strains. March and Olsen had been concerned to demonstrate that collective political action cannot be reduced to individual behaviour. They showed how the development of specific institutional structures and processes over time produce shared organisational cultures that shape the ideas, attitudes, and behaviour of those who work within them, influencing the way specific issues are perceived and tackled. This seems incompatible with the individualist assumptions behind rational choice theory. Yet some rational choice theorists found the institutional context was helpful in accounting for differences in policy outcomes among organisations. Thus they accept that institutions can make a difference while still focusing primarily on individual motivations and behaviour.

The new institutionalism is concerned not just with public administration but with all societal institutions that are important in the political process, including parties, pressure groups, and social movements. The new institutionalism is also more theoretical, placing specific institutions within a broader analysis of power in state and society. Thus, unlike old public administration that was sometimes perceived as an isolated and self-contained subdiscipline, the new institutionalism is more engaged with issues that are central to the study of politics.

THE REVIVAL OF POLITICAL PHILOSOPHY

Moral and political philosophy had been central to the study of politics for two and a half thousand years [see Section 1, above]. Nearly all the older great writings on politics, from the ancient Greeks to John Stuart Mill* in the 19th century, that are still read today come under the general heading of political theory or political philosophy. Yet by the middle of the 20th century political philosophy seemed at best marginalised, at worst no longer a legitimate field of enquiry. The rise of logical positivism to dominance in 20th-century philosophy meant that normative statements, statements of value rather than statements of fact, were no longer regarded as knowledge but merely expressions of feeling. Within the discipline of politics the behavioural revolution had shifted the focus of enquiry to the study of political behaviour, politics as it is practised rather than as it should be practised. The age-old questions about the ideal state, justice, freedom, political obligations and rights were apparently consigned to the dustbin (Laslett 1956).

Strangely, this total rejection of moral and political philosophy happened at the very time that ethical principles and human rights were widely enshrined in international documents, state constitutions, and laws. Thus, as we have seen [Section 1, above], countries freely signed up to the United Nations Universal Declaration of Human Rights (1948) and the European Convention on Human Rights (1951). Moreover, many countries spelt out these rights in written constitutions and passed specific laws affirming them, sometimes specifying penalties for their infraction and means of redress for injured parties.

In practice, some rights were only imperfectly implemented, particularly the rights of women and ethnic minorities. Gay rights, even when they were conceded, were often constrained by widespread social prejudices long afterwards. Thus pressure groups continue to campaign for the rights of women, for ethnic minorities, for gays, while some advocate animal rights. All this, indeed, is the essence of practical politics. Yet a strict behavioural approach, while allowing the study of pressure groups and movements campaigning for rights, excluded any exploration of the justification for those rights. Thus the behaviour of women campaigning for rights was a legitimate subject for scientific analysis, but the case for women's rights was not.

In practice, the rejection of political philosophy was never total. Many traditional universities continued to offer courses in political theory in the mid-20th century and onwards, although these courses focused largely on the great names of the past, from Plato and Aristotle through to Mill and Marx. Even so, there was a prevailing perception in the English-speaking world that political philosophy was hardly compatible with the new political science.

Rawls and the revival of political philosophy

It is argued by Brian Barry* (1979) and others that it was the publication of John Rawls*'s *Theory of Justice* in 1971 that successfully revived political philosophy, although not everyone agrees. Thus Bhikhu Parekh, (in Klingemann and Young 1996) strenuously maintains that the previous decades were far less barren than suggested in the study of ideas, pointing to the work of Oakeshott*, Arendt*, Popper*, Berlin*, and many others published in this period. Moreover, it should also be acknowledged that both the 'death' and the subsequent 'revival' of political philosophy was substantially an Anglo-Saxon phenomenon. On the European continent there was a ferment of ideas throughout the postwar period. Despite increased disillusionment with orthodox Soviet Marxism-Leninism, varieties of Western Marxism flourished, including Sartre's* existential Marxism, the structural Marxism of Althusser* and Poulantzas*, and the Critical Theory of the Frankfurt school, with influential work from Adorno*, Marcuse* and, later, Habermas*. Other ideas, subsequently grouped under the heading 'postmodernism', were already beginning to make an impact [see below].

Whatever the ultimate judgement of Rawls's work, it is difficult to deny the impact that it had on the study of political philosophy, particularly in the United States and the United Kingdom. To admirers, the *Theory of Justice* was an original work in the great tradition of moral and political philosophy that could stand alongside the classic texts of the past. Indeed, Rawls consciously connected with these works. His 'original position' and 'veil of ignorance' were a subtle reworking of the 'state of nature' and ensuing 'social contract' employed by Hobbes* and Locke*. His book also had considerable influence on thoughtful politicians on the centre left, for Rawls apparently provided strong theoretical support for the kind of wealth and income redistribution favoured by progressive liberals and social democrats.

Communitarians, neoliberals, and others

At the same time Rawls's work demanded a response from those opposed to his assumptions or his conclusions. One set of critics rejected his individualist assumptions. Those thinkers described as **communitarians** (e.g. MacIntyre*, Taylor*, Sandel*, and

Walzer*) objected that Rawls conceived of the individual as an isolated self-interested rational calculator, cut off from the social community to which he or she belonged and which shaped his or her values and behaviour. The communitarians instead emphasised the reciprocal ties and mutual sympathies and obligations between human beings and the communities to which they belonged.

There were plenty of others who shared Rawls's individualist assumptions but opposed his conclusions. These critics included free market neoliberals and rational choice theorists [see above], although as these were primarily economists rather than philosophers they took less notice of his work. Thus Hayek* had already supplied his own arguments against distributive justice in *The Road to Serfdom* (1944), well before the publication of the *Theory of Justice*. The main attack from a philosopher came from the extreme libertarian anarchist Robert Nozick*, who worked in the same philosophy department at Harvard University as Rawls. In *Anarchy, State and Utopia* (1974) Nozick advanced a labour theory of inviolable individual property rights derived from that of John Locke*, which effectively ruled out any redistribution of income and wealth and any notion of distributive justice of the kind favoured by Rawls. While Rawls provided a justification for state intervention of the kind supported by social democrats, Nozick's radical individualism ruled out such a role for the state.

New perspectives in political philosophy

In the last quarter of the 20th century Anglo-American political philosophy began to come to terms with some of the very different ideas emanating from the European continent, particularly France. Poststructuralism and **postmodernism** [see key concepts and below] emerged substantially among disillusioned former Marxists. As works of leading thinkers associated with postmodernism were translated into English, they had an increasing influence on American academics, feeding into feminist theory and new approaches to international relations [see under appropriate headings]. Arguments over military action in various circumstance revived old debates over the notion of a just war and the moral case for humanitarian intervention. Thus moral and political philosophy appeared more relevant than ever as the 20th century drew to an end and the 21st began.

There was also a notable revival of the long controversy surrounding human rights, for example the work of the British legal theorist H. L. A. Hart and the American legal and political theorist Ronald Dworkin*. Later, clashes between cultures and the growing importance of 'identity politics' reopened the issue of universal human rights, which had been apparently settled by the widespread consensus over such documents as the United Nations Universal Declaration of Human Rights (1948) and the European Convention on Human Rights. Feminists demanded equal rights for women [see below]. In many countries there were pressures for gay rights. The Canadian Will Kymlicka* has championed the group rights of minority communities, particularly indigenous peoples.

Not everyone agreed with some of these claimed rights. Bhikhu Parekh (2000) argued that there was a 'distinctly liberal bias' in the UN Declaration, which included rights that 'cannot claim universal validity'. He contended that these claimed 'universal values' might 'come into conflict with the freely-accepted central values of a cultural community', such as, for example, the Asian values of 'social harmony, respect for authority, orderly society, a united and extended family and a sense of filial piety'. In response, the liberal philosopher Brian Barry (2001b) objected that Parekh's approach was 'liable to be harmful to women and children in minority communities and to those within them who deviate from prevailing norms'. Thus cultural norms might be employed to trump universal human rights, including women's rights, gay rights, and even rights to freedom of speech.

An even more contentious debate has been opened up by the attempt of Peter Singer* and others to extend rights from humans to animals. Much of the moral case for animal rights and vegetarianism revolves around the exploitation of animals and the denial of their rights. This widening of concerns beyond the immediate interests of humankind might be seen as part of a wider environmentalism. Growing concerns over resource depletion and irreversible environmental pollution have made some perhaps surprising converts. Thus Brian Barry (1977) vigorously argued the case for 'justice between generations'. He maintained that 'those alive at any time are custodians rather than owners of the planet'. They 'ought to pass it on in at least no worse shape than they found it in.' He confessed that he felt 'great intellectual discomfort in moving outside a framework in which ethical principles are related to human interests'. However he concluded 'these are the terms in which we have to start thinking'. The concerns raised by Barry now seem even more urgent. The moral case for moving away from relating ethical principles solely to current human interests has been strongly urged by leading ecologists such as James Lovelock* and contemporary moral and political philosophers such as Onora O'Neill*, as well as those warning about the impact of human behaviour on the survival of other species.

Altogether it seems that political philosophy is very much back in fashion and at the centre of crucial continuing debates over values, rights, and freedoms which are as important or even more important than they have ever been. Bernard Crick in the 1950s had defended 'the normative and ultimately moral dimension to the study of politics' (Grant 2010, 34). Much of the modern academic politics community seems to have finally come round to Crick's position.

OBJECTIVITY AND BIAS IN THE STUDY OF POLITICS

The revival of political philosophy poses some issues for the theory and practice of political science. Any science should, in theory, involve a dispassionate search for truth. Arguably, this is true of much modern political science, although there are also some in-built, if perhaps largely unconscious, sources of bias in the study of politics. Partly this arises because we are studying ourselves, our own beliefs, institutions, practices, and behaviour, and this renders total objectivity virtually impossible.

Postmodernism

The most comprehensive challenge, not just to modern political science and philosophy but to the whole dominant Western understanding of the scientific revolution, the age of reason, the European Enlightenment and the modern world [see Section 1, above], came from **postmodernism**, linked particularly with Foucault*, Lyotard*, Derrida*, and Baudrillard* (although both Foucault and Derrida later dissociated themselves from the term). According to Lyotard, postmodernism involved an 'incredulity towards meta-narratives' (Lyotard 1984), in other words distrust of grand theories, ideologies and all claims to a higher knowledge. It was accordingly sceptical towards the claims of both traditional political philosophy and modern behavioural social science. Derrida stressed the need for deep analysis or 'deconstruction' of texts to reveal multiple interpretations, with the added implication that none of these had special validity. Baudrillard argued that modern mass communication made it almost impossible to distinguish the real from the unreal.

Some political scientists rejected the extreme scepticism of the postmodernists. Even so, it is possible to argue that postmodernism had a significant and generally salutary effect on the study of politics. Thus Hay (2002, 226) has persuasively argued that postmodernism 'is best seen as a heightened sensitivity to the opinions and world views of others – a respect for others and other perspectives'. Postmodernism rejects any single world view. It suggests that the world can be seen from many different perspectives, none of which should be granted privileged status. This explains the appeal of postmodernist ideas to minorities of all kinds and those who feel marginalised by mainstream orthodoxy. Thus postmodernism appealed to some radical feminists and to those considered deviant or abnormal by prevailing social norms.

Foucault explored the relationship between knowledge, language, and power. He maintained that conventional methods of defining, analysing, and treating social deviance (including activities labelled as mad, criminal, or 'unnatural') reflected forms of social control. The labels used to describe deviance, and social relations more generally, were not neutral but reflected social hierarchy and power.

Thus postmodernism has led to an often beneficial re-examination of some long-held assumptions and attitudes, to more humility in claims to knowledge and truth, and to increased respect for alternative views. Yet some critics allege that leading postmodernists do not express their ideas sufficiently clearly to enable others to understand them or seek to refute them. Accordingly, they fail **Popper**'s criterion of falsifiability. Indeed some postmodernists have pontificated in areas they do not know enough about, such as the physical sciences and mathematics, infuriating those working in these areas. Alan Sokal, a physics professor irritated by postmodernist rejection of scientific method, wrote a spoof article applying postmodernist ideas to science and mathematics, with appropriate postmodernist terminology and quotations from leading postmodernist thinkers, but also including glaring scientific howlers. The article was accepted and published by the prestigious US postmodernist academic journal *Social Text* in 1996. A week later Sokal revealed the hoax and his motives in an article for another journal. The story was a considerable embarrassment to the editors of *Social Text* and postmodernists generally. Sokal went on to challenge the postmodernist 'attack on science' in 'Intellectual Imposters' (Sokal and Bricmont 1998).

A broader criticism is that postmodernism is essentially negative, devoted to debunking and 'deconstruction'; postmodernists do not put forward constructive alternatives for others to criticise. While most postmodernists began on the left politically and some have continued to support progressive causes, their extreme scepticism and relativism have ultimately rather negative implications. If all narratives or discourses have equal validity (or invalidity), why should we prefer one over another? It may seem laudable to respect other world views and cultures, to regard them as different rather than inferior, but taken to extremes this might involve (for example) the tolerance of slavery or the subordination of women.

Gender bias and feminism

Some radical **feminists** applied a postmodern analysis to the way in which the language employed in mainstream history, literature, and politics reflected gender power relations. This was most obviously demonstrated in the way that masculine terms were routinely treated as the norm, as in 'the rights of *man*', '*mankind*', '*chairman*', or even '*his*tory'. Such language reflects a world in which male is the norm, female the exception, male is superior and female inferior. Those feminists who sought to replace gender-loaded terms such as 'chairman' with the more gender-neutral 'chairperson' of simply 'chair' were thus not indulging in 'political correctness gone mad' (as was often alleged) but making an important point of principle. As language reflects power relations, a change in language may help transform those relations and lead to more women chairing meetings at all levels.

Indeed, gender is a critical source of bias in the study of politics. Until the 20th century politics and government had been almost everywhere a male preserve, and women accordingly lacked political rights and opportunities. Even if women in the West may have won formal legal and political equality, they have largely failed to secure real equality in life, work, and power. Women still remain conspicuous by their relative absence in company boardrooms and in the higher ranks of the judiciary and the professions, as well as underrepresented in government.

If politics has long been, and substantially remains, male dominated, the same is true of the study of politics. Nearly all the leading political theorists mentioned in Section 1 were male. Most of the political scientists cited in this section and elsewhere in the book are also male [see key thinkers]. Arguably, this involves an essentially masculine interpretation of the nature and extent of politics, which focuses on 'high politics', the government of states, the management of public finance and expenditure, foreign policy and international relations. Indeed, a distinction is commonly drawn between a public sphere, where state intervention and political activity is legitimate and justified, and a purely private sphere of home and family from which the state and politics should be firmly excluded.

Radical feminists (e.g. Simone de Beauvoir*, Germaine Greer*, Kate Millett*) railed against the continued oppression of women. The radical feminist slogan 'the personal is political' implied a massive extension of the political sphere, involving ordinary everyday life, the experience of being a woman in the workplace, in the house, kitchen and bedroom. Personal relations between men and women, the role of women in the home and in nurturing, the physical and sexual abuse of women, and the harassment of women in the workplace became legitimate political issues. Power has long been seen as central to the study of politics. Radical feminists still focus on power but power throughout society, not only or even primarily power in government or the state.

A significant concern of most radical feminists was male sexual power. Andrea Dworkin* and Catherine Mackinnon* linked the harassment and sexual abuse of women with the pornography industry which they regarded as inherently degrading to women as well as legitimising violent and invasive sexual relations. Rape was perceived by the radicals not as a highly aberrant form of male behaviour but, as Susan Brownmiller argued, 'nothing more or less than a conscious process of intimidation by which *all men* keep *all* women in a state of fear' (1977, 15). Sexual dominance was at the heart of male power. Other feminists took up the link between language and power explored by Foucault* and postmodernist thinkers. Thus Dale Spender (1985) has argued that language was fashioned by men and reflects male dominance.

Much of this suggests that the radicals did not think that women were much the same as men. Perhaps the way in which some radical feminist approaches have departed most from previous variants of feminism is in their insistence that women are different from men, mentally and psychologically, not just biologically. Many radical feminists have been prepared to assert women's difference. From this perspective, competition and violent aggression are features of male nature rather than human nature. There is now some support for the proponents of female difference from other social sciences and the physical sciences. Thus the role of genes (including male and female genes) in influencing behaviour is increasingly recognised, as well as the importance of testosterone levels in explaining some masculine behaviour. Yet if male and female natures are significantly different (allowing of course for considerable differences within both sexes and overlap between them), this may have implications for skills and roles in society that are not always comfortable for feminists.

There has been a natural tendency for many women political scientists to focus on feminism as a rapidly expanding area of study, with obvious relevance to their own lives and beliefs. It is one field of the discipline where women very substantially dominate (although here there is a case for rather more dialogue with men). Yet increasingly women political scientists, while generally retaining an interest in and involvement with feminism, have chosen to work largely within other, still largely male-dominated fields, such as voting and political participation, public administration and policy, moral philosophy, state theory and international relations. In some surveys of these fields of study within the discipline of politics, there is an increasing acknowledgement of the 'feminist contribution'.

The notion of a specific feminist contribution to a range of fields of study or subdisciplines may appear artificial. As more women work alongside men, there may be no need to distinguish contributions by gender. Indeed there may be as much diversity among female political scientists as among their male counterparts. Yet if women do really hold different values and think differently, as many radical feminists maintain, they may bring distinctive and fresh insights to particular subject areas. Thus relatively few of the increasing number of women political scientists working on **international relations** belong to the realist school that has long dominated the discipline. The rising numbers of women political scientists in many more areas within the discipline may have a distinctive impact on the direction of research, scholarship, and theory.

Western bias

Any non-Western readers may already have perceived a pronounced Western bias in this book. Thus Section 1 on the evolution of the study of politics is centred on Western political practice and theory. This section, focusing largely on modern political science, refers principally to research in the United States, Europe, and the Western world. The key thinkers listed later are almost entirely from Europe, the Americas, and Australasia. While the study of comparative politics has always included the non-Western world, including the former communist bloc and the developing world, much of this is by Western political scientists imbued with Western perspectives.

Thus Edward Said in *Orientalism* (1978) argues that Western ideas and values are presented in terminology that implies they are the norm, while the 'Oriental' is described in such ways as to suggest deviance and inferiority. Here, Western terminology and analysis legitimises the dominance of the 'rational', 'enlightened' Western world over the 'inferior' and 'unenlightened' Orient, perpetuating colonial attitudes and postcolonial Western power. Said's work is a useful corrective to blinkered Western perspectives. Yet it is unlikely that this will change until Western political scientists engage in more extensive dialogue with those from other continents and cultures.

POLITICAL SCIENCE: INTO THE 21ST CENTURY

From the late 20th century and into the 21st century major political developments have contributed to a significant shift in the focus of the study of political science. One dramatic event, the fall of the Berlin wall in 1989, and the rapid collapse of the former Soviet empire had massive implications for international relations, for the government and politics of the successor states, and the old 'three worlds' typology of comparative politics.

Yet those who optimistically predicted a 'peace dividend' were to be sadly disappointed. The 11 September 2001 attack on the twin towers (9/11) was not the first terrorist atrocity and has proved far from the last, although it did bring home the vulnerability of even the most economically advanced and highly defended countries. That and the ensuing Western armed interventions in Muslim countries such as Afghanistan, Iraq, Syria, and Libya have ruined and divided those countries, caused a spiralling number of casualties, destroyed cities, and created a mass of desperate refugees.

Religion, long seen as of sharply declining significance for political division, has become once more a key driver of conflict. Religious differences both within and between states seem now of critical importance in the Middle East, north Africa, and large parts of Asia and increasingly also in much of Europe and America. Some would see this as part of a general shift in politics from economic class divisions to perceived identities, which might be related to religion, language, or other felt ethnic identities, often transcending state boundaries.

The main focus of this whole section has been on politics within states. It has always been the case that some key political issues and divisions transcend intrastate politics and are cross-national or international. While in established states there are institutions, procedures, and laws for resolving conflicts of interest, until relatively recently there have been few similar institutions and procedures to resolve conflicts between states, which were often ultimately only settled by war or the threat of war. Although government and politics within states normally proceeded within the context of widely acknowledged authority, law and order, international relations involved anarchy and many would argue still does, despite the development of international governmental institutions and international law in the 20th and 21st centuries, as well as an escalating number of nongovernmental organisations. (NGOs). International relations from the early 20th century onwards will be explored in the next sections, along with the growth of global capitalism and the increasing influence of transnational business corporations (TNCs) throughout the world. Increasingly also there are global political issues that may affect the whole future of the planet and its human and other inhabitants, including global warming, population growth, resource depletion, and pollution, and that require international co-operation. Thus the next section will focus on international relations and global politics.

PART 2   SECTION 3
INTERNATIONAL RELATIONS: POLITICS BEYOND THE WATER'S EDGE

Contents

INTRODUCTION

Most of the various approaches to the study of politics discussed in the previous section have focused on politics and government within states. Even comparative politics substantially involves comparing the internal political structures and processes of independent sovereign states across the world, rather than the politics of relations between states. Interstate politics, or international relations, has long been considered significantly different from intrastate politics, so much so that it has almost come to be regarded as a separate discipline. We have shown that some ancient thinkers such as Thucydides* were interested in interstate politics, but the academic study of international relations (often shortened to IR) really took off only with the First World War and its aftermath– although a number of earlier political thinkers, notably Machiavelli* (1469–1527), Hugo Grotius* (1583–1645), Hobbes* (1588–1679), Baruch Spinoza* (1632–1697), and Immanuel Kant* (1724–1804), contributed significantly to the stock of ideas. Politics among states often seemed to have little to do with politics within states, which normally involved a framework of law and order under a widely recognised sovereign power. By contrast, the whole system of relations among independent sovereign states appeared to be essentially one of **anarchy**, with no legitimate and effective international authority to arbitrate over disputes between states to prevent recourse to war.

In this section we trace the development of International Relations as a discipline. As always with such an endeavour we make choices about how to cover the material. Our choice is to mirror the way the discipline is traditionally taught in many universities. If you like, we take the standard history of International Relations route. However, it would be wrong for us to suggest this was the only way to view the history of the discipline. We accept that these are founding 'myths' that for many scholars do not really reflect the complexity of debate (see Schmidt 1998 and Wæver 1998 for alternative views). The nature of our discussion can also be argued to reflect the traditionally Western-centric approach to the discipline (Acharya and Buzan 2007; Friedrichs 2004; Hobson 2012). This manifests itself via its basis in Western political theory and the Eurocentric framing of world history. However, we take the position that you need to understand something to fully critique it and so, given that this is an introductory text, we follow the 'standard' path but introduce the debates/critiques as we go along.

This section aims to provide a brief introduction of the main theories of International Relations, whilst also linking them to major historical events/case studies. (Section 4 then develops this by examining international political economy before ending with a discussion of globalisation and the enduring pull of the nation-state.) As with most academic disciplines, the edges of political science and International Relations are blurred and so this 'story' must be read alongside the development of politics that we outlined in Section 2. To add to the mix, discussions of globalisation build upon sociology, whilst international political economy clearly links politics/International Relations and economics. Our historical approach also links obviously to history and there can be an interesting difference of opinion as to where history starts and political science/International Relations ends. Therefore the ability to see the links between different disciplines is a crucial element of university study.

WESTPHALIA TO FIRST WORLD WAR: THE FOUNDING THEORIES OF INTERNATIONAL RELATIONS

Given that International Relations has tended to start with a discussion of a state of anarchy, we return to Thomas Hobbes's* *Leviathan*, in which man is reduced to a state of nature. Within this approach, following Hobbes it has been accepted that the state has sovereignty over an 'exclusive jurisdiction'– law-making and law enforcement over people within a given territory. The territorial sovereign power would not be subordinate to any external authority. The Treaty of Westphalia established the principles of 'exclusive jurisdiction' and 'non-interference'. Each state's political independence and juridical equality is recognised by all, and there are accepted rules such as no intervention in internal affairs and relations regulated by treaties.

> **Box 2.4 Treaty of Westphalia**
>
> The Treaty of Westphalia ended the Thirty Years' War in 1648. It created a basis for national self-determination. The importance of the treaty is that it created the concept of coexisting sovereign states, which is central to international law and to the prevailing world order. As such, it is a fundamental event for the study of international relations.

Whilst the treaty merely codified changes that were already afoot in the global system at the time, it remains the 'base upon which the structures of anarchy are constructed' (Brown and Ainley 2009, 127). However, the treaty clearly did not stop states from intervening in each others' affairs, given the number of wars between states in the period. Up to the First World War the conduct of international relations revolved around concepts such as national sovereignty, national interest, and the balance of power. These did not relate closely to the political ideas and conflicts that dominated domestic politics, which often seemed to have few implications for foreign policy. Thus the rival alliances of the First World War did not initially consist of ideological bedfellows. Revolutionary and republican France lined up alongside autocratic Tsarist Russia. It could hardly then be described as a war to make the world safe for democracy, which only began to look like a credible claim from 1917 onwards after the entry of the USA on the side of the United Kingdom and France and the revolutions in Russia that took it out of the conflict.

Liberalism, failure of peace settlement and the Second World War

Even so, the unprecedented slaughter and destruction of the First World War had been the catalyst for stimulating new ways of thinking about international relations and applying liberal principles to the management of diplomacy and foreign policy, commonly described as 'liberal internationalism'. US president Woodrow Wilson* had taken the United States into war but saw it as 'a war to end war'. The Fourteen Points announced by Wilson in January 1918 provided a programme for a liberal approach to relations among states, or international relations. Wilson's programme included national self-determination, on the assumption that a world of democratic states would be the best guarantee of future peace (although wars inspired by nationalism in the previous century scarcely supported this expectation). The demand for 'open covenants openly arrived at' reflected the view that secret diplomacy had effectively committed states to war in support of allies, bypassing any attempts at effective democratic control by representative assemblies. Most important of all was to be a new international body, the League of Nations, to provide 'collective security' for all states. This, it was hoped, would remove the need for individual states to provide for their own security and protection through such traditional means as defence spending, promoting military alliances, and maintaining a balance of power. Instead the League of Nations would arbitrate in disputes between states. Thus there would be a wholly new system of international relations in which international order would replace anarchy and international law would banish war.

If the liberal or idealist approach to international relations was articulated in response to the horrors of the First World War, the alternative realist perspective was the direct consequence of the apparent failure of liberal international relations, with the breakdown of peace and collective security in the 1930s. It was this that provoked the British historian E. H. Carr* (ironically then the Woodrow Wilson Professor of International Relations) to write *The Twenty Years' Crisis* (1939), reviewing the developments that had brought nations to the brink of another world war. Against what he regarded as the 'utopianism of current political thought' he quoted with approval the realist philosophy of Machiavelli*. Carr argued there was no natural harmony of interest among nations. Statesmen pursued national interests, using the power at their disposal, although they sometimes cloaked their real aims in a more universal moral language.

The nature of competition at a global level also became evident in the political economy. The agricultural and industrial revolutions produced a situation where industrial society emerged in many states. This prompted a shift from self-sufficiency to a greater focus on trade. The protectionist view saw that states should compete economically, as economic might could translate into military and political power. Therefore the aim was to acquire a surplus in trade – in other words there would be winners (those in surplus) and losers (those in deficit). However, the liberal view of Adam Smith* and David Ricardo that international trade was a win–win came to dominate. Their arguments about how foreign trade contributes to the wealth of nations and the economic arguments about comparative advantage underpin much of modern classical economics. Ricardo's theory highlights that it is more efficient for countries to specialise in the economic activity where they have a comparative advantage. This notion, although criticised because the relative values of goods differ considerably, still underpins the regulation of the world economy through the rules of the WTO and the policies of many governments, especially in the Western world.

Compared with the First World War, the Second World War could more plausibly be related to ideological conflict, at least initially, when the parliamentary democracies of the United Kingdom, France, and their allies faced Nazi Germany and, a year later, fascist Italy. The subsequent defeat of France followed by the German invasion of Stalin's Russia complicated this battle of ideas, before the bombing of Pearl Harbour brought the USA and

Japan into the war. The Japanese government was also authoritarian and antidemocratic, like Germany's and Italy's. Yet Japan could plausibly claim to be championing oppressed Asian peoples against Western, and particularly British, imperialism. The United States, while united with the United Kingdom to defend democracy, was not fighting to save the British empire or other European colonial empires. Although important ideas were at stake in the Second World War, it can also be seen in terms of states pursuing what their leaders conceived as enduring national interests. Peace led to a new international authority, the United Nations Organisation, to replace the defunct and substantially discredited League of Nations. We also saw the birth of institutions designed to govern the global economy.

These changes produced theoretical reflections within international relations. The key figure in the development of a reaffirmed realist theory of international relations after the Second World War was Hans J. Morgenthau*, a German Jewish émigré who escaped from Hitler's Germany to settle in the United States. His key work was *Politics among Nations: The Struggle for Power and Peace* (1948). He argued that international relations essentially involve '*states*, pursuing *interests* defined in terms of *power*' (Brown and Ainley 2009, 30). States were not the only actors in the international sphere. Morgenthau conceded that other bodies such as international governmental and nongovernmental organisations could have an influence. However, he maintained that sovereign states remained by far the most important actors in the conduct of international relations. Thus the realist perspective is 'state-centred'. States act in accordance with their interests. In pursuit of those interests they have to rely substantially on their own resources, or self-help. Externally, the negative consequences of the state of anarchy could be averted if the state was strong enough to defend itself or was engaged in a relationship with another state that was mutually beneficial. Both Carr and Morgenthau considered their realist analysis of international relations more scientific than the liberal, idealist, or 'utopian' alternative.

THE COLD WAR AND REALISM

This realist perspective was articulated against the backdrop of the emerging 'Cold War' between the two 'super-powers' USA and the USSR and their respective allies. Peace and security could not be preserved by promises and agreement but only by the realistic threat of force, backed up by strong military capability and firm committed alliances between states. Aggression would be effectively prevented by the threat of massive retaliation from the escalating stockpiles of nuclear weapons, involving 'mutually assured destruction' (MAD).

The Cold War led to the pooling of sovereignty with the creation of the North Atlantic Treaty Organization (NATO) in 1949. NATO is an example of a collective defence grouping whereby the members committed to a unified response should one member of the group be attacked. A major premise was that this would act as a deterrent to Soviet aggression in Europe, especially towards what was then West Germany. One consequence of the formation of NATO was the counter response from the allies of the USSR, who created the Warsaw Pact in 1955.

Box 2.5 NATO Article 5

The Parties agree that an armed attack against one or more of them in Europe or North America shall be considered an attack against them all and consequently they agree that, if such an armed attack occurs, each of them, in exercise of the right of individual or collective self-defence recognised by Article 51 of the Charter of the United Nations, will assist the Party or Parties so attacked by taking forthwith, individually and in concert with the other Parties, such action as it deems necessary, including the use of armed force, to restore and maintain the security of the North Atlantic area.

This division into two blocs to some extent saw a return to discussions about the balance of power. The Cold War divisions were mainly formally focused on Europe, but the consequences of the divide were felt across the globe with American foreign policy dominated by a desire to contain the spread of communism. The Cold War divisions were played out in Africa, Latin America, and Southeast Asia in so-called proxy wars in which the two main powers supported different sides in conflicts. The existence of these types of wars became the subject of study for International Relations scholars. In particular, they were interested in why the Cold War between two ostensibly opposing ideological forces was played out via proxy wars and arms races.

Neorealism and Neoliberalism-neo-neo synthesis

Both Carr and Morgenthau considered their analysis of international relations more scientific than the liberal, idealist, or 'utopian' alternative, but both were criticised for their perceived methodological weakness. The behavioural revolution in American political science and the subsequent influence of the rational choice school on the discipline of politics [see *The influence of economics: Rational choice (or public choice) theory* above] produced a reaction within International Relations about the use of what its supporters as a more 'rigorous scientific methodology'.

Realists responded to this challenge by refining and rethinking their approach. Neorealists concluded that understanding the behaviour of states also involved understanding the nature of the international system. The key text associated with neorealism is Kenneth Waltz*'s *Theory of International Relations* (1979). Waltz argues that there are only two kinds of international system possible, a hierarchical system or an anarchical system, and that anarchy still prevailed in international relations, despite the increased role of international institutions of various kinds as well as nongovernmental organisations and transnational corporations. Within the hierarchical system two clear alternatives exist: bipolar or multipolar. Thus Waltz's approach remains state-centred. While he does not assume that states are necessarily aggressive in the pursuit of national interests, they are concerned to preserve their security, viewing other states as potential threats and adjusting their policies to the changing international situation. The key to their peace and security is the maintenance of a stable **balance of power** (a concept familiar to international diplomacy before 1914). Waltz saw the bipolar balance of power between the USA and the USSR and their respective allies as a fairly stable system, arguing that bipolar systems are more easily managed than multipolar ones. Waltz drew on neoclassical economics and **rational choice theory** to explain the behaviour of the main protagonists in the international system, comparing it to the role of leading firms in oligopolistic markets, regulating competition. Hence a key aspect is how the state is doing relative to other states rather than absolute gains.

Absolute gains are a central part of the neoliberal institutionalist perspective. These scholars stress a greater awareness of the importance of non-state actors and the importance of interdependence between states, for example, in the volume edited by Robert Keohane* and Joseph Nye* (1971) *Transnational Relations and World Politics*. Their **neoliberal** institutionalist approach to international relations built upon the liberal tradition of the past, highlighting the relative stability of the global economic system despite uneven distribution of political power. This approach, which can trace back to Kant*, stresses liberalism in terms of politics and economics. It refines the notion that states are key in international relations by stressing that whilst states are still the primary actors in the global system, other factors, especially international institutions, matter. This approach argues that anarchy does not prevent co-operation. The 'complex interdependence' among states helps prevent wars, as do economic ties. Their work on regimes adds a new dimension to the International Relations literature, as it brings international organisations into the picture. Krasner's influential study (1983) highlights how states are willing to compromise with other states to ensure mutually beneficial outcomes. NATO and the Bretton Woods institutions (which we discuss later) can be analysed using Krasner's approach.

Whilst the two 'neo' approaches share many commonalities, from basic assumptions about the nature of states and an acceptance of anarchy to methodological agreement about the scientific method, there are key areas of disagreement. A fundamental difference between the two approaches was how they saw international space – for Waltz this is fundamentally different and unchanging. However, the so-called neo-neo debate sets an agenda that is said to dominate much of international relations and connects the theories back to the debates we highlighted around political science.

This focus on the role of other factors in the international system takes us back to the concept of power once more. Much of the focus of the previous sections has been to examine 'hard' power, associated with military power and wars. Nye developed the concept of soft power (1990) as an alternative to the more realist-based notions of hard power, although he did not see a contradiction between soft power and realism. Soft power uses attraction and seduction to change behaviour. Nye argues that this is a more effective form of diplomacy, as states take on board the values and interests of the states wielding soft power, thereby leading to sustainable change. This is in contrast to forcing a country to change via hard power, where a state may not fundamentally change its position over time. This view of soft power is open to criticism. Hard power can be difficult to change quickly (e.g. building up arms before wars), but it is difficult to alter soft power too. If soft power was so successful, all states would have a 'Hollywood' to promote their values. It is also worth noting that values stick around longer than a state's position in the international system, for instance the United Kingdom has experienced a decline in political influence yet in many ways its cultural reach is still important. Whatever the evidence, governments still fund soft power projects via cultural bodies such as the British Council (the United Kingdom), the Goethe-Institut (Germany), and the Confucius Institutes (China). (See special edition of *Politics*, November 2015, 'The Soft Power of Hard States'.)

The end of the Cold War and the collapse of the Soviet Union

This section highlights the end of the Cold War and its consequences. In doing so it highlights how the different approaches offer insights into this key event of the 20th century. The sudden end of the Cold War with the fall of the Berlin Wall and the collapse of the 'Iron Curtain' dividing Eastern Europe from the West had major implications for both the practice and theory of international relations. While it could be viewed as a victory for tough diplomacy and Western defence policies that reflected a realist perspective, it had not been expected, nor predicted, and this was the cause of some anguished reassessment within the profession. The altered reality of the post–Cold War world assisted a new diversity of approaches in the study of international relations. The world had changed. The bipolar balance of power described by Waltz no longer existed. Instead there appeared to be just one surviving superpower, the United States. This prompted a discussion around US **hegemony**. This is one version of the concept and can be seen as one state playing a dominant political, economic, and security role.

Some optimists hoped that the end of the Cold War would lead to a 'new world order' and a 'peace dividend' as spending on armaments was diverted to other uses. Other saw the end of the Cold War as the ultimate victory for liberal democracy. Fukuyama's* "End of History" thesis argued that 'What we may be witnessing is not just the end of the Cold War, or the passing of a particular period of postwar history, but the end of history as such: that is, the end point of mankind's ideological evolution and the universalisation of Western Liberal Democracy as the final form of human government' (Fukuyama 1992). The reality soon proved otherwise. In many ways international relations after 1989 turned out to be more chaotic, unpredictable, and dangerous.

There were other, more immediate and dramatic, political consequences for the governments and peoples of the former USSR and its satellite allies in Europe. After the fall of the Berlin Wall, East Germany united with the German Federal Republic. Other one time members of the Warsaw Pact repudiated communism, embraced multiparty democracy, and joined the European Union. Parts of the former multinational Soviet Union broke away to become independent sovereign states, although in some cases their newly proclaimed democratic credentials soon appeared questionable, as was the case also with the now truncated Russian state, where first Yeltsin and later Putin effectively limited free electoral choice to establish what could best be described as imitation democracy. However, the Baltic states of Estonia, Latvia, and Lithuania, which had enjoyed a brief earlier period of independence between the wars, were rather more successful in converting to representative democracy. Altogether these new and restored states resulted in another significant influx of new members to the United Nations, following soon after the addition of many former Western colonies that had secured political independence [see below].

The end of the Cold War seemed to suggest that America and its way of life had 'won'. The EU has been able on occasions to match the United States' economic might but never its political might; it has not been able to replace the United States. The country that many commentators claim might replace the United States is China. Up until 1978 China was a closed country. In that year Deng Xiaoping started the process of 'building socialism with Chinese characteristics', a process that opened China up economically to the rest of the world. In the time since then China has grown to become the second largest economy in the world. Chinese finance, expertise, and technical know-how have since won friends over much of the developing world, offering an alternative development model to those proposed by the Bretton Woods institutions (see Brautigam 2009). Only in 2015 did the remarkable surge in China's economic growth slow, since when the Chinese stock market has experienced sizeable falls, with significant knock-on effects for older Western stock markets and financial centres (Hu 2015).

China is perhaps the best example of the transformations that have occurred in what was once described as the 'third world'. These changes have meant that the world has become far more diverse and differentiated. Some Asian states became especially prosperous economically. Hong Kong, Singapore, South Korea, and Taiwan all experienced rapid economic growth. These newly industrialising countries (NICs) were all relative small in area and hardly significant military powers. Other geographically extensive and populous states with fast growing economies, including Brazil, postcommunist Russia, and India, are now linked with (still nominally communist) China (to form the acronym BRIC), although in all these countries there has also been a marked increase in inequality, as the growing affluence was not widely shared.

South Africa was soon linked with the BRIC group. There, the release of Nelson Mandela* from prison and the rapid transition to majority rule marked the end of the legacy of colonialism and white rule in Africa and around the globe, which was of tremendous real as well as symbolic importance to non-white peoples everywhere. While the new South Africa has prospered economically and culturally, the living standards of most of its black citizens have not risen as far or as fast as many of them had hoped. Even so, the rising economic fortunes of the newly industrialising states and the BRICS group clearly transcends the outdated 'three worlds' division. Alongside the rise of the BRICS, some commentators are forecasting the next wave of states to be the MINTs (Mexico, Indonesia, Nigeria, Turkey). Here we see an interesting difference between economics and politics. On the whole all these countries have accepted the global economic rules set down after the Second World War. Therefore the vast majority of states are part of the International Monetary Fund (IMF), and 162 states have joined the World Trade Organisation (WTO). However, the political structures are more problematic. The UN Security Council permanent members reflect the postwar settlement and not political reality at the time of writing. Whilst this situation is unlikely to change quickly, the make-up of the Security Council does have issues for the legitimacy of the UN as a global body.

Box 2.6 Is the United States still the global hegemon?

US National Debt stands at 13 trillion dollars. China holds approximately 26% of US Treasury bonds, the single largest holder. Consider the implications of this for the USA's global role.

The world today is not the world envisaged by liberal international relations but, as with many of the concepts and theories in the study of politics and International Relations, open to your own interpretation. Interpretation leads us to a discussion of alternative theories of international relations, with the first approach being the constructivist school.

A NEW DIVERSITY OF APPROACHES: THE CONSTRUCTIVIST TURN

The failure to predict the end of the Soviet Union created much soul searching within International Relations, and the result was that the new intellectual ideas around norms and values gained momentum. As we discussed in Box 1.5 there is a fundamental debate within the social sciences about our role as observers of social phenomena. The realist/neorealist approach falls into the category of those who see the world as observable and hold that observable facts exist and can be tested. This approach is challenged by those who argue that human beings observing social phenomena can never be objective and rational because they bring their own assumptions and biases to the subject (i.e. knowledge is socially constructed). In International Relations the later approach was labelled the 'constructivist turn' by Checkel (1998). (It can also be seen as the normative turn.)

Constructivists, hostile to rational choice theory, emphasise rather the importance of social factors in international relations, the acceptance of norms and rules of the game that influence the actors' behaviour. In particular they have suggested that identity is important in international relations as in other spheres of politics, with feelings of shared identities often having considerable significance for the conduct of foreign policy (Wendt 1987). Alexander Wendt* (1958–) went on to outline his own Social Theory of International Politics (1999), a clear reference back to Waltz's seminal text.

In 'Anarchy Is What States Make of It: The Social Construction of Power Politics' (1992) he argues that all elements of state relations, including anarchy, are socially constructed. Wendt argues that in order to understand the actions of a state we need to understand the interests and identities held by key actors. Therefore, unlike the neo-neo approaches, for constructivists it matters who the actors are as this will determine how they act.

If we accept that key actors have interests and identities we also open International Relations to the study of other influential actors, not just states. The dominant actors, in this case states, are able to draw up a series of global rules and regulations that reflect their political priorities or normative preferences (see Ruggie 1998). Therefore, if we examine the so-called **Bretton Woods** institutions created at the end of the Second World War, constructivists would see the nature of the institutions as reflecting US priorities. The key institutions were the World Bank and the International Monetary Fund. Their aim was to set down a set of rules that would regulate the world economy to help re-build after the devastation of the war and also attempt to prevent future wars. The final institution that has evolved into the World Trade Organisation was set up to encourage free trade. The United States also ensured that it gained the most voting rights, giving it a veto over major policy decisions. The criticisms of the Bretton Woods institutions were that they cemented the US dollar as the dominant global currency and came to reflected a neoliberal view to trade and politics. In the 1990s this policy reached its height with what was known as the 'Washington Consensus'. The consensus promoted a neoliberal economic policy agenda, which often gave rise to major social issues, especially in developing countries. The institutions still exist today, although with perhaps a less dogmatic attitude to neoliberalism and with the role of the United States changed somewhat.

Martha Finnemore* (1996) also argues that international organisations play a role in the social construction of actors' perceptions of their interests. As a result, international organisations can also shape norms, such as in the field of human rights or gender equality. In *National Interests in International Society* she shows that the international structure shapes meaning and values. She developed her ideas with Kathryn Sikkink in 1998, when she highlighted the norm lifecycle. They identified three key stages – norm emergence, norm cascade, and finally norm internationalisation. This work is very influential in the field of human rights and shows the connection between the domestic and the international.

Understanding the connections between the domestic and the international is the stated aim of Foreign Policy Analysis (FPA). FPA to some extent does not fit neatly into our journey through International Relations theory, despite its focus on the nature of domestic politics being an implicit criticism of neorealism's state-centrism (see Mintz and DeRouen 2010). Kaarbo highlights that 'constructivism, liberalism, and realism largely divorced international politics from domestic politics and decision-making' (Kaarbo 2015, 193). Kaarbo goes onto argue that since the end of the Cold War we have witnessed a 'domestic politics turn' within International Relations, showing again that the divisions between politics and International Relations continue to narrow.

The field of FPA aims to understand the factors that determine how a country makes decisions in given foreign policy situations. The studies with the most longevity were formulated by Allison (1969, 1971) in his classic works on the Cuban missile crisis. This model attempts to understand how foreign policy decisions are made by examining the goals of the political leadership in a given country, the preferences of the bureaucracy and the preferences of previous governments. A commonly used method for applying the governmental politics model is by using two-level games (Putnam 1988), where both the domestic bureaucratic decision-making process and the subsequent international negotiations can be modelled in a single framework. Contemporary work in the field of FPA has tried to take the subject beyond North America (see Brummer and Hudson 2015), although much of the work still focuses on American foreign policy (see Milner and Tingley 2015). The FPA approach can be situated in the agency structure debate referred to in Section 1 and links us back into discussions around norms and values, which are implicit in FPA.

The discussion around norms and values takes us to the English School (most closely associated with the work of Hedley Bull*). In his key work *The Anarchical Society* (1977) he argued that nation-states remained the main actors in an international society characterised by anarchy, in the absence of any effective international authority. Yet anarchy did not necessarily involve the pursuit of state interests at all costs, leading to international disorder and war, as states recognise some obligations to each other, and from prudence and fear states seek to preserve a balance of power.

Within this school there is also more acknowledgement of the two-way relationship between domestic politics and the politics of international relations. Thus it is more widely accepted that there is not a single view of the national interest in international relations and that the balance between contending views can change to affect foreign policy (which can in turn have a major impact on domestic politics, as the Vietnam War and, later, the Iraq War demonstrate). The English school has conceptualised a 'society of states' or 'international society' in which states accept norms of behaviour (Bull [1977] 2002).

This approach moves the debate from states and systems to the possibility of an international society. There was a long-standing debate within the English School on intervention with the debate between pluralists (see Jackson 2000) and solidarists (see Wheeler 2001) centring on the responsibility of states within the international system. Pluralists believe that intervention could be seen as unethical, whilst solidarists see intervention as morally the 'right' thing to do. This general discussion of the English School, and the framing of the debate in broader terms of intervention and sovereignty and norms, is institutionalised in the principle of Responsibility to Protect (R2P), which was a response to the 'New Wars' of the 1990s which were seen to be identity based and involving non-states or failed states such as Somalia, Rwanda, and Kosovo. Global conflicts were seen to be changing – from wars between states to wars within them. Of the 89 conflicts between 1989 and 1992 only 3 were between states. This in turn led to a new basis for interventions: 'new interventionism or 'new humanitarianism', which challenged many notions of the sovereignty of states and the principle of nonintervention.

The principle of R2P argues that the 'duty to prevent and halt genocide and mass atrocities lies first and foremost with the State, but the international community has a role that cannot be blocked by the invocation of sovereignty' (United Nations 2005). Here again we see international organisations playing a role in shaping norms and values. The key element of R2P is that the principle explicitly charges the international community to take 'collective action' to protect populations, if the state cannot or will not (see Bellamy 2009; Ralph and Gallagher 2015). If we examine NATO we can see that the organisation has tried to reformulate its meaning and values in a post–Cold War context towards humanitarian intervention, despite the fundamental premise of the organisation being collective defence. Therefore NATO has been able to shape preferences of its members towards military intervention in Kosovo and Libya.

Box 2.7 Responsibility to Protect

The UN R2P website states that 'Sovereignty no longer exclusively protects States from foreign interference; it is a charge of responsibility that holds States accountable for the welfare of their people'.

The discussion around R2P reopens some of the debates we highlighted about global norms and universal values. The 'global' efforts to militarily intervene for humanitarian purposes or to prosecute war crimes in the International Criminal Court have been criticised as the imposition of Western liberal values on others. Critics highlight the locations of R2P actions or the nationalities of leaders sent to the ICC for war crimes as evidence of a bias in the decision-making (the United States is not even a participant in the ICC). There is also a broader critique from the BRICS, especially China which firmly supports the policy of nonintervention in other states' domestic affairs. Once again, how you understand the differing decisions taken by different states reflects different fundamental beliefs around the concepts of sovereignty, intervention, human rights, and the power of international institutions.

Security

The violence and terror which has been a recurrent feature in the politics of relatively remote parts of the world now threatens advanced Western countries. The attack on the twin towers of the US World Trade Centre in New York in September 2001 was only the most dramatic of a series of acts of terrorism around the world, followed by attacks in London, Madrid, Paris, and Brussels. The 'War on Terror' launched by the United States and its allies has increased political instability in Afghanistan, Pakistan, the Middle East, and north Africa and has also alienated and radicalised not only Muslims in countries directly affected but many of their co-religionists in the West (see Booth and Dunne, 2002). The world has become less stable, predictable, and safe and its future uncertain. It also changes how we view conflict. Traditionally we have understood security as being aligned with territory. So security models favoured the 'defence of the realm' and thus security was largely understood in terms of defensive capabilities (i.e. military hardware). This then linked into a specific view of war. Following the writings of Carl von Clausewitz we see war as being between two clearly defined enemies, with defined 'rules of engagement'. There is a clear chance of victory or, if not, the possibility for truce and negotiated peace. Clausewitz has been interpreted as a realist thinker because of the implication that might is morally right.

Chess has become a familiar metaphor for explaining the security situation, with different pieces having different hierarchical positions. War is therefore about territory and holding key positions. Certain pieces are of lesser importance and can be seen as the 'pawns of the game'. The Cold War security situation was epitomised in the language of Henry Kissinger as **Realpolitik**, but this militarism was challenged on the basis that threats no longer came from nation-states alone and that threats were more complex and societal. The useful distinction between old and new wars is important here. Mary Kaldor* (2012) argues that our old way of thinking about war, which is seen as wars between states, is being replaced by a type of 'new war', which could be described as a mixture of war, organised crime, and massive violations of human rights.

However, a closer inspection shows that the realist account of global power still speaks to modern events. The differing global efforts to counter the threat from Daesh reflect some of the Cold War alliances, with Syria and Russia working together whilst NATO maintains a watchful eye on Russian activities in the Ukraine, Turkey, and even the Baltic States. There are rumbling tensions in the South China Sea between nations over disputed territories. Iran and Saudi Arabia have regular skirmishes in the Arabian Peninsula, and the source of much global tension the Israeli-Palestine conflict looks no closer to a resolution. However, we are also witnessing some closure around long-standing tension points in the world. These include the first steps towards US-Cuban reconciliation, the Iran nuclear deal, and democratic elections in Myanmar. Some international co-operation and even intervention in other states' domestic affairs by China are visible in efforts to reduce the threat of nuclear weapons in North Korea.

We have seen alternative schools of thought advocate the deepening and broadening the meaning of security. In particular, the Welsh School (Booth 1991) and the Copenhagen School (Buzan 1991) pioneered a constructivist notion of security analysis of 'nonmilitary' threats leading to the advent of Critical Security studies. The Copenhagen School maintains some allegiance to the traditional approaches to security in the sense that threat must be seen to be 'existential', where as the Welsh School derives from Marxist and Critical Theory thinking. Despite differences, however, this debate has led to the military conception of security expanding to be accompanied by:

- Environmental Security
- Economic Security
- Societal Security
- Political Security

The broader definition of security has been adopted by many UN agencies and has helped refine liberal internationalism/cosmopolitanism. They argue that what matters is how an issue becomes a security concern, the so-called process of securitisation, although there is a debate about what needs to happen in order for a threat to life to be acted upon. Securitisation reflects a discursive construction of a threat whereby an issue becomes a security threat in part when the discourse around that threat becomes widely accepted (see Buzan, Wæver, and Wilde 1998). A key example would be when the threat from Islamic terrorism became securitised after 9/11. Although the threat had existed prior to the attacks (the 1998 United States embassy bombings in Dar es Salaam, Tanzania, and Nairobi, Kenya, are examples of this), the 9/11 attacks changed the narrative as the threat became widely accepted. The broadening or opening up of the concept of security brought a range of issues into focus. It has also opened up the discipline of international relations to new areas of study, such as global health (Davies et al. 2014).

Feminism

As we showed in Section 2, feminism encompasses many approaches. It is therefore unsurprising that the feminist approach to International Relations is not a single unitary theory but a distinct discourse made up of many competing theories (see Savigny and Marsden 2011). In terms of our theoretical discussions, most feminist critiques of realism and neo–realism have their roots in constructivism. They would argue that gender influences how you look at the world. This means that whilst feminism explores the role of women in international relations, it also studies the influence of male gender roles. For example many of International Relations' core concepts, such as war and security, are gendered. As we mentioned in the introduction, the main International Relations theories can be criticised for being based on the works of the dead white men that we outline in Part V. This means that the experiences studied tend to be those of the male elite. This can then lead to the criticism that much of this tradition produces artificial binary divides that can privilege one concept over others (see Tickner and Sjoberg 2011).

A key contribution to feminist international relations is 'Bananas, Beaches and Bases' by Cynthia Enloe* (1989). In this book she explores how the seemingly personal is actually the reality of global politics. She shows how through employment, the media, and their status in society, gender roles underpin all aspects of international politics. For International Relations to ignore these roles is to ignore the lived reality of many people across the world and to therefore only provide a 'partial' picture of international politics. A major critique of realism is that it fails to consider the experiences of women and thus excludes them from the discipline. For example, if scholars only focus on the male soldiers in war, they ignore the multiple roles played by women in conflict. Some scholars also focus on the male gender roles implicit in much of International Relations scholarship (see Carver, Cochran, and Squires 1998).

How elements of the mainstream discipline respond to the feminist challenge highlights the epistemological debates within the discipline. Keohane challenged feminist scholars to contribute to debates about what he sees as the fundamental concepts of the discipline, but he stressed the need to utilise empirical methodologies. This prompted criticism from C. Weber (1994) and Tickner (1997), who argued that Keohane's challenge revealed more about Keohane's assumptions than how feminist International Relations should evolve. The schools of feminist thought that take issue with the basis of classical International Relations theories often follow Marxist or Critical Theory perspectives, whilst stressing the particular role gender plays. As Daddow (2013) argues, this involves combining an analysis of gender with that of global political economy. Critical feminists also argue that notions of objectivity or rationality are constructs and thus help to reinforce gender and social hierarchies. It can be argued that the way we have covered the topic – very much like the token week on gender in many courses or chapters in textbooks – helps marginalise the study of gender (see Rowley and Shepherd 2012).

Box 2.8 How reality is socially constructed

Daddow (2013) offers an excellent example of how social expectations shape our behaviour. He highlights the example of boys' and girls' toys. If you watch adverts on children's television channels you can see adverts targeted at girls (the only actors you see are girl actors). These are often related to make up, dressing up, glitter, boybands, etc. The toys for boys tend to be football stickers, guns, and action figures. Our preferences can be shaped by societal norms associated with gender roles.

Marxism, International Political Economy, and Critical Theory

The theories outlined above to some extent form the canon of International Relations. However, we need to consider other perspectives that offer a fundamental critique as they challenge the assumptions of the nature of modern capitalist society. In an earlier section we showed the continued relevance of Marxism for politics today. Critical international relations and Marxism offer useful insights into structure and agency at a global level and the notions of power. As such they form the basis for many of the approaches that you will cover in your courses and have opened up new areas of study – such as globalisation and International Political Economy (IPE).

We have already introduced Marx* in earlier sections of the book. Although not specifically related to international relations, his ideas have influenced a number of writers who discuss relations between states and markets. The core assumption behind Marxism is that capitalism causes conflict between states as states facilitate the need for materials and new markets. As we showed in Section One, power and class are key concepts within Marxist thinking and so IPE is no different.

Marxism has inspired many authors but here we focus on just two. World systems theory, most closely associated with the work of Immanuel Wallerstein (2004) and André Gunder Frank (1967), stresses that the capitalist system and its economic relations rather than states should be the focus of attention. WST argues that the capitalist world system has a core (Western zones of affluence); a periphery (those who provide raw materials); and a semi-periphery (exploiters and exploited). The changes that have taken place in the global economy have challenged the international division of labour as there is no longer a clearly defined 'core' or periphery, and WST does not taken into account newer forms of production. Robert Cox* attempts to overcome some of the shortcomings in Marxist analysis of the global political order. His reinterpretation of the concept of **hegemony** has been important in providing a critical understanding of IPE.

He argues that the idea that modern capitalism meets the needs of humans is an example of hegemony. This definition of hegemony, derived from Gramsci*, differs from the definition offered by realists in relation to the dominance and power of states. In this context hegemony is defined by Cox as 'a form in which dominance is obscured by achieving an appearance of acquiescence…as if it was the natural order of things' (Cox 1994, 366). We see this at a global level, with states supporting the US vision of a global financial order as set out in the Bretton Woods institutions, or on an individual level. Overall, the Bretton Woods institutions offer an excellent case study on the role of ideas and norms but can also be seen through the lens of other theories. The realist interpretation focuses on the power of states as we showed above, but we can also see a Marxist view based on the concepts of class and hegemony [see below].

Savigny and Marsden (2011) explain that this results in workers seeing their interests as tied up with those of the system thus producing consent rather than conflict (this links back to Lukes's* three faces of power argument. We therefore hear people argue that they 'need' a new television or new iPhone, not because their old one does not work but because they wish to have the latest model – the system demands consumption! Marxists would also argue that the state becomes the mouthpiece for capitalism and the dominance of markets. Even social democratic parties sell their economic credibility at election time, proclaiming a message that they can run capitalism better than conservative or other parties. Particular economic policies such as fighting inflation and even austerity become the new orthodoxy that governments do not question. This debate highlights the contested nature of politics once again.

The key difference between Marxist and Critical Theory approaches to International Relations is the latter's rejection of the scientific method. As we showed in Part II, postmodernism is sceptical towards the claims of both traditional political philosophy and modern behavioural social science. Thus we get Critical Theorists challenging accepted notions of the 'truth' by showing that there are competing truths. A controversial example is the analysis of the Iraq War and 9/11, which examined the way the media constructs reality to frame events in a particular way and thus hide power relations (Savigny and Marsden 2011). Perhaps the two most important thinkers for critical international thought are Habermas* and Foucault*. Habermas's work on the public sphere has influenced some key critical thinkers (see Linklater 2007). Foucault's work argued that narrative and discourse reflected power.

Richard Ashley (1988) used Derrida's* method of deconstruction to re-examine the concepts of anarchy and sovereignty in international relations. It has long been argued that the prevailing condition in international relations is one of anarchy, in which independent sovereign states pursuing their own interests are the only actors that really matter. This implies a fundamental contrast between two mutually exclusive conditions, anarchy (violent, unstable, illegitimate) and sovereignty (peaceful, stable, legitimate). Ashley suggests that the terms are not opposites nor necessarily mutually exclusive. Other writers have argued that the ideal of the homogeneous sovereign nation-state associated with the modern understanding of sovereignty is part of the problem in modern international relations rather than the solution.

Postmodernist ideas have assisted the growing weight attached to agencies and movements operating outside and across state boundaries in international relations

Savigny and Marsden (2011) highlight the example of the 'rules of the game' in football. The constructed meaning associated with winning the game is to try and score more goals than the opposition. This is in contrast to other sports where the winning may be achieved by judges 'scoring' your performance on aesthetic or difficulty criteria. Therefore we cannot have one accepted way to do International Relations (or political science). The similarities between the two disciplines lie in the fact that both approaches tend to see changing the world as key, rather than just understanding it.

Global capitalism

The establishment of a global political economy, sometimes characterised as 'hyper-capitalism', has seen intensified business concentration and created not only global markets but cross-border mergers and acquisitions, leading to international oligopoly. To critics and opponents, much of this has appeared malign, due to cuts in welfare provision (Teeple 1995; Mishra 1999) and reductions in labour protection in many Western states. It is argued that within the new globalised economy, generous welfare provision and restrictions on hours of work can no longer be afforded, because of the impact of international competition from low-regulation, low-wage and low-tax economies. Some of the anti-capital protest movements have been stimulated by the erosion of accustomed levels of welfare and labour conditions, which has been blamed, not always fairly, on global capital.

In *Casino Capitalism* (1986), Susan Strange* outlines how the global currency markets resemble a casino with trillions traded in a high stakes, high rewards environment. Currency trading volume around the world has hit $4 trillion a day. These mind-boggling sums are greater than states can compete with. Some multinational corporations (MNCs) or transnational corporations (TNCs) have revenues substantially larger than the gross domestic product (GDP) of many sovereign independent states. Some employ more people around the world than the entire population of some of the smaller states represented at the United Nations. They are powerful players not just in global markets, business, and commerce but in state and international politics. Because they operate across national borders, they are not easily influenced or controlled by state governments. Some may choose to locate their headquarters in smaller countries such as Switzerland or Luxemburg or even tiny 'tax havens' to reduce their tax liabilities or avoid some forms of regulation. Indeed, higher taxes, stricter employment legislation, and closer regulation on grounds of health and safety may lead to the transfer of production to more tolerant competitor states. Accountability to shareholders is generally weak and ineffective. MNCs and TNCs are not entirely unaccountable, however, as they have a clear interest in maintaining their brand image and keeping their customers happy. Bad publicity about employment practices or tax evasion may on occasion affect sales and profits, so even huge global corporations need to look after their public relations.

Global corporations are increasingly wealthier than many countries, with Walmart, Apple, and Shell richer than Russia, Belgium and Sweden, according to research by the campaigning group Global Justice Now, which found that 69 of the world's top 100 economic entities were corporations rather than countries in 2015.

Box 2.9 Top 30 Economic Entities 2015

1.	Government	United States	$3,251,000,000,000
2.	Government	China	$2,426,000,000,000
3.	Government	Germany	$1,515,000,000,000
4.	Government	Japan	$1,439,000,000,000
5.	Government	France	$1,253,000,000,000
6.	Government	United Kingdom	$1,101,000,000,000
7.	Government	Italy	$876,000,000,000
8.	Government	Brazil	$631,000,000,000
9.	Government	Canada	$585,000,000,000
10.	Corporation	Walmart	$482,130,000,000
11.	Government	Spain	$473,600,000,000
12.	Government	Australia	$425,700,000,000
13.	Government	Netherlands	$336,500,000,000
14.	Corporation	State Grid	$329,601,000,000
15.	Corporation	China National Petroleum	$299,271,000,000
16.	Corporation	Sinopec Group	$294,344,000,000
17.	Government	Korea, South	$291,300,000,000
18.	Corporation	Royal Dutch Shell	$272,156,000,000
19.	Government	Mexico	$259,600,000,000
20.	Government	Sweden	$250,800,000,000
21.	Corporation	Exxon Mobil	$246,204,000,000
22.	Corporation	Volkswagen	$236,600,000,000
23.	Corporation	Toyota Motor	$236,592,000,000
24.	Government	India	$236,000,000,000
25.	Corporation	Apple	$233,715,000,000
26.	Government	Belgium	$226,800,000,000
27.	Corporation	BP	$225,982,000,000
28.	Government	Switzerland	$221,900,000,000
29.	Government	Norway	$220,200,000,000
30.	Government	Russia	$216,300,000,000

https://www.cchdaily.co.uk/corporations-dominate-worlds-top-100-economic-entities

Today much of the impact of large business enterprises may be described as beneficial, meeting human needs and wants and providing employment and income. Walmart has over two million employees and has many more millions of (generally satisfied) customers in its stores around the world. Altogether, such mega businesses provide much of the economic growth that improves national living standards and general prosperity – although inevitably also some of them are also responsible for increased exploitative labour practices, pollution, environmental degradation, and global warming, and a few enterprises have promoted the sale and consumption of products that have had damaging impacts on human health and wellbeing.

The larger multinational financial institutions have lent recklessly, shamelessly manipulated interest rates, and assisted widespread tax avoidance. It was not the reckless spending of national governments that caused the global financial and economic crisis of 2008 onwards, but the financial mismanagement of the banks. Too large to fail, they were bailed out by governments and ultimately taxpayers to avoid total economic collapse. Many of us are still living with the consequences.

Box 2.10 A truly global crisis?

The 2008 Crisis affected many countries. However, there is a debate around terminology. Many believe that 'international financial crisis' is more accurate than 'global financial crisis', as there were many countries that came through the period economically unscathed.

This discussion of global capitalism and international political economy takes us naturally to a discussion of globalisation.

Box 2.11 International relations and popular culture

The representation in film of many of the issues discussed in this section can add to your understanding of the concepts. A telling satire on the Cold War is found in *Dr Strangelove or: How I Learned to Stop Worrying and Love the Bomb* by Stanley Kubrick (1964). *The Battle of Algiers* (1966) explores issues around colonialism, independence struggles, and counter-terrorism. *Thirteen Days* (2000) offers a fictional account of the Cuban Missile Crisis in 1962. *Jarhead* is a 2005 film that illustrates many of the issues highlighted by our discussion of gender roles. *No Man's Land* (2001) and *Hotel Rwanda* (2004) offer some insights into the nature of modern conflict and peacekeeping. On a lighter note, *Independence Day* and other sci-fi films have been used to contribute to an understanding of how International Relations theories would understand an alien attack on the Earth. (See also the interesting literature on Zombies and International Relations in Drezner 2011). You can even understand much of what we discuss in this section by tracing the evolution of the 'baddie' in James Bond movies.

PART 2 SECTION 4
GLOBALISATION

Contents

INTRODUCTION

Globalisation has contributed to the normative turn in International Relations. As we shall see in this section, the changes in the world reflect a changing global landscape brought about by globalisation and changes in the nature of political economy. The globalisation thesis revisits arguments about the state-centric understandings of international relations. This section discusses the phenomena of globalisation.

Globalisation, simply put, denotes the expanding scale, growing magnitude, speeding up and deepening impact of transcontinental flows and patterns of social interaction. It refers to a shift or transformation in the scale of human organisation that links distant communities and expands the reach of power relations across the world's regions and continents. It is more than increased interconnectivity such as transactions or interdependency between countries which can be defined as internationalisation.

Globalisation is 'highly contested', with various schools advancing agendas that seek to promote, reject, reform or transform its operation. Many of the disputes are related to normative considerations, as we have shown throughout the book. Therefore for some it is an empirical reality, for others it is a social construct, and for others still it is a discourse (Savigny and Marsden 2011). However, it is clear that the concepts of international relations and IPE that we have discussed thus far do not conveniently map onto the debates about globalisation (see Diez, Bode, and Da Costa 2011), and so for ease of study we consider it in a separate section.

There are three broad schools of thought:

- The Hyperglobalist perspective
- The Sceptical perspective
- The Transformationalist perspective

The three perspectives engage with a number of key debates. These are that

- Globalisation is about the liberalisation and global integration of markets.
- Globalisation is inevitable and irreversible.
- Nobody is in charge of globalisation (left to benevolence of the market).
- Globalisation benefits everyone.
- Globalisation furthers the spread of democracy in the world.

Hyperglobalists

Hyperglobalists (see Ohmae 1990) see the current set of political and economic relationships as distinct from previous political relations. They also believe that national borders are increasingly irrelevant, especially in economic terms. The discussion above about the power of MNCs would be used by hyperglobalists to highlight the weakness of national borders. To many this is the ultimate expression of neoliberalism with markets dominating. This has political consequences for governments, as companies become mobile and have political power. As we discussed above, large businesses have long operated across national borders, wherever there are opportunities for expansion and profit. They may diversify into other parts of the production process or even other types of business. They may move some of their manufacturing capacity to other countries to take advantage of more favourable tax regimes or employment markets. Thus many become MNCs, operating in many countries and able to shift their operations around the world, owing no exclusive loyalties to any national governments or their citizens. While some may openly retain their headquarters in a particular state, others may become effectively transnational, with no clear national centre for their activities, and are described accordingly as TNCs, although the distinction is essentially relative rather than fundamental. In practice, some large international business organisations are described as either MNCs or TNCs, without discrimination.

Box 2.12 Globalisation and you

Look at where your clothes or your electronic goods were made. Were they made in the country in which you live? If not, think about the distance these goods have travelled and the price you paid for them.

Hyperglobalists argue that a key driver and specific element of modern forms of globalisation have been technological change. Globalisation is seen to have altered the relationship between speed and time – we can watch live TV broadcasts from Tokyo in Boston. We now have the ability to communicate and transact instantaneously with people across the world. We can record a gig or the aftermath of a terrorist attack and upload it to the internet almost immediately with a smart phone. A flight from London to Brisbane, Australia, for instance, the longest route available in 1938, took 11 days and included over two dozen scheduled stops. Today, people can make that journey in just 22 hours, with a single layover in Hong Kong. Technology is a key element in Thomas Friedman's *The World Is Flat* thesis (2005). He outlines three stages of economic globalisation:

'Globalisation 1.0' From about 1492 till 1800 when we saw the beginning of global arbitrage

'Globalisation 2.0' From 1800 till the year 2000 the great shrinkage of the world – spearheaded by corporations

'Globalisation 3.0' From 2000 Onward, which represents the technological flattening of the world.

It is clear that technology has impacted on how we view the world in 2017, but not all commentators agree that the impact of globalisation on politics and economics is as significant as in previous decades.

Sceptics

David Held and Tony McGrew produced some of the most influential texts on globalisation (Held and McGrew 2003). They say that the sceptical perspective on globalisation views current international processes as more fragmented and regionalised than globalised. Therefore we see regional groupings such as the European Union, ASEAN, or NAFTA as dominating economic life more so than a truly globalised economy. When we look at recent trade disputes, the main players tend to be nation-states such as China or regional groupings such as the EU. It was also clear that until recently the United Kingdom exported more to Ireland than it exported to the whole of the BRICS (Savigny and Marsden 2011). In fact, according to sceptical authors, the 'golden age' of globalisation occurred at the end of the 19th century (see Hirst and Thompson 1999). The extensive commercial trading activities of the East India Company, founded back in the 17th century, were largely responsible for the creation and expansion of the British colonial empire in India, which was only finally formally transferred from the company to the crown after the Indian mutiny of 1857. Other joint stock companies were closely involved in the development of the slave trade in the 18th century. Such trade, and the institution of slavery itself, was eventually abolished by states (which nevertheless felt bound to compensate former slave owners for the loss of their 'property'). Recent events such as Brexit, the election of Donald Trump, and the rise of populism have reignited the debates about globalisation and the nation.

An Alternative View – Transformationalism

Held and McGrew constructed a transformationalist perspective that aims to overcome the problems associated with the first two approaches. They argue that globalisation is a multidimensional concept with historical roots and specific modern elements. Where power is located becomes the key question for the school of globalisation. 'Globalisation can thus be understood as involving a shift or transformation in the scale of human social organisation that extends the reach of power relations across the world's major regions and continents. It implies a world in which developments in one region can come to shape the life chances of communities in distant parts of the globe.' However, unlike the hyperglobalists, transformationalists argue it is more than economics. (Held and McGrew, 2003, p. 4–5).

To sum up, globalists believe that globalisation is happening and is fundamentally changing the world, whilst sceptics point out that the nation-state is still the dominant entity for analysis. This fundamental distinction is a recurring theme throughout the debates. The challenge is that whilst the hyperglobalist and sceptical traditions appear flawed, the third-way view of globalisation has yet to fully articulate a coherent narrative.

The messy reality

What is clear is that the world has changed in some important ways and the benefits of globalisation are not distributed evenly across the globe or even within states. The oft-quoted phrase that there are 'more mobile phones in Uganda than light bulbs' highlights that the changes brought about by globalisation have been distributed unevenly across the globe. The disconnect between place and time can be seen in the nature of industrial production. In the heyday of industrial production in the United Kingdom people worked for companies that were generally owned by people who lived in the local area. A visit to any Northern British city will give you an insight into where the workers and owners lived, in different types of houses, yes, but in the same locality. At the time of writing this relationship is disconnected. Held and McGrew show that key sites of global power can be quite literally oceans apart from the subjects and communities whose future they determine. For example, people working for Nissan in Sunderland, the United Kingdom, and Barcelona, Spain, are ultimately under the charge of decision-makers in Yokohama, Japan.

This has prompted some scholars to apply network theory to the social world. This is the dominant theory for understanding complex systems, and its use in social systems has been pioneered by the work of Manuel Castells (1996). Castells, a former proponent of WST [see Section 3 above] wanted to move beyond the rigid structures of Marxism. In particular, Castells is interested in how the internet has changed modern society. Complexity is said to be made real by the advances in digital and information revolutions. Complex systems are defined by a networking logic, which creates changes. Network societies inevitably produce their own problems, and Ulrich Beck* places the concept of 'risk' central to these concerns. It is important to state that not all risk/uncertainty is bad, and for Beck the ability to take risks defines late modern notions of freedom. The challenge is that many risks, from Ebola, terrorism, climate change, etc., are risks that do not take national (or any) boundaries into account (what Beck terms 'de-bounding'). To tackle them requires a global imaginary. In other words they force us to search for global solutions, including notions of cosmopolitan democracy (see Held, 1995). Beck's work therefore presents further evidence for those who predict the demise of the nation-state.

THE FAILURE OF THE STATE

For some scholars globalization means that the concept of the state (which as we have already shown is a relatively recent concept) is redundant. If the state is redundant, then this has massive implications for International Relations as much of the discipline is built on the study of states and their interaction (the Westphalia system). Susan Strange*, a leading figure in the field of international political economy, argues that Westphalia is an 'abject failure' and re-labels it Westfailure. She argues that the state is not the supreme source of authority and that it fails to satisfy long-term conditions of sustainability. She identifies three key failures:

- environmental
- financial
- social/cultural

The major economic, social, political, and environmental problems/threats the world now faces are shaped by global forces that demand global responses and show that no state can or should work in isolation. This view also argues that the theory of sovereignty, which fundamentally rests upon the territorial integrity of nation-states, has never been matched by reality. We explore this argument by looking at the issues of environment, human development, and culture to see how the nation-state has responded to them.

The environment and human development

One of the most pressing and fiercely debated global issues today is the global question of the environment. It is not just the future of humanity that is at risk. It is increasingly clear that human consumption can have damaging or fatal implications for other species. Kolbert (2014) argues that human consumption is already contributing substantially to what she calls a sixth mass extinction, comparable in scale with earlier mass extinctions such as that of the dinosaurs. Yet the difference between the current mass extinction and its predecessors is that this one is largely the result of human activity. The escalating growth of the human population and consumption is threatening biodiversity and the survival of other species. Indeed, our species is not only transforming life on the planet but is even beginning to impact on its geology.

The environment would officially become a global problem following the Rio 'Earth Summit' in 1992, where for the first time issues such as climate change, biodiversity, resource depletion, and pollution were on the global political agenda. The global nature of environmental problems is that the environment knows no borders. For example the Nile basin encompasses 11 countries, so pollution in one part of the river can potentially have consequences in countries not responsible for the pollution (Box 2.13).

Box 2.13 Tragedy of the commons

The tragedy of the commons refers to a situation whereby shared resources are depleted by individual actors acting in a rational way. The key element is that individual self-interested actions run counter to the common good. Hardin (1968) applied the concept to environmental resources such as oceans or the atmosphere. A classic example is over-fishing. Each boat fishes in a self-interested way to maximise profits, yet their actions cumulatively lead to the collapse of the fish stock. You might encounter the tragedy of the commons in a shared kitchen – whose responsibility is it to keep the communal space clean? The political debate revolves around possible solutions to this tragedy – can the commons be regulated (see efforts to preserve fish stocks) or does the commons need to be owned to ensure their survival (referring back to our earlier discussion of Locke and property rights)?

Global warming is a classic political problem – the problem is global yet the causes (and possibly the solutions) are national. It has also impinged on wider public consciousness. It is now widely (although even now not universally) accepted that emissions particularly from the burning of fossil fuels are causing climate change, with cumulative implications for our weather and sea levels and for agriculture and biodiversity. There is now, some argue, a credible threat to future generations and perhaps the survival of our species. It is this that has led to a series of international climate change conferences, the most recent of which was in Paris in 2015, when representatives of states and organisations agreed to limit temperature increase to below 2% and 'pursue efforts' to limit it to 1.5%, although this will depend on subsequent ratification by the main states responsible for greenhouse gas emissions, and effective action to meet targets. (There are continuing doubts over the commitment of the USA.) The failure of past promises in earlier conferences does not augur well, although there does seem to be increased agreement on the urgent need for action, and there have been some significant changes in energy policy by leading states and organisations. However, we once again see that despite claims to the contrary the nation-state still dominates these types of international fora, and it is the action to achieve these targets at a nation level that will determine the success or otherwise of the agreement.

The challenge for the environment is that the issue is not always high on the political agenda. The perception of risk often relies on trust in scientific evidence, as environmental degradation is not always visible to the population. Other issues such as the economy or terrorism or migration demand a more immediate response. There is also a feeling that tackling environmental problems requires sacrifice today for the sake of future generations. The idea of intergenerational (between generations) justice (see Barry 1977) is important here – what legacy do we leave to future generations? Writers in this field of study tend to utilise concepts of justice and fairness as found in the works of J. S. Mill* or Bentham*. Barry and others would argue that it is unjust to leave a bad environmental legacy for future generations to clean up. The challenge is that the timeframe for many politicians is the next election, which is possibly only four or five years away. This, it is argued, limits politicians to only think about how to win the next election and therefore automatically gives preference to those people who vote, often the older generations. 'Jam* tomorrow, not today' is an election slogan that is going to be a hard sell in the modern world of democratic politics. Added to this is the irony that the power to tackle a problem that transcends national borders lies with the very nation-states that dominate the global systems of governance.

We also need to discuss intragenerational justice here. This is about fairness and justice within generations. Issues such as climate change exacerbate global challenges such as hunger and starvation. Marxists have pointed to the major inequalities that exist in the world today and blame the nature of the capitalist system. Oxfam has highlighted that 1% of the world's population owned more wealth than the other 99% in 2016, whilst research has focused on the 'the bottom billion' (Collier 2007), outlining why many states are unable to escape the chronic poverty trap, with around 767 million people living on less than $1.90 a day – the World Bank measure of poverty. This measure is calculated by working out the average of the national poverty lines of the very poorest countries in the world.

Globalisation has been blamed for the increase in inequality between the richer and poorer states worldwide. Free trade in many foods and raw materials has pushed down wage rates to near starvation levels in some countries, while the continuation of protection for Western industry and agriculture for other products has restricted the scope of competition from which poorer states might otherwise benefit. Dominated by the commercial decisions of powerful multinational corporations, whose turnover far exceeds their own gross national product, and burdened by debt to the wealthy nations and international organisations, poorer states appear helpless in the face of economic forces they cannot control. This massive global imbalance between rich and poor, or north and south, has fundamental implications for international relations. Richer states need to work to together to mitigate the worst effects of global poverty, and this is a priority for the relevant international agencies.

Other campaigners have focused on the efforts of the global community working together to tackle famine, and 'feed the world'. Development progress has been substantial, as illustrated by the annual Millennium Development Goals (MDGs) report. Extreme poverty has fallen from 47% of all people in the developing world in 1990 to 14% in 2015 – and the number in extreme poverty has fallen over the same period from 1.9 billion to 836 million. At the same time, global maternal mortality has fallen from 380 per hundred thousand live births in 1990 to 210 in 2013. And the primary school net enrolment rate in Sub-Saharan Africa rose from 52% in 1990 to 80% in 2015. Globally, the number of children of primary school age out of school halved between 2000 and 2015 (UNDP 2015). As Ban Ki-Moon, the former UN Secretary General observed: 'The global mobilisation behind the Millennium Development Goals has produced the most successful anti-poverty movement in history.' (UNDP 2015). An important implication is that 'development works'.

The MDGs expired in 2015 and were replaced by the Sustainable Development Goals (in place until 2030). This agenda is much more ambitious as the SDGs apply to all states and not just developing countries. The agreement is therefore a political achievement in itself, but the reality of such agreements is that the hardest task is the implementation. Therefore SDG 10 *Reduce inequality within and among countries* applies as much to the inequality within the United Kingdom and the USA as it does to the inequality that exists between the United Kingdom and particular parts of the world. This is a major challenge for states such as China and India, as the geographies of poverty show that larger numbers of people live in poverty in these newly industrialising countries (NICs) than in states, for example Sub-Saharan Africa, where Western political attention is more often focused (see Sumner and Mallet 2013). For democratic governments the 15-year timeframe promotes long-term thinking, but between now and then the USA could have had 4 different presidents which potentially runs counter to continuity in policy. The pressure to keep to targets can come from NGOs.

As the name implies, NGOs are not part of government (although sometimes state governments may help to fund them or give them other forms of support) and are commonly established and run by ordinary private citizens, organised at a local, national or international level. They are also not conventional 'for profit' organisations [see multinational corporations]. There are far more NGOs than intergovernmental organisations (IGOs). Many NGOs have negligible political influence, although some have become powerful international political players. They include major global charitable organisations such as *Médecins Sans Frontières*, Oxfam, Human Rights Watch, Save the Children, and Action Aid. Others are influential campaigning environmental organisations, such as Greenpeace or Friends of the Earth. Such bodies can change hearts and minds. Increasingly many more ordinary citizens are actively involved in such campaigning NGOs than in political parties. Their influence in modern politics is growing. However, they are just one voice in the global debates and their influence has to be weighed against the voice of business.

By examining these issues we once again see that writers with different perspectives will highlight evidence to support their own view of the world. Those in the realist tradition will highlight the enduring power of states, especially the most powerful states. Others will highlight the role of regimes in shaping state behaviour on issues such as climate change or global poverty. Other more critical perspectives will highlight the growing inequalities created by the capitalist system, how environmental damage affects the poorest disproportionally, how the global trading system is designed to maintain existing unequal relations. Issues connected to development can be seen to follow a 'West knows best' approach, imposing solutions top down onto recipients states, whilst debates about the role of women in different cultural settings highlight diversity within feminist approaches. This leads us nicely to a discussion about the role of culture and identity.

Culture and identity

A major debate within globalisation studies is around the impact on culture and identity. Demands for change within states is often driven by a recognition of specific groups' rights. The technological changes outlined above clearly impact on shared cultural experiences. In Edinburgh there is a pub that sits outside the city walls. It is called the World's End because for people living there in the 16th century, the world ended at the city wall. This localism was reflected in traditions and past times, where geography often restricted movement. In 2016, people living in the west of Europe, it is argued share more cultural experiences with others than ever before. This cultural globalisation is visible in the coffee shops we visit, the clothes we wear, or the films and television we watch. The homogenisation of culture is seen by the fact that we can visit the same coffee shops and burger restaurants, drink the same soft drink, and stay in the same hotel chains in many countries across the world. This coming together around a specific Western view of consumer culture is also often described as Americanisation because many of the symbols of this trend are American companies, such as McDonald's, Starbucks, or Coca-Cola.

Globalisation in many respects appeared to parallel and reinforce the end of the Cold War. Liberal capitalism was triumphant. There no longer appeared to be a credible alternative. Most former communist states eagerly embraced capitalism, the free market, and prospects for greater material prosperity. Global brands such as McDonald's that were already omnipresent in the West found an enthusiastic welcome in new markets in the East. Aspects of Western culture were widely imitated, although globalisation should not simply be equated with Westernisation (Scholte 2005, 58–59). Countries the world over appeared to be losing distinctive features and becoming more similar in interests and aspirations. In a more homogeneous world it might appear that old enmities would fade and there would be less to fight over between peoples who increasingly resembled each other. Indeed Scholte (2005, 198–199) observes that 'perhaps it is no accident that states with McDonald's outlets in their jurisdictions have only once gone to war against each other' (the sole exception was the war over Kosovo). This is an interesting variation on the often-made point that democracies do not fight each other.

The Westernisation trend creates tensions as it becomes harder to protect different cultures. The regionalist movements from the 1970s often had protection of language and culture at the heart of their demands. In the United Kingdom we see the creation of Welsh-speaking television channels. Globalisation and the rise of English challenges even major languages such as French. Actions to protect the French language include a law that forces radio station output to have at least 40% of their output in French.

These issues are intensely political but tend to be restricted to specific nation-states. A more visible reaction to the rise of Western culture has been the challenge offered by political Islam. In a challenging book Samuel Huntington (1996) argued that cultural (and religious) divisions transcending state boundaries had replaced ideological conflict between sovereign states in the post–Cold War world. Huntington's thesis was widely seen in the West as prophetic of the apparently growing threat to the West from radical Islam, as represented by the attack on the Twin Towers of 9/11.

Huntington's thesis is controversial. We showed earlier that, according to Edward Said*, Western studies of Eastern culture are warped by Western power and colonial dominance over the East. Said unsurprisingly criticised Huntington's thesis, for instance in an essay called 'Clash of Ignorance'. He argues that by trying reducing the global complexity to broad concepts such as the West and Islam, Huntington's idea 'mislead and confuse the mind, which is trying to make sense of a disorderly reality that won't be pigeonholed or strapped down as easily as all that' (Said 2001). The oversimplification fails to appreciate the political, social, and cultural aspects of, say, the tensions between religions in Pakistan or the political situation in Turkey. The demonisation of 'Islam' fuels the narrative of extreme right-wing parties and politicians in many countries, even those with sizeable Muslim communities.

Samir Amin (2010) also makes a major contribution to this debate with his works critiquing the Eurocentric view of history which ignores the contribution of the Arab Islamic world.

This discussion prompts a wider discussion about the nature of the intellectual diversity of modern international relations and political science. To misquote Daddow: 'Feminists ask "where are the women?" Marxists ask "where are the classes?" We also need to ask "where is the ethnic diversity?"' (Daddow 2013, 233). This is something we are conscious of in this book, given our own backgrounds. Postcolonial theory (which we use as a shorthand) is situated in the intellectual traditions like feminism and Marxism that pay attention to the power of language and critique the inequalities of the modern capitalist system. There is thus a critique of the behaviourist tradition and the focus on rationality, given that rationality is a constructed norm. Other constructed terms such as 'development' and 'growth' fail to engage with the unequal power relations that exist among different parts of the world.

THE DECLINE OF THE NATION-STATE IS EXAGGERATED

Reading much of the globalisation literature, you see a clear position that the nation-state is not fit for purpose. Yet the enduring hold of the nation-state is very evident. If international relations between 1945 and 1989 were dominated by the Cold War between the superpowers, the United States and the USSR, and their respective allies, the study of comparative politics in the whole postwar period was complicated by the unprecedented growth in the numbers of new independent sovereign states. There were just 51 member states of the new United Nations in 1945. By 1960 there were 104 members, by 1970, 127, by 1980, 154, and by 1990, 166.

Many of these new member states were former European colonies, now newly independent sovereign states although some still retained cultural and political ties with their former colonial rulers. A more damaging legacy of colonial rule was that boundaries had often ignored older tribal, linguistic, and religious divisions, and these posed continuing problems for the newly independent states, which commonly contained sizeable alienated and disaffected minorities and could hardly be described as 'nation-states'. In some cases this has led to successful or unsuccessful attempts at secession. Moreover, while democratic institutions evolved successfully in some former colonies, in others leaders and movements associated with the struggle for independence long dominated the new states and effectively excluded any effective competition for power.

After 1990 most of the new states that joined the United Nations were as a consequence of the breakup of the former USSR and Yugoslavia. By 2011 there were 193 UN member states. Some of these former one-party states have become relatively stable parliamentary democracies. Others, such as the new Russia and some of the other newly independent Asian successor states, have been described as illiberal democracies, as there is scarcely free and fair party and electoral competition.

Altogether, the whole period from 1945 until the present has involved an unprecedented explosion in the number of theoretically independent sovereign states. It is difficult to think of any remotely comparable period of rapid political change in global history. While the political maps of Europe had been substantially redrawn in 1815 and in the peace treaties after the 1914–1918 war, there has been nothing remotely similar to the almost continuous emergence of new independent states in the years after 1945.

On top of this there has been extensive regime change within many states, involving not just new political leaders but a radical overhaul of the whole system of government. Thus former dictatorships have been replaced by representative democracies in Spain, Portugal, and Greece, and communist regimes have been transformed into substantially genuine or imitation democracies in some of the former constituent states of the USSR and its East European satellites. Many Arab, African, and South and Central American states have experienced similar political convulsions.

The predictions of Fukuyama* about the victory of liberal democracy appeared to have been borne out by these global changes. The 2011 wave of democratisation that spread across north Africa (the Arab Spring) also appeared to support his central argument. However, the way the Arab Spring lost its optimism was for Fukuyama a failure of governmental capacity. His current thinking (2014) suggests that political decay can take away the great advantages that political order has delivered: a stable, prosperous, and harmonious society. Again we need to consider the role of language and the nature of concepts. Is the concept of democracy transferable into all political situations across the globe? Are human rights universal or constructed to reflect a particular view of the world?

This is a major challenge, given the enduring pull of the nation-state, which has been evident in the outcome of recent civil wars. The key aim in the East Timor and South Sudan conflicts was the creation of independent and new nation-states, both of which have been achieved. The stated desire of organisations like the ETA and the Tamil Tigers was to create independent states for a particular group of people. It is also not just armed conflicts that lead to independence calls. Populist parties, especially in Europe, often call for the creation of an independent state. For example, *Vlaams Belang* wishes to see the creation of a separate Flemish state. These demands are not the sole concern of the political right. A key long-term aim of the Scottish National Party is the creation of an independent Scotland. This call is premised on the belief that independence is the best way to ensure that Scotland is run in a socially progressive way. The resilience of the nation-state concept runs counter to many predictions within the globalisation literature. However, the resilience can be seen as a reaction to the global changes we are encountering. There is a potential paradox at play now: whilst the state has become too small to tackle the 'big' political issues we face today, the state has also grown too big for many of the 'small' or local issues we face.

All this has complicated considerably the study of comparative politics and helped to blur the line between the national and the international. There is also a growing disconnect between the 'winners' and 'losers' of globalisation. This manifests itself in two broad ways – between states and within states. In 2016 we saw the disconnect within states come into stark relief. First was the referendum decision in the United Kingdom to vote to leave the EU (Brexit); the second was the election in the USA of Donald Trump as president. It is too simplistic to say both decisions were a reaction against globalisation, but the effects of globalisation certainly played a role in many voters' minds. In particular, it can be argued that the sectors of society that have 'lost' as a result of globalisation were attracted to the economic nationalist rhetoric of 'bringing jobs back' and policies such as preventing companies moving factories to countries with cheaper labour/lower taxes. We see these nationalist narratives at work in countries as diverse as Russia, India, the Philippines, and Venezuela and coming from both the left and the right of the political spectrum.

The winners and losers of globalisation between states can be observed when looking at the issue of migration and refugees. War, famine, persecution, and environmental insecurity forced 65 million people from their homes in 2015. The key statistics, given the debate about migration in many Western countries, are that approximately three-quarters of that number are internally displaced and that most refugees end up living in developing countries. Therefore refugees are more likely to end up living in Lebanon or Kenya than they are in the United Kingdom or Australia. Although the disparity between states has narrowed in that the numbers of people living in abject poverty have fallen, the push factors from many developing countries have yet to be tackled by the global institutions or the nation-states. The global institutions such as the World Bank have launched campaigns to tackle global inequality by promoting 'shared prosperity'. Trying to reconcile these narratives with the 'retreat back behind borders' narratives popular in many states is going to be a key global issue going forward.

SUMMARY

If the practice of politics continues to change, often unpredictably, its study continues to evolve, in part reflecting what is happening in the real world. This is obvious in the study of global politics and international relations. Clearly the old typology of the West, the communist bloc and the residual category of the 'third world' is now obsolete. The second world imploded while the third has been effectively invalidated by the rise of the NICs and BRICS and no doubt by further novel acronyms. The key discussion revolves around the rise of the BRICS and their impact on the global balance of political power. Are we witnessing a return to a world best understood by neorealism? To what extent do these newly emergent powers utilise 'soft power'? Given the preference of some International Relations theories for a balance of powers in a bipolar world, what does the emergence of a multipolar world or a unipolar world mean?

Similarly, the study of international relations was thrown into some confusion by the end of the Cold War, which virtually none of its experts had predicted. Key concepts such as deterrence and mutually assured destruction (MAD) no longer seemed relevant. Not only were other fast industrialising states becoming important players on the international scene, but also there was increased recognition of the significance of international bodies, nongovernmental organisations, and multinational corporations.

It is perhaps worth reiterating that none of the issues described in this section would have been thought worthy of the attention of world statespersons before the late 20th century. There are now global political issues that, it is widely recognised, need addressing. To that extent the subject matter of politics and politics itself has changed.

There was also some in-built bias in much of the US-led study of the radical 20th-century changes in the real world, including the end of the Cold War; the emergence of newly industrialised states; a global financial and economic crisis; the disintegration of political order in failing states; terrorism, the Western war on terror, and the revival of faith-based political conflicts; and much else besides. All these changes have shaken and transformed the study of international relations and the global political economy especially. Yet globalisation has also opened up new divisions within states and societies and compelled some re-examination of political identities in the modern world. All these developments have massive continuing implications for the study of politics today.

While many had hoped that a new world order would emerge from the end of the Cold War, global politics increasingly seems better described as disorder. The disintegration of its only real rival has not ensured the dominance of the sole remaining superpower, the USA. On the contrary, its armed interventions in Afghanistan, Iraq, Syria, and Libya have been no more successful than in Vietnam and have been markedly counterproductive in promoting political stability.

Certainly global politics seem far more complex, with many more different kinds of players on the international scene. Once it appeared that the political world was essentially composed of a number of (largely nation) states, with weak international organisations attempting and often failing to keep the peace between them. Yet with few exceptions, state borders were widely agreed and respected, and there was, in most established states, a framework of internal law and order, if not always justice. Now, especially in north Africa and the Middle East, there are rogue states, failed states, and aspiring states. Prolonged civil war, internal disorder, and political chaos have become a feature of parts of Asia and Africa, with millions of refugees desperately seeking a better life, or indeed any kind of life, elsewhere. The so-called Islamic State claims the loyalty of some Muslims across existing frontiers frontiers that it does not recognise.

This overview of International Relations has taken you through from early 20th century to the present. The key points are that in many ways International Relations and mainstream political science followed distinct paths within our broader understanding of social science but that in recent years there has been a general coming together. The distinction between the domestic and the international has blurred, and this is reflected in the disciplines with the boundaries between them becoming much more fuzzy. This also reflects the reality of the world. The notion of a sovereign nation-state existing as an island (if ever true) is clearly no longer the case in a world that is more connected globally than before.

GUIDE TO FURTHER READING

There is no really satisfactory and up-to-date introduction to the whole development of modern political science or International Relations, so here we identify a range of books, although Savigny and Marsden *Doing Political Science and International Relations* (2011) is an excellent introductory text that takes on and develops many of the issues discussed in this book.

Useful, but difficult for beginners, is Colin Hay's *Political Analysis: A Critical Introduction* (2002). More comprehensive, but already a little dated, is Goodin and Klingemann (eds) *A New Handbook of Political Science* (1996). This contains an overview of the whole discipline, with separate parts devoted to political institutions, political behaviour, comparative politics, international relations, political theory, public policy and administration, political economy, and political methodology. A British book, Bealey, Chapman, and Sheehan *Elements in Political Science* (1999 is easier but less comprehensive. Lowndes, Marsh, and Stoker (eds) *Theory and Methods in Political Science* (2018) is rather more up to date. Also useful is Hay, Lister, and Marsh *The State: Theories and Issues* (2006).

On specific areas, Hague, Harrop, and McCormick (2016) provides the best up-to-date coverage of comparative government and politics. Hindmoor and Taylor (2015) discuss rational choice. The Canadian political philosopher Will Kymlicka (1990) has written a useful and provocative guide to contemporary political philosophy. On feminism, Valerie Bryson (2016) provides the most readable and comprehensive guide to feminist theory.

For useful reference books on politics and International Relations, see the guidance on further reading for other parts of this book, particularly Part IV (key concepts) and Part V (key thinkers). Many of the classic contributions to modern political science are discussed in these parts. If you wish to investigate any of them further, consult the key political terms and concepts in Part IV and key thinkers in Part V, follow the references cited in the text, and consult the bibliography.

Chris Brown and Kirsten Ainley's *Understanding International Relations* is a key textbook, and Daddow's *International Relations Theory* provides a very student-friendly introduction to the IR theories, plus it has some useful study tips. Both Cynthia Weber's *International Relations Theory: A Critical Introduction* (2014) and Douglas A. Van Belle's *A Novel Approach to Politics: Introducing Political Science through Books, Movies, and*

Popular Culture (2015) use films and popular culture to understand the concepts and theories of political science and International Relations. Daniel Drezner's *Theories of International Politics and Zombies* (2011) explains International Relations theories by showing how they would explain the consequences of a zombie attack on Earth. The final three will appeal to some of you, whilst others will find them a little gimmicky.

PART III

Your Degree, Study Skills, Methodology, and Research-led Employability

PART 3 SECTION 1

WHAT TO EXPECT FROM YOUR POLITICS OR INTERNATIONAL RELATIONS COURSE

Contents

THE MAIN ELEMENTS OF A POLITICS OR INTERNATIONAL RELATIONS DEGREE COURSE

Approaching a new topic can feel daunting. University study is no different. Many of you will be approaching aspects of your university programme for the first time. To make the most of your time you need to be able to navigate your way around your programme. On the surface it looks as if politics and International Relations courses vary considerably, both among countries and among universities. However a closer inspection reveals that most offer some broadly comparable main elements. Here we meet the first terminology barrier. In universities we can appear to use different terms to mean the same thing, which is confusing. In this book we will use 'programme' to mean the named degree programme you are studying. This is likely to be a BA with a degree title of 'Politics' or 'International Relations' (single honours) or a joint honours such as 'Politics and French' or 'International Relations and History'. You will be on a programme for a specific number of years. The programme will be made up of a certain number of courses or modules. These will last either a term, a semester, or all year. Each course is worth a specific number of credits and there is likely to be a minimum number of credits needed to pass the year/obtain your degree. Although structures vary, your first year of study is traditionally an introduction year (often mirrored in the titles of courses, e.g. Political Science 101, An Introduction to International Relations), with each subsequent year becoming more specialised. These main elements are explained below. It should, however, be appreciated that they may be described under rather different titles in some institutions, and the weight attached to each element may vary considerably among institutions.

The politics and government of particular states

The politics and government of the country in which the university is situated will constitute a core element of most politics degrees around the world. For 'home' students the politics of their own country will offer a familiar introduction to the study of the subject. For foreign students such courses provide a valuable opportunity to learn more at first hand about the government and politics of the host country. Thus virtually all degrees in politics in the United States involve students in undertaking an initial course in American government and politics, commonly followed by a range of more specialised American politics modules. Most politics degrees around the world expect or require students to learn about the politics and government of their country. Thus politics students take an introductory course in Canadian politics at the University of Ottawa, in Swedish politics at the University of Stockholm, in Australian politics at Melbourne University, and in Dutch politics at Leiden University (information from university websites). International Relations students will usually be expected to learn about domestic politics, as foreign policy decisions are made by governments, so how domestic politics informs those decisions can be key.

Comparative politics

The in-depth analysis of a single country's government and politics can be fascinating and illuminating, but it is now universally acknowledged that the study of politics should be comparative. Thus all university politics degrees involve some comparative politics. What this involves in practice may vary considerably. It may simply involve the in-depth analysis of the politics of one or more other countries. Thus a module in British politics offered by an American university or a module in American politics offered by a British university, might come under the heading 'comparative politics'. Such an analysis of another country's politics does involve implicit comparison, because students will inevitably compare its political institutions and behaviour with those of their own country with which they are already familiar, and similarities and differences will often be emphasised and made more explicit by tutors.

However, most specialists would argue that a truly comparative approach involves more systematic comparison across a whole range of countries on a regional or global basis. Thus legislatures or political parties, or pressure groups, or state bureaucracies may be examined across a continent or the world. The study of comparative politics can throw up considerable variations in political practice across countries. Major differences may become apparent, in, for example, levels of turnout in elections, or the finance of political parties, or checks on the power of central government, or media bias, or the extent of corruption. Cross-country surveys may throw up a wide range of political attitudes, loyalties, and values. Further analysis may suggest tentative hypotheses about the reasons for these variations, hypotheses that might be tested against the available evidence. Such work may help to illuminate why some peoples appear willing to engage in politics while others are more apathetic, why some political systems appear more durable than others, or why some countries have apparently managed the transition to democracy more smoothly than others (Hague and Harrop 2016).

International relations

While there is global scope for such comparison, comparative politics still focuses primarily on the government and politics of states, rather than interstate politics or the politics of transnational and international organisations. Yet many of the really big political issues, such as peace and war, terrorism, global inequality, the conservation of the environment, and the very survival of humanity, transcend state borders. They involve relations between states and also, increasingly, international government and nongovernmental organisations (NGOs) as well as powerful transnational business corporations (TNCs). The subject (or subdiscipline) of international relations examines the efforts of governments, organisations, and peoples to tackle the vital issues of international peace and security, global inequality, and the future of the planet. These are issues that naturally interest and concern students, who rightly expect them to figure prominently in any politics degree programme. As we showed in Part II Section 4, the lines between politics and International Relations have become blurred, and now it is very common to see a greater focus on foreign policy, security, and terrorism alongside a greater focus on globalisation and international political economy.

Political theory

Political theory almost invariably figures as another core study area in a politics or International Relations degree. Yet the broad label 'political theory' is somewhat problematic and can conceal considerable variations in content. It may not seem immediately obvious that political theory should be a distinct field of study within politics. Theories are integral to the study of politics. The analysis of political behaviour inevitably involves theory. The study of comparative politics certainly includes masses of theory at every level. Radically contrasting theories underpin the study of international relations. Why should those undertaking a university degree in politics be expected to take a separate course in political theory? 'Political theory' as a subject is commonly interpreted to mean the theories or ideas that key thinkers have had about politics over time. This time dimension can be very long – extending back to the political ideas of the ancient Greeks two and a half thousand years ago. Thus, in many universities political theory entails the study of the writings of great political philosophers of the past from Plato onwards, up to and sometimes including, the present day.

Such political theory can be fascinating but much of it is unashamedly 'normative', in other words involving how politics should be conducted, the best form of government, arguments for obeying authority, justifications for equality or inequality, rather than the more dispassionate or 'scientific' analysis of political behaviour as it is. This goes back to the distinction between normative political theory and explanatory political science discussed in Part I (see Box 1.5), which is a recurring theme in this book. Some of the early pioneers of the behavioural revolution in the study of politics and international relations rejected traditional political philosophy as unscientific. Yet the rigorous separation of 'fact' and 'value' appeared more difficult than these pioneers imagined, and much of the new political science involved implicit normative assumptions. Indeed, many of the key political issues facing the modern world clearly have an important ethical dimension (consider issues of human rights, global inequality, green politics). Moreover, political philosophy in recent decades has experienced a considerable revival and is no longer exclusively associated with the writings of 'dead white European males'.

Some political theory courses involve a thematic approach to explore issues of justice, equality, freedom, political rights and obligations, while others prefer to tackle these issues through a chronological treatment of key thinkers, such as Plato, Aristotle, Machiavelli, Hobbes, Locke, Rousseau, Kant, Mill, and Marx. Others politics courses prefer to focus more narrowly on the thinkers of the last two centuries and take in some of the pioneers of modern social science, such as Durkheim and Weber, and more recent thinkers such as Hayek, Dahl, and rational choice theorists, as well as the work of modern political philosophers such as Rawls and Nozick.

Public policy and public administration

Public policy and/or public administration is a core area of study in many general politics degree courses and is the main focus of some more explicitly vocational degree programmes, preparing students for a wide range of possible careers in public administration at various levels of government. The study of public policy and administration deals not only with political institutions and processes but with public bureaucracies and the outputs and outcomes of public policy. This involves examining the whole policy cycle from the identification of a problem, through the search for a solution, the emergence of policy, and on to implementation and subsequent monitoring and review. This approach gives more attention to actual policies, such as transport, health, or education policies, relatively neglected in some politics degree courses. Such a focus commonly reveals problems in implementing policy and the often unintended consequences of policy decisions. It has already generated significant academic debate and an impressive and extensive body of theory (Parsons 1995).

Research and study skills

It is increasingly likely that you will be introduced to the theories and methodologies of modern social and political science and deal with these in separate introductory modules. At some stage, research methods feature in most courses, commonly involving some statistics. [We discuss this in Section 4].

CHOOSING A UNIVERSITY, DEGREE COURSE AND OPTIONS

Where to study?

Many readers will have already chosen a degree course and indeed may well have started it. In that case you may prefer to skip this section. However, if you have yet to make a decision but think you would like to study politics at university, you may find that there is a bewilderingly large number of courses and institutions to choose from. It is worth considering your choice carefully. You are about to commit three or four years of your life to this course. The advice here is confined to educational issues. In practice there are many factors influencing the choice of university that may have little to do with purely educational issues. For instance, some students have to study near home and others want to, for personal or financial reasons, and this will considerably reduce the options available to them. Those who actively prefer to study well away from home, or even abroad, have a much wider choice. They may be more interested in what a particular city, area or country has to offer by way of amenities than the attractions of specific universities or courses.

To gain initial information about politics and International Relations degrees at particular universities, the first step is to examine in detail the courses that they offer, the staff responsible for teaching them and their research interests and publications. Search the website of the university. Visit the university and the city, as there is no substitute for sampling an institution first hand. Attend an 'open day' if you are given the chance. You will meet some of the tutors and ideally some current students, perhaps attend a sample lecture, inspect some of the teaching material, tour the library and facilities, and have the opportunity to ask questions.

Box 3.1 Questions to consider when choosing a university

What facilities are available? In particular, how good is the library?

What is expected of you in terms of work and attendance in lectures and seminars?

Can you get a sense of the overall pattern of assessment across the course?

Does the course include a compulsory or optional dissertation or long essay?

What degree classifications have recent cohorts of students obtained?

What did students do after graduating?

What further courses did they undertake and what jobs did they obtain?

Are there opportunities for a period of study abroad, perhaps at a partner institution, or for a placement or political internship in an appropriate department or organisation?

Students often complain that their university life goes by too quickly, but if you end up living in a place you do not like, your time there can seem very long. We suggest reflecting on what you like. If you prefer quiet and rural, then a major urban centre might not be the best place for you. If you like the option of enjoying city life, then a rural campus–based university might not be for you.

Increasingly we find that university departments are ranked and student 'reviews' are available on official and unofficial websites. Treat these reviews with some caution, as you would any review on a travel website. We advise against choosing a university because a world-famous professor is based there – he or she might not even figure in undergraduate teaching programmes. Avoid going there to study a specific module in, say, the final year. Students starting university in 2018 may not take their final year module until 2020 or 2021 by which time the module may have been replaced, the member of staff left or retired, or your interests may have changed. You will get to study courses and topics that you might not have thought you'd have enjoyed and yet you did. Perhaps the key issue to consider is the amount of choice you feel comfortable with and to what extent that choice is available to you at university. At a recent open day a prospective student discussed how she was comparing programmes based on their structure – did the programme offer her choice or did it limit what she could study?

Box 3.2 What's in a name? University schools and departments in politics

Politics and International Relations courses are usually provided by academic subdivisions of universities variously described as schools, departments, or sometimes faculties (although the term 'faculty' is more commonly reserved for groupings of schools or departments). From a student perspective these academic divisions can be confusing but are of little immediate importance. (Indeed some institutions make a habit of frequent administrative reorganisation.) Of little more significance are the names given to the various departments or schools. Almost everywhere in the United States and commonly in much of the English-speaking world and on the mainland of Europe, courses in politics are offered by a department (or school) of political science. However, in the United Kingdom and Ireland relatively few departments or schools employ the label 'political science' (Birmingham, University College, London, and Trinity College, Dublin, are among the exceptions).

Manchester, Essex, and Strathclyde have departments of 'government', as does the University of Cork in the Irish Republic. More common is the simple description 'Department (or school) of Politics' or 'Politics and International Relations'. The lack of reference to 'science' does not mean that the approach to the study of politics is any less scientific in these universities. Thus a department that specifically includes 'International Relations' or 'International Studies' should certainly cover these subjects more than adequately. Yet the absence of 'International Relations' from a department's title does not necessarily imply any neglect of a subject that is widely regarded as integral to the study of politics. However, some universities with a particular strength in the subject area have established separate departments of 'International Relations' (e.g. Aberystwyth in Wales, Sussex in England, and St Andrews in Scotland).

The discussion about choice can be linked to the size of university departments. Large departments will naturally employ more staff, with a wider range of scholarship and expertise, and may offer a greater range of courses and a far more extensive choice of specialist politics options. Smaller departments will inevitably reduce the range of choice, but there may be compensations. A more limited range of modules may fit together better in an integrated programme, and smaller institutions can be less impersonal and enjoy better staff–student relations.

Degrees of specialisation

One decision that you may have to take when initially choosing your course is how much politics or International Relations you want to study and what other subjects (if any) you might want to study alongside politics. This is a decision you may not always have to take immediately but can postpone until after you have begun your course, perhaps before you start your second level or year of studies. Commonly, university degree courses are initially broad in the first year or level and become more specialist as well as more advanced at subsequent levels. Sometimes this will involve studying a range of disciplines or subjects at foundation level, with students only opting for specialisation in a single discipline later.

In most universities you will be faced with key choices at various stages of your degree course, including whether to specialise in politics, or combine the study of politics with another discipline or disciplines, or take politics as a subsidiary subject. Thus an undergraduate in an American university may choose to 'major' in politics, or alternatively may prefer to make it a minor or subsidiary element of their degree programme, taking just a few politics modules. In the United Kingdom and some other parts of the English-speaking world there is often a choice between taking a 'single honours' (or 'pure honours') or 'joint honours'. A single honours course in politics will be devoted principally to the study of politics, although the study of some other subjects in associated disciplines, such as economics, sociology or law, may also be involved. In a joint (or combined) honours course, politics is studied in combination with one or more other disciplines, commonly drawn from other social sciences or the humanities, such as politics and anthropology, or politics and history, or politics and law. One popular degree title, used by some leading British universities, combines three major subjects, philosophy, politics, and economics (PPE). Some universities elsewhere in the English-speaking world employ the US terminology of 'majoring' in a particular subject alongside the British distinction between single and joint honours degree programmes.

A combined or joint honours degree programme course will clearly reduce the breadth and depth of the coverage of politics, although studying politics in conjunction with another allied discipline can frequently offer fresh insights into both. Partner disciplines may also significantly influence the approach to the study of politics. Thus where politics is combined with one or more of the other social sciences, such as sociology or economics, it is likely to be treated rather differently from politics studied alongside history or philosophy or law. The same may also be true of the disciplines with which politics is combined, particularly where they clearly overlap, as evidenced in composite subject labels, such as political economy or political sociology. Similarly, where politics is combined with a subject such as law this is likely to influence the content of both, with particular emphasis on constitutions, government and the legislative process, and human rights on the politics side, and on constitutional law and administrative or public law rather than private law.

The title of a single honours degree in politics may simply mirror the title of the department or school. However, very large departments may offer a range of specialist politics degrees, for example in public policy or international relations, as well as courses that combine the study of politics with another discipline or disciplines. These more specialist degrees may not always be quite as distinctive as their titles suggest. Thus a range of degree programmes may share some core politics modules and have access to some similar specialist politics options. Students who have studied many of the same modules may sometimes graduate with very different degree titles. Decisions on more specialist politics programmes require careful consideration. You will naturally be guided by your own interests, by your performance in particular modules, and by career considerations, as well as the advice you receive.

Often students see each week of study as a discrete bloc. It can be common to hear students refer to 'week 5 work'. Although courses have to be structured week by week, it is important to spot that each week builds on the last. This is important to remember as sometimes topics will be confusing at first and will only make sense, say, three weeks in. You need to see each week as a building block to your obtaining the knowledge for the course/module.

Box 3.3 Knowledge building

An Introduction to International Relations course will classically start with the theory of realism, as it is seen as the starting point of the discipline, before introducing you to other perspectives (see Baylis, Owens and Smith, 2016 as an example). It is hard to understand neorealism without having the building blocks of realism and its critics, as neorealism is a response to criticisms of realism. A political theory course will often start with liberalism and conservatism before moving onto more radical and/or contemporary thinkers.

You will also be building knowledge among courses. Thus in your first year you will often get a course on 'Introduction to Comparative Politics'. This survey course will give you the foundations to then take a course in your second year on 'Comparative Political Parties' and then a more specialist course in your third year on 'Radical Right-Wing Parties'.

It is also important to see the connections between your course on a specific year and of course the connections between modules you have studied in different years (see Box 3.3 above).

Specialist options

Whether you take a single honours degree in politics, major in politics or take politics in combination with another subject or subjects, you will still normally have a range of politics options to choose between at some stage in your course. A large university with a big politics department will normally offer not only more choice of degree courses (both specialist single honours and various combined honours programmes), but also a far wider range of specialist options.

Box 3.4 Course examples

This box shows both how different courses are structured and the range of options available at different levels of study. It is only possible here to give a few examples of the options offered by specific universities around the English-speaking world, but what this shows is that at their core most programmes cover similar topics – introduction to the subject in the first year of study, moving onto more specialist options in later years.

Politics and Governance: University of Cape Town, South Africa
Introduction to Politics A & B
Comparative Politics
Comparative Public Institutions
Politics of International Economic Relations
South African Politics
Politics of Africa and the Global South
South African Political Thought
Policy and Administration
Urban Politics
Conflict in World Politics
Global Governance

Politics: University of Liverpool, United Kingdom
British Politics
European Politics
Foundations in Politics
Foundations in International Politics
Media and Politics
Terrorism and Counter Terrorism
Security and Intelligence
International Institutions
Environmental Politics
British Political Ideologies
Parliament and Devolution in the United Kingdom
Comparative Peace Processes; Identity in Contemporary International Politics
Immigration and the State

Political Science: University of Illinois at Urbana-Champaign, USA

Introduction to Political Science
Introduction to US Government & Politics
The New Middle East
Introduction to Public Policy
Environmental Politics & Policy
Introduction to Political Research
Introduction to Comparative Politics
Comparative Politics in Developing Nations
Introduction to International Relations
Introduction to International Security

International Relations: University of Queensland, Australia

Introduction to International Relations
Introduction to Political Ideas
Introduction to International Inequality & Development
International Relations of the 20th Century
Global Security
International Organisations & Political Co-operation
Globalisation & International Political Economy
Australian Foreign Policy
International Relations of East Asia
Problems of Asia-Pacific Security
Terrorism & Insurgency in World Politics
European Political Issues
The United States & the Evolving International Order
Human Security and the Responsibility to Protect
Human Rights & International Politics
World Women: International Perspectives on Politics & Culture
Principles of Research: Social and Comparative Perspectives

Given the lists in Box 3.4, the choice of courses can seem daunting. Here are some of the points you might like to consider:

What exactly does the module involve? This is not always self-evident from the title or short description. Study any relevant published material, such as module handbooks (sometimes available online), ask your personal tutor, and talk to students who have taken it.

How will it fit with the rest of your studies? You may fancy a topic that is quite outside your experience and unconnected with much of the rest of your course, and why not? It might spark off new interests. More commonly you may want to consider options that connect with previous studies and may lead on to more advanced options (and sometimes even postgraduate courses or subsequent careers). Bear in mind that some choices may constrain what you can do in future. Thus some advanced options can only be taken if you have studied an earlier 'underpinning' intermediate option. Some more specialist degree titles may require that you take some relevant options.

Who is the tutor? This may be an important consideration. He or she may have a worldwide reputation in this subject, and you will have the opportunity to sit at the feet of an acknowledged expert (although he or she might not always be a brilliant and inspiring teacher!). You may have encountered the tutor previously in your course and know something of him or her. You may know nothing about him or her at all, in which case it is useful to seek information, including from students who have taken the module.

Is the option regularly available? Commonly, options only run if there is sufficient demand to make them economical. Sometimes options that feature in a university prospectus may not have been taught for years. Others may not run if the tutor is taking a period off for research (a 'sabbatical').

How is the option assessed? There is sometimes a fairly common pattern of assessment across modules, but in some universities assessment can vary quite considerably among modules. Some, for example, may be assessed entirely through an end of module unseen examination, while others might involve submitted essays, papers, or projects. Oral presentations may feature as part of some module assessments. The form of assessment can be critical for some students. Yet you would be unwise to reject a module that otherwise fits in with your interests and plans solely because of the assessment. If you are worried about it, seek further advice and find out how past students have fared.

IF YOU ARE NOT HAPPY WITH YOUR COURSE

However much (or little) advanced thinking and planning you do, you may at some stage feel dissatisfied with your chosen course. If so, do not make any hasty decisions. You may be temporarily depressed for reasons perhaps unconnected with your course. Alternatively, you may be experiencing problems with specific modules or pieces of work. Seek advice. Talk to your tutor, specialist advisory services, family, friends, and fellow students. It is possible that this will resolve your problems or put them in perspective. You may also be able to take a year out of your studies and resume later.

If you do ultimately decide that the course is not for you, it is not the end of the world. You may be able to switch to another course at the same university or to a different university. You may be better advised to drop out of university for a period and retain the option of returning to higher education later, perhaps to study politics, perhaps something quite different. Many 'second chance' students have subsequently done very well. Make sure you get it right next time, though. To misquote Oscar Wilde, to screw up on one course might be regarded as a misfortune; to screw up on two looks like carelessness!

PART 3 SECTION 2
STUDY SKILLS

Contents

INTRODUCTION

You may feel that you are ready to study at degree level, but often students find studying at university very different to school or college. Universities tend to have different teaching methods, larger classes, and a greater degree of independent learning than high school. Working out how to succeed at university by ensuring that you acquire the right skills is as important as ensuring you get on top of the course content. University is not dissimilar to a gym. Just buying a gym membership will not make you fitter or stronger – you need to make use of the membership, go to the gym and ensure you know how to use the equipment effectively. The same is true at university – you need to put work into both understanding the content of your course and developing the research skills you will need. Whilst your department and the wider university offer many forms of help to students, the primary responsibility for studying and learning lies with you – the expectation is that you will be self-motivated, you will organise your time effectively, and you will work to the best of your ability in an independent manner. If you don't know already, now it is time to find out how to become an independent learner. Most of the skills required for success on a university politics course are generic rather than subject-specific – in other words they are similar to the skills required in many subjects, particularly in other social sciences and the humanities (Dunleavy 1986). Moreover, many skills important for success on an academic course are also valuable in the world of work, and indeed throughout life.

We argue that there is a core set of research and study skills that students can and should develop as part of their politics or International Relations degree. Politics and International Relations students should have an appreciation and experience of carrying out research in politics: you should understand what the big questions in politics are and how academics are trying to resolve them; you should know how to find out who is doing what and where the major work is taking place. Crucially, for politics you should have the ability to deal with the greys in academic research rather than always looking for the black and white. Debates, challenges, and disputes can be found in any academic discipline; those in academic political studies overlap with and, in different ways and to different degrees, are entangled with debates, challenges, and disputes in the real world of politics.

WHAT SKILLS DO YOU NEED TO STUDY POLITICS AND INTERNATIONAL RELATIONS?

Each of you will bring a different skill set to the study of politics and international relations. In part the skill set will depend on how you have come to university (straight from school/college, after a gap year, after working for a while, or even after you have retired).

Students arrive at universities from diverse educational backgrounds, with an ever-increasing variety of qualifications and with different combinations and levels of skills, confidence, awareness, and ambition. The aim of this part of the book is to show that whatever background you come from, adjusting to life at university has challenges. Bearing in mind of the contestable nature of the topics that the discipline tends to study and the ways in which degrees in politics and International Relations are usually assessed – from essay writing to seminar presentations – this section offers a brief outline and discussion of the key skills that you are likely to find particularly important to make a success of your study.

Critical thinking

The need for critical thinking is crucial in the study of politics. If we go back to what politics is, Lasswell* sees it as being about 'who gets what, when, and how' (Lasswell 1936). This deceptively simple definition covers notions of decision-making, power, even ideology. It shows that politics is not just about government but that politics is an activity, a social activity. Politics reflects social diversity and involves differing interests coming together to make collective decisions. The key element is that politics involves choices, and those choices are often related to political positions based on ideology. As a result, lecturers may explicitly advise you to 'Question everything. Take nothing on trust, least of all from me.' Some students are uncomfortable with doubt and crave certainty. They seek right answers, and are unhappy when even their tutors do not claim to know what the right answer is, and positively invite criticism.

> ### Box 3.5 Motivations for study
>
> Think about why you chose to do politics or International Relations as a degree?
>
> Was it the subject matter? Good job prospects? Location? People study degrees in politics and International Relations for a number of reasons. Surprising, most students take their degree based on its potential to get them a good job. Only about a fifth choose their degree based upon the subject. Some students (admittedly a minority) don't care about their degree course – university is all about the social life, sports, or even political activities.

Criticism in an academic setting is not the same as in everyday life. Academic criticism or critical thinking aims to understand why someone made an argument or conclusion. Whilst we do this in many ways outside of university – choosing a phone package, a hotel, or even which university to study at – within politics and International Relations, critical thinking applies to arguments and conclusions. As Cottrell (2011) argues it is a process that includes:

- identifying other people's positions, arguments, and conclusions
- evaluating the evidence for alternative points of view
- weighing up opposing arguments
- identifying any assumptions made by the author
- drawing conclusions as to whether arguments are valid, based on evidence
- presenting a point of view in a structured, clear, and well-reasoned way that convinces others

As we have shown in the earlier sections, politics and International Relations are characterised by different ways of studying the world around us. In Part II, Section 3 we introduced the key schools of thought in International Relations. It is crucial you that identify whether the writer is a realist, a constructivist, a feminist, or a Marxist, as this will influence how they approach the topic in question.

Quality of reasoning matters: how good is the line of reasoning? Try and find out how the main argument fits together, and as you read or listen keep reminding yourself of the overall argument. You need to make sense of different pieces of information and try and understand how reasons and evidence make up the whole argument. Sometimes identifying the argument can be difficult; try and ask yourself what the point of the text is, what do you believe is the main message? What is it that the author wants you to believe and what reasons is he or she giving you to support his or her position? Critical thinking does not mean to just criticise everything. It means to try and understand the motivations of the writer or speaker to understand his or her position. Why did he or she argue his or her case in that way? In politics and International Relations this is crucial, as very quickly we move from facts to opinions based on values. So we need to distinguish between facts and values.

Facts and values

Indeed, as we have seen, politics and International Relations today are regarded as social sciences, aspiring, in some cases, to the same objective scientific approach as other sciences (although some academics will disagree with that opening statement – as you will see when we discuss methodologies later). Scientific method requires that hypotheses should be formulated in such a way that they can be tested rigorously against the available evidence. Research in politics, as in other sciences, should be capable of being replicated (or successfully repeated) by other researchers. Much scientific research is dependent on extensive quantitative analysis, and this is true of some political research, most notably on voting behaviour. With some other topics it is more difficult to test hypotheses using extensive quantitative analysis, yet a scholarly approach still requires that theories and causal explanations should be tested thoroughly against the available evidence. This is particularly important as we move into what is being labelled a 'post-truth' world. Here we see appeals to emotions as dominant, and questions are asked as to whether rebuttals are facts or merely assertions (Suiter 2016). We discussed the causes on p. 70, but the key to countering this trend is widen your reading and avoid just relying upon the echo chamber of social media.

Box 3.6 Facts versus values

Within politics and International Relations we see debates around the following:

Are there such things as facts?

Can we separate facts and values?

Why are concepts contested?

An example

'The Russian military intervention in the Syrian Civil War began on 30 September 2015, following a formal request by the Syrian government for military help.'

This information is 'factually' correct and can be verified by looking at reputable sources.

'Russian military intervention is focused on terrorist organisations.'

This is where we need to question the statement. 'Terrorist' is a value-laden term. You will be familiar with the famous statement that one person's terrorist is another person's freedom fighter. Who defines the terrorist organisation? If it is the Syrian government, then we need to know that. You might not agree, but critical thinking involves moving away from true/false or right/wrong to understanding of positions.

However, it is also the case that much of the study of politics over the last two and a half thousand years has been unashamedly normative, that is, it takes a political position in its approach, for example capitalism is intrinsically bad for the environment or intervention in conflicts in other countries a good thing. Modern political philosophy, like ancient political philosophy, is still about how we *ought* to behave or how society and government *ought* to be organised. Moreover (as should become patently obvious to anyone who reads this book), some of the most apparently rigorous, positive, and objective modern political science can still have normative elements, and some of the most celebrated modern political scientists straddle the positive/normative divide.

Box 3.7 Your own bias

You should acknowledge that your own upbringing, education, and the broader influences to which you have been exposed have inevitably shaped your political understanding and made you more predisposed to accept some political perspectives than others. Studying politics may not change your views, but it should make you more aware and understanding of the often very different assumptions of others. The Political Compass gives you an idea of your own political standing in relation to theories and real politicians in your country: http://www.politicalcompass.org/.

This presents some problems for you as politics students. How is possible to reconcile scientific objectivity with a more normative approach? Partly it is a problem with the social sciences generally. We are part of what we are studying. We bring our own preconceptions, interests, and preferences, sometimes unconsciously, to what we study, and scientific detachment is more difficult than with the physical sciences. Indeed, we would be (literally) inhuman if we failed to derive normative recommendations from some of our political analysis. International war, genocide, poverty, starvation and the destruction of the environment are all things that most of us would prefer to avoid. So perhaps we should also accept that the study of politics can embrace both a dispassionate analysis of political behaviour *and* recommendations for a better life for individuals and society (as indeed it did for Aristotle).

Yet if the discipline of politics involves the normative as well as the positive, it still demands obligations from students to examine evidence rigorously, not to ignore inconvenient facts, and to present arguments fairly. This is as true of political philosophy as it is of political science and International Relations. If we study modern political philosophers such as Rawls* or Nozick* we may come to agree or disagree with their arguments, but we should still outline them fairly first. The same is true of the study of political ideologies. We may strongly oppose some ideologies, but we still need to understand what they are and why and how they are held. That is true even for ideologies, such as fascism or racism, that most of us find abhorrent. We need to study as dispassionately as we can why many others have been attracted to fascism, just as today we need to understand why and how some are drawn to Islamic State and terrorism. Similarly, we need to try to understand the causes of less dramatic and extreme forms of political behaviour, such as political indifference and apathy.

As a student of politics or International Relations you need to adopt a questioning, dispassionate approach. This means that you can by all means criticise particular political institutions, thinkers or forms of behaviour, but you should do so from knowledge and not from ignorance. Always remember, when you are writing an essay, or presenting a seminar paper, that you are not making a political speech. You will often be invited to 'discuss' a particular statement. Normally this will involve exploring all sides of the issue, fairly and dispassionately, before finally reaching a balanced judgement. This may involve a reasoned support for a particular viewpoint. Yet how you are assessed will depend much less on the conclusion you reach than how you arrive at that conclusion.

Exercise 3.1 Identifying an argument

To make your own argument it is first helpful to identify arguments in other writers' work (see Cottrell 2011). Read this passage and identify the main argument and the reasons given for it:

> People are less politically aware now than they have been at any time in the past. For hundreds of years, people took great personal risks to fight for causes that would benefit other people more than themselves. This rarely happens today. As late as the 1980s, there were frequent rallies with people in one country demonstrating to show solidarity with people elsewhere. Now, rallies are more likely to be for personal gain such as better salaries or student grants rather than political issues of wider application. Even low risk activities such as voting in elections attract low turnouts. (Cottrell 2011, 53)

This is an argument making the case that 'people are less politically aware now than they have been at any time in the past'.

The purported evidence for this is:

- People used to fight for causes from which they didn't gain personally.
- People took more risks for political issues.
- Rallies had a more international perspective.
- Fewer people vote now in elections.

The support for your argument will be based on your reading and research – the topic that we move to next.

Finding what you need from books and articles

Academic reading is not like reading a novel or a popular work of nonfiction. You seldom need to start at the beginning and read to the end. A book or article is a resource from which you take what you need. You should already have some idea of what you hope to learn from it, perhaps questions you want answered, theories or approaches for which you seek explanations or criticisms. Do not read passively, hoping to 'soak up' knowledge, but actively and thoughtfully with an aim in mind.

Some passages that are less useful for your immediate requirements may be skipped or skim-read. Other passages you may need to re-read carefully until you have fully grasped their meaning. If there are words that you do not fully understand, you will have to look them up in ordinary or more specialist dictionaries. Once you have read the relevant chapters or pages, think about them, and then close the book and try to note down the key points [see section on note-making]. Then go back to check that you have included all that is necessary.

Reading is at the heart of critical thinking; you 'read for a degree' in social sciences, and you will have plenty of time to do so (Box 3.8). To develop as a critical thinker you have to be careful with the way you get the information you need; the most important literature will be given to you in module handbooks where you find reading lists and very important questions that will help you focus your reading, thinking, and listening. You need to focus on the key reading or what your tutors say is most important. In some modules you will find hundreds of recommended readings; you are not expected to read them all but to pick some. The readings may be listed alphabetically or by degree of importance (you will often find the list of the most important readings in the beginning of the handbook and an asterisk next to them there and under the weekly reading). You need to find a good place to work; familiarise yourself with the library as soon as you can. The library is a good work space for most and the best place to be for finding material and getting advice. Each faculty has its subject librarians who can help you find alternative and complementary reading, if what you are looking for is on loan. Librarians can also help you with many aspects of learning, from speed reading to referencing and efficient search of databases.

Box 3.8 Guide to effective reading

Articles
Browse abstracts – identify arguments.
Identify hypothesis.

Books
Skim sections.
Scan the introduction and final chapter.
Scan the beginnings and ends of chapters.
Decide on what you need to read more closely.
Use the index.

Exercise 3.2 Identifying authors' positions
To read critically and efficiently you need try to identify authors' positions. This exercise asks you to identify the argument in the extract below. When reading it, ask yourself:

What is the point of this text?
What is the main message?

What does the author want me to accept/ believe?
What reasons has the author given to support her/his position?

This article considers the World Bank as a political thinker. This involves an interpretation of the values, methodologies, and theoretical references contained within the Bank's governance documentation. Generally, the Bank steers away from a serious engagement with the nature of states, or the dynamics of reform execution, even in its more detailed policy documents in reform areas such as administrative reform. But, by looking at the World Bank's involvement in African states, we can understand the ways in which the World Bank works with certain expectations concerning how reforms will work. The article critically analyses the Bank's 'political vision' by comparing it with prominent theories of African politics. The article concludes that the World Bank's governance agenda misses three pivotal aspects of African politics: the unity of political and economic power, the extreme openness of African states to external pressures, and the salience of historically-embedded cultural and political relations. These three points directly raise important questions about the prospects of good governance reforms in Africa, and the involvement of the Bank therein. Harrison, G. (2005) 'The World Bank, Governance and Theories of Political Action in Africa', British Journal of Politics and International Relations 7: 240–260

What is the point of this text?
To consider the World Bank, a political/economic institution, as a political thinker.

What is the main message?
The World Bank has certain expectations concerning how the reforms it promotes in African states will work. This message runs counter to the view that the World Bank is an economic body and therefore 'neutral'.

What does the author want me to accept/believe?
That the World Bank has a 'political' vision that underpins its activities in Africa, particularly in the field of governance.

What reasons has the author given to support her/his position?
The author argues that by missing three pivotal aspects of African politics, the reforms promoted by the World Bank form a 'political vision'.

To recap: to identify what reasons the authors use and their conclusions you should start by reading the abstract, the conclusion, and the introduction; then you know what you are looking for. You need to analyse how authors select, combine, and order reasons to come up with a line of reasoning. You need to evaluate if their reasons support their conclusions; are their reasons well founded – based on evidence? Can you find flaws in their reasoning? All this is very hard at the beginning of a degree, but you will learn. Make sure you fill your time with reading and thinking. In politics and International Relations it is very important that you follow the news and are aware of current political development and changes.

When reading anything academic, always use a quality check. Think about: Who is the author? What constitutes the author's expertise in the field? Is the information presented up to date? Is the argument presented in a logical, structured, and coherent way? Where is it published? What are the limitations of the research and have these been mentioned? What are the strengths/weaknesses of the approach? Are statistics used in a misleading way? How selective is the material?

A key aspect of the quality check is to compare the conclusions with those from different sources. Do other people agree with what the writer is saying? What counter arguments are presented? What are the limitations of the research?

This allows you to develop your own judgement. Is what is presented believable? Do you agree with the writer – why and why not? What are counter arguments proposed by the writers and are these counter arguments more convincing?

So if we apply the quality check to the article by Graham Harrison, we find that he is a professor at the University of Sheffield in the United Kingdom. The piece was published in a peer reviewed journal, *The British Journal of Politics and International Relations*. Both of these things suggest that the article is written by an expert in the field. However, as hinted at in the abstract of the article, his interpretation of politics is shaped by his political beliefs. A little research finds his website where he shows that he is a Marxist. Therefore when reading his work you would also need to consider how a non-Marxist might approach the topic.

Exercise 3.3 Academic debates

This exercise highlights the nature of debates in politics and international relations as having no 'right' and 'wrong' answers. Academics will disagree – the divisions may be informed by ideology but most often they are a result of methodological approaches, which leads us to a discussion of methodology later in this chapter. This means that there are often multiple sides to every debate and key disagreements in the various fields about certain topics. If you do not read widely, you will miss these debates, uncritically accepting one position as the definitive position. This exercise asks you to read selected sources around a number of debates and highlights the nature of these disagreements.

1: Consider this three-part debate on how radical was Thatcherism:

Moon, J. (1994) 'Evaluating Thatcher: Sceptical Versus Synthetic Approaches', *Politics* 14 (2): 43–49.

Marsh, D. and R. A. W. Rhodes (1995) 'Evaluating Thatcherism: Over the Moon or as Sick as a Parrot?', *Politics* 15 (1): 49–54.

Moon, J. (1995) 'Evaluating Thatcher: Did the Cows Jump Over? A Reply to Marsh and Rhodes', *Politics* 15 (2): 113–116.

2: This following conversation between Tickner and Keohane is an excellent example of an academic debate. Tickner is critiquing International Relations' (and to some extent Keohane's) lack of engagement with feminist perspectives, especially around the concept of security. Note the fact that Tickner thanks Keohane for commenting on her paper, so whilst they might disagree it does not mean they just criticise each other's work.

Tickner, A. (1997) '"You Just Don't Understand": Troubled Engagements between Feminists and IR Theorists', *International Studies Quarterly* 41: 611–632.

Keohane, R. (1998) 'Beyond Dichotomy: Conversations between International Relations and Feminist Theory', *International Studies Quarterly* 42: 193–198

Tickner, A. (1998) 'Continuing the Conversation...', *International Studies Quarterly* 42: 205–210.

3: A debate over whether the United States could have intervened to stop the Rwandan genocide in 1994:

Wertheim, S. (2010) 'A Solution from Hell: The United States and the Rise of Humanitarian Interventionism, 1991–2003', *Journal of Genocide Research* 12 (3–4): 149–172.

Melvern, L. (2011) 'A Response to Stephen Wertheim's "A Solution from Hell: The United States and the Rise of Humanitarian Interventionism, 1991–2003"' *Journal of Genocide Research* 13 (1–2): 153–157.

Wertheim, S. (2011) 'On Moralism and Rwanda: A Reply to Linda Melvern', *Journal of Genocide Research* 13 (1–2): 159–163.

DEVELOPING GOOD ACADEMIC ARGUMENTS IN ESSAYS AND OTHER ASSIGNMENTS

Having applied critical thinking to your research you need to apply it in your academic writing/argumentation. Greetham (2013) argues that good academic writing has five stages:

- interpretation of the question
- research
- planning/structure
- writing
- revision

Interpreting the question

You have been set an assignment on a specific topic that you need to research. How do you set about it? Step 1 is preparation. Firstly, you need to figure out what it is that you're looking for. Think about what the question is asking or what you want to research. It is likely that this topic has already been covered in a lecture and/or a seminar, so re-read your notes. Think about the core themes and theory that have been covered in the module and relate your answer to them.

There are a variety of question forms used in academic assessment. These range from open-style questions 'Is torture ever justified?' to more closed questions such as 'Provide three reasons why the United Kingdom voted to leave the European Union in 2016'. The key is to ensure you understand the question and met the requirements of the question. In the closed example, providing only two reasons why will only give you two-thirds of the answer, and the need to provide three reasons should drive your argument structure. In contrast, the first example is asking you to identify the main arguments and to structure your essay accordingly (Hathaway, 2015).

Research

Your research will involve primary and secondary sources. Primary material is official publications, laws, official speeches, manifestos, or interviews. If this is the official version, why do we use secondary sources? It's not *just* to give us an understanding of a particular topic. In addition, you're using sources to:

1. Support your arguments.
2. Give you something to argue against/for/modify.
3. Outline key thinking in the field, and then situate yourself accordingly.
4. Provide an idea to develop, expand, or refine.

Therefore a key skill to master is how to research.

Researching topics – using libraries and the internet

Using the Library

Hopefully most of the books and articles you are you are recommended to read may be found in your university library or from other libraries to which you can gain access (such as a city reference library). You should be able to access the library catalogue giving full book details, location, and availability. Familiarise yourself thoroughly with the layout, facilities, and regulations of your own university library and other useful libraries. The majority of the texts we cited in Part I were books.

You may already be aware of the Dewey cataloguing system, which helps you locate a book from the catalogue. Most politics books will be found catalogued from 320 to 330, although you may find other useful texts under different headings (e.g. 'public administration' from 350). You will often need to look on the shelves housing subjects linked with politics, such as sociology, economics, law, and history. If you cannot find the books you need in your university library, you should be able to order them on interlibrary loan. Very recent books, not yet purchased or catalogued by your library, may sometimes be perused quickly in bookshops (but it is not usually easy to take notes!).

Exercise 3.4:

Using your library's system find at what location Cynthia Weber's *International Relations Theory: A Critical Introduction* (2014) is housed.

What is the classmark (or class number) for books on Chinese Foreign Policy?

Do not neglect the library reference section. The downside is that you cannot normally take reference books out, but the compensating advantage is that you are more likely to find the books you need on the shelves (or after a short wait if they are in current use). Ordinary dictionaries and even encyclopaedias may not be sufficiently specialist for your purposes, but you will normally find some more specific politics dictionaries, sourcebooks, yearbooks, handbooks, collections of statistics, and journal abstracts. For some assignments these resources are invaluable.

You should start by reading the textbooks before you start reading journal articles, because these are often more specialised and will have detailed discussions on specific areas within the wider concept. By comparison a textbook introduces a topic and will explain how the concept can be applied to case studies. A textbook also introduces the main theoretical discussions and the positions of individual scholars in relation to the theory. Some important developments in the discipline have sometimes first appeared in journal articles. Publication in prestigious journals is highly prized in the profession, and students who use such sources can feel they are at the frontiers of knowledge and research. Sometimes it is possible to follow the course of a major academic controversy through a series of journal articles.

Researching online

You are highly likely to be very familiar with searching the internet for information with Google and other search engines. However, we find that many students need to learn how to use these skills in an academic setting. Admittedly, many of the general rules apply – would you buy a plane ticket from the first site listed on Google? We would hope you would shop around and check for the best price and/or the quickest route. Search engines use an algorithm to search and can be manipulated to ensure a higher placing when the results are displayed. Therefore just because something is first does not necessarily mean it is the best/most relevant.

One problem with the internet is that there is no effective quality control. Anyone can publish material on the internet. Thus entries on Wikipedia and other similar sites are not subject to an extensive process of peer review, as journal articles are. Some material may be one-sided or simply wrong. So do not rely on it uncritically, and check against information in published sources. Some students today are overdependent on the internet and do not read enough books and articles. Use the internet by all means (you would be foolish not to), but use it critically and never as a substitute for other more traditional sources of information.

Our advice is to utilise Google Scholar when searching for academic information. It's much better than a normal Google search because it only gives you reputable academic literature (Box 3.9). It also gives you more up-to-date literature, as to have cited something you would have had to have read it! The downsides of Google Scholar are that it is not subject specific; there is an overwhelming quantity of information; and it does not include articles from journals that are print only or books or book chapters (unless on they are on Google Books).

Box 3.9 Google versus Google Scholar

If we are interested in the question 'Should NATO have bombed Libya?' a Google search turns up information from these sources:

Wikipedia, NATO, *Huffington Post, Russia Today*, Antiwar.com Blog, theintercept. com, belfercenter.ksg.harvard, libyaagainstsuperpowermedia.org.

There is nothing 'wrong' with these sources; it is just that you need to treat them with some caution – they may be written from a specific political viewpoint that is hard for you to discern, or they may contain factual mistakes.

A Google Scholar search on the other hand turns up information from these sources:

Ethics and International Affairs, International and Comparative Law, International Security, Guardian, Washington Post, Survival, Centre for European Reform Essays, Journal of Strategic Security.

The majority of these sources are peer-reviewed journal articles. That means they are more trusted academic sources and more suited for use in academic assignments.

Using Google Scholar or other more sophisticated search engines such as JSTOR, Web of Knowledge, and Web of Science can help you expand your reading lists in a very quick and efficient way. Using Cynthia Weber's *International Relations Theory: A Critical Introduction* (2014) again we can see that if we put the citation into Google Scholar the book has been cited 395 times by other authors. If you limit the search (using the tools on the left) to since 2015 you can see that the list has been reduced to 43. Not all will be relevant for your purposes but 'cited by' can be seen as low-hanging fruit that helps build up your reading list and find articles (Box 3.10).

Box 3.10 Better information searches

Putting words inside quotation marks, e.g. 'Rwandan genocide', is called a phrase search and it tells the search engine that you want to look for these two words together as a phrase and not separated.

Using a star or asterisk at the end of a word helps you to find all the different versions of it, so flood* will find flood, floods, flooding, flooded.

You can use the word AND to narrow your search, so you can search for 'Rwanda AND coffee' to make sure the computer searches for both key items together, not one or the other. If you want to widen your search you could use OR, e.g. 'Rwanda OR coffee'.

Planning and structuring your argument

The structure of an argument is always organic – it is dependent upon the argument you wish to make, rather than being something that can be universally applied (Hathaway 2015). Remember it is not just telling the reader everything you know about a particular topic. So if we take the torture essay question from page 70 we can identify two basic structure types. The first is a kind of yes/no structure. The first section might argue that torture is never justified before going onto a second section that says that torture can be justified. This works to a large extent, although there is a risk of repetition as points raised in the first section might need to be repeated to ensure the reader makes a connection in the second section (Hathaway, 2015 provided the inspiration for this section).

For example in section one you might argue that torture is never justified, even if other people's lives are at risk (the ticking bomb scenario). However, if you then discuss other points related to the never justified aspect of the question you risk losing the reader's attention. An alternative structure would be to compare how different political theorists such as Kant and Beetham approach the topic. That way you get the arguments for and against placed next to each other, making the discussion easier to follow.

Another example would be addressing the question 'Compare and contrast realist and constructivist definitions of anarchy'. This could set out the realist perspective and then the constructivist perspective. In that way you would be comparing. However, that approach can make it hard to address the contrast element of the question. An alternative approach would be to comparing the two theories by breaking your comparison into three parts, based on three aspects of the theories. So you might focus on areas of agreement, such as the centrality of the state, before highlighting areas of disagreement, such as the nature of the international system (competitive/consensual) and the role of ideas. This E-IR student essay highlights a hybrid approach (Dornan 2011), showing that structure is organic.

Even the best argument will be undermined by poor structure, so make sure you give time to your structure. You can think of your essay being split into three broad sections: introduction; body; conclusion. The body of your essay needs to put forward points that support your main argument. The different points you present in the body of your essay will resemble mini essays, each with its own short 'introduction' and 'conclusion', and you will need to demonstrate the links between the points you present and why and how they support your argument.

Introductions

Don't think that stating your argument in your introduction is like spoiling a surprise ending for your reader. The anticipation in an academic essay comes not from waiting to see what the argument is, but waiting to see how the argument is developed.

Example 3.1 A good introduction

In the field of health policy there are multiple tensions between the interests of the pharmaceutical industry, national health systems and citizens/consumers. The issue of direct-to-consumer advertising for prescription drugs (DTCA-PD) touches on all of these tensions. For advanced industrial countries, DTCA-PD is currently only allowed in the United States and New Zealand. It is banned in the EU. Earlier attempts by the pharmaceutical industry to overturn the ban in 2000–2002 were soundly rejected. However, using new industry-funded patient groups (for example, European Patients Forum), a Commission-supported 'Pharmaceutical Forum' and strong support from DG Enterprise, between 2006 and 2008 the industry once again tried to prise open the ban. However, it was again defeated in the European Parliament (EP), a decision that was later confirmed in the June 2008 Council. Later attempts to recycle the issue in 2009 and 2010 under 'Patient Information' proposals were also unsuccessful. In both periods, a powerful European/global economic interest that was supported by DG Enterprise and key member states was unable to push through a pro-market deregulatory policy. For observers of EU health policy this raises key questions. Can this outcome be explained within the general framework of EU health policy, and what does this imply for our understanding and the future of EU health policy? To explore these questions this article will briefly review and identify five key elements in the development of EU health policy. It will then define DTCA-PD and review the arguments for and against it. Next, using a review of primary and secondary sources and interviews with EU health policy NGOs and European Parliament and Commission actors, the article goes on to provide a brief overview of EU health policy and a detailed review of the two recent attempts by the pharmaceutical industry and its allies to overturn the ban in the 2000s. Following this, it will try to address the aforementioned key questions by examining how the five elements of EU health policy affected the development of DTCA-PD policy, and what the case of DTCA-PD policy implies for the understanding and future of EU health policy. (Geyer 2011, 567–568)

Writing your essay

Critical writing has all the features of persuasive writing (i.e. facts + your point of view), plus the added feature of at least one other point of view. Many academic texts that you write will have some parts that are more analytical or descriptive and other parts that are persuasive or critical (see University of Sydney guide to academic writing http://sydney.edu.au/stuserv/learning_centre/help/analysing/an_distinguishTypes.shtml). For example, an empirical thesis needs critical writing in the literature review to show where there is a gap or opportunity in the existing research. However, the methods section will have many paragraphs that are mostly descriptive, in order to summarise the methods used to collect and analyse information. In the results section of an empirical thesis or a research report there will be a mix of descriptive and analytical writing, while the discussion section is more analytical, as you relate your findings back to your research questions, and generally also more persuasive, as you propose your interpretations of the findings.

We have discussed the high-order elements of writing such as argument – structure – introduction – conclusion above. It is also worth remembering the low-order elements: sentence structure – word choice – punctuation – presentation. High-order elements and low-order elements need to work together for an essay to be successful; one set of elements is not more important than the other. For example, if your sentence structure is unclear or overly complex, you can't expect your argument to be effectively communicated to your reader.

In order to keep a reader interested and engaged in your writing it is always a good idea to use a variety of sentence types and lengths. In fact, sentence variety is one of the most important things you have to control the rate at which a reader moves through your work. Simple sentences speed up the rate of reading. Complex sentences slow down the rate of reading. As the introduction is meant to be a clear overview of your essay, if you use complex sentences here, you will have slowed down and overcomplicated what should have been your simple opening statement.

Poor word choice and punctuation can really confuse the argument you wish to convey. Be cautious about using a thesaurus to try and make yourself 'sound smarter'. If you don't know what the word means, don't use it!

Example 3.2:

This then leads us to some examples where students fail to demonstrate these facets of academic writing and critical thinking in essays/assignments.

Uncritical writing presents the views of different authors so each paragraph becomes a description of a view rather than a synthesis. This is an example.

Although legal victories by women's organisation have gone some way in preventing discrimination against women in the legal realms, Turkey remains a very patriarchal society (Lake 11 2005:115–123). There are a number of cases that show how women are still treated unequally in Turkey by ordinary citizens rather than by government authorities. Lake gives the examples of 'honor killings' that he suggests still take place in Turkey to show the discrimination still faced by Turkish women. One such example is that of a woman who had become the second wife of a married neighbor after he had made her pregnant and was then savagely stoned by her relatives for disgracing the family honor (Lake 2005:122). Although these are not discriminations made by the authorities in Turkey, they do represent a traditional perception of 'women that is still held in Turkey' (ibid.).

Ideally, the student would have critically engaged with the work of Lake and looked to see if there was an alternative literature either arguing against Lake's assertion or refining it (for instance there might be a urban–rural division). Here is an example of a writer who has synthesised the work of key authors.

> For example, large member states including Germany, France and Italy, have been labelled strategic partners of Russia (Leonard and Popescu 2007: 2), who maintain a 'tradition of having their own Ostpolitik towards Russia' (Aalto 2006: 102). This position contrasts with other member states such as the three Baltic states, who are more likely to operate at the EU level on the Russian relationship (Fernandes 2007: 40) and support harsh EU statements about the human rights standards in Russia (Romanova 2009: 63).

Contradicting yourself

'Terrorism is a contested concept. In this essay I define terrorism as…' This student gets that terrorism is contested but is not showing how and why the concept is contested. Reviewing different definitions before showing why he or she had settled on one (and acknowledging that definition's limitations) would be a better example of quality academic writing.

Lack of evidence

The most common feedback we see on essays relates to use of evidence. We might see tutors put 'reference?' or 'evidence?'. Too often we read student essays with statements such as 'Some people argue that International Relations ignores feminist debates'. This does not tell is who is arguing a particular point – the marker might assume you are referring to feminists, but you might not be. A better way would be to say 'Feminist critics argue that much mainstream international relations ignores feminist debates'. An even better way is to follow the latter statement by providing key references, so that the sentence reads like this: 'Feminist critics argue that much mainstream international relations ignores feminist debates (Enloe 1989; Steans 2003; Weber 1994).'

Not referencing

The way you demonstrate the breadth of your reading is via your references. The way you do this might be set down by your university, but the key advice is not to get bogged down with the nuts and bolts of referencing (although we will give you tips on that below) but to source all quotations and research findings, as well as theories and concepts associated with particular authors. These should be cited in the text and then complied into a full bibliography at the end of your essay.

Not knowing what you should reference

You must reference any direct quotation that you provide. If you are summarising in your own words the argument or theory of a particular writer or comparing and contrasting the views of different writers, you should give references. You do not have to provide a source for all the information you provide if it is uncontroversial and reasonably well known, but if you cite data or claims from academic research you should give the source. Beyond that, you should hope to cite a range of sources in your text that will figure in the final bibliography. You should not dishonestly inflate your bibliography with sources you have not read or hardly used, but you should not sell yourself short by failing to list all the various sources you have consulted. It is quite legitimate to list a source you have skim-read in a library or bookshop, as long you have derived something from it. Where relevant, you may want to list websites or other relevant material, such as a newspaper article or television programme (for which you should supply relevant details and dates). The key is to provide a range of sources.

Poor writing style

Although writing style is something personal, there are some key things to avoid. These include slang, colloquialisms, and abbreviations used in everyday speech (e.g. 'didn't', 'could've'). We would also urge against making your writing too flowery or complicated. Do not use long rare words when short common ones will do. But all disciplines use a specialised vocabulary, and politics and international relations are no exceptions. Many key concepts [see Part IV] are either unfamiliar or use familiar terms in an unfamiliar specialised sense. You do need to show you have mastered the appropriate terminology.

Do I use 'I'?
Some advise avoiding the first person. Certainly it should only be employed sparingly, if at all, perhaps in an introductory 'signpost' paragraph. Avoid peppering your essay with 'I think' or 'I consider'. Such phrases are redundant. The whole essay should be what you think.

No conclusion
How can you have an argument without a conclusion? You need a clear section at the end of your essay that sums up your main points and then provides a clear answer. So in the essay on torture we would expect to see an explicit engagement with the question, something along the lines of 'This essay has argued that torture is only justifiable in extremely rare cases, such as the ticking bomb scenario'.

No proofreading
Make sure you thoroughly proofread you essay. Poor spelling and and gramar and inaccurate details show a careless, unscolarly approach and will be penalised. Make sure proper names are speled correctly, dates and other figures are acurate, and quotes are exact. Variations in font and text size also show a lack of care, as does neglecting to including page numbers (as this example shows!).

Not acting on feedback

Once we have marked essays, it is common for students to get some form of feedback that outlines why the mark was awarded. It used to amaze us that many students failed to collect this feedback, as without it the raw mark does not tell you anything. Without the feedback you will not know how you achieved your 62% and more importantly how to improve that mark. It reminds me of the number 42 which, in *The Hitchhiker's Guide to the Galaxy* by Douglas Adams, is calculated by an enormous supercomputer named Deep Thought over a period of 7.5 million years as 'The Answer to the Ultimate Question of Life, the Universe, and Everything'. Unfortunately, no one knows what the question is. Was your 62% because of good research but poor structure? Did you fail to fully understand the question? Did your research show the full range of arguments? Sometimes the feedback is only relevant to that particular piece of work, but in our experience, more often than not, students repeat the same practices in essay after essay.

Revision

Greetham (2013) emphasises that to properly revise your work you need to move from thinking about your work as the author and start thinking about it as an editor. He has some excellent tips on how to do this and suggests at least five revisions to ensure the highest quality essay. A checklist developed by Hathaway (2015) suggests that any revision focus on the following aspects:

Argument:

Have I answered the question?
Is my argument clear throughout?
Are all points fully developed? If not, are the points integral to the argument?
Do my examples support my points well?

Writing:

Are certain words and phrases repeated? Can these be rephrased?
Do my paragraphs separate my points?
Will my audience understand what I've written?

Structure:

Would a different ordering of points make more sense?
Is every paragraph relevant to the question?
Does each section (introduction, body, and conclusion) do what it is meant to?

Presentation:

Do all my citations have references?
Are the pages numbered?
Is all the formatting the same (font, alignment, typeface)?

This advice works for all forms of written work, including more substantial and sustained individual pieces of work such as dissertations or long essays, in which students select their own topic within broad parameters, conduct a literature search, and choose a research question that they can proceed to test against evidence that they collect and analyse (see Cottrell, 2014 for advice on undergraduate dissertations).

HOW TO REFERENCE

There are various approved methods of scholarly referencing. One common form involves footnotes or endnotes (at the end of chapters, articles, or books) relating to small superscript numbers in the text, thus.[1] This is a well-tried system and has the advantage that the flow of the text is not interrupted, but it can mean much tedious repetition of details of a frequently used source in footnotes or endnotes. Such repetition can be avoided by using approved abbreviations of Latin phrases referring to earlier entries (ibid. and op. cit.), but this is not easy for the reader, who has to search back for the first citation of the source. Rather more common today is the *Harvard* or author–date system of referencing. Here you cite just the author or authors (or first author where there are four or more authors and et al. to cover the others) and the year of publication and page number in parentheses in the text, for example (Dunleavy 1986, 131–2). You then provide, at the end in the 'bibliography' or 'references', a detailed reference with names and initials of all authors, full title in italics, place published and name of publisher, as follows:

Dunleavy, P. J. (1986) *Studying for a Degree in the Humanities and Social Sciences,* Basingstoke: Macmillan.

With journal articles the author's name and initials and date of publication (in parentheses) are provided, then the title of the article (in quotation marks, rather than italicised) followed by the journal title in italics, with volume and page references, as in the following example:

Lindblom, C. (1959) 'The Science of Muddling Through', *Public Administration Review* 19: 79–88.

Word-processing systems cope with traditional footnotes and endnotes well, automatically renumbering when you insert an extra note. Most modern books and journals, however, use the Harvard method, which is easier on the reader. Using a system such as Endnote for your notes helps you with your referencing and comes highly recommended. Whatever you do, find a good system of storing your references, as otherwise you waste lots of time looking up needed references that you no longer have to hand, if you have failed to record the details earlier. (The last point reflects bitter personal experience. We do not always follow our own advice, and we always regret it!)

PLAGIARISM (AND HOW TO AVOID IT)

Plagiarism is copying work from books, articles, the internet, fellow students, or other people and passing it off as your own. It is a particularly obnoxious form of cheating in that it is the negation of everything that education is about. It is also unfortunately a serious problem in many universities, particularly in assessed course work, long

---

[1] Dunleavy, P. J. (1986) *Studying for a Degree in the Humanities and Social Sciences,* Basingstoke: Macmillan.

essays, and dissertations. Some institutions provide their own clear guidance on plagiarism, which you should study closely. (If you still do not understand what constitutes plagiarism, see Cottrell (2013). It is the clearest explanation we have come across). Universities have also developed their own checks and formal procedures for dealing with the problem (Box 3.11). Detecting cheating has become a minor industry. Those who are caught can expect no sympathy, certainly not from university staff and not from the vast majority of students, whose own achievements are devalued by the cheats.

We would prefer to believe that anyone reading this book is most unlikely to contemplate deliberately cheating in this way. Yet inexperienced students who have no intention of cheating can sometimes, almost unconsciously, appear to copy someone else's work and find themselves accused of plagiarism. How could this come about, and how can it be avoided?

You should of course use your own words. There are some students, perhaps conditioned by expectations in other subjects at an earlier level of education, who naïvely assume there are 'right' answers to questions they are set on politics courses (as there might be a right answer to a maths question). They further take it for granted that they will earn credit by copying out the 'right' answer, which they assume is the answer given in a lecture or textbook. Some indeed have even been taught that way. We have confronted students who have copied out whole paragraphs word for word from a book and who protest vehemently that they have 'always written essays like that' and 'no one had ever told them it was wrong'.

There are others who understand that copying is wrong but can be drawn into it unconsciously. It can result from writing an essay with a key book open in front of you. You may not mean to copy, but you may be drawn repeatedly into using similar phrases, because you cannot think of a better way of putting a point than as it is expressed in the book. By all means refer to books as you need them when writing an essay but avoid writing with books continuously open in front of you. That will force you to use your own words and help you to think about the arguments and to understand them.

Poor note-making can sometimes lead to essays that too closely resemble passages in a book or journal. A student conscientiously seeks to note a key source, perhaps a recommended textbook, and, unable to make a brief summary of the salient points, virtually copies down every other word. The essay is subsequently based on the notes, and as the latter are expanded again to make proper sentences, inevitably resembles the original text. You can avoid being accused of plagiarism in this way by improving your note-making, by not becoming too dependent on a single source or limited range of sources, and by developing your own essay planning and writing skills [see under relevant headings elsewhere in this section].

The fact that many journals are accessible online creates a specific problem – the issue of cut and paste from a PDF file. Having a PDF version of an article is extremely helpful in that it allows you to search for key words or phrases (the ctrl f function was a revelation!) and it can allow you to copy and paste key elements. However this means your note taking must be spot on as otherwise it becomes very easy for these sections that have been cut from an article to find themselves into an essay, especially if your time management is poor and you end up rushing the essay. In our experience this is the most common cause of plagiarism.

Box 3.11 Turnitin and detecting plagiarism

Many universities now ask students to submit their work via Turnitin. We often hear that Turnitin detects plagiarism. That is not the case. Turnitin detects similarity between the work you submit and other sources, including other student essays submitted via Turnitin (worth noting if you are ever tempted to buy an essay). Plagiarism is detected by academics using Turnitin who judge whether the source has been used appropriately. So the quote from Geyer [above] would show up on Turnitin, but the fact that it is indented and properly referenced would mean it was not plagiarised.

Citing your sources with extensive accurate references [see heading on referencing] should ensure that you never face an accusation of deliberate plagiarism, although you may be urged to 'use your own words' if some of your own writing sometimes appears too close to that of a source you have cited. Those who set out to cheat commonly do not reveal the source material they have copied from, either in the text or in their bibliography. Indeed the discovery of chunks of material closely derived from an unlisted source provides fairly clear evidence of a conscious intention to plagiarise. One student who was found guilty of plagiarism at an institution with which we were connected was found to have copied almost all of his dissertation from two sources that were not listed in his bibliography and were not even in the institution's library. Needless to say, once this was proved, he did not get a degree.

Plagiarism cannot be tolerated, because it devalues the efforts and ultimately the qualifications of honest, conscientious students. Ultimately, if it became suspected that cheating was widespread, degree certificates would become as worthless as forged banknotes. Unfortunately problems with plagiarism have already led some institutions to reduce or discard some educationally valuable forms of assessment (such as dissertations) and return to traditional unseen examinations, where cheating is much more difficult.

TIME MANAGEMENT

Critical thinking and academic criticism are core skills for a politics or International Relations degree. However, all of the above takes time. Therefore it is worth discussing time management and taking responsibility for your own learning. On a politics or International Relations course (as in most degree courses in the humanities and social sciences) the hours of class contact per week may be relatively light, with long gaps in between. There is a strong temptation to retire to the student union or coffee bar between classes, passing your time chatting, drinking, or playing cards or games on your iPad. Yet the university will expect you to spend much of this 'spare time' studying – reading and researching in the library, note-making, preparing for classes, and working on essays, reports, seminar presentations, and other projects. There is almost always a link made between the credits you are studying and how much time you need to devote to your studies outside of the formal class setting. These vary, but one hour in class = three hours preparation is a minimum in many US universities. Commonly, most of the work on which your assessment and progression is based is 'end-loaded' in the form of end-of-semester, end-of-term or -year examinations or course work. Even if deadlines seem pleasantly distant, you need to get started early, in plenty of time. If you do not adequately prepare for this work, you risk not meeting the required standard. You risk failure. Indeed the most common reason given for plagiarising is lack of time and a panic to finish.

You need to acquire good working habits, from the start if possible, and keep to them. Commonly you will be given course or module handbooks full of advice and instructions. Read and digest all the material you are given on what is expected of you. Make sure you know submission dates for course work and the exam timetable. Draw up a daily schedule of work and keep to it. You can reward yourself with planned free time, which will be enjoyed all the more if you have earned it following hours of productive study. Do not rely on 'burning the midnight oil' to complete course work or on last-minute cramming before exams.

Here we provide a fictitious working week based on the one hour = three hours preparation model. However, this is just a working week (an old-fashioned Monday–Friday) as it is clearly important that you also have free time (and time for lunch!).

Exercise 3.5: Making the most of your time

	Monday	Tuesday	Wednesday	Thursday	Friday
9–10	Class preparation/reading	Group work	Skills session	Comparative Politics lecture	Assessment preparation
10–11	Class preparation/reading	Meet tutor	International Relations seminar	Class preparation/reading	Assessment preparation
11–12	Class preparation/reading	Theory lecture	Assessment preparation	Class preparation/reading	Assessment preparation
12–1	Assessment preparation	Assessment preparation	Assessment preparation	Class preparation/reading	Paid employment
1–2	Assessment preparation	Class preparation/reading	Co-curricular activities/sport	Theory seminar	Paid employment
2–3	International Relations lecture	Class preparation/reading	Co-curricular activities/sport	Careers search	Paid employment
3–4	Tutor feedback	Class preparation/reading	Co-curricular activities/sport	Research seminar	Paid employment
4–5	Environmental Society	Class preparation/reading	Co-curricular activities/sport	Research seminar	Paid employment
5–6	Environmental Society	Comparative Politics seminar	Co-curricular activities/sport	Paid employment	Paid employment

Style Code
Class Time: (CAPS)
Class Preparation/reading: (Small caps)
Assessment Preparation: (Bold)
Academic Development: (Bold italic)
Co-curricular activities: (Italic)
Paid employment: (Roman)
For every hour in class we recommend you spend a minimum of three hours preparing.

MAKING THE MOST OF LECTURES, SEMINARS, AND TUTORIALS

Given what we have said about contact hours, it is vital that you make the most out of them. Much like membership of a gym, you will not get fit for study if you do not turn up for lectures and seminars. The hours of formal class contact may vary considerably among institutions and over the period of study. (Commonly, more class contact may be expected in the first year, less in the final year). These formal timetabled sessions may take various forms, for example, lectures, seminars, and tutorials. Here we come up against a potential terminology barrier. You will often see 'lecture' and 'seminar' on your timetable but may not be sure what the difference between them is. It is probably easiest to see the lecture as large-group teaching (in some universities a first year lecture can have over 300 students in it) and seminars or tutorials as small-group teaching. Both types of classes have different functions, and this section sets out to give you tips on how to make the most of both forms of teaching.

Lectures

Lectures are an efficient way of reaching a large group so they are widely used at university. The common view is that the lecturer is the 'sage on the stage', the person who will provide all the answers. This can often mean that students fail to make the most of lectures.

Why do we use lectures?

Lectures are criticised for the fact that students find it hard to concentrate for long periods. Human beings tend to have a concentration span of around 20 minutes, so a 50 minute lecture is a stretch. Given this information why do we still use lectures? They:

1. Give a way in to a topic – an intro or overview.
2. Summarise the key ideas, principles, or controversies.
3. Stimulate your own thinking.
4. Provide you with reading and ideas to follow up afterwards.

As the gym analogy is common in this section, we liked this description of a lecture from the University of Reading: 'You might think of lectures like the warm-up stretches you do to prepare yourself before playing sport or doing exercise. You need them to get moving, but you then go on to do more active training (or studying)' (https://www.reading.ac.uk/internal/studyadvice/StudyResources/Seminars/sta-lectures.aspx). We also think of them as providing hooks on which to hang your knowledge on as otherwise you approach the new topic with a blank slate.

Getting the most from lectures

As we discussed above, adopt a questioning approach. Do not take material on trust. Sometimes lecturers seek to provide a balanced overall summary of different views; sometimes they express their own distinctive approach; sometimes they take a deliberately provocative line. What was your lecturer attempting to do? Compare the analysis of your lecturer with that in textbooks and more specialist books. Discuss lectures with fellow students formally and informally. You may find they react very differently to the same material.

Make full use of any accompanying material supplied. Most lecturers will provide at least a list of the lecture topics, and some helpfully supply a synopsis of each lecture, either in a pre-circulated module or subject handbook, or in material distributed during each lecture, or provided online.

Make brief notes during the lecture, concentrating on key points and important supporting evidence. If a lecture outline is provided, you may be able to make marginal notes on this. If not, most lecturers provide some hints on what is worth recording. Do not try to record every word. If you do, you will be writing too frantically to be able to concentrate on understanding the lecturer's argument.

Go over your notes as soon as possible after the lecture to identify key points while it is still reasonably fresh in your mind. It has been claimed that students who do not review the lecture material remember less than 10% of it after three weeks. Write down any questions that occur to you or points that need clarifying in your own mind. You may have opportunities to follow these up in seminars or tutorials.

Box 3.12 The authors' experience

In preparing to write this book I (Lightfoot) re-read my own university notes and realised I had been guilty of not revisiting – too many times I had notes like this:

Three points about Marx's *Eighteenth Brumaire of Louis Bonaparte*

1. Napoleon Bonaparte as emperor

2. ??

3. class struggle and immaturity of proletariat

File your notes, so that you can find them again when you might need them (for example it is important to have a full set of notes to revise from). Learn from and reflect on the style and technique of good lecturers. They may provide good role models for oral presentations [see later] that you may be required to undertake. (You might learn what to avoid from some lecturers!).

Seminars

A seminar is a small-group session often held in a classroom rather than a lecture hall.

Seminars commonly involve a seminar tutor and a small group of students, say around a dozen (although rising numbers of students and resource constraints mean that seminar groups in some institutions are becoming larger). Seminars may be scheduled to follow lectures, pursuing and developing material from the lecture, or they may involve a quite distinct programme of activities not closely related to the lectures. The seminar is usually the place where you get to discuss ideas/think about concepts, etc., in small groups. The onus is on you to participate in seminars because that way you'll be developing a wide range of both academic and employability skills. In seminars we want you to develop your own ideas based on the lecture and more importantly your reading. How do you evidence those skills? Through articulating them verbally in the seminar.

Box 3.13 Examples of seminar participation

Formal Presentations

Putting questions to students who have made presentations

Putting questions to the seminar tutor

Responding to what other students say

Answering the set seminar questions

Responding to the seminar tutor's questions

Discussing set questions in groups

Each week you are normally assigned some key reading for the seminar. It sounds obvious, but it is important to do the required reading each week. Without the reading you may struggle to participate in the discussion. Participating in seminar discussions aids your learning process, because it requires you to engage in more active learning than in, for example, lectures. In seminars you are expected to develop your own ideas and thoughts about the topic based on your readings. Seminars are not just an informed chat about aspects of politics and international relations. They introduce you to the key concepts and debates within the disciplines you are studying. Active participation in seminars is valuable in itself. Not only are seminar activities excellent preparation for tackling formal in-course assessments or examinations but the skills you acquire and refine over your university life are great skills for employment and life.

Box 3.14 Seminar top tips

1. Preparing for seminars – do the reading!

   Read at least two to three texts from the reading list.

   Try to make sure that your reading is varied so that you get an idea of the debates/different opinions.

   Take time to consider your reading in relation to any seminar questions.

2. Ask questions!

   Come prepared with some questions based on your seminar reading. This also helps overcome fears of speaking in public.

   Feel free to ask questions and to say when you don't understand something.

3. Say something!

   Your opinion is just as important as the most talkative student and sometimes a few words are more valuable than lots of talk!

   Actively participate in seminars by contributing to class discussions. When making your points, try to use examples and/or refer to the lectures and/or readings you have done.

   Be respectful of others' opinions while critically engaging with them in an informed discussion.

PRESENTATIONS

It is odd to give advice about what makes a good presentation in a written form, but we hope these tips are helpful.

Focus on the content

Research the topic for your presentation thoroughly, until you feel in command of your material. The gaps in your own understanding may only become clear when you need to explain something to others (as any teacher will tell you). Therefore approach finding information for a presentation in the same way as you would for an essay or exam [see section above]. Your presentation needs structure, including a brief introduction and conclusion.

Focus on the presentation

An oral presentation is a very different form of communication from an essay and requires different skills. You will be speaking to an audience, and you must consider their needs. Do not plan simply to read out an essay, but organise your talk around a clear framework with headings and bullet points, using cards, overhead projector transparencies or PowerPoint slides. The delivery may be less fluent than if you read every word from a full script, but it will appear more natural and be easier for your audience to follow, especially if the key points are on screen. When your presentation has to be delivered, take your time. Most nervous speakers are far too fast. Remember that you can normally count on a sympathetic audience who have either suffered a similar ordeal themselves already or have it to come. Throughout, hold your head up, make eye contact and speak directly to your audience (avoid focusing on one friendly face though!). Try to appear confident even if you don't feel it. Practice and have something with you to time yourself. Pace and pitch are everything. Vary the tone of your voice, using your voice to emphasises key points. Monotone presentations are very boring!

Use visual aids carefully

A PowerPoint or Prezi can be very helpful. Visual aids can help reinforce points and help the audience follow your argument. However, you need to think carefully about how you are going to use visual aids and whom they are for. Too often we see presentations with too much text, in too small a font, that are then just read out by the presenter.

Be realistic

You are very unlikely to cover 28 PowerPoint slides all with information on them in five minutes. On our computers the default font for PowerPoint is Calibri size 32. Our estimation is that using that font size a slide with four sentences of two lines maximum on it will take about a minute to read out. To be realistic is key. You need to structure a presentation just as you would an essay. What are the key points you are trying to make? Whatever you do, always obtain feedback on your previous performance if possible.

REVISION AND PREPARATION FOR EXAMINATIONS

Examinations assess not only, or principally, knowledge, but insight and understanding. Most politics examinations still involve a choice of essays, and these test the ability to structure relevant and coherent answers to specific questions under time pressure. Therefore most of the advice we have provided on essay writing holds true for exams, providing a *structured argument that answers the specific question set*, although there is rarely the expectation for you to provide references as you would in an essay. However, there are specific elements of the exam that are worth focusing upon.

The prospect of examinations can provoke apprehension or even terror, even among conscientious students who fear they may not be able to do themselves justice. However, good preparation can take some of the worry out of exams. The following advice largely assumes that you are tackling the traditional unseen essay-based examinations. For other types of examinations follow the specific recommendations and advice of your tutors and look at past papers.

- Draw up a revision schedule [see below] well in advance of the exams, allowing plenty of time for sleep and recreation, and keep to it. A training plan for a 10k run has rest days, and these are crucial to allow your body to recover and rebuild. You need down time to allow your brain to process and make sense of the information you have fed into it during your revision. It is therefore best to avoid relying on last-minute revision. There are even apps to help you manage your revision time!
- Get hold of copies of past papers. It is important to 'know the enemy' and become familiar with the structure of the paper and type of questions. However, avoid learning rote answers to last year's exam questions – the clue is in the name; they are last year's questions and therefore are highly unlikely to be repeated.
- On many modules you will not need to revise all topics. If, for example, you are required to answer four questions from ten that roughly cover the syllabus, revising six major topics should normally be enough to ensure that you can answer four decent questions.
- Equip yourself to answer any conceivable question on your chosen topics. (You need a margin of safety in choosing topics, because sometimes a major topic may not come up at all or may appear in a form that you had not anticipated and cannot immediately see how to answer.)
- Revise *actively* not passively. This is the advice given most emphatically by Dunleavy (1986, 148–150). Do not spend hours re-reading lecture notes and textbooks and hoping that some of it will stick. (It usually does not!) Instead engage your mind and *practice outline answers* to past questions. When you find difficulty in answering a specific question, *then* go back to books and notes to fill in gaps in your knowledge and understanding. The key to good exam performance is *technique*, and technique can be improved by *practice* in drafting answers to specific questions.
- Obtain feedback on previous exam performance (if such feedback is available).

Box 3.15 Exam tips

If, as is commonly the case, all questions carry equal marks, make sure you answer the number of questions required. The extra time given to fewer answers is most unlikely to provide marks to compensate for those you have lost by failing to answer a whole question. We often see mark breakdowns like this for exams (in this case answer three questions in three hours): 64, 60, 58. The first mark is often higher because the student picks the question he or she feels most comfortable with. The last question is often the one with which he or she feels least comfortable. What is important is that all three marks are in the same rough band as the way the mark is calculated is to add the marks up and then divide the total to get an average – which in this case is 61%. If you spend too long on the first question you risk gaining a mark breakdown like this: 70, 56, 48 = 58%. This example also highlights the importance of getting something down on paper, even if it is just a plan.

In the exam room once you turn over the paper, make a brief plan – perhaps just five or six points (or even just key words) to be developed into paragraphs. Remember it is an essay, so structure is key. It is also worth beginning with a brief 'signpost' paragraph indicating how you are proposing to answer the question set; then get on with it.

PART 3   SECTION 3
METHODOLOGY

Contents

QUALITATIVE AND QUANTITATIVE SKILLS

The subject matter of politics essentially involves the study of human beings, how they interact with one another and the power relations among individuals and among groups. Politics is therefore a social science. It is increasingly important that as undergraduates you have an appreciation of how we as social scientists conduct research. There are a number of methods used to study politics and international relations and you are likely to encounter most, if not all of them at university, especially in your reading.

The key terms you are likely to come across during your time at university are qualitative and quantitative methodology. As part of your degree you may take a research methods course, and a dissertation can involve some original empirical research.

Box 3.16 What is methodology?

Methodology means a way of approaching the world – how do we know the world around us? (Moses and Knutsen, 2012) It can be seen as a very broad theoretically informed framework for research practice, which provides a coherent and logical approach or process for undertaking particular types of tasks or solving particular problems. Each perspective assumes a menu of research methods (though many research approaches adopt a mix of different methods).

The methods are linked to different methodological approaches within the discipline.

The two key research traditions are **positivism** and social **constructivism**, and these traditions have important implications for research design. Both traditions are visible in politics and International Relations, although International Relations scholars have described this division between these two traditions as 'a fundamental division within the discipline' (Burchill et al. 2013).

Quantitative methods

Quantitative Methods are built upon a positivist philosophy of research. This is an 'approach to the creation of knowledge through research which emphasises the model of the natural sciences: the scientist adopts the position of the objective researcher, who collects "facts" about the social world and then builds up an explanation of social life by arranging such facts in a chain of causality, in the hope that this will uncover general laws about how the society works' (see John 2010 for a fuller overview).

This methodology argues that:

- Events and behaviour are observable phenomena.
- Observable phenomena are measurable.
- Measurable phenomena are causal.
- Causal sequences are deterministic or probabilistic.

If quantitative methods focus on the measurement of human activity, then we need observable data. This means that classic quantitative methods include the use of statistics gathered from voting records in parliament, election data, public opinion data, etc. Within politics we see this tradition best represented by political scientists such as Downs* and in International Relations by thinkers such as Hans Morgenthau*, who argued international politics was governed by 'objective laws'. Lamont (2015) argues that there are three core characteristics of International Relations empiricism: (1) that international politics can be studied as an objective reality, that is as a world 'out there' and distinct from the researcher; (2) theories are held to the standard of predictive validity; and (3) hypotheses tested in International Relations research should be falsifiable.

Example 3.3 Examples of quantitative research

1: This research studies public support for war. It runs a survey experiment embedded in a major internet survey of British foreign policy attitudes (N = 2,205) to explore how international backing affects public support for military action. It finds that the absolute number of troops involved matters far less than the proportion of total troop numbers to be contributed and that the perceived strength of the enemy predicts support only when the British are to contribute a large proportion of total forces.

Johns, R. and Davies, G. A. M. (2014) 'Coalitions of the Willing? International Backing and British Public Support for Military Action', *Journal of Peace Research* 51 (6): 767–781.

2: This research (co-written by a politics lecturer!) was a study of whether the introduction of three points for a win in senior football makes football more exciting. This is a fascinating topic because, as the authors acknowledge, concepts like 'exciting' are highly subjective and therefore hard to measure. To overcome this they construct an excitingness index based on two factors. The first is that more matches should be decided, rather than drawn. The second is that more attacking play should lead, on average, to more goals per match. Their preliminary findings were that three points for a win does seem to boost football's excitingness (as measured in part by the number of goals scored), but that the improvement takes four to five years to take full effect. You might simply *assume* that increasing the points available for a win is bound to increase the attractiveness of the win for the team, but what the Aylott and Aylott study shows is that your assumption has statistical validity! Also, depending on your viewpoint, reducing football to these two operationalisable variables ignores the complexity of 'the beautiful game'. Aylott, M. and Aylott, N. (2007) 'A Meeting of Social Science and Football: Measuring the Effects of Three Points for a Win', *Sports in Science* 10: 205–222.

Qualitative research

Qualitative methods tend to focus on gaining a deep understand of why human beings act the way they do in politics and international relations (see Vromen 2010 for a fuller introduction). These methods give a role to the researcher to interpret the world, underpinned by interpretivist and constructivist positions. They ask 'Is there a truth to find?' Within International Relations this type of research was promoted by thinkers such as Robert Cox*. The method focuses on meaning and especially how people make sense of physical events and behaviour that are taking place. For example, does your gender, race, religion, class, or sexuality influence how you view an event. Qualitative researchers try to understand how individuals construct their own reality within their social context. Lamont (2015) argues that within International Relations interpretivism focuses on understanding social meanings embedded within international politics by unpacking core assumptions that underlie the positivist image of the world in an attempt to counter the perceived empiricist orthodoxy in international relations. Interpretivist research agendas seek to understand identities, ideas, norms, and culture in international politics (see, for example Ashley 1998; Cox 1987). Therefore this method tends to focus on interviews, Participant Observation, Documentary Data analysis, Focus Groups, and Field research.

Example 3.4: Qualitative research in politics and international relations

1. The book by Duncan McCargo *Tearing Apart the Land: Islam and Legitimacy in Southern Thailand* (Cornell University Press, 2008) focuses on a conflict in southern Thailand. The rebellion in Pattani and neighbouring provinces and the Thai government's harsh crackdown have resulted in a full-scale crisis. The research for the book is based on a year's fieldwork in Thailand, with interviews conducted in the area and unpublished Thai-language sources.
2. This article by Zeng, Jinghan and Breslin, Shaun, 'New Type of Great Power Relations: A G2 with Chinese Characteristics?' *International Affairs* (2016) examines how China sees its own role in the world, especially in relation to shaping norms. The authors use content analysis to examine official documents. Via this method they are able to detect how Chinese documents evaluate their own power.

When you undertake research your choice of research question will generally drive your choice of method.
Researching the Arab Spring: Empirical or Interpretive? (Lamont 2015).

- I want to explain the causes of revolution or I want to understand how revolution transformed local identities.
- I want to explore the political role of Islamist movements before and after the revolutions or I want to understand the symbolism of self-immolation in the context of the Tunisian Revolution.
- I want to examine the constitution drafting processes in postrevolutionary Tunisia or Libya or I want to understand Western perceptions of the Arab Spring and how these have been shaped by recent transformations.

Based on this, think about the research examples above and consider whether the research could have been conducted in a different way.

STUDENTS AND RESEARCH

Students often choose to do a questionnaire survey; this is certainly an option, but unless the questions are carefully selected, framed, and tested and a substantial representative sample of the target audience obtained, the results may be virtually worthless, even if they are attractively presented.

One alternative is to conduct a small number of semi-structured interviews with, for example, local party or pressure group activists, public officials or elected councillors. Such interviews need courteous initial contacts and careful advance planning. Prepare your questions and discuss them with your tutor, but be ready to diverge from your script if the occasion demands. Note-taking can be difficult. If you can, persuade interviewees to let you tape the interviews. Whatever you choose to do, try to ensure that your own empirical research reflects your earlier theoretical framework and that the whole dissertation hangs together.

SUMMARY

This section is designed to give you a flavour of the various research skills you will either need to develop or hone to succeed in your politics or International Relations degree. We should stress that everything we say must be considered alongside the advice and rules of your specific university or course. Their rules must be obeyed. What we hope this section does is show you that you are researchers-in-training and that the skills you are developing and using are the same ones being used by the people teaching you. We have to answer questions, research the topic, choose a research method, structure our arguments, and present our research findings.

The skills we outline are also not just academic skills. They are key skills for the workplace. Graduate jobs, as we will discuss in the next section, require employees to demonstrate a range of core skills. The ability to think and write critically, to write logically, and to present your findings to other people are all extremely common in the 21st century. University is a great place to practice in relative safety!

PART 3   SECTION 4
RESEARCH-LED EMPLOYABILITY

Contents

INTRODUCTION

We identified a range of skills that you need to develop or hone whilst at university earlier in this section. This section now discusses how these are key skills in the workplace and outlines how various employability skills are embedded in your politics or International Relations degree. Politics and international relations graduates do not have a career path that some other degrees might have. Most (if not all) chemical engineers become chemical engineers. But students of politics or International Relations face a breadth of career choice that can be confusing. To try and guide you, we draw a distinction between those careers that can be seen as politics related (the civil service; local government; the European Commission; working with an elected politician, a political party, a political lobbyist, a pressure group, or a think tank) and other careers. We also highlight avenues for further study after your undergraduate degree.

WHAT SKILLS DO EMPLOYERS WANT?

It is evident that many employers do not hold any preferences with regard to degree discipline from their candidates but instead focus on the skills that graduates can articulate and demonstrate. The ten key competences that UK employers look for in graduates are (as outlined in Table 3.1): communication; teamwork; integrity; personal development; innovation, creativity and problem solving; research; flexibility; organisation and time management; leadership and decision-making; critical analysis. Evidence from the United States supports the point about the title of your degree: nearly all the employers surveyed (93 percent) say that 'a demonstrated capacity to think critically, communicate clearly, and solve complex problems is more important than [a candidate's] undergraduate major' (HART 2013).

Linking these skills with your degree

We have a table that shows the skills sets that many employers are looking for. The key for you as a student is to identify and articulate these skills. Employers want you to provide evidence. It is not enough to say 'I have group working skills', you need to provide evidence of that skill. In this section we break down the skills identified above and show you where they can commonly be found in a politics and International Relations degree. It is important to link these skills with the ones you develop outside of university in so called co-curriculum activities such as paid work, placements, or roles in clubs or societies, but many studies show that students often only focus on the skills they acquired from working outside the university and fail to highlight their full skill set as a result. The links between academic skills and employability remain opaque to students within the social sciences. To give yourself a head start in the job market it is clear that you need to understand and appreciate how the skills you develop researching and writing essays, sitting exams, making presentations, etc., map onto key employability skills outlined above. You need to be fully aware of, and be able to articulate, the skills you acquire at university and to understand how these can be applied in the workplace/further study, especially in job applications and interviews.

Table 3.1 Graduate Skills sought by UK Employers

	Total number of employees in firm			Grand Total
	1–99	**100–999**	**1000+**	
Communication skills	88%	86%	82%	86%
Team-working skills	85%	84%	84%	85%
Integrity	81%	86%	82%	83%
Intellectual ability	81%	84%	78%	81%
Confidence	80%	81%	78%	81%
Character/personality	81%	79%	60%	75%
Planning and organisational skills	74%	72%	75%	74%
Literacy (good writing skills)	68%	72%	75%	71%
Numeracy (good with numbers)	68%	67%	69%	68%
Analysis and decision-making skills	64%	67%	73%	67%

Source: The Council for Industry and Higher Education (CIHE) (2008).

Developing and demonstrating skills

A document produced by the UK National Union of Students and the business group CBI argues that the key skills are the 'skills which…will always be in demand and will underpin success throughout a career whatever the field'. Within this section we identify generic skills and subject-specific skills.

Box 3.17 UK Civil Service Graduate Scheme: Key Competencies

Flexibility, thinking on your feet, working with others, being persuasive, confident and articulate and taking charge of your own development.

Source: FastStream website https://www.faststream.gov.uk/.

If we look at the skills above, we can see that they are generic skills, that is skills that are not related to a specific subject or discipline. However, the nature of your subject means that as a student you will be asked to analyse, examine, compare, contrast, argue, and evaluate. This may be in seminar discussions, in essays, in group work, or in exams, but it is clear that the skills you gain as a politics or International Relations graduate give you both the generic skills looked for by employers PLUS the means to evidence them. The ability to research for information, evaluate arguments, debate and argue your position are key strengths as we will show.

Communication skills

The UK Political Studies Association highlights communication as a key element of a political science or International Relations degree. It stresses that communication is learning how to discuss and argue from an informed point of view. Students make presentations and develop skills in summarising arguments. They learn to communicate effectively through writing essays, reports, and reviews. Oral communication skills are developed every time you speak in a seminar but can also be evidenced by presentations (individual or group). These skills complement the communication skills you might develop in a job, such as communicating with customers. In your curriculum vitae (CV) you can therefore stress communicating to different audiences in different settings.

Team-working skills

Working with other people is often the trickiest element of university life or the workplace. Many students have to undertake a group project. This can often be stressful, as it involves relying on other people to provide information or to contribute sections of a presentation. Working with others involves trust and compromise. We laugh when skills such as working with other people are labelled 'soft skills', as working with people is often the hardest thing you'll ever do! Hence using a group project is a great way to evidence team-working skills. Remember, employers are not looking for the mark you got, more how you managed the process.

Integrity

This may be seen just in relation to its everyday meaning associated with honesty. However, politics and International Relations students can also discuss the nature of the human condition through their study of political thought and/or philosophy.

Intellectual ability

This can be evidenced by your marks and your overall intellectual engagement with the theoretical and empirical implications of your degree.

Planning and organisational skills

You have three 2,000-word essays due in on April 8th. You are also the secretary of the United Nations Society and you work 15 hours a week in a café. The fact that you manage your time to submit the essays on time is an excellent testament to your planning and organisational skills.

Literacy (good writing skills)

Essay writing allows students to demonstrate a wide range of competences from the way the essay is written (communication skills) to the depth of analysis in the content. Every essay that is produced during a politics or International Relations degree will require research, innovation, creativity and problem solving, written communication, and critical analysis.

Numeracy (good with numbers)

An increasingly important aspect of politics and International relations degrees is learning to feel comfortable with data and the methods used to analyse the data.

Analysis and decision-making skills

Analysis is about learning how to analyse evidence and arguments. Students may focus mainly on texts or perhaps on quantitative data, but either way they learn vital skills in critical evaluation, which is an key element of your degree. 'Politics is about the analysis of complex and often contradictory data and being able to construct and defend arguments derived from such data. You will be able to articulate and defend your arguments in the face of criticism' (PSA nd).

Box 3.18 Studying politics

Studying political science or international relations teaches you 'to rigorously analyse problems and to understand the big picture but not lose focus on the small details' (Karan Chadda, Client Development Manager, Populus in PSA nd).

Research

Politics and International Relations degrees offer the chance to do research. Students learn how to locate, assess, and analyse information – key skills for many of today's jobs.

Box 3.19 Student experience

The thoughts of three University of Leeds students articulating the skills they feel they obtained from a politics or International Relations degree.

> You are asked to give a presentation with two other students in a seminar. Between the three of you, you divide the question into three specific aspects (team-work, planning skills, and flexibility – you might have to compromise on what is done!). The aim of the presentation is to convince the class that 'democracy is good for gender equality' (persuasion skills). The three of you work together to produce a PowerPoint presentation outlining your key arguments based upon your research (presentation and research skills) which you then present orally to a class of 20 students (communication skills). After the presentation, you must answer questions (which requires you to think on your feet). Afterwards you reflect on how it went. You felt nervous and read from your notes which made your presentation hard to hear. You decide to book a session at the skills centre on effective presentations.

STUDY ABROAD, PLACEMENTS AND INTERNSHIPS

Most universities also offer the chance to study in another country in a partner institution for part of your course. The terms used vary from study abroad to a junior year abroad. Drake (2014, 20) highlights the benefits of the ERASMUS study abroad scheme in the United Kingdom. She notes that the students 'valued the scheme... for its "employability" potential'. The benefits of study abroad are that employers see students who undertake such an experience as potentially more flexible, more adaptable, more open to new ideas, more able to handle a challenge, and more resourceful. Study abroad can also offer a way to distinguish their academic career from other equally suitably qualified applicants. These were all benefits of the study abroad scheme as articulated by the students in the Drake article: study abroad would be 'a unique point to put on a CV' and 'it is important to employers to look like you are willing to try new places and travel' (ibid.). Experience in a different country can also bring benefits in terms of language learning, which can be an advantage especially in the European context. Overall then, study abroad can be a great opportunity to broaden your horizons, although the personal, financial and academic implications will need to be weighed carefully.

Alternatively or additionally you may have the option to undertake a semester or year to gain practical experience of work in government or the public or voluntary sector as part of your degree course on a placement or 'internship'. Both the term and the practice of internships were originally applied to medical training in hospitals, particularly in the United States. It has been extended to cover practical work experience in other fields of study and in other countries, especially in the English-speaking world, although the term 'placement' is still more familiar in the United Kingdom. This links back to a distinction between careers that can be seen as politics related (the civil service; local government; the European Commission; working with an elected politician, a political party, a political lobbyist, a pressure group, or a think tank) and other careers. Whilst discipline-related placements are clearly beneficial for students, any work experience is seen as important. Most graduate recruiters stress the need for work experience in their adverts.

Some students are aware of the distinction between politics-related and other careers, as one of Lightfoot's work placement students argued:

Whilst I enjoy the politics I study in my degree, I feel that the real skills I will leave university with are good presentation skills, analytical skills, and the ability to conduct independent research as part of a project. All of these skills are highly relevant to my internship with L'Oreal and will allow me to develop them further. As a result I feel this opportunity will make me stronger in all areas for my final university year, as well as making me more employable in the future. I have never had a desire to use my politics degree to be a politician, but to use it help me further my career in a more business-based organisation, such as L'Oreal. For these reasons I feel my placement is relevant to my degree and I will be using and improving the skills gained during my politics degree. (Lightfoot 2015, pp. 149–50.)

Examples of political internships for students

Working

- for an MP in the Australian Federal Parliament
- as a placement clerk in the Parliament of Queensland
- in the Australian Permanent Mission to the United Nations
- for the United Nations in Geneva.
- as an aide in the US Congress at Washington in the Scottish Parliament
- in a public relations company
- for an NGO
- for a political lobbyist in Brussels

Box 3.20 Graduates with a politics or International Relations degree go on to...

'Politics and International Relations graduates are typically employed by:

> accountancy and banking organisations
>
> charities
>
> councils
>
> law firms
>
> local and national government
>
> retail and media companies.

They are also employed by a range of commercial businesses, particularly within marketing departments.

Other employers include the United Nations (UN), the European Commission, the Civil Service, non-governmental organisations (NGOs), lobbying, campaigning, and voluntary organisations and the public sector in general'.

Source: https://www.prospects.ac.uk/careers-advice/what-can-i-do-with-my-degree/politics-and-international-relations.

But I want to be a lawyer?

During university students often discover that they want to pursue a career in a specific area but do not have a degree in that field. Many professions recognise this and offer conversion courses, for instance in the case of law in the United Kingdom or specific training for teaching. Others will have obtained a job in a particular field such as finance or accountancy and then undertaken professional training (often in-work qualifications). The director of finance for the University of Leeds is a history and economics graduate who then trained as an accountant.

In many professions there are further qualifications that may be useful or essential in progressing your career, but these similarly can often be obtained while you work or on a period of secondment from work or by studying part-time in the evenings or at weekends. These days it is highly unlikely that any skills acquired from a university degree will equip you for a lifetime at work. The new mantra is 'life-long learning'. You will need to acquire new skills and maintain, refresh, and develop old skills over the course of a working life. Yet the generic skills you have developed on your politics degree should stand you in good stead for a lifetime.

Selling yourself

This can be tricky for students (and authors of books). It often feels that you need to sell yourself by exaggerating your skills. That is not the case. Try and stick to the facts – you got a 67% in a policy brief, you were captain of the football team, you ran for office in student union elections, you spent six months studying in Ghana.

Choosing a career

This is a difficult section to write, as the world of work has changed. It is perhaps best to leave more detailed advice on choosing a career to specialist careers advisers, although one or two general points can be made. One of the problems is that we tend to be influenced initially, perhaps too much, by the role models we have among our immediate family, friends, or teachers. It is natural enough to want to stick with what is familiar. Without some knowledge or experience, it is very difficult to imagine what an unfamiliar career would be like as, for example, a lawyer, a journalist, or a business manager. Some politics degree courses offer short work placements, and these may give some taste of what some careers are really like. You may get a chance to do part-time or vacation work in an area of employment you are considering and find out more about it. Your extracurricular activities at university can also be helpful. The key is to keep an open mind – most of Lightfoot's friends do jobs that he did not know existed when he graduated in the 1990s.

If you have not already firmly made up your mind what you want to do, keep an open mind and be prepared to do some research. Attend sessions with university careers advisers and go to careers fairs, where you can seek information and advice without obligation. Make sure you understand what a specific career involves in terms of basic qualifications, opportunities to train on the job, working conditions, and prospects before you make any serious applications.

APPLYING FOR POSTS

Writing job applications and compiling CVs is inevitably time-consuming. There is no point in providing detailed advice here, as plenty should be available from your own institution, including examples of good practice. Seek advice, take time and trouble, and get someone to read your application to check it. Word-processing packages make it much easier to produce professional-looking letters and CVs, and computer spell-check facilities help to avoid some of the grosser errors that might lead to your immediate rejection. Many employers have old-fashioned ideas about spelling, grammar, and punctuation. One personnel manager, describing how he sifted applications, told me he immediately binned any with spelling mistakes. Make the most of yourself, but avoid exaggeration and do not on any account invent experience or qualifications that you do not have. Others may do it, but do not imitate them. It is not worth it. It can be at least extremely embarrassing when you are found out, and it could lead to more damaging consequences.

For interviews, again there is plenty of advice available, often illustrated by appropriate video clips. Prepare for the interview by rehearsing answers to the kind of questions you might expect. Think of questions that you can ask the interviewers yourself. Dress smartly, attend promptly, behave courteously. Try to look keen and interested. Do not be too distressed if you are given a hard time. Friendly interviews do not always promise success. A hard grilling may surprisingly be the preface to a job offer. Do not despair if things go badly. Sometimes they do, often for reasons outside your control. You will get better at it as you go along, although if you already have plenty of experience of oral presentation you should have learned much about presenting yourself and communicating confidently.

If you are made an offer and you are not sure that you want to accept it, ask if you can have time to think about it. This may not be what the interviewers want to hear, but it is better than accepting and later taking back your word or, worse, starting a job and pulling out in few weeks.

FURTHER STUDY

One option you may consider is further study. You may decide not to go straight into full-time employment immediately after graduating but to take another course, perhaps a higher degree, either at the same university or another institution. Some graduates may understandably feel that they have already had quite enough education to last them a lifetime and have no inclination to prolong their studies any further. Instead, they are eager to throw themselves into a 'proper job', earning 'real money', as soon as possible. Others are quite the opposite. They have enjoyed student life so much that they never want it to end, and would sign up to any postgraduate course on offer to postpone the evil day of their entry into the 'real world' of work.

Both groups are liable to be disappointed. The 'Peter Pans' will discover that they cannot remain perpetual students but have to grow up sometime and earn their keep. Their more worldly and materialist contemporaries will almost certainly find that they cannot turn their backs on education completely, as most careers involve the need for some serious further study at some stage. The notion of 'life-long learning' has become something a cliché, simply because it reflects reality. New knowledge and new skills will be necessary to adapt and survive in a fast-changing world.

There is thus not a stark 'either–or' choice between full-time employment and further study. Nearly all graduates can expect to have to do both. The only questions are, when and how? You can take another full-time course immediately after graduating. You can return to full-time study in a few years' time after a period in full-time employment. You can carry on part-time study while working, or take on a part-time course later. If you have learned to be self-motivated and self-directed you may be able to cope with what is now more commonly described as 'distance learning'.

All these options have advantages and disadvantages. 'Distance-learning' is commonly much cheaper than full-time courses, but it also requires much more determination and persistence. Yet as long as you appreciate the self-discipline that will be necessary, distance learning does have the advantage that you can fit your studying around work and family commitments, whenever you can find the time. Moreover, there are now some excellent courses run on a distance-learning basis, such as those developed by the UK's Open University. Indeed many prestigious traditional universities now offer some courses by distance learning.

Part-time courses involving college attendance require a regular commitment of time, which can be a problem, particularly if you miss a few weeks. Yet there are not only social benefits from attending classes, as tutors and fellow students help to keep each other going. Returning to full-time study later may be more rewarding but almost certainly much more expensive, both directly (in terms of course fees) and indirectly (in terms of lost earnings).

Thus if you want to extend your education and improve your qualifications there is something to be said for doing it sooner rather than later, before you will notice the substantial reduction in your living standards and before you have a family of your own whose needs must be considered. You will also be used to studying and regularly producing work to be assessed. Those who return to study later sometimes find it difficult to cope with the demands of assessed work, and particularly examinations. Yet if you choose another full-time course immediately after graduating, do it for positive rather than negative reasons – because you really want to do a specific course or really need a particular qualification. Do not undertake further full-time study simply to postpone a decision on what you are going to do for the rest of your life.

An 'academic' or 'professional' course?

One option is a higher degree, such as a master's course, in politics or a related subject. This can be a natural progression – carrying on your studies, commonly in a more specialised way at a more advanced level. There may be plenty of courses to choose among, and plenty of universities and staff only too eager to enrol you because they need a sufficient number of students (and their fees!) if a particular course is to become and remain viable. So you may not have a problem with gaining acceptance. You may be able to opt for either 'part-time' or 'full-time' study, although at the postgraduate level the distinction between these two terms is relative, even more than at the undergraduate level, as nearly all postgraduate students will need to undertake some part-time work to maintain themselves.

That is one reason you need to think carefully about why you want to do it. Is a further qualification going to significantly improve your employability and prospects? In some cases the answer may be clearly 'Yes'. If for example you are keen to pursue an academic career at the university level, higher degrees are essential. Yet if you are thinking of becoming a school teacher or further education lecturer, a teaching qualification is more important than a higher degree, which may make only a marginal difference to your employability.

A LIFETIME'S INTEREST AND INVOLVEMENT IN POLITICS

This part of the book has necessarily concentrated on the important business of earning a living. Yet it is to be earnestly hoped that paid employment is far from all you will have gained from undertaking a university course in politics or International Relations. It should be an interest that you will carry with you for the rest of your life. Moreover, even if you do not pursue a political career full time, you will inevitably be involved to some extent in politics, beyond simply casting a vote periodically. The knowledge and understanding of politics you have picked up at university may prove unexpectedly valuable at various stages of your life.

You may become involved in a particular interest or cause and in the practical business of pressure group politics. You may be aroused by a specific decision, such as new airport runway, or road, perhaps a hospital or school closure, and find yourself organising opposition and demonstrations. Unforeseeable developments in your own life or that of your immediate family may impel you to seek a remedy for an injustice or advance a specific cause. You may become an active member of a political party, canvassing for support, and seeking to influence its policies and strategy. You may even seek election yourself. You make seek to influence the wider political debate by articulating your views in the media. Now, it is certainly true that you can do all this without studying politics at university, and so it should be, if democracy has any meaning. You should not need a degree to participate in politics. Yet your knowledge and understanding should help you to participate more effectively and with more satisfaction.

However much or little you participate directly in politics yourself, politics in all its variety remains a subject that is not only intrinsically important but full of absorbing and never-ending interest. Hopefully you can be an advocate for the study of politics and international relations to counter the trend for 'hating politics'. It will be surprising if you do not retain a keen concern in the subject, not only closely following political news around the world but reading serious political analysis, perhaps even returning to its academic study at some later date. It is an interest you should be able to continue well into retirement after your full-time work is finished (just like one of us!).

GUIDE TO FURTHER READING

The Palgrave series on study skills is generally excellent, although you might feel we would say that given that this book is published by Palgrave (critical thinking!). Cottrell (2013) has a broad scope. It is particularly good on some topics (e.g. plagiarism). The overall design is a matter of taste. Some may find the approach engaging and accessible; others perhaps a little patronising. Her book on critical thinking (2011) follows a similar vein but has some great examples. *The works by Daddow (2013), Greetham (2013) and Hathaway (2015) were very helpful in helping us write this section and this inspiration is acknowledged with thanks.*

Also published by Palgrave is the best book we have come across on methodology:

Jonathon W. Moses and Torbjorn L. Knutsen *Ways of Knowing: Competing Methodologies in Social and Political Research* (2012). If you are looking for the classic book on methods within political science, see Vivien Lowndes, David Marsh, and Gerry Stoker, *Theory and Methods in Political Science* (2018). For a book on International Relations, we would recommend Christopher Lamont (2015) *Methods in International Relations* (published this time by Sage).

PART IV
Key Political Terms and Concepts

Contents

INTRODUCTION

This part of the book explores some of the key terms and concepts that students of politics may encounter in their reading and research. Most of the terms and concepts discussed here have already been introduced in earlier parts of the book and some have already been discussed extensively; where the latter is the case there seems little point in duplicating earlier analysis here, so use the index to locate further information and analysis in the rest of the text.

While some definitions are reasonably straightforward and relatively widely agreed upon, many others are *essentially contested* concepts: there are competing interpretations, sometimes reflecting very different political perspectives. These terms and concepts are explored in rather more depth.

References to related concepts in this part of the book are printed in bold and references to key thinkers discussed in Part V are asterisked. (The dates of these thinkers are not included here, as this information is provided in Part V.)

KEY TERMS AND CONCEPTS

Absolutism

The doctrine (associated with Bodin* and Hobbes*) that the **power** of the **sovereign** in a state should be absolute or unlimited. While the term 'absolutism' can be applied to any system of government where the power of the sovereign body is theoretically unlimited, it is most commonly used to describe the 'absolute monarchies' of continental Europe in the early modern period (particularly the 18th century). The saying attributed to King Louis XIV of France 'L'état, c'est moi' ('the state – that's me') encapsulates the notion of an absolute ruler, responsible and accountable to no one. A few 18th-century thinkers (such as Voltaire*) were inclined to defend absolutism, as some of these absolutist monarchs were patrons of the arts and philosophy and appeared to take their responsibilities seriously. These were sometimes described as 'benevolent' or 'enlightened' despots.

Accountability

The notion that those who hold an office or position are accountable or answerable to others for their behaviour. Thus in a parliamentary **democracy** state officials are accountable to ministers, ministers to a **legislature** or parliament, parliament to electors. The terms 'accountability' and 'responsibility' are sometimes confused. Accountability flows upwards, responsibility downwards. Thus officials are *accountable to* ministers who are *responsible for* their officials. Accountability may involve a formal requirement to render an oral or written account, for example to answer questions and/or submit written reports to a parliament or a legislative assembly. Thus those responsible for a particular action (or inaction) can be called to account.

Administration

This term is confusingly used in a number of different ways. Thus 'the administration' is sometimes a synonym for the government and the leading politicians in charge of the government, while sometimes it is used to mean the bureaucracy or civil service, and sometimes merely the detailed implementation of government policy.

Agency

(See under **Structure and Agency**.)

Anarchy and anarchism

Anarchy (literally 'no rule') is a term commonly used as a synonym for chaos and a complete breakdown of law and order, as may happen, for example, in the midst of revolution or civil war. Some political theorists (e.g. Hobbes*, Locke*, Rousseau*) imagined early humans before the development of society or the state living in a condition of anarchy without government or law, and went on to argue that people needed a **state** of some kind to maintain order and protect **property**. The concept of anarchy is also important in the theory of **international relations**, in which it is commonly argued that relations between states essentially involve anarchy as there is no effective power to keep them in order, despite the recent growth of international law and international organisations.

Anarchism is a political ideology that rejects government and authority. Anarchist thinkers (e.g. Godwin*, Proudhon*, Bakunin*, Kropotkin*) argue that states are inevitably oppressive and limit freedom. Humans are not naturally aggressive and competitive but social and co-operative, and they would realise their true nature in voluntary association in stateless societies. Anarchists are hostile to all forms of authority, such as established religion, and most are against private property and **capitalism** and are thus usually located on the far **left** of the political spectrum, (although the label 'anarcho-capitalism' has been given to some **neoliberals** who seek to limit the role of the state to a minimum).

A key question for anarchists is how their ideal is to be realised (the problem of **agency**). While some anarchists (e.g. Bakunin) have justified violence as a means to promote an anarchist revolution, others (e.g. Kropotkin, Tolstoy) have been **pacifists**, opposed to all violence. Anarchism has had a strong following in some countries (such as Spain, Italy, and Russia for a time) with anarchist political parties attracting

significant support. In the Spanish Civil War (1936–1939), most anarchists concluded that defeating Franco was the immediate problem and not only fought on the side of the Republic but even participated in the government. (There was for a time an anarchist Minister of Justice.)

Aristocracy

'Aristocracy' (a term derived from Greek) means literally 'rule of the best', although over time it has come to mean a governing **elite** or **class** whose status depends on hereditary descent, normally combined with possession of extensive landed **property**. (In practice, however, successful merchants or manufacturers were often able to buy their way into this ancient landed aristocracy). Once, this land-owning aristocracy constituted the effective ruling class in many states (e.g. 18th-century Britain, France, and Austria). Today an aristocrat is, in common parlance, a person with an aristocratic title, such as Duke or Baron. Some such titles are ancient and inherited, while others are recently bestowed, perhaps to honour outstanding achievements or sometimes, allegedly, in return for money or political favours. Although aristocratic status remains a source of influence and even power in some modern states claiming to be democratic (such as the United Kingdom), the aristocracy in general are no longer *the* ruling class. Some thinkers in the past defended aristocracy (e.g. Burke*, Coleridge), but only eccentric mavericks do so still.

Authority

Authority is a **power** that is (willingly or reluctantly) acknowledged and accepted by those over whom it is exercised.

Max Weber*, the German sociologist, distinguished among three main types of authority: traditional, charismatic, and legal-rational. Traditional authority rests on long-established usage or custom – such as the authority of a tribal chief or hereditary monarch. Charismatic authority derives from the compelling personal qualities of an individual (for example the authority exercised by Napoleon or Hitler or, more positively,

Mahatma Gandhi*, Martin Luther King*, or Nelson Mandela*). Legal-rational authority is authority based on formal rules. Thus the authority of elected politicians or appointed government officials may be accepted and obeyed, not because of custom or personal qualities but because it is acknowledged that they legitimately hold their office under accepted rules and procedures; it is essentially the office or post rather than the person who occupies the post that is obeyed. Weber considered that legal-rational authority is the characteristic modern form of authority. Both modern bureaucracy and representative democracy involve legal-rational authority. Note that Weber's three types of authority are not necessarily mutually exclusive. Thus an elected politician (legal-rational authority) may have some charismatic authority and, if he or she occupies an ancient post, an element of traditional authority also.

Balance of power

The creation, restoration or preservation of a balance of power between states has been a concern of some thinkers and statesmen in the conduct of **international relations**. From the early modern period to the beginning of the 20th century the main preoccupation has been the balance of power in Europe. After the Second World War the concern was the global balance of power between the USA and the USSR and their associated allies. The threat of nuclear annihilation through mutually assured destruction (MAD) reinforced the balance of power, which disintegrated with the end of the Soviet Union in 1989.

Behaviouralism, Behavioural revolution

Behaviouralism is an approach to the study of politics and other social sciences that focuses on the observable (individual and social) behaviour of humans.

Behaviouralism was influenced by the methodology of the natural sciences, and by **positivism** in philosophy. Both implied the rejection of **normative** approaches and the adoption of a more rigorous scientific methodology, involving the collection and analysis of (largely) quantitative data. The behavioural revolution in the social sciences that developed in the USA from the 1940s onwards marginalised or rejected older approaches to the study of politics that had focused on the study of political ideas. While early behaviouralists assumed the need for a purely inductive approach, modern neo-behaviouralists acknowledge that some preliminary hunch or hypothesis to be tested normally guides the collection of data. [For more on behaviouralism, see Part II, Section 2].

Bourgeoisie

'The bourgeoisie' was once simply a name for town dwellers in France. Later it came to be applied to well-to-do merchants, a rising middle **class**, whose wealth was coveted but whose social pretensions were mocked by older aristocracies. Marx* used the term 'bourgeoisie' to refer specifically to the owners of **capital** in an industrial society. He also used the term 'petty bourgeoisie' (in French 'petit bourgeoisie') to describe the 'middle class' of small employers, shopkeepers, professionals, and others between the capitalists and the workers, although he did not use the term very precisely or consistently. Today the term 'bourgeoisie' is still employed by **Marxists** to mean the capitalist class but is more commonly used to describe an (undifferentiated) middle class. The adjective 'bourgeois' is often used in a disparaging way to describe conventional middle-class values, tastes, and attitudes.

Bretton Woods

The Bretton Woods Institutions are the World Bank (WB) and the International Monetary Fund (IMF). They were set up at a meeting of 43 countries in Bretton Woods, New Hampshire, USA, in July 1944. Given the experience of the Second World War, their aims were to rebuild economies, especially in Western Europe and set down rules for monetary and economic cooperation among states. Heavily influenced by the work of Keynes*, the system operated until the early 1970s. The Bretton Woods system was criticised from the political right for its attempts to regulate markets and from the left for cementing the US dollar as the dominant global currency. Ultimately, the institutions began to promote a neoliberal approach to trade and politics, becoming known in the 1990s as the 'Washington Consensus'.

Bureaucracy

'Bureaucracy' was a term coined (originally in France) to mean government by permanent officials; from the start it had pejorative (or hostile and critical) connotations, and it is still commonly used in the same sense today. Thus to describe someone as a bureaucrat is to disparage him or her. Bureaucracy became a byword for officious, inflexible, and insensitive treatment of people by the letter of rules and regulations. It is particularly associated with the **state** and with public officials.

The German sociologist Max Weber* employed the term 'bureaucracy' in a more neutral or even positive way. For him, bureaucracy was an efficient and effective means of running any modern large organisation in either the public or private sector. It involved recruitment and promotion of officials by merit and qualifications rather than by patronage, a clear chain of responsibility and **accountability** in hierarchical organisations, and decisions made impartially in accordance with written rules rather than through personal favours or bribery. Bureaucracy was thus both more efficient and fairer than traditional forms of organisation. Weber was well aware that bureaucracy (rule by permanent officials) might be more of a reality than **representative democracy** (rule by the people's elected representatives) in the modern state, but bureaucracy and democracy both involved what he characterised as legal-rational **authority** and were theoretically compatible.

Yet it is often argued that behind the façade of democracy in modern states lies the reality of bureaucracy and that permanent state officials have more influence on key decisions than the elected ministers whom they serve. Economists of the **rational choice** school assume that state bureaucrats pursue their own interest rather than the public interest. Thus William Niskanen* and others claimed that state bureaucrats had a vested interest in the expansion of their own departments and budgets, leading to increased public spending (and taxation). This analysis was a key element in **New Right** thinking in the United States and Europe, leading to measures to cut back the state, increase competition, and pursue **privatisation**.

Capitalism

'Capitalism' is a term used to describe a largely free market economy where the means of production are privately owned and controlled by the relative few, who employ the bulk of the working population as wage labourers to produce and purchase the goods and services required for their own subsistence. Capitalism accompanied by industrialisation rapidly superseded the feudal and agrarian economies of, first, the West and, later, much of the rest of the world. Capitalism was extensively analysed by Marx* and Engels* and their followers. While Marx was aware of the unprecedented productive capacity of the capitalist system, he argued that it would ultimately be destroyed by its own internal contradictions, as competition would force the capitalists to intensify the exploitation of the industrial workers until these were driven to **revolution**. For Marx, political **power** reflected economic power. Thus a capitalist society and economy where wealth and income were concentrated in the hand of the few could never become a genuine **democracy**.

In practice, capitalism has been more adaptable and resilient than Marx predicted. While it is certainly arguable that inequality widened under capitalism, the appeal of revolution declined as the living standards of European industrial workers rose rather than fell. (Lenin* among others argued this was a consequence of imperialism and the increased exploitation of colonies.) Capitalism also survived the emergence of a rival

socialist command economy, first in Russia and later in Eastern Europe, China, and elsewhere. The 'Cold War' between the two systems ended with the collapse of communism in the former Soviet Union and Eastern Europe and its transformation through market reforms elsewhere (notably China).

Capitalism is now seen as a global phenomenon. Today major **transnational corporations (TNCs)** operate across state borders, able to take advantage of favourable tax and regulatory regimes and incentives for new investment. Global capitalism still provokes much hostility, particularly for its impact on the environment and for its contribution to widening the gulf between rich and poor. Yet there no longer seems to be any viable alternative. Attention has focused more on rival versions of capitalism, such as Anglo-American free market capitalism, or the social market capitalism, sometimes referred to as Rhineland or German capitalism, involving more partnership and state regulation of labour markets. A third model is East Asian capitalism of which Japan has long been the standard bearer, to be joined by Singapore and, remarkably, China. East Asian capitalism involves active state guidance and a more paternalist relationship between business firms and their employees.

Christian democracy

Christian democracy has been an important and sometimes dominant ideology in the party systems in Western Europe (e.g. Germany, Italy, France, Belgium, Netherlands, and Austria) in the post–Second World War period. It has also had some impact in South America. Formerly the Roman Catholic church in particular had appeared hostile to democracy and reform. After 1945 reformed Catholic and cross-denominational parties became fully engaged in electoral competition, economic management and welfare reform, adopting a moderate state interventionist approach. A similar centre or centre–right approach has been evident in the European People's Party in the European Parliament. Yet more recently Christian democracy has been a declining force (except in Germany).

Citizen and citizenship

A citizen is a member of a state, who by virtue of citizenship has both rights and obligations. The term 'citizen' implies active involvement in the **state**, as compared with the term 'subject' that suggests passive obedience to a sovereign. As such, the term has become closely bound up with the **republican** tradition and was used by the American and French Republics following their **revolutions** towards the end of the 18th century. In contemporary politics, citizenship has become a key concept across the ideological spectrum, although the term is used in different senses, implying very different underlying assumptions and implications. Those who advocate participative **democracy** stress the political rights and duties of the citizen. **Neoliberals** emphasise the freedom of individual citizens to make their own choices without interference from the state and other citizens. **Social democrats** by contrast emphasise the economic and social rights of the citizen in a modern welfare state. **Communitarian** thinkers (e.g. MacIntyre*, Sandel*, Taylor*, Walzer*) stress the obligations of citizens to the wider **community**.

Civil disobedience

Civil disobedience involves deliberate and open disobedience of the **state** and is generally justified on moral grounds by those who use this political strategy. The term was first used by the American Henry David Thoreau* in the mid-19th century to justify disobedience to a government that upheld the institution of slavery. Peaceful civil disobedience was later extensively used by Gandhi* in his ultimately successful campaign to promote the independence of India from British colonial rule and by Martin Luther King* as leader of the civil rights movement to end discrimination against African Americans. Non-violent campaigns are less likely to be successful against a powerful and ruthless government. Peaceful civil disobedience was tried for years unsuccessfully against the apartheid regime in South Africa; Nelson Mandela* among others advocated the switch to armed struggle that was to lead to his long imprisonment on Robben Island.

Civil society

Particularly in liberal thought, the term 'civil society' is distinguished from the **state** to describe the 'private sphere' of business, voluntary bodies, interest groups, faith groups, clubs, and families. Thus **liberals** generally argue that the state should not interfere with the **freedom** of autonomous individuals and organisations in civil society. The liberal defence of civil society was contrasted with **totalitarianism**, involving no limits to the authority of the state and the effective abolition of the private, independent realm of civil society.

Yet from other perspectives the clear separation of the state and civil society can allow the perpetuation of injustice, discrimination, and even violence against individuals and minorities and irreparable damage to the environment. **Socialists** and trade unionists have sought state intervention to ensure health and safety at work, to protect workers from unfair dismissal or bullying, and to provide a legal minimum wage, and other interference with the freedom of employers to manage their businesses as they saw fit. **Green** activists have campaigned for greater controls over the freedom of individuals and businesses to pollute the environment. **Feminists**, proclaiming 'the personal is political', have sought increased state intervention to protect women from violence and abuse at work and in the home. Many modern liberals have campaigned vigorously for laws against discrimination on grounds of **race** or **gender**, thus preventing landlords and private clubs from exercising their freedom to exclude whom they wanted from their premises. While many oppose what they see as unwarranted interference with the freedom of the individual by the 'nanny state', extensive state intervention is advocated and defended for a whole range of reasons. Thus the notion of 'civil society'

as a sacrosanct sphere, free from state interference, is contested. However, many would still argue that a flourishing civil society is necessary for a healthy **democracy**. (See also **social capital**.)

Class

Economic or social class has been a key concept in modern political analysis, although some now argue that it is of declining significance. For Karl Marx* politics was all about the struggle between conflicting class interests. Under **capitalism** there were only two classes that mattered, and their economic interests were diametrically opposed and irreconcilable. These classes were those who owned and controlled the means of production, the **bourgeoisie**, and those who owned only their only labour and were forced to sell it on disadvantageous terms to survive, the industrial working class or proletariat. Marx acknowledged that there were other classes, including the old landowning **aristocracy**, the petty bourgeoisie of professionals and small business owners, and the peasantry, but all these were of declining significance and in process of being absorbed into the two important classes.

Conventional analysis of class involves distinguishing among upper, middle, and lower or working classes, sometimes with intermediate groups such as 'upper middle' or 'lower middle'. The upper class may be identified with the traditional landed aristocracy and/or with those who are sufficiently wealthy not to depend on their labour for their income. The middle class is a broad category covering a wide range of income and wealth that includes not only business owners (Marx's bourgeoisie) and shopkeepers but professionals and all 'white-collar' workers (or those who work with their brains rather than their hands). The working class includes all 'blue-collar' or manual workers and their dependants but may be further subdivided among skilled, semi-skilled, and unskilled.

Although these categories are imprecise and unscientific they still have some significance for students of politics, not least because many people are prepared to define themselves in these terms. Such subjective assessments of an individual's class may be important for political attitudes and behaviour (particularly party allegiance and voting). Others such as advertisers, government statisticians, and social scientists have sought a more practical classification of social divisions for their own purposes. Thus advertisers need to know not only newspaper and magazine circulation figures and television viewing figures but also something about the social class and purchasing power of each audience. Government statisticians seek to break down the population into employment categories for a number of purposes, such as assessing the impact of government policies on particular sections of the population. Social scientists may use the categories devised by advertisers or official government statisticians or devise their own. Whatever classification they use, they generally find significant correlations between particular social or occupational groups and political attitudes and behaviour. Thus in some countries there is marked correlation between social class and voting. Other analysis may show that a disproportionate number of elected representatives and appointed state officials come from a restricted class background.

Although class remains important to an understanding of politics, it may be of reduced significance. This may be partly due to economic change, including the decline of mining and manufacturing and the rise of service industries. It also may reflect the growth of new divisions within and across class divisions. Thus age, **gender**, **nation**, religion, and **ethnicity**, always important in some countries, may now be of increasing significance even in those countries where class divisions once dominated politics. Some argue that the politics of identity have increasingly replaced the politics of class.

Collectivism

Collectivism emphasises the importance of pursuing the interests of the whole of society or the whole community rather than individual self-interest. It is commonly associated with state ownership and state planning on behalf of the community. Thus collectivism rejects leaving the distribution of goods and service to **free market** forces. The growth of the **state**, of state services and state expenditure, is commonly seen to involve the growth of collectivism.

Collectivism is commonly associated with the **left** of the political spectrum and **individualism** and the free market with the **right**, but the relationship of specific creeds to collectivism is more complex. **Socialists** and **communists** on the left favour collectivism, but so do **fascists** on the far right, while classical **liberals** and **neoliberals** deplore it. On the moderate right, European **conservatives** and **Christian democrats** have often supported state welfare provision and some intervention in the management of the economy, while maintaining general support for private enterprise.

Communism

Communism in the broadest sense means the common ownership of wealth, and an absence of private **property**. Thus Plato* in *The Republic* advocated common ownership for the guardians of his ideal state, to ensure they pursued the interest of the community as a whole rather than their own private interests. Thomas More (1478–1535) similarly envisaged common ownership in his *Utopia*. The Diggers attempted to establish a communist colony in 1649–1650, following the English Civil War. Various early **communists**, **socialists**, and **anarchists** in many countries advocated the abolition of private ownership. Today, however, communism is largely associated with the theories of Karl Marx* and his followers and the political systems established in the Soviet Union, China, and other states under the broad heading of **Marxism-Leninism**.

Communism is often distinguished from democratic **socialism** and **social democracy**, although the relationship between these terms is complex and contentious (see **socialism**). Marx and his 19th-century followers used the terms 'communism', 'socialism', and 'social democracy' almost interchangeably. Lenin*, drawing on and developing a distinction made by Marx in *The Critique of the Gotha Programme,* treated socialism as a transitional phase leading ultimately to the final institution of communism. Marxist socialists in the West commonly referred to the socialism of the Soviet Union and its satellites as admittedly imperfect but nevertheless 'actually existing socialism', to be defended against the alternative liberal **capitalism** of the United States and 'the West' more generally. Other democratic socialists and social democrats in the West distinguished sharply between their own socialism and what they regarded as a perverted interpretation of socialism in communist states, involving one-party **dictatorship**, centralised state control of the economy, and the denial of individual freedom. Some communist parties in Western Europe, notably in Italy, pursued their own distinctive version of Eurocommunism, which accepted parliamentary democracy and co-operation with other parties of the left and centre in a multiparty system.

For much of the 20th century communism of the Marxist-Leninist form appeared a viable alternative to Western liberal **capitalism.** The fall of the Berlin Wall in 1989 was followed swiftly by the collapse of communism in Eastern Europe and the implosion of the Soviet Union itself. Some former Communist parties in the West have been renamed. In China, where the Communist Party still rules, there has been an increased acceptance of **free markets** and private ownership, although this has not been accompanied by political liberalisation.

Community and communitarianism

A community may be defined as any group of people who have something in common and feel a sense of a common identity. It is generally but not exclusively related to specific geographical localities, particularly small face-to-face local communities, although the term 'community' is also freely linked with much larger geographical areas not involving face-to-face contact, such as the 'national community', the 'European community', and even the 'international community'.

The word is also sometimes used in a sense that transcends a physical location, as in the 'business community', 'academic community', 'professional communities', or 'Muslim community'. Here it implies common endeavours, perhaps entailing a common outlook, common interests, or common values.

It should be clear from the above examples that the term 'community' is used extensively, with little precision, and carries some strong **normative** associations. 'Community' is widely perceived as 'good'. It is a word freely employed by politicians across the political spectrum. It is also often used as an all-purpose warm, sanitising term to encourage the acceptance of particular institutions and policies. (British examples include 'community care', 'community hospitals', 'community policing', and even the 'Community Charge', the official name for an unpopular local government tax that has since been abolished.)

'Community' sometimes implies more uniformity of attitudes and behaviour than exist in practice. Thus within the 'Muslim community' or the 'Jewish community' or the 'Christian community' there are deep divisions of opinion and behaviour. There are similar differences within the 'business community' and the 'academic community'. Even small local communities can be deeply divided. The 'national community' commonly comprises numerous subcultures, often involving considerable mutual antipathy. Some would argue that the concept of an 'international community' is virtually meaningless and in practice is employed to describe the views or interests of the governments of the most powerful states or international business.

At another level 'community' and community rights and interests are commonly contrasted with the emphasis of **liberals** on the rights and interests of the **individual**. Communitarianism is a political philosophy that emphasises the importance of the common good, common values, common interests, and the reciprocal rights and duties bound up with membership of a community, contrasted with the atomised **individualism** and pursuit of self-interest associated with classical liberalism. Leading communitarian thinkers include Alasdair MacIntyre*, Michael Sandel*, Michael Walzer*, and Charles Taylor*. Their ideas have been popularised by Amitai Etzioni (1967) and have been taken up by some **social democrats**, '**third way**' thinkers, and **conservatives**. They have also influenced the approach of some modern scientists, including the ideas of Robert Putnam* and his emphasis on the importance of **social capital**.

Comparative politics

A feature of modern political science is a more systematic comparative study of political institutions and practices across countries. This has involved, for example, exploring voting behaviour, political culture, parties, pressure groups, and executives and legislatures across countries rather than within a single political community. However, the growth in the number of independent states from 1945 has rendered comprehensive comparisons increasingly difficult. In practice, political scientists have either focused their studies on broad areas (e.g. African studies) or types of political regimes (e.g. military dictatorships) or specific institutions (e.g. executives, legislatures, parties).

Consensus

Consensus means agreement or compromise. While politics is often seen in terms of conflicting interests and sharp disagreement over values and goals, others emphasise the pursuit of compromise and the establishment of a broad agreement over values and procedures and often also over specific policies. Thus political leaders may seek to build a consensus through persuasion, bargaining, and compromise. Politicians and parties may also try to ascertain what is the public consensus (or what most people think) and adapt their programme accordingly. Thus they will seek to occupy the 'middle ground'.

Some have argued that the politics of sharp ideological conflict gave way to the politics of consensus in the period after the Second World War. This consensus has been variously described – as a **social democratic** consensus in Europe generally,

or as the Keynes–Beveridge consensus in the United Kingdom (from the names of the economist John Maynard Keynes* and the welfare reformer William Beveridge*). Thus there appeared to be a broad consensus in favour of state welfare provision and government macroeconomic management, with often some state ownership of industry in what was seen as a mixed economy. However, there was always some disagreement over the extent of consensus (a societal or just an elite consensus?) and even over its reality. Subsequently it appeared that consensus politics had widely broken down, with the reappearance of sharp ideological divisions from the late 1960s and the 1970s onwards, although periodically observers have identified the emergence of a new consensus.

Inevitably there are those who do not share in the consensus or feel excluded from it. Left-wing **socialists** deplore the abandonment or watering down of socialist commitments by party leaders pursuing consensus and **power**. Similarly, the **New Right** rejected the main planks of the postwar consensus and sought to destroy it. The British Conservative Prime Minister Margaret Thatcher, charged with abandoning consensus politics, responded that she was a conviction politician: 'For me, consensus seems to be the process of abandoning all beliefs, principles, values and policies.'

Consent

Consent, or agreement, is a key liberal democratic concept. **Liberals** from John Locke* onwards have argued that only the consent of the governed can provide governments with **legitimacy**. Similarly, it is maintained that consent is the basis of an **obligation** to obey laws and government; citizens should obey laws to which they have consented, either in person or through their own elected representatives.

There are practical problems with the notion of government by consent. Citizens could reasonably object that they have not personally consented to government. Locke, rather unsatisfactorily, argued that government rested on *tacit* consent. By staying in a country when it was possible to leave, the citizen was giving tacit consent to obey the government and laws of the country. Yet, as David Hume* and others have objected, leaving a country is commonly not a realistic option for most people.

Also, peoples' ideas can be moulded and manipulated by governments or dominant interests to secure consent. **Dictators** have sometimes legitimised their rule by **plebiscites**, often held under conditions in which the expression of contrary views was not permitted and sometimes involving blatant intimidation.

In some representative democracies popular consent, through a **referendum** or plebiscite, is required for **constitutional** change. In others the express consent of the **legislature** may be required for some **executive** actions and appointments. Thus in the United States the 'Advice and Consent' of the Senate is required for treaties and the appointment of ambassadors, ministers, and members of the Supreme Court.

Conservatism (and neo-conservatism)

As the name implies, conservatism as a political doctrine or ideology means conserving, keeping things as they are. Historically, conservatives have been suspicious of change, hostile to the new ideas associated with the **Enlightenment**, industrialisation, constitutional reform, and above all **revolution**. Conservative thinkers such as Burke* and Oakeshott* have valued tradition and emphasised the limitations of human reason, preferring the known to the unknown and practical experience to intellectual speculation. 'If it ain't broke, don't fix it' is a familiar expression of conservative **pragmatism**.

However, in practice, conservatives have often embraced limited or gradual reform as the best means of maintaining stability. While conservatives were initially hostile to representative **democracy**, they ultimately embraced it, once it appeared clear that it did not necessarily involve social revolution nor a substantial threat to existing **property**. They have nevertheless continued to emphasise the need for strong **leadership**,

with limited potential for democratic participation in politics beyond voting.

Traditional conservatism has been critical of the **liberal** emphasis on the freedom of the individual and self-help and self-reliance within an environment of **free market** forces. Instead conservatism has emphasised a more organic view of human society, with humans locked together in ties of mutual **obligation** and dependence. Conservatives have generally viewed **human nature** as inherently selfish, acquisitive, aggressive, or (in religious terms) sinful, requiring a strong **state**, effective leadership, and **authority** to maintain law and order. Conservatives have also largely defended inequality and the existing property rights, particularly landed property, against the demands of socialists for greater **equality**, redistribution, and **social justice**. Instead, conservatives have emphasised the need for the propertied classes and ultimately the state to acknowledge a proper responsibility towards the deserving poor. However, in the late 20th century a **New Right** combined elements of traditional conservatism with the free market, minimal state convictions of **neo-liberals.** In the international sphere conservatives have generally vigorously defended what they perceived as national interests.

Although the appeal of overt conservatism generally declined in the 20th century, it thrived in the United Kingdom, partly because British conservatives embraced social reform, but partly also because **nationalism** and even **imperialism** seem to have won votes across social classes. In the United States there has been a revival of conservatism. Its exponents are sometimes described as neo-conservatives (or 'neocons') who (for example) have asserted national interest and realism in **international relations** and have become particularly influential in US administrations in the late 20th and early 21st centuries.

Constitution

In the study of politics a constitution is simply a set of basic principles, rules, and processes for the government of any state. Today these are normally set out in a single authoritative document, following the celebrated American Constitution (1787 onwards). Thus constitutions may contain some statement of fundamental principles, perhaps including a declaration of human or citizens' **rights**. They normally include rules governing the relationships among the various parts and levels of government, for example between the **executive, legislature**, and **judiciary** and, in a **federal** government, between federal and state institutions. the United Kingdom, almost alone among modern states, does not have such a written constitution in the sense of a single authoritative document, although parts of the British system of government are contained in authoritative written sources, so that the British constitution is better described as 'uncodified'.

Written constitutions can inspire reverence and confer legitimacy on a system of government, although they are not always a reliable guide to political practice. Over time, all written constitutions require supplementing with conventions or accepted usages, while some parts of a constitution may fall into disuse. Thus even parts of the American constitution (notably the electoral college for choosing a president) are virtually defunct. In the last analysis a constitution offers little protection against individuals or groups who have acquired effective **power** and do not scruple to use it as they see fit. Thus the model constitution of the Soviet Union 1936 bore very little resemblance with the actual practice of government under Stalin, while the model constitution of the German Weimar Republic established after the First World War could not prevent the rise of the Nazi dictatorship.

Most constitutions contain provisions for amendment. Some are relatively flexible and thus fairly easily modified, while others are much more inflexible, with all kinds of built-in safeguards designed to provide checks against hasty ill-considered change. Thus a constitutional amendment commonly requires more than simple majority in a representative assembly, often a two-thirds or three-quarters majority (in both houses

in a bicameral system), with sometimes additional provision for popular approval in a **referendum**. (There is provision for referendums on constitutional changes in, for example, Australia, France, Japan, Spain, and Switzerland). The United Kingdom's unwritten constitution appears extremely flexible, requiring only a simple majority in Parliament, effectively in the House of Commons. Even so, a number of constitutional reforms have been additionally legitimated by referendums (in theory only advisable, but in practice binding).

Federal systems will also require the approval of all or most of the states within the federation. Thus amendments to the US constitution require a two-thirds majority in both houses of Congress and the agreement of three-quarters of the states in their own legislative assemblies. Despite these hurdles, a number of important constitutional amendments have been passed, from the first ten adopted in 1791 (and known as the Bill of Rights), down to the present day.

Constructivism (also social constructivism)

Constructivism is the notion that knowledge does not necessarily reflect some external reality but is socially 'constructed', in other words reflects the particular social and cultural context from which it comes. There is a clear affinity between constructivism and **postmodernism**. Both are relativist theories. A constructivist perspective can be and has been applied to many disciplines (for example, education, psychology, sociology, and cultural studies).

Within political science constructivism has been particularly applied to the study of **international relations**, most notably by Alexander Wendt*. In a key article 'Anarchy Is What States Make of It: The Social Construction of Power Politics' (1992), Wendt showed that some central concepts in **international relations** were socially constructed rather than simply reflecting some objective reality. He applied the argument more systematically in his book *Social Theory of International Politics* (1999), where he emphasised the importance of **identity** and norms in international relations. There are now many International Relations scholars applying constructivism in various ways (Reus-Smit in Burchill et al. 2013). Constructivists argue that international relations are not influenced only by the objective rational material interests of states and rulers but also by the norms, ideas, and identities of political leaders and peoples. These often transcend state borders. Thus, for example, shared ideologies, cultures, or religions may favour friendly relations or formal alliances between states and peoples. Following the terrorist attacks in the United States on 9/11, the importance of culture has become even more evident in international relations, particularly in issues around international **terrorism**.

Corporatism

Corporatism involves incorporating major organised socioeconomic interests into the process of government. What is now sometimes described as liberal corporatism or societal corporatism is generally distinguished from the state corporatism associated particularly with Mussolini's **fascist** state, which involved the functional representation of major economic interests rather than the representation of individual voters through electoral areas (or constituencies). The dictators Salazar (in Portugal) and Franco (in Spain) pursued a variant of this fascist corporatism.

A liberal form of corporatism has been pursued in some democracies in Western Europe in the postwar period, particularly Austria but also to some extent in Germany and Sweden. the United Kingdom, particularly in the 1970s, experimented with a modified version of corporatism, sometimes described as tripartism (decision-making by government, business, and trades unions).

Corporatism stimulated the growth of a formidable academic literature in Europe (less so in the United States). For some, corporatism involved partnership, co-operation, and consensus politics, all deemed beneficial. Corporatism was hailed as an improved system of decision-making and by some even as a new economic system. Although, like **pluralism**, corporatism assumed the representation of interests, corporatism involved the interaction and collaboration of a relatively few 'umbrella' or 'peak' groups rather than the countless multitude of freely competing groups of pluralist theory. Philippe Schmitter (1979) provided an influential distinction between corporatism and pluralism.

Corporatism has been criticised from various perspectives. Some condemned it as a top–down process of decision-making that bypassed parliament and people. Marxists saw it as the response of capitalism to falling profits. Thus, incomes policies involved restraining wage increases to the benefit of business owners at the expense of workers. The **New Right**, by contrast, considered that corporatism conceded too much influence to producer groups, and particularly trade unions, at the expense of consumers and taxpayers.

In the United Kingdom, corporatism was not deemed a success; it was abandoned by the incoming Thatcher government of 1979 and has not been revived since. Other European states have had a more fruitful experience of corporatism over a longer period and have viewed it more favourably.

Corruption

Corruption in general terms means physical and particularly moral decay. In politics it refers to the illicit purchase of influence or favours from politicians or state officials. Thus an offence may be overlooked in return for a bribe, a government post or contract may be secured by financial or other inducements, inside information may be misused for private gain, votes may be bought. In some political systems, corruption appears to be endemic; in others it is assumed to be rare, although some critics suggest that the occasional case in which corruption is found is only the tip of the iceberg. While it may be impossible to eliminate corruption completely, appropriate rules and procedures may limit its extent, although the best safeguard is a **political culture** in which all forms of corruption are regarded as unacceptable.

Culture and political culture

Culture in general terms means the attitudes, beliefs, and values acquired as a consequence of living in a specific human society, as opposed to inborn human nature. State citizens may appear to share a common national culture, although there may be distinctive regional subcultures or other minority cultures, perhaps based on a distinctive religion or language or ethnic background. Sometimes a distinction is drawn between 'high' and 'low' culture or 'elite' and 'mass' (or 'popular') culture.

Political culture refers to the attitudes, beliefs, and values of people that affect their political behaviour. Thus some political communities may appear to be relatively deferential towards authority and officialdom; others much more resistant. Some political cultures may favour active engagement in the political process, while others might incline to political apathy. There may be big differences between political cultures over attitudes to such values as **freedom**, **equality**, social **justice**, or **toleration**. Political culture may have a crucial influence on political behaviour. Thus it has been argued that **democracy** may only thrive within a suitable political culture.

Gabriel Almond* and Sidney Verba (1963, 1980) subjected a range of five national political cultures (USA, the United Kingdom, Mexico, Germany, Italy) to comparative analysis. They suggested that what they called a 'civic culture' (a blend of aspects of the US and UK political cultures) was most compatible with representative democracy. Their work was hugely influential but also attracted criticism, (the neglect of divergent subcultures within nations, for example).

Because the concept of political culture seemed difficult to operationalise, it subsequently somewhat fell from favour. However, more recently, interest in it has revived. Ronald Inglehart* (1971, 1990) has detected a significant shift among the younger generation in postindustrial societies towards 'post-material' values, with significant political implications. The work of Robert Putnam* on **social capital** (e.g. 1995, 2000, 2002) also seems to belong under the broad heading of political culture. Moreover, those researching **democratisation** have rediscovered the importance of political culture for consolidating and stabilising new democracies.

Decentralisation

Decentralisation within a state normally involves the transfer of **power** downwards from central government to regional or local institutions. Sometimes a distinction is drawn between political **devolution**, involving a transfer of power to elected regional or local authorities, and administrative decentralisation, which is widely assumed to be beneficial. Thus governments often promise to decentralise and give more power to local people over their own lives or more authority to 'front-line' workers.

Yet decentralisation can have a downside. Where real discretion is given to local politicians or officials, one inescapable consequence is variations in decisions and service levels. Thus effective decentralisation can detract from the ideal of social justice – that all state citizens in the same circumstances should be treated equally. Indeed, one consequence of decentralised decision-making is the growth of complaints about a 'postcode lottery', where the level of service or even the availability of a service depends on where one lives.

Democracy, direct democracy and representative democracy

Democracy means government by the people, or in Abraham Lincoln's slightly expanded formula, 'government of the people, by the people, for the people'. A form of democracy existed in ancient Athens in the 5th century BCE. Athenian democracy excluded women, resident foreigners, and slaves, but it also, more positively, involved direct citizen participation in government. This system of **direct democracy** was memorably eulogised in words put into the mouth of the great Athenian statesman Pericles* by the historian Thucydides*. It was criticised by Plato*, who castigated democracy as the rule of the ignorant.

Such direct democracy, feasible for small city states, was scarcely practical for the more extensive states of later centuries. Thus until the late 18th century democracy scarcely existed anywhere and was widely perceived as undesirable as well as impractical. Even those who, like Rousseau*, advocated democracy were extremely pessimistic over its prospects.

Representative democracy was the form of democracy that emerged in the 19th century and became the system widely, almost universally, approved by the end of the 20th century. This involved government not by the people themselves but by the elected representatives of the people. Representative democracy was advocated by such thinkers as Tom Paine* and Jeremy Bentham* and implemented in the newly independent United States, whose democracy was sympathetically described by the French aristocrat Alexis de Tocqueville*, although he raised some concerns over the potential 'tyranny of the majority', as well as the treatment of black slaves and native Americans.

In leading Western countries the vote was extended to most adult men in the course of the 19th century and to women from the early 20th century. Not everyone accepted that the right to vote meant that real **power** was effectively transferred from the few to the many. **Marxists** continued to argue that even in parliamentary systems, political power reflected economic power, which remained highly concentrated. Classical **elitists**, such as Pareto*, Mosca*, and Michels*, argued that power was still held by the few, and ridiculed the notion of rule by the people. Joseph Schumpeter* (1943) subsequently attempted to redefine democracy as a limited choice between alternatives promoted by political leaders, in an approach described by David Held (2006) as 'competitive elitism'. Others, from John Stuart Mill* to Carole Pateman* have advocated a more participatory democracy and active **citizenship** that goes well beyond just registering a vote in infrequent elections. Indeed, pluralists such as Robert Dahl* argued that power was more effectively dispersed through the activities of countless pressure groups. One formal mechanism for giving more direct power to the people is through using the **referendum** (used quite often in some democracies such as Switzerland), plebiscite, or initiative (in some US states).

Despite periodic challenges from other versions of democracy, Western-style 'representative' or 'parliamentary' democracy has become the generally approved model. This suggests the necessary conditions for democracy are regular, free and fair elections, contested by competing parties and individual candidates. These conditions are not always met. In some countries elections are patently rigged, party competition limited or absent, and voters denied an effective choice. Elsewhere there are on-going debates over electoral systems and party finances.

A focus on the mechanics of elections implies that democracy is all about process, although it is also widely assumed that democracy entails some core values, such as individual **freedom** (including freedom of expression), **toleration** of dissent and minority opinions, political and legal **equality**. Yet if democracy means simply the rule of the people or the rule of the majority of the people, it does not necessarily follow that the majority will tolerate the views and behaviour of minorities.

Democratisation

Democratisation is the process of extending and consolidating **democracy**. Samuel Huntington* (1991) has identified three main periods or 'waves' of democratisation (with intervening 'reverse waves') over the last century or so. While most countries and most peoples now live under systems that are described as democratic, 'new democracies' have not always been successfully consolidated and stabilised. There are continuing questions over the extent to which many 'new' and some 'mature' democracies fulfil the basic criteria of a liberal representative democracy. The term 'illiberal democracies' or 'imitation democracies' is sometimes applied to these political systems (see P. Anderson 2015).

Devolution

Devolution involves the delegation of powers by an upper level of government to a lower level. Unlike **federalism,** devolution, in theory, does not involve any transfer or division of **sovereignty**. Devolution was the term used to describe the transfer of powers by the United Kingdom government to representative assemblies in Scotland, Wales, and Northern Ireland. Devolution is also an appropriate term to describe the introduction of regional political institutions in other unitary states (e.g. Spain) wishing to avoid a fully federal system.

One motive for introducing devolution is to satisfy peripheral nationalist pressures within a state. However, **nationalism** normally involves demands for sovereign independence rather than simply more autonomy, and it is questionable whether devolution will satisfy the national sentiment of (for example) many Scots or Basques. Thus some critics fear (while others hope) that devolution involves a slippery slope towards the disintegration of states such as the United Kingdom or Spain.

In theory, as sovereignty is not transferred, **power** devolved is power that might be recalled. Indeed, the United Kingdom government has several times suspended devolved institutions and resumed direct rule in Northern Ireland. However, it would appear politically difficult if not impossible for the United Kingdom government to reverse devolution in Scotland and Wales (except in the unlikely event of this becoming the settled preference of the Scots and the Welsh). Indeed all the pressures are the other way, to devolve more powers. Thus some argue that the United Kingdom is already a quasi-federal state, and the sovereignty of the Westminster Parliament effectively dead. (See also **decentralisation**.)

Dictators and dictatorship

'Dictatorship' is today a term used to describe the absolute rule of a single individual, who has seized **power** (generally unlawfully) and exercises it unconstrained by constitutional or other checks. The term originated in the time of the Roman Republic when, however, dictatorial powers were initially granted only for a limited period to deal with a specific emergency and the dictator could be called to account subsequently. Since then the term has been more commonly used for those who have taken power by force of arms. In the 20th century some of the most notorious rulers widely described as dictators, such as Mussolini, Hitler, and Stalin, owed their position not to the support of the army but to their effective exploitation of modern mass communication to win and retain substantial popular support. This arguably enabled them to exercise power more extensively and completely than dictators in the past. (See also **totalitarianism**.)

The term 'dictatorship of the proletariat' was coined by Marx* to suggest the need for a temporary period of class rule after a socialist revolution to prevent counter-revolution. The term was later used by Lenin* to justify his own concept of democratic centralism and subsequently, after the Bolshevik revolution, the exclusion of other parties from the political system.

Ecology, ecologism

(See under **environmentalism**, **ecologism**, and **green thinking**.)

Election

Elections have become the most widely used method of choosing those who are to exercise responsibilities of government at different levels around the world. While the vote or franchise was in the past often restricted to those with a property qualification, it is now, in modern parliamentary democracies, exercised by all adults of both sexes. It is now also generally assumed that elections should be free from intimidation and bribery and fair in the sense that, as far as possible, all votes should count equally, although this depends on the electoral system used. Thus the United Kingdom and USA both use a single member, simple plurality (or 'first past the post') system that does not lead to a close correspondence between votes cast and seats won. Other electoral systems involving more proportional representation ensure a much closer correspondence between votes cast and electoral seats won, but the results may make it difficult to form and maintain a stable government if many smaller parties are represented in the parliament or assembly, so some systems have a minimum threshold (e.g. 5% in Germany) for votes to secure assembly seats.

Elites and elitism

An elite is any small group in society that by virtue of some attributes or qualities (real or imagined) has prestige, political influence, and **power** beyond its numerical strength. An elite group may in practice be a priesthood, a traditional hereditary **aristocracy**, a military caste who have acquired power and prestige through their control of weapons, organisation, and expertise, a business elite who have gained wealth and influence through trade or manufacturing, or a **meritocracy** whose influence is based on education and formal qualifications.

Elitism is the belief that political power is effectively concentrated in the hands of elites, or a single elite, even if it is formally controlled by, or accountable to, the whole people or the majority of the people. Thus real power, even in a state that is supposed to be democratic, is effectively in the hands of the few rather than the many. For some elite theorists, such as Pareto*, elitism is not only an inescapable fact of political life but is also a normative principle: power should be in the hands of the few. For radical elite theorists (e.g. Mills*) the concentration of power in the hands of elites in modern democracies is wrong and should be ended. [See also the discussion of elitism and pluralism in Part II, Section 2.]

Empiricism

Empiricism is the philosophic and scientific doctrine that all knowledge is derived from the direct experience of the senses. Theories and hypotheses require testing by repeated observation and experiment. Locke*, Berkeley, and Hume* were three key figures in what is known as the British empirical tradition. The empirical approach underpinned the subsequent development of **positivism**, **behaviouralism**, and modern Western political science.

Empiricism is often linked with induction or inductive reasoning – inferring a general rule from a number of particular instances – as opposed to deduction – deriving logical conclusions from initial assumptions. Empiricism is also sometimes associated with **pragmatism**, which emphasises the importance of practical application ('what matters is what works') rather than relying on abstract theory.

Environmentalism, ecologism, and green thinking

Environmentalism is one of the labels (other labels include ecologism and green thinking) used to describe the political ideology that places a special priority on the protection of the environment. Although the roots of environmentalism can be traced back a long way, it is essentially a new ideology that has only acquired political significance over the last half century or so. It has articulated a number of specific concerns (over, for example, population growth, resource conservation, environmental pollution, and animal rights) and woven these into a coherent and distinctive political philosophy. Greens place the environment at the centre of their political philosophy; they are ecocentric. Mainstream ideologies are anthropocentric. They focus on the presumed interests, needs, or rights of humankind or a particular section of human society. Environmentalists focus instead on the planet.

The environmental movement has spawned a number of influential green pressure groups (such as Friends of the Earth and Greenpeace) and green parties. These have had considerable success in alerting people to the dangers of specific problems such as unrestricted population growth, depletion of nonrenewable energy sources, irreversible pollution of the environment, and climate change. Some of this has impacted on mainstream ideologies and parties, to the extent that these have acquired a greenish tinge and incorporated some green policy proposals. Yet green parties and pressure groups,, have generally dismissed these as too little, too late.

Green parties have won some electoral support, most notably in Germany where the Green Party was briefly a junior partner in a coalition government. Elsewhere they have had less impact. They have a difficult message to sell, which is at odds with prevailing political assumptions about the pursuit of individual or group or class interests. There are some internal differences among greens over the compatibility of environmental preservation with economic growth and living standards. Greens assume some restrictions on growth at least, and many greens concede that it will involve what most people would see as a reduction in their standard of living, with less air travel and less car use. Most political parties promise to make people better off. Greens, in effect, are promising to make them materially worse off to prevent a catastrophe others think may not happen, or at least may not affect them in the foreseeable future, if at all. Environmentalists also express concerns for interests that have no vote and no voice, for generations yet unborn, for other species, for planet earth. It is difficult to see how these interests can be taken into account in the current economic and political marketplace, unless humans show far more altruism than social science models of their motivation and behaviour generally assume.

Equality

'Liberty, equality, and fraternity' was the celebrated slogan of the French Revolution. There was some potential for conflict among these principles, particularly between **liberty** and **equality**. Thus increasing equality might entail some restraint on individual freedom, while increasing freedom might lead to more inequality. Separately, each of these principles was problematic, but **equality** has been the most contested.

It had long been argued by some political thinkers (including Hobbes*) that all men were equal in their original condition, or state of nature. Religious texts suggested that all were equal in the sight of God. **Liberals** went on to argue that all men (and later women) were, or should be, equal before the law, and some went on to demand equal political rights, including the right to vote and stand for election. Yet formal legal and political equality have not ensured that everyone in practice is treated equally before the law, and certainly has not entailed guaranteed equal political influence. Thus although women in many countries now enjoy the same rights as men to vote and stand for political office, they remain substantially underrepresented in politics and government almost everywhere.

Both **conservatives** and liberals stress equality of opportunity, rather than equality of outcome. Indeed they defend substantial inequality of outcome, as this provides incentives and rewards for effort and initiative. Equality of opportunity amounts to the opportunity to become unequal. This may result in a **meritocracy**: those who deserve to succeed will do so. Those who show greater ability, energy, and initiative will be appropriately rewarded. Yet in practice this is a race in which the competitors do not start equal. Conservatives stress the right to bequeath and inherit property and commonly rail against inheritance taxes. They also defend the right of parents to purchase a better education for their children. While these are advantages that in theory could be removed, it would be virtually impossible to eliminate all the advantages of nature and nurture that ensure some children have a far better chance of success than others.

While conservatives and liberals defend inequality, **socialists** argue for equality and social justice. Indeed, equality is perhaps the term most associated with socialism. Socialists point to the massive inequality existing in almost all societies and advocate for a substantial redistribution of income and wealth, either through revolution, or more gradual reform. Yet while a few socialists and **anarchists** have championed the total abolition of private property and the equal rights of all to the fruits of the earth, most socialists and social democrats have argued not for communism, nor for absolute equality, but greater equality. As critics such as Hayek* have observed, absolute equality at least provides a clear criterion for the socialist planner, while the goal of 'greater equality' provides no practical guidance for distributing income.

How far socialists have succeeded in their aim of making society more equal is debatable. Socialist revolutions have commonly involved a substantial redistribution of income and wealth, although critics suggest they have created new forms of inequality. The evolutionary social democratic route appeared to achieve some more modest redistribution over time through the tax and benefits system, particularly in the decades immediately following the Second World War, but more recently inequality has grown, even in countries with social democratic governments (see the analysis of Piketty 2014, among others).

Radical critics today place more emphasis on global inequality, the massive differences in living standards between societies rather than within them. While such differences existed in the past, they are now far better documented and far more publicised. The consequences of this inequality are more dramatic. In many countries people suffer from absolute rather relative poverty, lacking basic necessities. This global inequality involves the danger of further humanitarian disasters, as well as threats to peace and the environment. Yet tackling global inequality seems far more difficult than tackling inequality within countries.

Ethnicity and ethnic minorities

The definition of 'ethnicity', and how far it can be distinguished from terms such as '**nation**', '**community**', and (most contentious of all) '**race**' is problematic. The term 'race' long involved the now totally discredited notion of biological differences among humans. The term 'ethnicity' refers not to biological but to cultural differences between communities, relating to their origins and development over time, involving distinctive language, beliefs, customs and traditions. Thus Jews may be considered to constitute an ethnic group and a distinctive

ethnic minority in many states (and an ethnic majority in the state of Israel). Minority religious groups or those speaking a different language may be regarded as an ethnic minority.

Commonly, a relatively recent immigrant minority might be considered a distinctive ethnic group. Thus Italians, Poles, or Greeks who have settled in the United States might be regarded as **ethnic minorities**, although the term is most commonly applied to those distinguished by skin colour (e.g. black or Asian) or religion (e.g. Muslim). While an ethnic group may be defined by others, it may also be defined by its own members, who may passionately assert their own distinctive identity. Such an ethnic identity may be compatible with loyalty to the state, particularly a multicultural state. Hyphenated or multiple identities (e.g. Irish-American, French-Canadian, Muslim-British) might be regarded as an increasingly common phenomenon in the modern world. However, members of a distinctive ethnic group that dominates a particular geographical area may indeed regard themselves as a separate nation and demand political independence (although this is not an easy option for more widely dispersed ethnic minorities).

Executive

In the study of politics the executive is the branch of the state responsible for day-to-day government. Thus it administers laws and determines and executes policy, including responsibility for defence and foreign relations. The executive functions of the state are distinguished from the **legislative** or law-making functions, and from the **judicial**, or law adjudicating functions under the influential ideal of the '**separation of powers**'. In many countries the separation of powers is imperfect in practice, and in some dictatorships and totalitarian systems it does not exist even in theory.

In democracies the executive is normally either directly elected or emerges from, and is responsible to, an elected parliament or assembly. The executive can be a single person (who may be called president), but it can also be a committee or cabinet (a plural executive), perhaps headed by a leading minister or prime minister but in theory involving 'collective responsibility' for policy.

Generally, the form of the executive and the powers of the executive (and limitations to those powers) are spelt out in a state's constitution. Thus the American constitution vests executive power in the president, describes how the president is elected and the limits to the president's term of office, and sets out the president's most important functions.

The US president both is the formal head of state and holds real executive power. In many other countries (e.g. the United Kingdom, the Netherlands, Sweden, Spain, Germany, Ireland, Italy) the role of formal head of state (sometimes a constitutional monarch, more commonly a directly or indirectly elected president) is separated from the effective executive. Thus the ceremonial head of state does not control the government. France (under the constitution of the Fifth French Republic) unusually has what is sometimes described as a dual executive, with a directly elected president with real powers (particularly in foreign affairs), and a parliamentary executive headed by a prime minister. In the United Kingdom, which lacks a written constitution, the executive is generally identified with the cabinet, but the growth of prime ministerial power suggests to some critics a quasi-presidential system, while others define a broader 'core-executive', covering the cabinet, junior ministers, leading civil servants and advisers.

Fascism and Nazism

Fascism is the name of a political ideology that had antecedents but essentially developed in Italy at the end of the First World War and spread to other countries, particularly in Europe and South America. The name 'fascism' was derived from 'fasces', the bundle of rods carried as a symbol of **authority** by the lictors in ancient Rome. The name and symbol was adopted by the former socialist Benito Mussolini, whose fascist party came to power following the so-called March on Rome in 1922, amid the confused state of parliamentary democracy in postwar Italy.

Mussolini soon established a one-party state, with himself as 'Duce' or leader. His fascist state appeared to restore order, achieved some initial success in foreign policy and economic policy, and won some admiration abroad.

Fascism was presented as a new and distinctive political philosophy, offering a 'middle way' between **capitalism** and revolutionary **socialism**. As such, it appealed particularly to those classes in society, particularly the lower middle classes and peasants, apparently threatened on the one hand by big business and on the other by militant trade unionism and socialism. Mussolini made much of his brand of '**corporatism**', involving the functional rather than the territorial representation of interests. These corporations combined employers and workers, (whose old free trade unions were banned). Mussolini also emphasised total allegiance to the **state** (see **totalitarianism**). More obvious elements of fascism included aggressive **nationalism**, **militarism**, and **dictatorship**. Mussolini sought to build a new 'Roman Empire' with himself at its head. This culminated in the Italian invasion of Abyssinia and the alliance with Hitler's Nazi Germany.

Among scholars there is some disagreement as to how far **Nazism** can be distinguished from fascism. Nazism shared many of the characteristics of fascism but added virulent racism and particularly anti-Semitism, initially not shared by Mussolini but subsequently imitated by him. Thus Nazism and fascism became, in effect, a single creed, diametrically opposed to **liberalism** and **democracy**. Fascist and quasi-fascist movements appeared in many other countries, although in Europe these mostly only came to power briefly as a result of external pressure or occupation. Even so, liberal democracy seemed in general retreat between the wars, and the main threat came from the fascist **right** rather than from the **communist left**.

There is further debate over whether fascism in some shape or form survived its defeat in 1945. Certainly, quasi-fascist regimes survived for a time in Spain and Portugal and periodically flourished in South

America. Subsequently 'neo-fascist' movements have won some significant support in several countries more recently – in Italy, Germany, France, and Greece. These place an emphasis on some familiar fascist ideas – including the cult of **leadership** and extreme **nationalism**. However, little remains of Mussolini's own conception of fascism, which has become simply a generalised term of political abuse. The core element of the various neo-Nazi and neo-fascist movements, and the only element that remains significant is **racism**, sometimes still directed against Jews but more often against blacks and Asians and generally against immigration.

Federalism

Federalism involves the division of supreme power or sovereignty in a state between two or more levels of government, each of which is (in theory) supreme in its own sphere. Commonly, there is a federal government responsible for the interests of the federation as a whole and in addition governments for each of the states that belong to the federation. Thus a federal system virtually requires a written **constitution** laying down the powers and responsibilities of each level of government. For example, in the American Constitution the powers of the federal institutions are outlined, reserving all other functions to the constituent states and the people. In practice there are commonly ambiguities and tensions over respective responsibilities. In many federal systems it appears over time that more power accrues to the federal government at the expense of the states. In some others the federal authority is relatively weak and the states exercise most key functions.

Federalism is an attractive solution where close co-operation between states or peoples is needed for their mutual defence or to yield economies of scale in production and trade, but where religious, linguistic, or other cultural divisions between peoples render closer union impractical and potentially damaging for minorities. (Examples include Switzerland, Canada, Belgium, Germany,

and Brazil.) In many countries today there are pressures to devolve more power or allow more autonomy to regions, and where these are conceded a 'quasi-federal' system may develop (examples currently include Spain and the United Kingdom). The term federalism is also often applied to the European Union, in a way that appears unproblematic to member states used to federal arrangements within their own countries but appeared threatening to the United Kingdom. (See also **devolution**.)

Feminism

Feminists seek women's liberation from male domination or **patriarchy**. Like other ideologies, feminism involves a critique, an ideal, and a programme. The critique contains an analysis of the discrimination and injustices suffered by women in existing society. The ideal is justice for women, generally but not exclusively interpreted to mean full **equality** between the sexes. The practical programme has included action to secure for women political and legal **rights**, equality in the economic sphere, the elimination of sexual discrimination in education and the workplace, a more equitable division of domestic and child-rearing duties, and protection against physical and sexual violence.

Literature on feminism commonly refers to 'waves' of feminism. The first wave extended roughly from the late 18th century to the 1920s, culminating in many Western states with the extension of legal and political rights to women, in particular the right to vote. The second wave of feminism, from the 1960s onwards, focused on the continuing discrimination still suffered by women in practice despite their formal legal and political equality. More recently, scholars have described a third and a fourth wave of feminism. The older literature also distinguished between three main types of feminism: liberal feminism, Marxist (or socialist) feminism, and radical feminism.

Early liberal feminists, such as Mary Wollstonecraft*, Elizabeth Cady Stanton and John Stuart Mill*, applied liberal theory by extending the 'rights of man' to women, demanding their full equality. Liberal feminists were ultimately successful in securing formal legal rights for women and some practical advances, particularly for a minority of educated middle-class women enabled to compete in a man's world. They have been criticised for accepting essentially male values and concentrating on the 'public sphere' of law, politics, and employment, while largely neglecting women's role in the private world of home and family, which is to many feminists the very centre of women's exploitation and subordination.

Socialist feminists such as Juliet Mitchell and Michelle Barratt employed Marxist methodology to explain the subordination of women in modern capitalist society. The unpaid domestic labour performed by women was related to the requirements of **capitalism**. As part of the paid workforce women could also be used as an 'industrial reserve army of labour' to swell the ranks of workers in times of boom and to undercut the wages of male workers. It followed that the emancipation of women could only be achieved with the abolition of capitalism and the **bourgeois** relations between the sexes associated with capitalism. Socialist feminists sought to reverse the inequality and discrimination women faced in work, campaigning to involve women in trade unions and to secure the provision of nurseries and workplace crèches. Some advocated wages for housework. Socialist feminists have been criticised for assuming women's exploitation was a function of capitalism, and that therefore the gender issue was secondary to the class issue, and for their relative neglect of the domestic sphere.

Radical feminists such as Kate Millett*, Germaine Greer*, Andrea Dworkin*, and Catherine MacKinnon* focused on the concept of **patriarchy** to argue that the problem for women was not essentially an inadequate political and legal framework, nor capitalism, but simply men and male power. For radicals it was the sex war rather than the class war that was fundamental. At its heart were the everyday relations between men and women in the home, family, and bedroom. This involved not so much a retreat from politics as a deliberate widening

of the political sphere, as implied in the radical feminist slogan 'The personal is political'. A key target was violence against women, particularly rape, including rape within marriage, and pornography, which appeared to legitimise the degradation of women. Influenced by **postmodernism**, some radicals argued strongly that language and literature reflected an orthodox 'malestream' discourse that diminishes women. Radical campaigns changed attitudes and significantly influenced the portrayal of women in the media, although some women were alienated by their criticisms of traditional feminine tastes, the family and motherhood. Radical feminists have also sometimes been accused of universalising their own circumstances as typical of women everywhere, overlooking the very different needs and problems of women from different cultures.

Among the diverse strands of modern feminism may be included such categories as black feminism, eco-feminism, linking environmentalism with the caring, nurturing role of women, and the so-called new feminism, articulated by Natasha Walter (1999) among others. She criticises the radicals for reinforcing the hostile stereotype of feminists as lesbian man-haters and for rejecting fashionable clothes and make-up, which Walter argues can help to make women feel good and thus empower them. Germaine Greer has dismissed these new feminists as 'lipstick feminists'.

Freedom or liberty

Freedom or liberty has long been a key political concept, and an inspiring political ideal. 'Give me liberty or give me death!' the American revolutionary Patrick Henry declaimed in 1775. In contrast to the unfree slave or serf, a free citizen appears to have control over his or her own life. State **constitutions** and international charters of human **rights** spell out specific freedoms, commonly including freedom of speech, freedom of religion, and freedom to own, obtain, and dispose of property. But liberty is not license to do as one pleases, regardless of harm to others. While **liberals** and **socialists** tend to an optimistic view of the capacity of humans to pursue their interests rationally and peacefully with only limited external control, **conservatives** have more generally assumed that most humans are inherently quarrelsome, governed by the passions rather than reason, and thus require strong **government** and the rule of **law**, vigorously enforced, to keep them in order.

Isaiah Berlin* famously distinguished between two kinds of liberty: negative, involving essentially freedom *from* external control, and positive, involving freedom *to* enjoy something worth enjoying and fulfil one's own potential. Older liberals such as Herbert Spencer* and **neoliberals** such as Hayek* have championed the freedom of the individual from interference or oppression (including government oppression). However, progressive or 'new' liberals such as T. H. Green* and Leonard Hobhouse*, as well as **socialists** and **social democrats**, support the notion of positive freedom to enjoy the benefits of employment, housing, health, and especially education to enable people to develop their true potential. Yet, of course, the freedom of all to enjoy these benefits entails increased state intervention and at the very least a heavier burden of taxation, which reduces the freedom of individuals to choose what to do with their own money.

Although liberals assume that freedom is highly desirable, some thinkers, such as Erich Fromm, have expressed the notion of a psychological 'fear of freedom', arguing that freedom creates uncertainty and anxiety. Similarly, Theodore Adorno* described the 'authoritarian personality' of those who prefer a framework of **leadership**, order and obedience, without freedom of choice. Such notions may help to explain why millions appeared willing to surrender democratic freedoms to follow without question leaders such as Mussolini* and Hitler*.

Free market

A free market is a market free from interference by state governments or by monopoly powers. Thus the free market assumes unrestrained competition. For **liberals** and **neoliberals** only a free market is compatible with economic efficiency and growth, but it is also seen as a key element of individual freedom. **Conservatives** have sometimes been prepared to justify interference with the free market to protect some interests or preserve social harmony and stability, for example advocating protection and 'fair trade' rather than 'free trade'. **Socialists** have commonly sought to interfere with free market forces to secure objectives such as full employment, greater equality, and social justice and have claimed that state planning is more efficient. They would also argue that state provision of services can enlarge freedom.

Gender

Although the terms 'gender' and 'sex' are often used interchangeably, most **feminists** make a clear distinction between them. While 'sex' refers to the physical or biological differences between men and women, 'gender' describes the socially and culturally conditioned roles of men and women. Thus assumptions about men's and women's different nature, aptitudes, potential, rights, and duties are part of socially conditioned expectations of different gender roles, rather than biologically determined. The inferior position of women, compared to men, in many fields of employment and in politics, is a consequence of assumed gender differences rather than real biological differences. Similarly, women's considerably greater burden in child rearing and caring for elderly or infirm relatives arises from socially conditioned expectations of gender roles rather than biological differences. Increasingly gender perspectives are utilised to understand **international relations** (Enloe*). For many feminists, gender is the most fundamental social and political division, more important than social **class** or **ethnicity**. Thus feminists seek gender equality.

Yet while most feminists deny that there are any socially or politically significant differences between men and women and that the two sexes are substantially similar, some feminists are prepared to assert that women *are* different, not just physically but mentally. They argue women may be less aggressive, more co-operative than men, more sharing and caring (with implications for the social and political roles). Some leading male political theorists (for example Plato*, Rousseau*, and Mill*) have speculated on male and female nature. The same/difference debate among feminists has brought a new dimension to this old argument.

Globalisation

Globalisation has become an extremely important but contentious concept in the study of politics. It refers to the increasing impact of global trends and pressures on the lives of everyone, transcending state borders (and some would even argue, making the **nation-state** obsolete) and creating a globalised economy and culture. Important manifestations of globalisation include increasing global communications (creating what Marshall McLuhan* described as a 'global village'), expanding international trade and investment, the increased recognition of the global impact of environmental pollution and the exploitation of scarce resources. The growing power and influence of **transnational enterprises** (TNCs) and a range of **nongovernmental organisations** (NGOs) and international institutions appear to have significant implications for the politics of the nation-state. Global **terrorism** is the latest manifestation of the globalisation of politics.

Although globalisation is often presented as a very recent phenomenon (the concept is not included in older dictionaries of politics), Marx* in the mid-19th century drew attention to the global impact of industrial **capitalism**, anticipating some of the concerns expressed about global capitalism in the modern world. Globalisation may have intensified more recently and its effects may be more widely recognised, but it is hardly new. National economies have long been subject to events and trends in the wider world over which state governments have little or no control. The economic depression initiated with local bank failures in 1929 rapidly became an international phenomenon whose consequences were felt in remote relatively undeveloped states and colonies. Similarly governments have often in the past found it difficult to resist the impact of political developments outside their borders. Thus rulers found it difficult to immunise their countries from religious reformations in the 16th and 17th centuries and political revolution in the 19th century.

Yet if globalisation is not new, its impact has increased and it has become more evident, particularly perhaps following the end of the Cold War and the apparent victory of the values of liberal capitalism. Some would argue that the politics of the nation-state is effectively obsolete. State governments cannot ignore or withstand global economic developments. They may appear to be at the mercy of decisions of transnational corporations, some of which have a greater market value than the national income of many nation-states. Individual state governments are also increasingly subject to international and transnational institutions, such as the World Trade Organisation, the World Bank, and the G8 group of leading states.

Nonetheless some would argue that the impact of globalisation has been exaggerated. States retain considerable power and significant autonomy. Global capitalism has not obliged states to abandon welfare provision or significant economic regulation. International institutions are created by states and can only succeed if states continue to support them. Large and powerful states can ignore them. Nongovernmental organisations may influence opinions but have little power or authority unless state governments choose to acknowledge them.

There may be a range of massive global problems that require co-operation on a global scale if they are to be tackled effectively. Such problems include global warming and other actual or potential environmental threats, global poverty and inequality, nuclear proliferation, global terrorism, as well as the more long-standing threats of famine, disease, and war. Yet effective international co-operation and strong international institutions are not created by the existence of a need for them. There has been some resurgence of interest in notions of world government and global democracy, but although these may be desirable ideals, they seem a long way from current reality. Indeed, hostility to globalising trends has been one factor in the appeal of the politics of ethnic and religious identity. [See also discussion of globalisation in Part II, Section 4.]

Government and governance

To govern is to exercise control over others, and some form of **government** can be identified in any organisation. In the study of politics the term is particularly applied to the formal institutions for maintaining public order and making, executing, and adjudicating on laws in any state. Yet in popular usage the term 'government' is used more narrowly to mean only the **executive**, while 'the Government' is used to describe those individuals who constitute the executive at any particular time. Both terms are most commonly used to describe the national or central government, but it is accepted that government may take place at various levels within a **state**, such as federal, state, regional, and local government.

While the need for government of some kind is widely acknowledged (although not by **anarchists**), there is considerable disagreement over both the scope of government (extensive or strictly limited) and the form of government. The government of states can take many forms. Greek thinkers identified three main types: the rule of one (**monarchy**), the rule of the few (**oligarchy**), and rule of the people (**democracy**), with many subvariants. Government may be characterised as legitimate or illegitimate, constitutional or unconstitutional, limited or absolute. Key liberal concepts implying legitimate, and limited (or constitutional) government include the notion of government by consent, and the separation of (**executive**, **legislative**, and **judicial**) powers.

'Governance' has sometimes been used simply as a synonym for government, but it has become a fashionable term to describe the process of governing rather than the institutions of government (Osborne and Gaebler 1992). Governance blurs the distinctions between governors and governed, the public and private sectors, the **state** and **civil society**, because we are all more or less involved in that process. It implies the delegation, **decentralisation**, and fragmentation of power rather than the concentration of sovereign authority in the hands of a single national government within a unitary state. The term 'governance' is compatible with partnerships, networks, and other forms of collaborative activity rather than the unified chain of command and control associated with much traditional government. The term 'multilevel governance' suggests that these processes can and perhaps should take place at different levels.

Hegemony

The term 'hegemony' has been used to describe any form of dominant influence, for example of one state over another. **Marxists**, following Antonio Gramsci* have used the term more specifically to describe the ascendancy one **class** may acquire over other classes, not just from its ownership and control of economic resources but though the permeation of its dominant **culture** and **ideology** throughout society. Thus, subordinate classes accept the perspective of the dominant class and regard it as their own. This cultural and intellectual hegemony allows the dominant class to rule by apparent **consent** rather than coercion. In **International Relations** the term is used in two ways. (Neo) **Realists** define a hegemon as a **state** that dominates a particular region and can impose its will on other states because of its economic and military power. Robert Cox*'s reinterpretation of the concept of hegemony has been important in providing a critical understanding of **international political economy**.

Human nature

Human nature refers to the inborn characteristics of human beings, as opposed to those produced by upbringing, education, and social conditioning. Thus 'nature' is contrasted with 'nurture'. Underpinning most perspectives on politics are sometimes implicit, but often explicit, assumptions about human nature. Aristotle* assumed that men were by nature social and political animals and that the **state** (or political community) also exists by nature. However, many later political thinkers posited a (historical or hypothetical) 'state of nature' before the emergence of society or government. Hobbes* reckoned that humans were aggressively competitive and hypothesised an original 'state of nature' involving a war of every man against every man. Rousseau*, by contrast, viewed the 'state of nature' with some regrets. His 'noble savage' was free from social and political constraints and was capable of pity and sympathy for his fellow creatures.

Assumptions about human nature underpin ideological perspectives. **Liberals** see humans as self-interested and competitive but also rational and enlightened. They assume that the pursuit of enlightened self-interest by individuals will promote the greatest common good (an assumption shared by modern **rational choice** theorists). **Conservatives** are more sceptical about the capacity of most humans to be guided by reason, rather than passion or emotion, and commonly perceive a need for **authority** and strong government to control the evil streak (or 'original sin', from a Christian perspective) in humanity. Yet, in marked contrast to liberal individualism, conservatives also emphasise the family, **community**, and national ties that bind people together in mutual dependence and solidarity. **Socialists** similarly stress the social nature of humankind, rejecting liberal **individualism**. They are more hopeful than conservatives about human capacity for fruitful co-operation for the common good. Selfish competitive behaviour is seen as the product of **capitalism**, rather than a universal human characteristic. **Anarchists** optimistically assume that humans could live together peacefully and co-operatively without the coercive and corrupting role of government. **Fascists** make some fairly cynical assumptions about the pliability of ordinary human beings and the potential for their manipulation.

Many older writers commonly referred to the nature of 'man', either ignoring women or tacitly assuming that male and female natures were fundamentally similar. Yet some political theorists did suggest that women's nature was markedly different from men's. Indeed, this assumed difference between the sexes was commonly used to justify refusing women political and other rights. To counter such arguments in his own day, John Stuart Mill* maintained that 'what is now called the nature of women is an eminently artificial thing – the result of forced repression in some directions, unnatural stimulation in others' (Mill [1869] 1988, 22). Yet while liberal feminists tacitly assumed there were no significant differences between male and female nature, some modern radical feminists have been more ready to assert that aggression and violence are essentially male characteristics, while women are naturally more caring and sharing (see also **gender**).

Idealism

Idealism in philosophy and political theory is contrasted with **materialism**, **empiricism** and, in **international relations** theory, with **realism**.

Plato* argued that knowledge involved understanding perfect unchanging ideals or forms, rather than the imperfect transient world of our sense perception. Thus his ideal state, explored in *The Republic*, was for Plato more 'real' than actual imperfect states, subject to constant change and decay. Kant* and Hegel* similarly denied the empiricist claim that real knowledge of the world could only be derived from experience, assuming instead that there were eternal values and ideals that could be validated by human consciousness.

In politics 'idealism' is associated with the pursuit of abstract ideals or principles and is contrasted with '**pragmatism**'. Some argue that politicians and parties should be guided by clear ideals and principles, rather than by pragmatism. By contrast, policies are sometimes castigated for being 'too idealistic' or 'unrealistic'. In **international relations** the label 'idealist' has been attached to those **liberals** who sought to end war and promote international harmony through the development of international law, collective security, and the establishment of international institutions. To 'realists' such as E. H. Carr* and Hans Morgenthau* this involved a naïve neglect of the reality of international **anarchy**, conflicting national interests, and **power**.

Identity and Identity Politics

Subjective or felt identity may be contrasted with the supposedly more objective categories employed by statisticians, social and political scientists, such as occupational class. Such felt identities may have a greater influence on political behaviour than more material interests. Thus it is suggested that in some political communities felt identities based, for example, on ethnicity, gender, religion, or language, are replacing class loyalties or material interests. (However, some may still identify strongly with a particular social class.)

Ideology

The term 'ideology' is problematic and contested. Ideology may be loosely defined as any system of ideas directing political action. The key words here are 'system' and 'action'. An ideology involves firstly an interconnected set of ideas that forms a perspective on the world – what the Germans call *Weltanschauung* (world outlook). Secondly, ideologies have implications for political behaviour – they are 'action-oriented'.

Political ideologies normally contain three key elements: an analysis of existing social and political arrangements, a political ideal or vision of the future (that for some might involve a return to the past!), and a strategy for realising that ideal. However, the balance among these three elements inevitably depends on the extent of satisfaction with the current state of affairs and of optimism over the possibility of change.

Karl Marx* commonly employed the term ideology in a pejorative (or negative) sense, identifying it with illusion. Because, he argued, the prevailing ideas in any society will reflect the interests of the dominant class (through, for example, its control of education and the mass media), it follows that subordinate classes will not recognise

their own exploitation but will hold a distorted view of their own interests. This 'false consciousness' he described as ideology. Much of the prevailing wisdom of his own day, including classical economics and conventional bourgeois morality, Marx considered ideological rather than scientific. His own method, he considered, involved science rather than ideology.

Much of modern American political science takes a diametrically opposed view. For them, Marxism, along with other 'isms', is dogmatic, unscientific, and 'ideological' compared with their own detached, value-free, rigorous empirical research. Ideology was particularly identified with 'closed' **totalitarian** systems of thought. Daniel Bell* (1960) proclaimed 'the end of ideology'. **Conservatives** and **liberals** commonly denied that their own political ideas were ideological. Yet some critics suggested that Western politics was characterised not by the end of ideology but the dominance of a particular ideology, liberal **capitalism**. Indeed some commentators identified an ideological **consensus** in the West, based on Keynesian* economics and welfare reform, sometimes identified as a **social democratic** consensus. This consensus, (if it ever really existed), was challenged by new ideological perspectives (such as **feminism** and **environmentalism**) and the revival of an old one (**neoliberalism**).

The end of the Cold War and the break-up of the Soviet empire seemed to some to mark the 'end of ideology' (the end of history as ideological conflict – see Fukuyama*) and the victory of liberal capitalism, although it soon became apparent that new political divisions based on **culture**, **ethnicity**, and religion were replacing the old Cold War split between **communism** and **capitalism**.

Today most commentators prefer a more neutral non-pejorative understanding of ideology. Thus **liberalism**, **conservatism**, **socialism**, **nationalism**, **feminism**, and **environmentalism** all commonly figure in surveys of political ideologies (e.g. Leach 2015), sometimes alongside other older or more recent political doctrines. It is also generally accepted that ideologies may be expressed at various levels and with different degrees of sophistication, for example by political thinkers, practising politicians, the media, and the wider public.

Imperialism

Imperialism involves the expansion of the state beyond its boundaries to secure domination over other countries and peoples. Empires have been established throughout history – notable examples being the Egyptian, Chinese, Persian, Alexandrian, and Roman empires of ancient times. More recently, from the 16th to the 19th centuries, European states, such as Spain, Portugal, the United Kingdom, France, and the Netherlands acquired colonial empires in other continents, and relative newcomers Germany and Italy became involved in the 'scramble for Africa' in the late 19th century.

The case for imperialism was variously advanced. **States** commonly justified their own imperialism as a civilising mission, spreading the benefits of Christianity and Western **law** and **culture** to 'heathen' native peoples – the 'white man's burden' in the poet Rudyard Kipling's words. Others saw it as a competitive struggle for power and influence in the world; thus, if the opportunities for imperial expansion were neglected, other states would seize them, in what was perceived as a kind of Darwinian survival of the fittest. Imperialism could also be seen as an extension of **nationalism**, validating the claims of superiority made for the nation. An additional advantage for ruling **elites** was that both nationalism and imperialism appeared useful in diverting the working classes away from revolutionary **socialism**.

Others again argued that the motive for imperialism was essentially economic, part of the industrialising nations' search for captive sources of raw materials and markets for finished goods. Lenin* argued in *Imperialism as the Highest Stage of Capitalism* that imperialism was an economic necessity for capitalist states. Exploitation of colonies enabled imperial powers to postpone the increasing poverty of their own working class

that would otherwise spark **revolution.** Yet some colonies appeared an economic burden, and it has been argued that empire was more of a political distraction and a drain on resources than a benefit.

From the perspective of the colonised there was a glaring inconsistency between the **liberal** and **democratic** ideals preached by their colonial masters and imperial practice. They were treated as subject peoples rather than equal citizens within an imperial state. Colonial subjects used the language of their conquerors to demand their own **freedom** and self-determination. In the course of the 20th century empire increasingly appeared an anachronism. When Mussolini's Italian **fascist** government invaded Abyssinia in 1936, it was only doing what other European powers had done in the 19th century, but the aggression was almost universally condemned. The remaining European empires were rapidly liquidated in the decades following the Second World War, which had reduced the power and prestige of the old colonial powers. Apart from a few tiny anachronistic survivals, the age of empire, at least in its traditional form, appears over.

However, some argue that the relationship today between the economically developed states and the developing world is a profoundly unequal one, amounting to economic and cultural exploitation without direct political control that is sometimes described as neo-colonialism or neo-imperialism.

Incrementalism

Incrementalism is a model or theory of policy-making that suggests that most policy involves a limited choice between relatively few options and only a small (or incremental) change from past policy. It is associated particularly with Charles Lindblom* who developed his incremental model in opposition to the rational model of decision-making linked with Herbert Simon*. For Lindblom, incrementalism was both a descriptive and prescriptive model of the policy making process. He not only thought that most policy was made incrementally but that policy was better for being made in this way. Provocatively, he described it as 'the science of muddling through'. Incrementalism avoids the potential risks of radical reform. It also assumes accommodation and compromise among different interests, a process Lindblom described as 'partisan mutual adjustment'. His understanding of incrementalism is thus linked with **pluralism**. Incrementalism also has obvious affinities with the cautious approach to reform associated with some conservatism, the gradualism of Fabian **socialism** of Beatrice and Sidney Webb*, and the 'piecemeal social engineering' recommended by Karl Popper*.

Critics have argued that while incrementalism offers a realistic description of much policy-making, particularly the budgetary process, it does not explain sharp switches, as sometimes demonstrated in foreign policy. As a prescriptive model, incrementalism has been criticised for its in-built conservative bias, when radical change might sometimes be required. Other theorists, such as Amitai Etzioni and Yehezkal, have recommended more complex models of decision-making, drawing on the insights of both Simon and Lindblom.

Individualism

Individualism involves an assumption of the prime importance of individuals over any social group. Society is seen as no more than an aggregate of individuals. All theorising about politics and society begins with the individual, and the rights and freedom of the individual are seen as paramount. The former British Prime Minister Margaret Thatcher expressed an extreme form of individualism in her much-quoted (and frequently misquoted) remark, 'There is no such thing as society. There are individual men and women, and there are families.'

Individualism is a key concept in classical **liberalism** and most forms of modern liberalism. It also underpins the social contract theory of Hobbes* and Locke*, the utilitarianism of Jeremy Bentham*, and much modern economics, including **rational choice** theory. Traditional **conservatism**, by

contrast, commonly involved a more organic conception of society, over and above the individuals who at any one time constitute society. **Socialism** assumes both the importance of social pressures on individual consciousness and behaviour and the need to consider the interests and welfare of wider society, and not just the self-interest of individuals. **Communitarians**, as the term implies, emphasise the importance of the wider communities to which individuals relate and the values these involve.

Institutionalism and new institutionalism

In the study of politics and (especially) **public administration**, traditional institutionalism involved a focus on the formal organisations involved in **government** and the **state**. From a **behaviouralist** perspective this approach was atheoretical and too descriptive and involved an often uncritical acceptance of the letter of the law and the constitution in defining the role of government institutions. in the political process. However, critics thought the behaviouralists underestimated the role of institutions in the political process. March and Olsen (1984, 1989) coined the term new institutionalism. This took a broader view of institutions, to include organisations outside government, social institutions, and informal organisational networks. Institutions of all kinds involve norms, rules, and 'standard operating procedures' that are internalised by those who work within them and thus affect their behaviour. The new institutionalism has influenced not just the study of public administration and public policy but mainstream political science, including (to a degree) **rational choice theory** and **International Relations**. [See also Part II, Section 2 on the new institutionalism.]

International law

International law is commonly divided into public international law, involving rules governing the relations between states, and private international law, concerning the adjudication of disputes between nongovernmental organisations from different states.

It is public international law that has attracted more interest from writers on **international relations**, although private international law is of growing importance in an era of increasing **globalisation.** The problem for international law, as compared with state law, has long been the absence of a generally acknowledged international body to make law or enforce it. Thus the 'rules' governing relations between states have commonly amounted to little more than descriptions of practice on the one hand or pious expectations on the other.

Hugo Grotius* is widely considered to have laid the foundations for the study of international law. He sought to derive not only state law but law governing relations between states from a universal natural law. Rather less ambitiously, he argued that states should uphold treaty obligations freely entered into. It is such treaties and other agreements between states that constitute the substantive body of international law. These initially involved agreements between a few (two or more) sovereign states, but over the last century some of these agreements were international in scope.

A number of international organisations have been established whose **authority** to make law is widely if not universally acknowledged but whose power to enforce this law against powerful states often appears lacking. Thus, while **liberal** theorists of **international relations** championed the growth of international institutions and international law, the failure of these between the wars provoked the **realist** counter-assertion that international relations involved states pursuing interests, defined in terms of **power**. According to this realist perspective, liberal **idealist** notions of international justice and international law were a chimera. Relations between sovereign states necessarily involve a Hobbesian state of **anarchy**.

A number of factors have nevertheless led to renewed interest in extending and strengthening international law. These include the growth of **transnational corporations** (TNCs) and **nongovernmental organisations** (NGOs) and the erosion of state **sovereignty** by globalising trends, as well as continuing wars, humanitarian disasters, major trade concerns, and rising worries about irreversible damage to the environment. There is no longer a **balance of power** to provide a framework of order and security. The world has become less predictable and safe. There appears to be more willingness to pursue and abide by international agreements, although enforcement remains a problem.

International political economy

International political economy (IPE), also known as global political economy (GPE), is a field that links politics/**International Relations** and economics. The main focus is the links between various political forces such as the state's interaction with economic forces, especially the power of **markets**. IPE and **globalisation** studies have overlaps, given that prominent IPE thinkers such as Susan Strange* and Robert Cox* focus considerable attention on the way modern politics and especially the **nation-state** have political choices restricted by the power of international **capital**.

International Relations

International Relations is sometimes regarded as a separate discipline, more usually as a very important specialist subdiscipline within political science. It involves the political interrelationships of states (and increasingly also a growing number of non-state institutions). A number of older writers, including Thucydides*, Machiavelli*, Grotius*, Spinoza*, and Kant*, had much of interest to say on the political relations among states and issues of diplomacy, peace and war. However, international relations only became more systematically studied in the 20th century, initially as part of a sustained initiative to apply **liberal** principles and the notion of **international law** and collective security to interstate relations. It was widely hoped that this would make war redundant.

The events leading up to the Second World War seemed to mark the failure of this liberal international relations. Following the work of E H Carr* (1939) and Hans Morgenthau* (1948), a rival realist theory of international relations gained widespread acceptance in the Cold War era, suggesting that states use their resources to pursue their interests. Some critics suggested that mainstream international relations theory was too state-centred, neglecting the influence of international institutions and other **nongovernmental organisations** (NGOs). It also neglected the influence of domestic politics on foreign and defence policy. Waltz* (1979) developed a theory of international relations (dubbed 'neorealism') that took some notice of other influences. However, the sudden end of the Cold War (that scholars had not predicted) has led to a wider range of theories, including the **constructivist** approach of Alexander Wendt* and others and a revival of liberal international relations. [See also Part II, Sections 3 and 4 on international relations and **globalisation**].

Judiciary

The judiciary is the part of the state that deals with legal disputes, both criminal prosecutions, normally brought by the state, and civil cases, involving disputes between private citizens or organisations. The judiciary consists of a body of judges, whose detailed organisation and functions may differ from state to state. Commonly there is a hierarchy of judges dealing with different levels of courts, with the highest level dealing with the most important cases, often including constitutional issues, as well as appeals from inferior courts. Increasingly, however, state judicial systems are subject, to some degree, to the decisions of supranational courts, such as European Court of Justice, the European Court of Human Rights, and the International Court of Justice.

Important issues surrounding the judiciary are judicial independence and neutrality, the recruitment and possible bias of judges, and judicial powers, relating especially to the **constitution**, **legislation**, and judicial review of **executive** action. Judicial independence may be regarded as part of the principle of the **separation of powers**. However, even liberal democracies where the executive and legislative functions of the state are interdependent proclaim the independence

and political neutrality of their judiciary. To reinforce the principle of judicial independence, recruitment is restricted to those with appropriate professional legal qualifications and experience, and there is normally security of tenure (sometimes appointments are for life, sometimes to a relatively late retirement age). Thus it is very difficult to get rid of judges and influence their decisions, except in '**totalitarian**' **dictatorships** where the judiciary is controlled by the regime.

The judiciary in theory adjudicates on the law rather than makes the law, which is the function of the **legislature** (although the executive may in practice take a major role). However, judges inevitably have some discretion in interpreting the law. In common law systems, where past court decisions constitute a body of case law that guides subsequent judgements, judges may be effectively making rather than merely declaring or interpreting the law.

In some states the highest judges are guardians of the **constitution**. Thus the Supreme Court of the United States and similar supreme courts or high courts in other states can declare laws passed by the legislature or decisions of the executive to be unconstitutional and null and void. The judges have no such power to strike out laws in states where parliament is sovereign. Even in those states where judges have no power to strike out unconstitutional law, there is commonly provision for judicial review of decisions and actions of the executive. Citizens who are aggrieved by a particular action of a minister or government department or other public body may be able to appeal to the courts for a judicial review of the decision.

If the judiciary is normally free from executive control, this does not necessarily mean that the judiciary is free from political bias. In most countries senior judges are predominantly male, elderly, and come from a relatively narrow social background, and this inevitably (if only subconsciously) influences their outlook and their judgement. Thus it is sometimes alleged that they may be unduly lenient in dealing with white-collar crime and they may be too inclined to trust the word of those in authority and the police. Some argue that the judiciary has an in-built conservative (with a small 'c') bias and is out of touch with modern values and modern life. This raise issues over the recruitment of the judiciary. In some countries there are pressures to recruit more women and members of **ethnic minorities** in an attempt to make the judiciary more socially **representative**.

Justice

The term 'justice' is used in a range of different but overlapping senses. Aristotle* distinguished between 'distributive justice', the proper distribution of goods within a community, and 'commutative justice', the treatment of individuals in respect of their behaviour towards each other and the community, commonly involving punishment (criminal justice). Both involve notions of fairness or justice: income and wealth should be distributed fairly or justly, those accused of crimes or civil wrongs should be treated fairly or justly, according to the law. Yet criminal justice essentially requires fairness in procedures (a fair trial), while distributive justice (sometimes called economic or social justice) involves more difficult and questionable assumptions over what constitutes 'fairness' or a just distribution of scarce resources. It is distributive (or economic, or social) justice that has more exercised political theorists, moral philosophers, and economists.

Distributive justice has commonly been linked with some notion of **equality**. Aristotle* argued that equals should be treated equally, incidentally justifying the unequal treatment of inferiors (including, on his assumptions, women and slaves). **Liberal** theory asserted the equality of man and, originally, equal **rights** to the fruits of the earth and had some problems in explaining and justifying substantial differences in income and wealth in practice. Locke* justified unequal **property** rights in terms of individual labour mixed with natural resources. Subsequently, liberals emphasised equality of opportunity rather than outcome (and some later extended this principle of equality of opportunity to women as well as men).

Marx* used the labour theory of value derived from Locke* and Ricardo to denounce the exploitation of workers, demanding initially 'from each according to his ability, to each according to his work' but ultimately 'from each according to his ability, to each according to his needs'. **Socialism** in all its variants involves some assumptions about redistribution. While a few socialists argued for the abolition of all private **property** and a form of primitive **communism**, most demanded simply 'more equality' rather than complete equality of outcome (a compromise that, while understandable, poses obvious theoretical and practical problems). Many progressive (or social liberals) and modern **social democrats** enthusiastically endorsed the influential theory of justice as fairness, expounded by John Rawls*, which appeared to offer a way out of these difficulties. However, conservative thinkers from Edmund Burke* to Michael Oakeshott* have defended inequality, while both the neoliberal Friedrich Hayek* and Robert Nozick* have denounced the very principle of distributive justice.

Laissez-faire

Laissez-faire may be roughly translated as to 'leave alone' or 'let be'. From at least the early 19th century onwards some argued that the best governments were those that did least, and in particular those that refrained from interfering with the **free market**.

Law and the rule of law

Laws are public rules, today normally made by the **state** through a recognised legal process. They take precedence over other rules. They are compulsory, and supported by penal sanctions, but also widely accepted as binding by state subjects. It is generally conceded that it is better to be ruled by consistent and impersonally executed laws rather than the arbitrary decisions of human rulers. This is a key element of the rule of law. Rulers are bound to uphold the law. No one, not princes, nor politicians, nor public officials, is above or outside the law. Government actions without legal authority can be challenged in the courts. The **judiciary** is supposed to be independent of the **executive** and impartial in its adjudication. The rule of law is also generally held to embody key principles such as natural **justice**, fairness, and reasonableness.

Yet there have often been cases when individuals or groups have felt strongly that a particular law is unjust, to the extent that they feel may justified in defying it (see, for example, **civil disobedience**). Those who defy the law of the state may claim that it is against a higher law, such as the eternal law of nature or the law of God. Some have maintained that human law should be derived from **natural law** or divine law (with the implication that it is human law that should give way if there is a clash). One obvious problem is that there is far from universal agreement over what is natural law. Bentham* attacked the whole notion of natural law and the associated idea of **natural rights**. Since then there has been a strong tradition of 'positive law' that suggests that laws are simply those rules made by those entrusted with legislative authority. However, the return to fashion of the language of rights (if now universal human rights rather than natural rights) and the incorporation of such rights into law suggests that the natural law tradition is far from dead. The modern American legal and political philosopher Ronald Dworkin* has championed natural law and natural rights.

The broader relationship between law and morality remains contentious. Some maintain that state law should uphold public morality. However, many modern jurists would deny that it is the role of the state, and the state's laws, to enforce public morality, following the arguments of Mill* that the only justification for interfering with the freedom of the individual is to prevent harm to others.

Leadership

Leadership implies a natural rather than imposed **authority**, derived from qualities that make the leader willingly followed and obeyed. While leadership is commonly highly prized not only in politics but also in many other spheres (e.g. business, the armed forces, schools), criticism is sometimes levelled at those who are 'too easily led', implying a culpable lack of independence and self-reliance. This is particularly evident with political leadership. While Pericles*, Lincoln, Gandhi*, or Churchill are commonly cited as positive role models, other 'strong leaders' such as Hitler and Stalin* are now widely execrated and those who obediently followed them condemned.

Thus attitudes to leadership vary considerably. In **fascist** ideology the leader was viewed as a kind of superman, the *Duce* or *Führer*, inspiring an almost religious devotion among his followers. **Communist** leaders were similarly elevated to a quasi-divine role, their images placed everywhere in life, and even in death their bodies embalmed for the faithful to file past. Nationalist leaders have sometimes inspired a similar reverence. Such leaders commonly 'emerge' and may be effectively self-appointed, although personal charisma (see **authority**) as well as **power** may attract willing followers who provide a kind of **legitimacy** for their leadership.

Democratic norms require that political leaders should be chosen by and accountable to, and ultimately removable by, those they lead. There may be a preference for collective rather than individual leadership. **Conservatives** who assume a natural hierarchy and inequality in human society tend to revere strong leaders, but those with more egalitarian assumptions regard leadership with greater ambivalence – leaders should not be too powerful. Democratic **socialists**, while reluctantly recognising the need for effective leaders, not least in winning power, have sought to constrain them, recurrently fearing betrayal of party principles. Some radical **social movements**, such as the women's movement, the peace movement, and the **green** movement have commonly avoided identifying leadership roles. For **anarchists** the whole notion of leadership is inimical to everything they believe in (although even so, some anarchists have clearly had a personal charisma that inspired a following).

Left and right

The labels 'left' and 'right' are still widely used to classify ideologies, political parties, and intraparty factions and to describe the position of individual thinkers and politicians. (The terms derive from the seating positions in representative assemblies following the 1789 French Revolution.) Today, on the conventional left–right political spectrum **communists** are placed on the far left, **socialists** and **social democrats** on the left, **Christian democrats** and **conservatives** on the right, and **fascists** on the far right. **Liberals** are generally located somewhere in the centre, although the term 'liberal' today covers a wide range.

left–right, conventional scale

far left	left	centre	right	far right
communists	socialists	liberals	conservatives	fascists

Other ideologies are more difficult to place. **Nationalism** is today more commonly associated with the right, although in different times and places it has been linked with ideas and parties from across the ideological spectrum. **Green** thinking is generally linked with the left, although greens themselves often claim to be off the scale – 'not left, not right, but forward'. **Anarchism** was usually regarded as far left, although some extreme free market thinkers described as anarcho-capitalists are associated with the right. **Feminism**, like green thinking, cuts across the left–right spectrum, although many feminists have been linked with the left.

If degrees of 'left' and 'right' can be marked on a scale it is by no means clear what that scale is measuring. Attitudes to change? Attitudes to **authority**? Attitudes to **capitalism** and the **free market**? None of these seems to fit closely the way in which the terms 'left' and 'right' are actually used. Consequently, some argue the terms are confusing and should be abandoned. Others have suggested a more complex two-dimensional system of classifying political ideas, with attitudes to authority on the vertical axis and attitudes to change on the horizontal axis (Eysenck 1957). Whatever the merits of such more complex systems of classification of political attitudes, it is unlikely that they will ever displace the more familiar language of left and right.

Legislation and legislature

A legislature is in theory a state institution responsible for law-making (or legislation). Legislation is one of the three main functions of the state – the others being the **executive** function (essentially governing and administering the law) and the **judicial** function (adjudicating). According to the doctrine of the **separation of powers** these three functions should be entrusted to different institutions.

In many countries a directly elected parliament or assembly is primarily responsible for legislation, and these bodies are commonly described as legislatures or legislative assemblies. However, it is widely argued that executives have gained in power at the expense of legislatures. In practice, the executive (particularly where it is a parliamentary executive, drawn from and dominating the legislature) is often the main source of legislative proposals, and the role of many parliaments or assemblies involves more deliberation and discussion than the initiation of laws. Also, particularly in countries with a common law tradition, the **judiciary** has a key role in making and not just adjudicating on the law. Thus, although legislatures may be closely involved in making the law, they are not the sole, nor even necessarily the main, source of new law.

Legitimacy

'Legitimacy' is a term that can be used in a literal sense to mean lawfulness. Thus a government or an order or a ministerial act may be considered legitimate if derived from **law** or exercised under lawful **authority**. Thus lawyers distinguish between *de jure* authority which one is legally obliged to obey and *de facto* **power** which is not lawful (although it may be prudent to obey or acknowledge it). Sometimes a government in exile is recognised as the legitimate government, even if another government wields effective power over the territory. Yet commonly a claim to legitimacy cannot long survive effective loss of power, while a *de facto* government over time gains recognition and legitimacy.

For political theorists issues of legitimacy are bound up with the grounds of political **obligation** – why should I obey the state? Some asserted the ruler's authority was derived from God, others assumed an original contract between people and government. Today, in the West it is widely argued that only governments deriving their authority from free and fair elections are fully legitimate. Besides these legal and philosophical arguments, popular acceptance of legitimacy is in practice very important for national unity and the maintenance of law and order, as can be plainly seen where the majority or a sizeable minority do not accept a regime's legitimacy. Thus in Northern Ireland much of the large Catholic minority never accepted the division of Ireland and the legitimacy of the old government of Northern Ireland, nor the authority of the police. In many other parts of the world (e.g. Palestine, Ethiopia, Afghanistan, Iraq, Libya, and Syria) there has been long-running violence and sometimes full civil war arising from the rejection of the governing regime's legitimacy by a substantial section of its inhabitants.

Sociologists from Max Weber* onwards have been more interested in how a popular belief in legitimacy arises – why do people in practice regard some power as legitimate? Weber distinguished between three main types (or causes) of authority: traditional, charismatic, and legal-rational. While the first and third might be acknowledged by lawyers, charismatic authority on its own has no legal basis, although it may be widely acknowledged without coercion.

Liberalism

Liberalism is sometimes viewed as the dominant or hegemonic **ideology** of the modern Western world. Indeed most other Western ideologies, including some versions of **socialism** and of **conservatism**, might be regarded as 'variants of liberalism'.

Like all ideologies, liberalism has evolved over a long period and has varied considerably over time and space. Although the term 'liberalism' was not coined until the 19th century, its roots can be traced back much further. It drew inspiration from the religious reformations of the 16th century, the 17th-century Scientific Revolution, and the 18th-century Enlightenment. Industrialisation from the late 18th century onwards transformed economic and social relations and created new class interests with a commitment to a liberal political programme of reform. This generally included constitutional reform, religious toleration, national self-determination, and free trade.

From a Marxist perspective liberalism was the political creed reflecting the **class** interests of the rising **bourgeoisie**, the owners of capital, as against the interests of absolute **monarchy** and the old landed **aristocracy** on the one hand and industrial workers on the other. In practice, liberalism also received considerable support from the professions, shopkeepers, and skilled workers.

Key liberal concepts include **freedom**, **individualism**, **rationalism**, **toleration**, and the **free market**. For the liberal, individual human beings, rather than nations, races, or classes, are the starting point for an theorising about society, politics or economics. Society is seen as an aggregate of individuals, who should be free to pursue their own rational self-interest. No one else, not rulers, nor priests, nor civil servants, are capable of determining the individual's interest for him or her. Individuals should concede a similar freedom to others to pursue their own economic, political, and religious interests in their own way.

In the early 19th century liberalism was widely perceived as a revolutionary creed posing a threat to states and governments almost everywhere. As liberals also favoured economic freedom, free trade and free markets, they opposed government intervention in the economy that was commonly exercised to protect domestic agriculture and industry. Yet the extension of the franchise, substantially the result of liberal pressure, and the growing acceptance of **representative democracy** helped transform the attitudes of some liberals to the state. Thus the New Liberals in the United Kingdom increasingly favoured increased state intervention to provide education, health are, and unemployment insurance, while elsewhere in Europe traditional liberals retained a dogmatic attachment to the **free market**. More recently, the revival of free-market ideas from the 1970s onwards has been associated with what has been described as '**neoliberalism**' (a creed diametrically opposed to the interventionist New Liberalism of the early 20th century).

Today there is no longer any clear agreement over what the terms 'liberal' and 'liberalism' mean. Liberals are generally placed somewhere in the centre of the left–right political spectrum. Yet in the United States the term 'liberal' has been widely used as a derogatory term for those who are perceived to be 'soft' on **communism** and favour 'socialised medicine'. Thus in American terms a liberal is on the left of the political spectrum. Some European liberals, such as the British Liberal Democrats see themselves as progressive or centre-left. Others such as the Free Democrats in Germany might be more accurately described as centre-right. Such diverse thinkers as Keynes*, Hayek*, and Rawls* have all described themselves as liberals. Any discussion of liberalism today requires some definition of terms and the use of a number of hybrid labels such as 'economic liberal' or 'social liberal' to differentiate between conflicting interpretations of the creed. Eccleshall (1986) provides a useful reader on liberalism, and Arblaster (1984) gives a critical account from a socialist perspective. [See also **Neoliberalism**.]

It is also important to consider that liberalism and neoliberalism in **International Relations** refer to a specific way of viewing world politics. This concept is often seen as the counterpoint to realism in that it argues that international organisations shape state behaviour (see Keohane*).

Liberty

(See **freedom** and also **liberalism**.)

Mandate

A **mandate** is an instruction or command that has to be obeyed. Thus a delegate to a conference or assembly may say that he or she has been 'mandated' by the members he or she represents to vote in a particular way. The concept of the mandate is more specifically used in politics today by elected governments, to argue that they have a popular mandate, an endorsement from the people, to implement specific policies in their **political party election** manifesto. Opposition parties may sometimes argue that the government has no mandate for policy proposals that were not foreshadowed in their manifesto. Governing parties may however argue that they have a more general mandate from the electorate to govern.

Although the concept of an electoral mandate is widely employed, it raises some problems. Party manifestos are commonly long on general aims and short on specific commitments. Few voters read them, and many may be ignorant of the details of the party programme. Voters cannot discriminate between particular policy pledges – agreeing with some and rejecting others – but have to accept the whole package. Thus, even if most voters have preferred a party to its main competitors, this does not mean they have necessarily endorsed its whole programme. Often a party may be elected in spite of, rather than because of, specific policy commitments. Also, circumstances may change after the election, justifying a government in acting contrary to a specific manifesto pledge.

The notion of a mandate is more difficult to apply in multiparty systems involving coalition government. To form a government, parties have to bargain and compromise and are sometimes obliged to jettison key elements in their programme to reach agreement with potential partners in government. This is a process from which voters are normally excluded, and it is difficult for such a coalition government to claim an electoral mandate.

Marxism and Marxism-Leninism

Marxism is a term that clearly involves the ideas of Karl Marx*, elaborated over a lifetime and also as interpreted during his life and after his death by his close collaborator Friedrich Engels*. It is a term that more broadly encompasses the ideas of the numerous and diverse followers of Marx and movements inspired by Marx in the 19th and 20th centuries. How far Marx himself would have endorsed all these ideas and movements is contentious and clearly unknowable in regard to developments after his death, although Engels reported that Marx observed of French 'Marxists' in the 1870s, 'All I know is that I am not a Marxist' (Engels [1890] in Feuer 1959, 396).

There were (and still are) many variants of Marxism around the world. The most influential was **Marxism-Leninism**. This involved the interpretation of Marx's ideas by the Russian Bolshevik leader Lenin*, both before and during the Bolshevik revolution, and the subsequent practice of the government of the Soviet Union by Lenin himself and his successor, Stalin*. It became the orthodoxy of **communist** parties around the world and a model to be followed by communist regimes that came to power after the Second World War, although some of these pursued a distinctive path ('Titoism' in the former Yugoslavia; 'Maoism' after Mao Zedong* in China). Broadly speaking, Marxism-Leninism in practice involved one-party **dictatorship** and extensive state control of the economy.

Some Western Marxists substantially endorsed Marxism-Leninism and what they regarded as 'actually existing socialism' in Soviet Russia and Eastern Europe, although some who continued to revere Lenin rejected Stalinism. Others followed the ideas of Stalin's defeated rival Trotsky*. Others again followed the ideas of Bernstein* and subsequently Kautsky* and endorsed a parliamentary route to socialism, which was denounced by Marxist-Leninists as 'revisionism'. The Italian Communist Party, influenced by the ideas of Gramsci* and operating in a liberal parliamentary system, pursued its own version of 'Eurocommunism'. There were also influential academic strands of Marxism, particularly the Critical Theory of the Frankfurt school (Adorno* Marcuse*, Habermas,* although some of these effectively moved away from Marxism), the existential Marxism of Sartre*, and French structuralist Marxism (Althusser*, Poulantzas*).

Mass media

The term 'mass media' refers to all those forms of communication where large numbers of people are exposed to an identical message. They include the print media – newspapers, magazines, and books – and the electronic media – film, radio, television and, increasingly, the internet.

The 1960s media guru Marshall McLuhan* argued that 'the medium is the message', implying that each medium of communication has its own characteristics that shape the message that is received. Thus television is primarily a visual medium, and the main message is conveyed by the pictures. Radio, although an oral/aural medium, abhors silence, so that in interviews and debates prompt, short answers work best – there is no time for considered reflection. Print can discuss serious ideas in more depth, although tabloid journalism deals in headlines, slogans, and pictures.

A free and diverse media expressing a range of political views is widely seen as an essential precondition of a pluralist **democracy**. Thus media control and media bias are major concerns of political analysts. The concentration of newspaper empires and television channels in the hands of a few powerful media magnates (such as Rupert Murdoch or Silvio Berlusconi) and their control of editors and journalists is a particular concern. Some television channels and many newspapers exhibit a strong and persistent political bias. The internet offers more scope for the expression of a wide range of views and real debate, but its impact on politics until more recently still lagged behind that of the press and mainstream television.

Does media bias matter? Some argue that people do not expose themselves to messages they do not agree with or filter out or reinterpret messages that do not fit their preconceived views. Many may ignore politics altogether in the media, not watching news and current affairs programmes on television. Yet it seems likely that the constant reiteration of a particular message has some effect, even if the main impact is subliminal. There is some evidence, for example, that newspapers can influence voting and perhaps on occasion swing elections. At another level radicals of all kinds argue that the mass media are biased towards establishment values, masculine attitudes, capitalism and consumerism, and it is this that legitimises and reinforces the status quo.

Materialism and dialectical materialism

Materialism in philosophy emphasises 'matter' over 'mind'. In political theory it implies that only the material or physical world is relevant for the explanation of political and social phenomena. It implies a rejection of abstract moral, religious or spiritual values for a concentration on material interests and welfare. Materialism can thus be contrasted with the idealism of Plato*, Kant*, and Hegel*, for whom knowledge related to intangible ideals or ideas. For Marx, all ideas, religious, moral, economic, were expressions of material interests: 'It is not the consciousness of men that determines their being, but on the contrary, their social being that determines their consciousness.' Thus Marx adapted Hegel's dialectic, applied by Hegel to the development of ideas, to the conflict between economic class interests over time, hence 'dialectical materialism' or historical materialism.

Meritocracy

'Meritocracy' was a term coined by Michael Young (in *The Rise of the Meritocracy*, 1958) to describe the rule of those with merit. 'Merit' might be held to involve a combination of aptitude and effort. This could be interpreted as rule of the deserving, the natural consequence of equality of opportunity and social mobility (although Young was actually rather critical of meritocracy). Indeed, recruitment and promotion based on merit, rather than bribery or social connections, may be regarded as a key principle of modern **bureaucracy,** as described by Max Weber*. Yet talents are unequally distributed, so a meritocracy is by definition an **elite** and not socially **representative** of the mass of the people. There is the added implication that meritocrats know better what the masses really want and need than the masses themselves. Thus meritocracy has questionable implications for democracy.

Militarism and military dictatorship

Militarism involves extolling military virtues, military discipline, and military power. Ancient Sparta is often cited as an example of a militaristic state, along with some more recent or contemporary political societies. High spending on the armed forces, and a readiness to use them, might be taken as an illustration of militarism. The military may be extremely influential even in a **democracy**, because the armed forces are themselves big business, and the manufacture and sale of arms may be important to the national economy. Critics refer to the power of the military-industrial complex.

Where the armed forces are sufficiently well equipped and numerous, their leaders may be tempted to seize political power and install a **military dictatorship**, as often happened in the past and is still not uncommon in the modern world (Finer 1962). Generals may seize power in a time of (perceived) chaos, promising order and prosperity and, ultimately, the restoration of civilian democratic rule, although they are often reluctant to relinquish power. A military dictatorship may be terminated by a counter-coup among the armed forces, to be followed by a new dictatorship under different personnel. It may ultimately collapse as a consequence of economic failure or (ironically) military failure. Thus the military junta in Argentina was brought down by its military defeat in the Falkland Islands (or Malvinas) in 1982.

Model

In politics and the social sciences generally the term 'model' is used to describe a scaled-down simplified version of reality. Such models may be only verbally described, although they may also be portrayed in diagrammatic form, involving highly simplified and abstract portrayals of significant relationships among institutions or variables. Particularly in economics, models can be developed into workable computer simulations, into which key statistics are fed to produce predicted outcomes. (The British Treasury has developed and used such a model.) In politics, models are generally more simple and illustrative. Some models involve rival hypotheses about the working of the political system as a whole (e.g. **elitism** and **pluralism**).

Monarchy

Monarchy is another term derived from the ancient Greek, literally rule by one. In practice the Greeks distinguished between monarchy (a traditional or legitimate single ruler) and tyranny (dictatorial rule by a usurper). Monarchy was the dominant form of government in Europe from the Middle Ages through to the 19th century. In the Middle Ages the effective power of monarchy was often limited by the power of nobility and/or the church. While most kings owed their position to heredity, there were some survivals of (very limited) forms of elective monarchy (e.g. in Germany). Subsequently, monarchy became identified with rule by a single person, owing his (or, rarely, her) position to hereditary descent from previous rulers. In the 17th and 18th centuries some of these hereditary rulers appeared to have unlimited or absolute power (see **absolutism**). In the 19th and 20th centuries monarchy was overthrown in some countries and limited in others. The few surviving kings and queens are constitutional monarchs. They reign but no longer rule. Some argue that monarchy retains some advantages for the role of formal head of state; others that the hereditary principle is inconsistent with democracy.

Multiculturalism

The term 'multiculturalism' can be used in a largely descriptive way, simply suggesting that many societies and nations involve peoples with different cultures, languages, and faiths living together. Multiculturalism in this descriptive sense is increasingly a feature of the modern world. From the 1970s onwards the term has also been used in a more prescriptive or normative sense, suggesting that the diversity involved in multiculturalism has positive benefits and that governments should protect and support cultural diversity, rather than encourage the assimilation or integration of **ethnic minorities**. Multiculturalism in this normative sense recognises and respects distinctive minority cultures. Indeed it is commonly argued that a variety of dress, food, customs and beliefs can enrich the whole community, creating an interesting and vibrant diversity. One consequence of multiculturalism has been the increasing acceptance of hyphenated identities that suggest a dual allegiance such as Irish-American or British-Muslim or Black-British. Multiculturalism accommodates such multiple identities and fits easily within the more complex interlocking political allegiances.

Some fear that multiculturalism is dangerously eroding formerly common national values and identities. Others are less resistant to the ideal of multiculturalism but point out that in practice those from different cultures commonly have minimal contact with each other, living separate lives in largely segregated communities, and that these are breeding grounds for damaging intercommunal conflict. Beyond that there are some concerns that multiculturalism, in so far as it legitimises the continued use of minority languages and other distinctive cultural practices, may reduce the economic opportunities of those from minority backgrounds. Faster integration might enable them to compete more successfully, on equal terms.

Others again fear that multicultural values can be used to ignore or trump what they consider to be universal **human rights**. Thus, under the influence of multiculturalism, a blind eye may be turned to practices unacceptable in a liberal democracy, such as forced marriages, the persecution of homosexuals, even limitations on freedom of speech. It sometimes appears difficult to reconcile respect for distinctive community identities and cultures with widely accepted individual rights, although critics (e.g. Bhikhu Parekh 2000) suggest that some 'universal' human rights involve a strong Western cultural bias and undervalue alternative traditions.

Nation, nation-state, and nationalism

A nation may consist of a community of people, bound together by some characteristic they all share and regard as important, such as a common language, religion, **ethnicity**, or **culture**. Yet ultimately there are no objective criteria. A nation exists where a people feel they constitute a nation. Thus nations exist in the minds of their members. They are 'imagined communities' (B. Anderson [1983] 1991).

The term 'nation' is sometimes used almost interchangeably with the term '**state**', but while a nation is a community of people, a state is a political and governmental unit. The term 'nation-state' is used for a state whose subjects or citizens comprise those who belong to a single nation, however that is defined. Many older states were (and some today still are) multinational as a consequence of past conquests, marriage alliances, and/or conventions governing the hereditary succession of rulers. Debates over the power of nation-states in global politics form the basis of much of International Relations.

Nationalism is the political doctrine or ideology that nations should form states and states should consist of nations. A distinction is sometimes drawn between separation nationalism and unification nationalism. Separation nationalism involves a national minority within a multinational state seeking independence or national self-determination. Historical examples include Greece, Finland, and Slovakia. Current examples of nationalist movements seeking independence include Quebec (from Canada), the Basque separatists (from Spain), and Scottish nationalists (from the United Kingdom). Unification nationalism involves peoples from separate states with a common sense of nationhood seeking to combine to form a new political union. Examples include Italian and German unification in the 19th century and, more recently, the re-unification of East and West Germany following the fall of the Berlin wall.

There is disagreement over the emergence of national consciousness and nationalism. Some argue that a sense of national consciousness or national identity emerged in some communities many centuries ago (e.g. Greenfeld 1992). Others suggest that a sense of nationhood is more recent, the product of industrialisation, **mass media**, and mass education, and often shaped by states or ruling **elites** in their own interest. Gellner (1983, 55) observes 'It is nationalism that engenders nations, and not the other way around.'

Some political thinkers (e.g. Mazzini*) hoped that national self-determination would lead to a new international era of peace and co-operation among nation-states. Yet most nationalists seem less interested in national self-determination as a general principle than in the rights and grievances of their own particular nation. For such nationalists 'the interests and values of their nation take priority over all over interests and values' (Breuilly 1993, 2). Sometimes this has taken the form of an aggressive nationalism, under which the success of the nation in competition or conflict with other nations vindicates its superiority.

The US President Woodrow Wilson* tried to apply the principle of self-determination in the peace settlement at the end of the First World War. In practice some new 'nation-states' established then contained substantial minorities with different national identities and an enduring sense of grievance.

Nationalisation and privatisation

Nationalisation involves **state** (rather than private) ownership and control of key economic enterprises. The 'common ownership of the means of production' was a key **socialist** objective from the 19th century onwards, as a means to secure a more equal society and a more efficient planned economy. Some socialists hoped this would involve effective 'workers control' or producer co-operatives, although these hopes were substantially disappointed. In the 20th century some **liberals** and **conservatives** in western Europe accepted **pragmatic** arguments for taking specific industries into state hands, particularly in wartime and the aftermath of war. Thus industries regarded as of strategic importance (for defence or other national purposes) and declining industries requiring rationalisation were nationalised. In France some firms that had collaborated with the Germans, including the car manufacturer Renault, were taken over. A state-run industrial sector became part of the postwar **consensus**. Yet even socialist governments did not pursue wholesale nationalisation. Other parties, such as European **Christian Democrats** and the British **Conservative** Party largely accepted the notion of a mixed economy.

The record of nationalised industries is contentious, although many were losing money before they were nationalised. Neoliberal critics argued they were inherently inefficient, as they were effectively state monopolies, not subject to the discipline of the **free market** and liable to endless political interference in key management and investment decisions.

The erosion of the postwar consensus and the rising influence of the free market ideas of neoliberals and the **New Right** led to the privatisation (or denationalisation) of many formerly state-run undertakings. Privatisation brought in capital receipts for governments and the prospect of reducing the continuing burden on state finances of largely loss-making undertakings. Increased competition, it was argued, could only benefit consumers. In practice some state monopolies became privately owned and run monopolies, requiring the maintenance of some state **regulation** to protect consumer interests and in some cases considerable on-going state support, while other nationalised industries were forcibly broken up, causing problems for co-ordination. Governments soon discovered that denationalisation did not depoliticise key issues around these industries.

Nature, natural law, and natural rights

In political philosophy nature, what is natural or inborn, is contrasted with **convention**, meaning custom or practice. While nature is universal, custom and practice vary between and within societies. Some political theorists, including Aquinas*, Grotius*, and Locke* argued that behind the varied positive laws of particular states there lay a universal natural law, with the implication that natural law provided a standard against which the laws of **states** could be measured. There was a further implication that where natural law and positive law clashed, it was natural law that should prevail. It was also commonly argued that there were universal and inalienable natural rights (see also **rights** and **law**).

In practice there were rather different understandings of what was natural. For some it was to be identified with an assumed original state of nature before the establishment of human society, government, and civilisation. For others nature was what was perceived to be common to all persons and societies. For religious thinkers, nature was simply what God intended for humankind and thus natural law was, in effect, divine law.

Critics such as Jeremy Bentham* ridiculed the whole notion of natural law and natural rights. Law and rights had to be enforceable to be effective, and there was no means of enforcing natural law and natural rights. In practice, he argued, the concepts of natural law and natural rights were used to undermine positive law and legal rights.

Neoliberalism

'Neoliberalism' is a term used to distinguish modern economic liberalism from the progressive or social liberalism that had become dominant in some parts of the Western world in the last century. The ideas were not new – they were derived from the **free market** economics of classical **liberalism**. Such free market ideas had become unfashionable in the decades immediately after the Second World War. Economic crises in the 1970s provoked a rethink and support for the free market or neoliberal ideas of Hayek*, Friedman*, and the **rational** or **public choice** school of Buchanan*, Tullock*, and Niskanen*. Some politicians and thinkers combined this economic liberalism with some features of traditional conservatism (see **New Right**).

NB: Neo-liberalism within international relations is a very different concept-see ??

New institutionalism

(See under **Institutionalism**.)

New Right

The 'New Right' is a term used to distinguish ideas and policies adopted from the 1970s onwards by politicians, parties and movements on the **right** of the political spectrum from many of the ideas and policies pursued by traditional right or **conservative** parties. The novel ingredient was the **free market liberalism** or **neoliberalism** of Hayek*, Friedman*, and the **rational choice** school, rather than economic ideas of the old right (more wedded to **nationalism** and economic protectionism). However, the New Right involved a blend of neoliberal economics with elements of traditional **conservatism**. Leading converts included Keith Joseph and Margaret Thatcher in the British Conservative Party, and the Republican administration of Ronald Reagan in the United States. New right ideas also increasingly challenged the formerly dominant interventionist policies of **Christian democracy** and **social democracy** in much of western Europe.

Nongovernmental organisations (NGOs)

'Nongovernmental organisation' (or 'NGO') is a term used principally in the study of international relations to describe international voluntary organisations that are neither part of government nor the commercial sector. They include organisations such as the International Committee of the Red Cross, Médecins Sans Frontières, Oxfam, Amnesty International, and Human Rights Watch. The number of registered NGOs had risen to 37,000 by the year 2000 (Brown and Ainley 2009, 223). Some NGOs work closely with intergovernmental organisations (IGOs), such the United Nations. They have had some success in pressuring national governments, and transnational corporations (TNCs), particularly on human rights and environmental issues. The increasing importance of NGOs has been one element in the criticism of realist and neorealist state-centric theories of international relations.

Normative and normativism

The term 'normative' is used to describe the *prescription* of rules (or norms). Much traditional political theory is normative, involving the prescription of preferred forms of government, political principles, obligations and rights. Modern political science, by contrast, aspires to be **positive** or objective, avoiding *prescription* in favour of accurate *description* and *analysis*. However, the distinction is far from watertight. Some traditional political thinkers (e.g. Aristotle*, Machiavelli*) combined both prescription and an attempt at scientific analysis. Some modern political scientists (e.g. Downs*, Dahl*, Putnam*) often seem to straddle the divide between positive analysis and normative recommendations.

Obligation

An obligation in general terms is any duty or behaviour involving moral assumptions. Thus a father may be considered to have an obligation to look after his children, an employer an obligation of care for his or her workers, a borrower an obligation to repay his or her debt. A distinction may be drawn between a legal obligation, backed by clear enforceable sanctions against noncompliance, and a moral obligation, depending on individual conscience and social pressure.

Political obligation is commonly more narrowly defined in terms of the question, why and how far is a citizen obliged to obey the state or government? This was a far from academic question in a world of political instability, involving frequent conflicts between rival claimants to political authority, revolution and civil war. Social contract theorists such as Hobbes* and Locke* derived the obligation to accept the authority of a government and obey its laws from a prior historical or hypothetical promise. Thus government rested on the consent of the governed. For some contract theorists the obligation to obedience was conditional only, depending on how far the sovereign kept to their terms of the agreement. Accordingly, Locke (but not Hobbes) conceded a limited right of rebellion. Yet regardless of whether such a contract or promise had ever been made, clearly most existing subjects had never formally promised obedience, as contract theorists generally acknowledged. Thus they argued (essentially following the arguments in Plato's* *Crito*) that continuing to live in a state amounted to a tacit promise to recognise its authority.

The philosopher David Hume* mocked not only the notion of an original contract but the derivation of political obligation from a promise. His argument was simply that we should obey the state because society could not otherwise subsist, a **utilitarian** argument. Yet the notion has endured that a government can forfeit the obligation of subjects to obey it. Indeed, **international law** and the proceedings of war crimes tribunals do not accept the familiar defence of those accused of war crimes that they were simply 'obeying orders', implying an obligation to disobey established political authority in certain circumstances.

Oligarchy

Oligarchy means literally 'rule by the few'. Oligarchy may be contrasted with **monarchy** (the rule of a single person) and **democracy** (rule of the people). Aristotle* distinguished between **aristocracy** (literally 'rule of the best', in the common interest) with oligarchy

(rule of the few in their own interest). The rule of the few rather than the many was once regarded as normal and even desirable, but with the widespread acceptance of representative democracy 'oligarchy' has become a pejorative term. Writing in the late 19th and early 20th centuries against the democratic tide, the classical elitists (Pareto*, Mosca*, and Michels*) argued that oligarchy was in practice inevitable, even in states that claimed to be democratic, and Pareto certainly believed that oligarchy was also preferable. More recently, radical **elite** theorists and **Marxists** have pointed to the continuing concentration of power in the hands of the few in modern supposedly democratic states, which they condemn and wish to transform.

Pacifism

'Pacifism' means the rejection of violence and war even in the face of aggression. Thus pacifists have refused to join armies and have resisted compulsory conscription, often facing prison or death where a right to conscientious objection was not recognised. More recently, this right has been more widely conceded, at least in liberal democracies. Political leaders who have renounced all violence and preferred to use peaceful resistance or **civil disobedience** include Gandhi* and Martin Luther King*.

Patriarchy

'Patriarchy' means literally rule of the father. The patriarchal principle supported the inheritance of titles and property through the male line and was considered to have implications for political authority. Thus the rule of the father of the family for Aristotle* prefigured and justified the rule of kings over states. Filmer (1588–1653) derived the divine right of kings from the original gift of authority by God to Adam.

Today the term 'patriarchy' is used by **feminists** to mean male domination over women generally. While they argue, like Aristotle, that male power in society and government stems from the power of fathers within the family, unlike Aristotle they reject the whole principle and practice of patriarchy. For radical feminists patriarchy is all-pervasive, underpinning male domination throughout society, even if there are formal legal commitments to gender equality.

Plebiscite

(See under **Referendum**.)

Pluralism and neo-pluralism

Pluralism implies a broad range or plurality of organisations, interests, and values rather than a monolithic or **totalitarian** society and state where differences are not tolerated. Pluralists argue that power and influence are (and should be) widely diffused rather than concentrated in the hands of the few or a single **elite**. While these assumptions are highly compatible with democracy, pluralists also emphasise the importance of opportunities for ordinary citizens to influence the political process in other ways than voting, particularly through involvement in **pressure group** activity, in addition to their (inevitably more limited) role as voters.

Pluralists maintain this pressure group activity aids and improves the democratic process rather than subverting it (as some early critics had argued). In an open democratic society there are ample opportunities for anyone who wants to defend an interest or promote a cause to organise with others to influence decision-makers and the wider public. This will commonly encourage those who take a different view to establish opposed groups, leading to a balance of interests (sometimes described as countervailing power). The information and arguments put forward by conflicting interests and causes puts more relevant knowledge in the public domain, improves the quality of debate, and aids decision-making. Pluralists see this competition for influence among countless groups as the essence of **democracy**. Some see governments as responding to the sum of group pressures, acting as neutral arbiters among conflicting interests in society.

Pluralism is closely linked with mainstream American political science. It grew out of the group theory of A. F. Bentley*,

developed and extended by David Truman, Nelson Polsby, and especially Robert Dahl*. Radical **elite theorists** and Western **Marxists** are among their critics. Briefly, critics of pluralism argue that there are massive inequalities in resources and influence among groups and that the state is not neutral but encourages some interests while effectively excluding others.

Part of the argument has focused on case studies of specific local political communities, both in the United States and elsewhere. However, this community power debate has tended to confirm the initial assumptions of theorists on each side. Pluralists discover that influence is widely dispersed, while those who believe that power and effective influence are concentrated find evidence is support of their assumptions. Thus some conclude that case studies can only be illustrative and do not prove anything. Critics suggest that research on specific decisions ignores issues that are effectively excluded from the political agenda, or are not even considered as issues, because of a systematic bias in the political process.

Some of the criticism of pluralism has been recognised by those dubbed 'neo-pluralists', including Charles Lindblom*, J. K Galbraith*, and Robert Dahl* himself in his later writing. Thus neo-pluralists accept that the state is not a neutral referee but an active participant in the game. While continuing to maintain that power and influence is fairly widely dispersed, they acknowledge that some interests, particularly business interests, have considerable practical influence, while others may be virtually excluded from the political process. According to some interpretations, **corporatism**, a policy process involving a few peak or umbrella groups in a relationship of mutual dependence with government, is more prevalent than free and open competition for influence among countless groups (Schmitter 1979).

Police and police state

The **police** enforce the criminal **law**, and effective policing is important in any political **community**, particularly for those who are most vulnerable, including the very young, the old, and minority groups, although a professional police force, separate from the armed forces, is a relatively modern development.

Effective policing requires extensive powers and resources (including weaponry) to deal with lawbreakers, some of whom are among the most dangerous and ruthless elements in society. In some circumstances police powers may be exceeded or abused. Unnecessary force may be used, correct procedures ignored, and in extreme instances evidence fabricated or bribes taken. This raises the issue of *Quis custodiet ipsos custodes?* (Who guards the guards?). While it is widely recognised that the police should be free from the detailed supervision of politicians, questions arise about police accountability and control that states have sought to address in various ways. There are also questions surrounding the recruitment and composition of police forces. Where the police are drawn from a relatively narrow segment of society or exclude ethnic minorities, they may not enjoy the confidence of some **citizens** who may view them as the enemy rather than their protectors.

Some countries are described as police states. Here the function of the police is to control rather than protect the public. Such abuse of police power is often associated with **dictatorships** and one-party states. Here the police are used to suppress opposition in a blatantly partisan way, and there is no pretence of even-handedness. (Historical examples include the role of the Gestapo in Nazi Germany or the KGB in the Soviet Union.)

Political parties

Political parties play an important role in modern democracies. Once, party was widely condemned. Thus Thomas Jefferson*, regarded party and faction as a damaging source of disunity in state and society. While party politics is still often deplored, parties feature in virtually every modern democratic system, even where the prevailing political climate was initially hostile. This suggests that political parties are integral to **representative democracy** and perform important functions. These include:

- Political choice and representation – it is largely through parties that voters are given an effective choice at elections between competing teams of political leaders, with distinct policies and ideas. Although voters can choose independent candidates, overwhelmingly they prefer candidates with party labels. Thus in practice **representation** is through parties.
- Political recruitment – it is through parties that individuals are recruited and trained for political office (as elected representatives, government ministers, etc.).
- Reconciling and aggregating interests – while **pressure groups** 'articulate' or promote their own special interests, parties 'aggregate' or bring together a range of interests and help transform a mass of sometimes conflicting demands into a coherent programme that can be placed before voters at elections. (Larger parties inevitably involve coalitions of interests, with some internal tensions.)
- Political participation – joining parties provides another opportunity for ordinary citizens to participate in the political process. Party members can help to select candidates for elections in their area, may contribute to the choice of party leaders, and influence party policy.
- Political identity – parties have provided party members and voters with a sense of their own political **identity**.
- Political communication – parties provide a two-way channel of communication between political leaders and their supporters. Party leaders seek to convince members of the merits of contentious policies, while the views of party members may constrain party policy proposals.
- **Accountability** and control – as government is effectively party government, it is principally through parties that government, at various levels, is held accountable for its performance, particularly at election times.

Some of these functions – particularly political recruitment and communication, are also performed by parties in one-party states, although these will crucially not involve effective democratic choice and only limited accountability and control.

While leading political parties in the mid-20th century were mass parties, with millions of paid-up members, party membership and active involvement has fallen markedly almost everywhere, to such an extent that at local level party organisation may be moribund. [See Part II, Section 2 for more on parties and party systems.]

Politics

[See Part I for a discussion of different perceptions of politics.]

Populism

The term 'populism' has been used to describe specific political movements in the USA and Tsarist Russia in the late 19th century and, more recently, in South America and Europe, although it has been more generally applied to political programmes designed to appeal to ordinary people. This might appear to be the essence of **democracy**, although the term populism is commonly employed in a pejorative way to mean pandering to popular prejudices on issues such as capital punishment or immigration. Thus it is often argued, against populist demands, that elected politicians should lead rather than follow public opinion and should exercise their own judgement rather than follow blindly the views of their constituents or the wider public (see Burke*).

Populist parties and movements are critical of established parliamentary elites and parties. They argue that the people rather than parliament should decide on key issues through **plebiscites** or **referendums** (plebiscitary democracy). Populist politicians may have what Max Weber* described as charismatic authority. While older and some modern populist movements might be considered on the **left**, many today are more associated with the **right** of the political spectrum (e.g. the US Tea Party, the French National Front, and UKIP in the United Kingdom). They appear to be of rising significance around the world today.

Positive, positivism, and logical positivism

Positivism is a philosophical approach that argues that observable facts are the basis of reliable social research. The approach stresses the objective nature of the researcher and is thus independent of the study. The overall aim of a positivist methodology is to explain and predict. A positivist approach tends to suggest the use of quantitative methods and statistics. Key positivist thinkers include Comte*. In political science and international relations positivism is connected with approaches such as rational choice theory and realism. The approach is criticised by supporters of (social) **constructivism**.

Positivism, as expounded by Comte* in the 19th century emphasised the importance of observation of the real world, as opposed to theology and metaphysics, facts rather than values. Thus the study of economics or politics or sociology should study quantifiable data and ignore normative claims and values. Logical positivism in philosophy in the early 20th century rejected any propositions that were unverifiable and thus much traditional philosophy and political theory.

Postindustrialism

'Postindustrialism' (or 'postindustrial society') is a term commonly used to describe a society or economy no longer largely dependent upon mining and manufacturing but on services, knowledge, information, and communication. Most modern Western economies may be described as postindustrial. Many countries in the developing world remain pre-industrial, while others are rapidly industrialising. Yet it is also possible for societies to play a key role in the knowledge and information 'postindustrial' society without ever having been extensively industrialised (for example, India). A postindustrial society may have extensive social and political implications for population distribution, class structure, interests, power, ideas, and values. Daniel Bell* wrote an influential text, *The Coming of Post-Industrial Society* (1976), that explored the concept and its implications.

Post-materialism

Post-materialism is a concept used to describe attitudes or cultures that are no longer largely concerned with increasing material wealth and prosperity but with personal fulfilment and maintaining and improving the quality of life and the environment. Post-material attitudes are commonly associated with advanced Western economies where basic needs have been substantially met and much of the population enjoys material prosperity. According to Ronald Inglehart* (1977, 1990) such a post-material culture is particularly evident among the younger generation in advanced capitalist economies.

Postmodernism

'Postmodernism' is a term that has been widely applied to developments in art, architecture, aesthetics, and literary criticism, as well as psychology, philosophy, and political theory. As with other terms with the prefix 'post' (e.g. **'postindustrialism'**, 'poststructuralism', 'post-**feminism'**) there is some ambiguity over the relationship with the original term. Postmodernism may imply either a following on from or a rejection of modernism and modernity. Yet with regard to politics, postmodernism generally involved a repudiation of the Enlightenment and its trust in human progress, reason, and science. Postmodernists adopted a sceptical attitude to the claims to objectivity and truth made by both natural and social scientists, including political scientists. Postmodernism thus involves an extreme form of relativism or, as some critics would argue, nihilism.

Both postmodernism and the closely related term poststructuralism became influential from the late 1960s onwards in French intellectual circles. Key thinkers associated with postmodernism include Lacan, Foucault,* Lyotard*, Derrida*, and Baudrillard*, although both Foucault and Derrida subsequently dissociated themselves from the term. Some of them also vigorously disagreed with each others' ideas. While none of them were primarily political thinkers, they nevertheless had an important influence on the study of politics, both in Europe and the United States.

Lyotard* famously characterised postmodernism as involving 'an incredulity towards meta-narratives', by which he meant any theory, ideology, science, or religion claiming to provide a general explanation of the world. He argued that faith in such total doctrines had 'lost their credibility' in the post–Second World War era. No single theory could be given privileged status above others. Derrida* is associated with the key postmodernist methodology of deconstruction that re-emphasised the relativist message. Any text, such as a novel, poem, historical account, or political document (e.g. a constitution) had multiple interpretations, among which none should be regarded as authoritative, not even that of the author. Such texts should be 'deconstructed' by readers to reveal other hidden meanings and often contradictory interpretations. Foucault's* early work on the history of madness raised questions about the relationship between normality and abnormality, reason and unreason, while his later work explored the connection between the use of language and **power**. Baudrillard* suggested that in the era of modern mass communication, media images had replaced reality, to the extent that it was often virtually impossible to determine what was real and what was unreal.

In some respects, such scepticism might be regarded as healthy (and indeed scepticism towards traditional authority was a feature of the Enlightenment and the **liberal** tradition that postmodernism rejected). Thus postmodernism particularly appealed to those who felt marginalised by mainstream Western ideas, such as some radical **feminists**, and those belonging to all kinds of minorities. However, the thrust of postmodernism was subversive of all theories, including radical alternative perspectives, and all kinds of knowledge.

Power

Power is a key concept in politics. It may be defined as the capacity to achieve desired goals Yet power is difficult to pin down and even more difficult to measure. Sometimes power is equated simply with physical force. Thus the Chinese **communist** leader Mao Zedong* declared 'Political power grows out of the barrel of a gun.' Yet political power does not always take such overtly coercive forms. The notions of business power, or the power of the church or of the press, or simply the power of ideas imply that power can involve more subtle forms of control or influence than physical compulsion. Indeed, a distinction is often drawn between 'hard power' and 'soft power' (or 'smart power'), the latter associated with persuasion and attraction rather than physical force.

Power can be exercised unlawfully or illegitimately (for example the power wielded by a robber, a rapist, or a warlord). Other power may be accepted and regarded as **legitimate** by those over whom it is exercised. **Authority** is the term commonly used for legitimate power. Lawful or legitimate power may be exercised by a recognised government, particularly today one that has been democratically elected. Yet even if power is willingly accepted and acknowledged, without any appearance of coercion, this may be the consequence of a more subtle exercise of power (see Foucault* 1977), that effectively tells people what to think (for example, through control of education or the **media**, and the whole process of political socialisation).

The American **pluralist** Robert Dahl* defined power in terms of A getting B to do something he would not otherwise do. Dahl sought to measure this by studying decision-making, exploring the influence of various interests on political decisions, and concluded that political power was fairly widely diffused in the communities he studied. Yet it is impossible to prove that the activities and influence of a particular group caused a specific outcome. Moreover, critics have objected that this focus on overt decision-making ignores the capacity of dominant interests or **elites** to shape and influence the opinion of others, so that some issues do not come onto the political agenda at all (Lukes 1974). Alternative approaches to the focus on decision-making, for example tracing the links between members of elite groups in a political community to suggest the existence of a dominant single ruling elite or establishment, may be suggestive but hardly more conclusive. Thus political scientists continue to disagree over the extent to which political power is diffused or concentrated in any society or community. [See also discussion in Part I.]. Power is a key concept in International Relations. Realists such as Morgenthau* see power in terms of influence over outcomes. Power is often focused on military or 'hard' power, although Nye* introduces the concept of 'soft' power, whereby states influence norms to achieve outcomes.

Pragmatism

Pragmatism in politics involves hostility to theory and **ideology** and a preference for practical experience. 'What matters is what works.' This approach has been most commonly associated with **conservative** thinkers (such as Burke* or Oakeshott*) and politicians, although it has also been linked with some politicians on the centre-left. Critics equate pragmatism with lack of principle and with following public opinion rather than leading it. For advocates it is about judging issues 'on their merits' rather than in accordance with preconceived ideas. It is however impossible to escape all theoretical assumptions. As the economist Keynes* ([1936] 1964, chapter 24) declared, 'Practical men, who believe themselves exempt from any intellectual influences, are usually the slaves of some defunct economist.'

Pressure groups

In the study of politics a pressure group may be defined as any organised group that seeks to influence **government** and public policy at any level. They are *organised*, thus they are not just a section of the public with an interest in common. They commonly have elected or appointed officers and paid up members and sometimes a formal constitution. They are thus to be distinguished from broader and looser **social movements**. Unlike political parties they seek *influence* rather than direct control of power, nor do they normally contest elections (although some have done, generally to advertise their case rather than with any realistic expectation of winning). While pressure groups 'articulate' interests, parties 'aggregate' interests. This means that pressure groups campaign for a specific interest or cause, whereas political parties must have a wide range of policies appealing to many different interests, which in turn requires accommodation and compromise.

The literature on groups is bedevilled by the absence of a generally agreed terminology. 'Pressure groups', 'organised groups', 'interest groups', and simply 'groups' are among the many terms commonly used to describe essentially the same phenomenon. 'Groups' and 'organised groups' seems too broad and insufficiently related to politics. 'Interest groups' has the disadvantage of cutting across a common distinction made between types of group – 'interest' and 'cause' groups. 'Pressure groups' has the merit of emphasising the role of groups in the political process, bringing pressure to bear on government, although it perhaps exaggerates the importance of such pressure compared with the other roles of many groups that do not exist primarily for political purposes. They may be seen as voluntary organisations, part of **civil society**, and outside government and the **state**.

Analysis of pressure groups widely distinguishes between groups *defending* the (self) *interest* of a particular *section* of the community, and groups *promoting* a *cause*. This distinction between interest and cause groups is generally useful, although there are some problems of classification at the margins. Another common distinction focuses on the relationship with government. Some are *insider* groups, with regular access to government, while others are *outsider* groups, excluded from consultation by government (Grant, 2000).

Beyond these issues of definition and classification there is an extensive debate over the role of pressure groups in the political system generally, and more specifically their contribution to **democracy**. (Some of these issues are addressed briefly under other key concepts, such as '**elitism**', '**pluralism**' and '**power**' and in more detail elsewhere in this volume, under **behaviouralism** in Part II, Section 2.

Privatisation

(See under **Nationalisation**.)

Property

Entitlement to property and its distribution has been a central issue in political theory. Some thinkers have envisaged an original state of nature in which there was no private property and where the fruits of the earth were enjoyed in common. In *A Discourse on Inequality* Rousseau* imagines 'The first man who, having enclosed a piece of land, thought of saying "This is mine" and found people simple enough to believe him, was the true founder of civil society' (Rousseau ([1755] 1984, 109). Rousseau appears to regret it, arguing the human race would have been spared endless miseries and horrors if the claim had been resisted, but goes on to suggest that the acceptance of the institution of private property was perhaps inevitable.

Conservatives have seen few problems with private property, particularly land, once the most obvious source of status, wealth, and income. While **liberals** have sometimes expressed strong reservations over the distribution of landed property in particular, they have generally strongly asserted the right to enjoyment of private property. Some **socialists** and **anarchists** have opposed all private property, arguing instead that goods should be held in common. The French socialist anarchist Proudhon* famously declared that property was theft. Marx* and Engels* specifically targeted **bourgeois** property, the private ownership of the means of production. Both Soviet **communism** and, at one time but to a lesser extent, Western **social**

democracy sought to replace private ownership of industry with public ownership.

Although the majority of the population once had negligible private property, property ownership has become more widely diffused in some societies. It is no longer unusual for ordinary working people to own their own homes, a range of luxury consumer goods, and even stocks and shares and other forms of wealth. This suggests to **conservatives** that a 'property-owning democracy' is now a reality. Critics on the **left** of the political spectrum however argue that the distribution of income and wealth is more unequal than ever (see Piketty 2014). Redistribution to secure more **equality** and **social justice** is strongly resisted on the **right** – particularly taxes on wealth and inheritance and progressive income tax.

As well as arguments over the distribution of property, there are also increasingly arguments over its use. While at one time it was suggested that a man and at times also a woman was entitled to do what he or she wished with his or her own property, regardless of the social or environmental consequences, this has long not been the case. Today there are increasing legal restrictions on the uses to which property can be put.

Public administration

Public administration is a term used to describe the organisation and management of services for which government (at any level) is responsible. The term is also used to describe the study of the organisation and management of public services.

Public choice theory

(See under **Rational choice theory**.)

Public good

A public good is a good that has to be supplied to everyone if it is supplied to anyone and from which no one can be excluded. Examples of such public goods include clean air, national defence, public parks, lighthouses. The market cannot be relied upon to supply such public goods, as charging is ineffective because it is impossible to prevent 'free riders' who have not paid for the good or service from benefiting from it. Such public goods may be supplied by public authorities, although they may also be provided by public subscription or private philanthropy.

Public interest

The public interest may be defined as the common interest, or the interest of the majority, or the 'common good'. Governments, individual politicians, and public officials may claim to serve the public interest. Sometimes a particular decision or policy is claimed to be 'in the public interest', while an alternative is 'not in the public interest'. Yet it is difficult to identify the public interest definitively. Very few decisions or policies can be said to benefit everyone.

Rational choice and **public choice theorists** are particularly sceptical over the claims made by politicians and public officials that they serve the public interest. These theorists do not recognise such apparently altruistic motives but assume that all individuals, whether working in the public sector or the private sector, pursue their own rational self-interest. Thus ministers or officials claiming to serve the public interest would really be pursuing their own interests, for example seeking to advance their own careers.

Quango

'Quango' is an acronym (widely used in the United Kingdom) for **q**uasi-**a**utonomous non-governmental **o**rganisation. Exactly what organisations should be counted as quangos is contentious. Some quangos have important executive functions, some are quasi-judicial, some regulatory, while some are purely advisory. Examples of British organisations that have been described as quangos include the Arts Council (executive), the Employment Tribunal (quasi-judicial), the Audit Commission (regulatory), and the White Fish Authority (advisory).

Quangos are best described as appointed (rather than elected) agencies not directly controlled by elected politicians. In the United Kingdom the official description is 'nondepartmental public bodies', indicating that they are not part of the government departments nor staffed by civil servants. Other terms used to described these institutions include 'ad hoc bodies' (suggesting they are not part of the permanent machinery of government) and 'para-state organisations'. However, the acronym 'quango' has become the most familiar, even if the 'nongovernmental' part of the description is rather misleading, as quangos can be funded out of taxation and ultimately (regardless of their 'quasi-autonomous' status) function as part of government.

The growth of quangos has been widely criticised, from the centre and left on the grounds that these organisations are not democratically elected and are only weakly accountable to parliament and public, and on the right as part of a disguised and undesirable growth of government and public spending. A key issue is patronage: how are people appointed to quangos and on what criteria? Pejorative terms to describe the phenomenon include 'the quango state', 'quangocracy', 'the appointed state', and 'the new magistracy.'

Yet it is generally conceded that some public functions (e.g. funding the arts and much state regulation) need to be administered independently of the government of the day, to promote public confidence in their neutrality. Also many advisory quangos usefully and cheaply tap expertise not necessarily available within the permanent government bureaucracy.

Race and racism

Race is a concept that reputable thinkers now recognise has never had any scientific validity. In the 19th century it was widely believed that humankind could be classified into distinctive races (crudely identified by skin colour labels: white, yellow, brown, red, and black) with measurable physical and mental differences. In Nazi Germany 'scientific racism' became a state-sponsored orthodoxy used to justify the treatment of 'non-Aryans' as inferior species and, ultimately, the extermination of the Jews in the Holocaust. Today, scientific racism is totally discredited, although the term 'race' is still widely and loosely used, sometimes to distinguish cultural rather than biological differences. **Ethnicity** has become the approved term to describe such cultural differences, although official sources sometimes still use the term 'race', as in 'race relations'. Descriptions based supposedly on skin colour ('blacks') or broad geographical background ('Asians') are also widely used and even to a degree accepted by minority communities themselves, although they involve gross oversimplification and ignore substantial differences within these crude categories.

Racism, discriminating against those perceived to be of different racial origin, remains a feature of many modern societies, despite legislation outlawing discrimination and prejudice. Some writers have associated racism with economic deprivation and class relations under capitalism. Thus most 'blacks and Asians' in countries where 'whites' are in the majority are employed in low-status manual work and live in racially segregated deprived urban areas. Here they compete for jobs, houses, and services with working-class whites inhabiting the same deprived environment. Both white working-class racism and the aggressive response of some young black and Asian males to white racism can be seen as a symptom of economic decline and deprivation. Yet economic deprivation hardly explains one of the most persistent forms of racism displayed by all classes over the centuries, anti-Semitism.

Some argue that racist attitudes are deeply embedded in popular culture, as a consequence of the historical experience of slavery and racial segregation in some countries (e.g. the USA) or colonial domination and exploitation in others (e.g. the United Kingdom, France, Spain). American writers describe this culturally embedded racism as institutional racism, whereas in the United Kingdom the term is commonly applied more narrowly to persistent racist attitudes embedded in particular institutions, such as the police or the armed services.

Racism is routinely denounced by mainstream politicians, although some have not been above employing coded language to appeal to those concerned about ethnic tensions and immigration. Indeed, much of the expressed concern over 'immigration' and 'bogus asylum seekers' thinly conceals racist attitudes. The 'war on terror' has exacerbated anti-Muslim feeling, and although this is strictly a religious rather than a 'race' issue, it has had some impact even on Asians who are not Muslim. There have been periodic concerns over rising support for racist parties in a number of countries.

While some would see integration and a colour-blind approach as the long-term answer to racism, others assert the value of distinctive ethnic identities and the benefits of diversity and argue for a positive acceptance of **multiculturalism**. Then again some fear that the perpetuation of difference may hinder mutual understanding and toleration and reinforce prejudice, eroding any sense of a common national identity and allegiance. Others respond that multiple identities and allegiances are a feature of the modern world.

Rational choice theory and public choice theory

Rational choice theory is derived from classical economic theory and assumes that **individuals** pursue their rational self-interest. Thus the starting point of analysis is the individual, not groups of people nor society as a whole. Each individual is deemed capable of recognising his or her own self-interest and pursuing it rationally. This assumption can be applied to voting, implying that individual voters will choose candidates and parties most likely to look after what they perceive as their own interest (lower taxes if they pay high taxes or improved public services if they are beneficiaries of such services).

Public choice theorists (e.g. Buchanan*, Tullock*, Niskanen*) apply the assumptions of the pursuit of rational self-interest to the **state**, the public sector, and public policy. They assume politicians, ministers, and public officials are motivated to pursue their own rational self-interest in the same way as consumers and producers in the **free market**. In the absence of profits, however, those operating in the public sector will seek to advance their own careers, pay, and conditions by expanding their own departments and agencies ('bureau maximisation' instead of profit maximisation). Thus politicians and officials in the public sector will favour increases in the size of government, public spending, and taxation, without fearing the disciplines of the free market (ultimately, business failure and bankruptcy). Voters and special-interest groups who benefit from public services and subsidies but who do not have to bear the full cost as taxpayers may support such public spending and taxation. Public choice theory provides a plausible explanation of rising public spending and taxation in the postwar decades. It has become influential both in government circles and in the study of politics generally, but particularly in the USA.

Critics of rational choice theory and public choice theory may argue that individuals can act altruistically, preferring to pursue another's interest rather than their own. Or they may deny the assumption of rationality, suggesting that humans often follow their instincts or passions. They may reject the individualist assumptions, suggesting that individuals may be socially conditioned to act in the interests of others. Finally, it is possible to accept the assumptions but reject the conclusions derived from the assumptions. Thus it is possible to argue that the pursuit of rational self-interest by public sector bureaucrats does not necessarily entail 'bureau maximisation' (Dunleavy 1991).

Rationalism

Rationalism assumes humans are, or should be, guided by reason rather than instinct or emotion. It is a key assumption of the Enlightenment and **liberalism**. Liberals go on to assume that humans pursue their own rational self-interest and that they are the best judges of their own interests. It has been commonly argued that reason is what distinguishes human beings from other sentient creatures, although it is far from generally agreed that all humans are capable of rational thought and conduct. Thus Plato* argued that only a tiny minority of humans are ruled by reason; the rest are governed by emotions or base appetites. Only those who are themselves ruled by reason should be entrusted with ruling others. **Conservative** thinkers such as Burke* and Oakeshott* have not only doubted the extent to which people are guided by reason, rather than instinct, **tradition**, or prejudice, but have explicitly criticised reason and rationalism. Thus for Oakeshott* rationalism in politics is to be avoided. **Fascism** elevated commitment and emotion above reason. **Postmodernism** has questioned the Enlightenment trust in reason, knowledge, and progress.

Some modern political science seems to suggest that human behaviour is not very rational (for example, some of the analysis of voting behaviour and some theories of political communication). However, Herbert Simon* advocated for and defended a rational model of policy-making against the rival **incrementalist** model of Charles Lindblom*. Moreover, rational choice theory assumes the pursuit of rational self-interest in the public as well as the private sector. Some other approaches, particularly variants of **Marxism**, assume that the ideas and behaviour of individual humans are extensively socially conditioned and thus they may be unable to recognise and pursue their own rational self-interest.

Realism and *Realpolitik*

Realism, in politics, is commonly contrasted with idealism. Realism means seeing the world as it is rather than as one would like it to be. Machiavelli* and Hobbes* have sometimes been cited as exemplifying the realist approach.

The term realism has been applied particularly to an influential interpretation of **international relations**. The study of international relations was initially given impetus by idealist assumptions about the potential to end war through collective security and the development of appropriate

international institutions. The failure of these hopes between the two world wars led to the dominance of the realist interpretation of international relations associated with the work of E. H .Carr* and Hans Morgenthau* and later the neorealist work of Kenneth Waltz*. (These realist assumptions have remained strongly in evidence among American neo-conservatives.) Realists and neorealists have seen international relations as remaining essentially anarchic and have stressed the continuing central role of states pursuing their own national interest through a readiness to use the military and economic resources at their disposal. Realists and neorealists are sceptical about the efficacy of international institutions and international law in dealing with threats to world peace. However, the growing importance of non-state actors (especially **nongovernmental organisations** and **transnational corporations**) in a globalising world, coupled with the transformed international landscape following the collapse of Soviet communism, has led to a variety of challenges to the hitherto dominant neorealist interpretation of international relations.

'*Realpolitik*' is a German word that expresses a hard-headed realist approach to domestic and international politics, involving a readiness to use all resources available, including military force, to attain one's ends. It has been associated particularly with the diplomacy of the 19th-century Prussian and German chancellor Bismarck in his pursuit of German unification.

Referendum, or plebiscite

A referendum or plebiscite allows voters themselves to decide directly on particular issues, rather than leaving them to the decisions of elected representatives. It has been used particularly to decide constitutional questions but also on a wide range of other issues in some countries (e.g. in the United Kingdom so-called Brexit from the European Union, 2016). Thus a referendum may be held to determine whether a particular territory should become independent or exercise devolved powers. In some US states (e.g. California), under a device called the 'initiative', a proportion of citizens can force an issue (for example tax cuts or the legalisation of cannabis) onto the ballot paper for a decision by voters.

The referendum and other similar devices inject an element of **direct democracy** into a system of representative or parliamentary democracy and appear to give more power to the people. It allows people to vote on specific issues that affect them, rather than leaving the decision to representatives. It is also argued that the public debate around referendum questions submitted to the electorate helps to educate the public on the issues involved.

However referendums can involve problems. Firstly, who decides issues to be determined by referendum and who frames the questions? **Dictators** and charismatic leaders have sometimes made use of referendums to legitimise a preferred course of action. A question may be cleverly worded so as to encourage a desired answer. Equal time and equal resources may not be given to advocates of both sides, so the public debate may not be balanced and fair. A particular problem is that many issues cannot be easily framed to provide a straight choice between 'yes' or 'no'. There may be unanticipated problems in implementing the electorate's choice, particularly on tax and public spending cuts.

At another level it is argued that there is a conflict between the ideas of direct and representative democracy and between those of popular and parliamentary **sovereignty**. It is not easy to combine two methods of decision-making based on different principles. One compromise solution that apparently preserves the principle of parliamentary sovereignty, and is used in the United Kingdom, is to consider referendums advisory only. This preserves the principle of parliamentary sovereignty. Yet in practice it would be politically very difficult to disregard a clear majority decision on a reasonable turnout in a referendum, and UK governments have in practice regarded referendum results as binding (e.g. the UK vote to leave the EU).

Representation

Representation is a key but contentious concept in modern politics. Broadly, it involves a means by which an individual or small group are formally entrusted with promoting and defending the views and interests of many people (who may directly choose or elect them). It has been argued that the ancient world was unfamiliar with the concept of representation. Whether this is true or not, representation has become the crucial element of the modern conception of **democracy**. Instead of direct rule by the people themselves, government is subject to the control of elected representatives of the people. Some would urge that these elected representatives should faithfully 'represent' the views of those they were elected to serve, even where they strongly disagree with those views. Others (following Edmund Burke*) have argued that a representative is not a delegate and should use his or her own judgement of the **public interest** rather than reflect the views of electors. This has become orthodoxy, although it might be noted that socialists and trade unionists have been more inclined to regard representatives as delegates. (See also **democracy**, **referendum**, and **mandate** for arguments about representative and direct democracy and the problems of combining elements of both.)

Another issue is how far any representative institution should be broadly socially representative, as well as formally elected. In practice, many representative bodies at national, regional, and local levels are not socially representative. In most representative democracies women and **ethnic minorities** are underrepresented. Some occupations are overrepresented (commonly, law and education) while others are underrepresented (e.g. manual workers).

It is argued that an elected body can hardly be expected to be a microcosm of the electorate, unless the electors' freedom to choose is considerably restricted. Others would argue that it is more important that representatives have the political skills necessary to serve their electors effectively, and these skills are inevitably unequally distributed in the population. There is some force in these arguments. Even so, if most representatives have no direct knowledge of the life and experience of those they represent, there may be an important element missing from their debates and decisions.

Republic and republicanism

The familiar meaning of republic today is any state that is not a **monarchy**, in other words, most states in the modern world. A republican is someone opposed to, or seeking to abolish, monarchy. The term republic does however have other associations. It derives from the Latin *Res Publica* ('the public concern' or 'public affairs'). The original Roman Republic was established after the expulsion of the last of Rome's kings in 509 BCE and lasted until the formal establishment of the Roman Empire under Caesar Augustus in 31 BCE. This Roman Republic involved a mixed but substantially aristocratic system of government, headed by two elected consuls and the Senate, (an assembly of patricians or noblemen), but with tribunes of the plebs looking after the interests of the common people. Writers such as Cicero* identified the Roman Republic with **liberty** and public service, and this became a model to be idealised and copied in subsequent ages. Thus republics flourished intermittently among the cities of Renaissance Italy, in the Dutch Republic from the late 16th and 17th centuries, and in England briefly in the middle of the 17th century. The republican ideal was later taken up with enthusiasm in the American and French revolutions, and by their subsequent imitators. In political thought this republican tradition is represented by thinkers such as Machiavelli* in Renaissance Florence, Paine* in the 18th century in England, and Madison* (particularly) among the founding fathers of the United States of America. For Madison, a republic involved a representative but essentially mixed system of government rather than a pure democracy. Subsequently both in America and particularly in France 'republic' became synonymous with 'democracy'.

(Note that the translation of the title of Plato's* best known work *The Republic* is misleading. It has nothing to do with the republican tradition described above.)

Responsibility

While accountability flows upwards, responsibility flows downwards. Thus government ministers may be held responsible for everyone employed in their departments and everything done in their name. In the past, ministerial responsibility sometimes resulted in resignations for serious failures, even where the minister had no personal involvement or knowledge of the matter, but now it is unusual for a minister to 'carry the can' for mistakes by subordinates.

The UK doctrine of collective cabinet responsibility requires all ministers to support, or at least not publicly oppose, government policies that they may personally dislike. Such collective responsibility is a principle widely practised by other governments, because open internal divisions are damaging to public confidence and can lead to government breakdown.

Revolution

In politics the term 'revolution' is commonly used to describe a substantial popular uprising that secures not just a change in the government but a change in the whole system of government, or 'regime change'. (Note, however that the term is sometimes employed more loosely to describe, by analogy, any major change, e.g. 'the Industrial Revolution', 'the behavioural revolution'.)

A political revolution may be distinguished from a 'coup', the term used for a takeover of government at a more limited elite level. Key political revolutions that became models to imitate and/or examples to avoid were the American Revolution, the French Revolution of 1789, and the Russian Bolshevik Revolution of 1917. The English Civil War is sometimes described as a revolution, although this term is more commonly given to the replacement of King James II by William of Orange in 1688, the so-called Glorious Revolution, which was more of a coup than a revolution. Revolutions involving significant regime change have been a recurring feature of the last two centuries around the world.

The causes of political stability and change have been explored by political thinkers from Plato* and Aristotle* onwards. It has become a major theme in the modern study of comparative politics. Theda Skocpol* (1979) made her name with a comparative analysis of the French, Russian, and Chinese revolutions. More recently, scholars have focused on the anticommunist revolutions of 1989 onwards in the former Soviet Union and Eastern Europe. Ralf Dahrendorf wrote *Reflections on the Revolution in Europe* (1990) in conscious homage to the essay of Edmund Burke* on the French Revolution two hundred years previously.

Rights

Rights involve an entitlement to something – a right to life, a right to education, a right to free expression, a right to work. They may be enshrined in specific **laws**, as for example a right to equal pay for men and women is in many countries. In some countries they may be listed in a charter of **citizens**' rights or may form part of the state **constitution**.

It is often argued that these legal rights and citizen rights reflect some prior natural rights or universal human rights. Thus the American Declaration of Independence claimed that 'all men are created equal and are endowed by their Creator with certain unalienable rights and that among these are life, liberty and the pursuit of happiness'. Rather more specific are the rights listed in the Declaration of the Rights of Man and Citizen made by the French revolutionaries in 1789, and more detailed still are the United Nations Universal Declaration of Human Rights (1948) or the European Convention on Human Rights (1951).

If rights were indeed 'self-evident' or universally acknowledged, there would be no need to proclaim them. Many of the rights that have been proclaimed as natural or inalienable human rights (for example freedom of expression or gender equality) have been far from universally recognised

over time. They are proclaimed to persuade people that they *should* be recognised.

Not everyone finds the notion of rights helpful. Jeremy Bentham* mocked the whole notion of natural rights as 'nonsense on stilts'. The only right he recognised was a legal right. Marx* criticised not so much the principle but the particular rights enumerated in the *Declaration of the Rights of Man*, particularly the emphasis on rights to property and security. These were, he considered, the rights of egoistic man, 'an individual withdrawn into himself, his private interest and his private desires and separated from the community' (Marx [1840s] 1975, 230–231). Some (e.g. Bhikhu Parekh 2000) argue that 'universal human rights' are only the rights recognised by dominant liberal Western culture and that the right of other cultures to be different should be respected. A problem here is that the rights of religious or ethnic communities may be employed to trump the rights of individuals and minorities within these communities (Barry 2001a). Thus respect for a particular cultural tradition might involve acceptance of discrimination against women or gays.

While some would deny the universality of human rights, others seek to extend rights further. The notion of animal rights implicitly conflicts with some traditionally recognised human rights, but there are some influential moral philosophers today (e.g. Peter Singer*) who champion animal rights.

Secularism

Secularism arose from the movement towards religious toleration from the 18th-century Enlightenment onwards. It involved the separation of government from religious institutions and beliefs, state neutrality in matters of religious belief, and toleration of different faiths. This principle was enshrined in the First Amendment to the US constitution, which declared that Congress 'should make no law respecting an establishment of religion, or prohibiting the free exercise thereof'. It was also associated with the government of France of the Third Republic onwards, where the principle has been interpreted to mean that no religious clothing or symbols are permissible in state schools and specifically the ban on Muslim girls wearing the hijab (sometimes mistranslated as 'veil').

There has been a strong modern trend towards secularism, particularly in the Western world but also elsewhere. Thus Kemel Ataturk founded the republic of Turkey as a secular state, while India gained independence as a secular state, which was seen as particularly necessary for a country with substantial religious divisions. However, more recently there have been some reversals of this trend towards secularisation and the separation of politics from religion, particularly in parts of the Islamic world and in India, which has seen some resurgence of Hindu nationalism.

Separation of powers

The term 'separation of powers' means that the main functions of the state – **executive**, **legislative**, and **judicial** – should be clearly distinct and wielded by separate institutions. Hobbes* and others forcefully declared that **sovereignty**, supreme **power** within the **state**, could not be divided. Other thinkers, following Montesquieu*, have argued that the main powers or functions of the state could and should be maintained in separate hands in order to preserve the liberty of citizens and protect them from tyranny. Montesquieu considered that British government involved such a separation of powers, with the king (or queen) and his (or her) ministers constituting the executive, parliament the legislature, and an independent judiciary. Other observers (e.g. Bagehot* [1867] 1963) subsequently concluded that the executive and legislative functions in British government were interdependent and essentially fused, while even the judiciary was not truly independent.

It was the American **constitution** that first embodied the principle of the separation of powers. This declared that legislative powers were invested in Congress, executive powers in the president, and judicial powers in the Supreme Court and other inferior courts. Besides this apparently clear separation of the main powers or functions of the state, the US constitution also involved a separation between different levels of government, **federal** and state. In practice, the separation of powers in the American system of government did not and could not involve a complete separation of powers, as they were necessarily interdependent, but instituted a system of 'checks and balances' designed to prevent the accumulation and centralisation of **power**. These checks and balances are still widely approved in the United States, although over time there have been some criticism that the power of the presidency has increased at the expense of Congress and the federal government at the expense of states' rights. By contrast, there are periodic concerns over 'gridlock', resulting from conflict within the system, commonly between president and Congress, frustrating the process of government.

Social capital

The term 'social capital' is used by the American political scientist Robert Putnam* to mean the extent of social interaction and community engagement in any society. Thus active involvement in a bridge club, parent teacher association, trade union, church, political party or gun club would all count as part of social capital. Putnam has documented a marked decline in social capital in the United States, with, he argues, adverse implications for a healthy functioning **democracy**. However, critics suggest that Putnam underestimates the positive potential of new methods of communication via the internet which do not require physical association.

Socialism and social democracy

'Socialism' has been variously defined. Socialists in the 19th century emphasised **equality**, general social welfare rather than individual self-interest, co-operation rather than competition, planning rather than **free market** forces, common ownership (or more specifically, collective ownership of the means of production) rather than private **property**. Thus socialism was seen as an alternative to **capitalism**. Arguably, socialists disagreed more over strategy than over values, some advocating a *revolutionary* route to socialism, others placing their faith in a more gradual *evolutionary* socialism to be achieved through the ballot box and **representative** institutions, although this disagreement partly reflected differing political circumstances in particular states. Thus while both German and Russian socialists had been inspired by Marx's* brand of revolutionary socialism, the two movements developed very differently. The German socialists openly organised a mass **political party**, which won substantial electoral support and parliamentary representation, while their (much less numerous) Russian counterparts were constrained to operate clandestinely and mainly in exile. While the German party largely came to terms with a parliamentary system and the norms of representative **democracy**, the Russian party remained committed to **revolution**.

Both these parties were called social democrat, and before the First World War the terms 'socialism' and 'social democracy' were commonly used interchangeably. All socialists (including Marx) considered themselves democrats. The successful Bolshevik revolution in Russia deepened the division between those committed to parliamentary socialism and those seeking revolution. This split was institutionalised into rival international socialist organisations: the (social democratic) Second International and the (Soviet-dominated) Third International.

Since then, 'social democracy' has become the term widely used term to describe a moderate, reformist (or revisionist), parliamentary socialism, rather than revolutionary or explicitly **Marxist** socialism or **communism**. Between the two world wars there was much bitter mutual antipathy between communists and social democrats in Europe, interspersed with limited periods of co-operation in 'popular front' coalitions. After the Second World War the split between the socialism practised in the Soviet Union and Eastern Europe and that championed in the West was emphasised by the 'iron curtain' between them. In

Western Europe the values of social democracy were apparently so widely endorsed (even by other parties) that commentators talked of a 'social democratic consensus'. This consensus involved the acceptance of a mixed economy with a substantial state sector, increased welfare provision, and progressive taxation, all expected to lead, over time, to a more equal society. It was challenged by a revival of neoliberal free market ideas in the West in the 1970s and 1980s, while the alternative 'actually existing socialism' of the Eastern bloc rapidly imploded after 1989. One commentator, Ralph Dahrendorf (1990, 38) declared, after the revolutions of 1989 that socialism in all its variants (including social democracy) was dead.

The survival of socialism or social democracy depends on how these terms are defined. Parties describing themselves as socialist or social democratic have since been returned to power for significant periods in Sweden, France, Germany, the United Kingdom, and elsewhere. Yet most of these have not only come to terms with capitalism and free market but have also sometimes actively pursued the privatisation of formerly state-owned enterprises. Political leaders argue they are maintaining traditional socialist or social democratic values but reinterpreting them to meet altered circumstances. Certainly it is difficult to identify social democracy any more with **collectivism** and **nationalisation**. Fairness or **equality** are still enthusiastically endorsed by social democrats. Yet it is questionable how far greater equality has been achieved to any appreciable degree (see Piketty 2014).

Social movements and new social movements

The term 'social movement' is commonly used to describe a relatively loosely organised and informal combination of individuals and groups supporting a broad interest or cause. While a **pressure group** commonly has a formal organisation and identifiable leaders and members, a social movement may lack any coherent structure, being composed instead of a fluctuating body of supporters and sympathisers, many of whom may not belong to any organised group. An example of an older social movement is the labour movement, which contains organised union members but also their families and sympathisers.

The term 'new social movement' has been used to describe a number of political movements that became prominent from the 1960s onwards, including the women's movement, the peace movement, the **green** movement, and more recently the anticapitalist movement. While all of these included some formally structured pressure groups, they also contain unattached supporters and sympathisers. Indeed, a loose informal movement was partly preferred for ideological reasons. Thus some **feminists** associate formal organisations, involving rules and hierarchies, with a male preference for order, **authority**, and status and seek less directed, more spontaneous and co-operative methods of working. Similarly, some peace campaigners and green activists positively reject leadership roles. The supporters of such new social movements commonly favour alternative forms of political activity, often including direct action rather than traditional pressure group methods. For movements operating on the fringes of legality (such as parts of the anticapitalist movement or the animal rights movement) a lack of formal organisation may have some practical advantages, making it more difficult for the authorities to determine who is responsible for what.

While these new social movements are associated with the **left** of the political spectrum, it should be noted that there has been a rise of right-wing protest movements in many countries, such as movements objecting to immigration or opposing restrictions on traditional countryside pursuits (such as hunting).

Sovereignty and independent sovereign state

'Sovereignty' means supreme power. Within a state it refers to the ultimate source of legal authority. While some thinkers (e.g. Hobbes*) insist that sovereignty in a state cannot be divided, others (e.g. Locke*, Montesquieu*) argue that it can and should be. Thus many modern states follow the United States in separating the **executive**, **legislative**, and **judicial** functions of the state, and some also have imitated the United States in dividing sovereignty between a **federal** and state level. The United Kingdom's political system, by contrast, was supposed to involve the principle of parliamentary sovereignty within a unitary state, and the power of the Westminster Parliament was in theory unlimited. This parliamentary sovereignty is inconsistent with the ideal of the **separation of powers** (embodied in the American and many other constitutions). Some critics have attacked the principle of parliamentary sovereignty, while others have argued that recent developments in British government (**devolution**, the increased use of **referendums**, and the Human Rights Act) have substantially eroded parliamentary sovereignty.

When used of the external relations of states, sovereignty refers to a state's ability to function as an independent entity free from external control or interference – as an **independent sovereign state**. The traditional interpretation of **international relations** as practised from the Treaty of Westphalia (1648) onwards has revolved around the interrelationship of such independent sovereign states. Today some supposedly sovereign states are perceived as the puppets of other states, while other states fail to maintain a monopoly of the legitimate use of physical force within their own borders. Moreover in an era of **globalisation**, international relations are complicated by the growing importance of international institutions, **nongovernmental organisations** (NGOs) and **transnational corporations** (TNCs) that appear to constrain the freedom of action of sovereign states. Within the study of international relations, idealists welcome these trends, involving the increasing acknowledgement of international obligations and international law. Realists, however, insist that the extent of change is exaggerated and that independent sovereign states, with their own economic and military resources, remain the crucial players in the game of international diplomacy.

State

The state may be briefly defined as a compulsory political association that has ,supreme power (**sovereignty**) over a particular area. According to Max Weber* 'the state is a human community that (successfully) claims the monopoly of the legitimate use of physical force within a given territory'. The concepts of force or **power**, **sovereignty**, and **legitimacy** are closely bound up with most accounts of the state. The state may be defined narrowly, to include just the formal institutions of central government, or rather more broadly, to cover local authorities and any other organisations funded by taxation. For some **Marxist** thinkers the state comprises any social institutions that appear to fulfil the functions of the state (including the church or even the mass media).

'The state' in everyday language is sometimes used simply to mean 'the government', but while governments come and go, the state continues (unless destroyed by conquest, revolution, or breakdown). States in practice have taken a wide variety of size and type, from small city states to extensive empires, from traditional autocracies to modern representative democracies, from unitary states to federal states (see **federalism**).

The functions or responsibilities of states vary in both theory and practice. Minimum (or 'night watchman') states largely confine their activities to defence and the maintenance of internal law and order. Others seek to exercise extensive powers over the outward behaviour and expressed beliefs of subject or citizens. **Welfare states** have assumed wide responsibilities for the provision of social services.

Attitudes to the state vary widely, reflecting widely different ideological assumptions. **Anarchists** argue that states are inevitably oppressive, restricting **freedom**. People would be better off relying on peaceful voluntary co-operation in stateless societies.

At the other extreme **fascism** was associated with a **totalitarian** theory of the state, under which the state was all-embracing and excluded from no sphere of activity. **Conservatives** have generally emphasised the need for a strong state to protect people from external threats and internal crime and disorder. **Free market liberals** have tended to see the state as a necessary evil but have sought to limit the power and scope of the state, excluding it from much economic and social activity and sharply distinguishing between the sphere of the state and **civil society** or the state and the market. **Social democrats** have generally seen the state more positively and have sought, through the electoral process, to capture and use the institutions of the state to achieve social reform. This is compatible with the **pluralist** assumption that the state is neutral among the various interests and pressures within a political community, as opposed to the **elitist** perspective that assumes that the state is controlled by and serves the interests of a ruling elite or elites. **Marxists** contend specifically that the state in a **capitalist** society is bound to serve the interest of capital (although some Marxists allow that the state has 'relative autonomy' in pursuing that aim).

These different perspectives on the state also suggest very different answers to the questions posed by political theorists: why and how far should we obey the state? For some (e.g. Bodin* and Hobbes*) this **obligation** is unconditional. For others, such an obligation depends on the state's **legitimacy**. For democrats, legitimacy depends on the willing **consent** of the governed. For **nationalists**, to be legitimate the state has to be a **nation-state**, comprising all those who feel they belong to the **nation** (however defined). Revolutionary Marxists seek the overthrow of the capitalist state. Anarchists reject all states.

International Relations as a discipline has long involved the study of the interaction of independent sovereign states. Until recently no other actors seemed to matter. Within the last century or so the growth of international organisations and international law have sometimes appeared to constrain states. The increased role of **transnational corporations** (**TNC**s) in an increasingly global economy and the growing influence of **nongovernmental organisations** (NGOs) have arguably limited states' freedom of action still further. Indeed, some argue that **globalisation** heralds the end of the nation-state (Ohmae 1996). For others the implications of globalisation have been exaggerated and real power in international relations still lies with independent sovereign states. Yet in the modern world some states are clearly far more powerful than others. Some struggle vainly to maintain order within their own borders. Failed states may lead to prolonged civil war, external intervention, and humanitarian disasters.

Structure and agency

The relative importance of structure and agency in politics has become a key theoretical debate. It is closely related to the old issue of free will and determinism. 'Structure' may be defined as the context or environment in which individuals or groups operate. 'Agency' refers to the ability of individuals or groups to affect political outcomes. Some theorists suggest that the capacity of any individuals or groups to change history is highly constrained, owing to economic and social factors over which they have little or no control. This suggests that there is no point in examining too closely the ideas and behaviour of politicians such as presidents, prime ministers, or chancellors. Instead we should seek to understand the whole economic, social, and political system and examine the deep underlying structures that shape political change. Others implicitly or explicitly maintain that individual or group action can make a decisive difference. Both **pluralists** and **rational choice** theorists assume that individuals on their own or in combination shape political outcomes. '**Structuralist**' is the name given to those political theorists who emphasise the importance of structure and context over human agency.

Terrorism

'Terrorism' is a term with which the world has unhappily become reacquainted, but it is nevertheless difficult to define uncontentiously. It has become a cliché that one person's terrorist is another person's freedom fighter. Thus the German occupiers of France and the Vichy French government regarded those French who actively resisted the occupation as terrorists. Later, these same 'terrorists' were regarded as heroes and liberators.

Much the same was true of nationalist leaders rebelling against colonial **governments** and **racist** regimes. Nelson Mandela* was widely regarded as a terrorist, not only by the apartheid government in South Africa, which successfully prosecuted him for treason and sentenced him to life imprisonment, but also by many in the West, who later venerated him. Mandela justified sabotage, targeted against **property**, though not violence against persons, because there were no legitimate and effective means of opposition that were open to non-whites.

Terrorism is generally envisaged to involve random and indiscriminate attacks on people, including not only rulers, government officials, and the armed forces but ordinary **civilians**. The shock effect of such attacks achieves considerable publicity of a kind not easily secured by more peaceful means, although the suffering of innocent victims can arouse revulsion and damage the cause.

While terrorism is usually associated with opponents of the **state** and dominant **classes**, the term 'state terrorism' suggests that governments also can use terror deliberately to create a climate of fear and crush opposition. Thus Robespierre in **revolutionary** France and Stalin* in the Soviet Union employed terrorism as deliberate policy.

There has been much recent discussion of global terrorism, acts of terror perpetrated across the world's continents. Thus the al Qaida network of Islamic fundamentalists inspired terrorist atrocities in New York, East Africa, Bali, Saudi Arabia, Istanbul, Madrid, and London. More recent acts of terrorism, involving filmed beheadings and more indiscriminate massacres, have been linked to the Islamic State. The continued threat of global terrorism has had massive implications for domestic policy on security and civil **liberties** and even more far-reaching consequences for Western foreign policy. Some argue that the Western 'war on terrorism' has stimulated an increase in terrorism rather than checking it. Counterterrorist activities within Western states sometimes involve restrictions on individual **freedoms**, including, some argue, freedom of speech.

Third way

Broadly speaking, the 'third way' is a term that has often been employed to describe a different option, making unnecessary a choice between two unpalatable alternatives. Thus Mussolini presented **fascism** as a 'third way' between Soviet **communism** and **free market capitalism**. Others have used the 'third way' in the sense of a 'middle way' or centrist philosophy between **left** and **right**. The then **Conservative** rebel Harold Macmillan used the term 'middle way' in the 1930s to describe his own brand of progressive conservatism. In the 1990s the term 'third way' was linked with, among others, Blair's 'New Labour' in the United Kingdom, Bill Clinton's Democrat administration in the United States, and the Social Democrat–led government of Gerhard Schröder in Germany. Schröder used the term 'new middle'. Blair argued that 'The solutions of neither the old Left nor the new Right will do. We need a radical centre in modern politics.' The British sociologist Anthony Giddens* (1998) described the third way as updated **social democracy**, while some critics saw it as a cloak for the acceptance of **neoliberal free market** ideas by social democratic parties. Other considered there was more rhetoric than substance in the term.

Toleration

Toleration means not persecuting those who have different ideas or beliefs, as long as they do not involve harm to others. The principle of toleration is commonly expressed in relation to religious observance, and more broadly in favour of freedom of speech, a principle expressed in words commonly (but not entirely accurately) attributed to Voltaire*: 'I disapprove of what you say, but I will defend to the death your right to say it.'

Although the principle of religious toleration is now widely accepted, at least in the West, this was certainly not the case in the past. Religious heresy was regarded as a threat to the established order that also endangered the immortal souls of the people. Thus, religious minorities suffered persecution or even extermination. Catholics in Protestant states and Protestants in Catholic states were seen as potential traitors or terrorists. The carnage involved in the wars of religion in the 16th and 17th centuries in Europe did something to change attitudes. Spinoza*, Locke* and, later, Voltaire championed religious toleration – although even for Locke toleration did not extend to Roman Catholics or atheists. In the 19th century John Stuart Mill* ([1859–1861] 1972) advanced the classic case for full freedom of speech. For Mill this did not just involve freedom from legal penalties or government restrictions but freedom of the individual from the stifling control of public opinion, the 'tyranny of the majority'.

Religious toleration no longer appeared an issue in much of the modern world until recently, when a number of *causes célèbres* raised once more the scope and limits of religious toleration. In the United Kingdom the fatwa declared by Ayatollah Khomeini in Iran against Salman Rushdie's *The Satanic Verses* forced the author into hiding under police protection for years. The death threat was real. Criticism of the Muslim faith by the director Theo van Gogh in Holland led to his murder by an Islamic fundamentalist. In France cartoons published by the magazine *Charlie Hebdo* provoked the brutal murder of its journalists in 2015.

Some argue that freedom of speech should not involve the licence to insult the deeply held beliefs of others. Respect for minorities in a **multicultural** society, it is argued, requires some restraint on what have been described as 'communal libels'. Yet religious toleration is an argument against the persecution of believers because of their beliefs, not for their protection from any criticism of their religion that they may deem offensive.

Totalitarianism

Totalitarianism was a label initially applied to Italian **fascism** and German Nazism to describe a new kind of **dictatorship** involving a monolithic and all-embracing **state** controlling every aspect of political and social life. 'Everything for the state, nothing outside the state, nothing against the state', as the Italian fascist leader Mussolini put it. Thus the totalitarian state dissolves the **liberal** distinction between the **state** and **civil society**. The term 'totalitarianism' was later employed in the West to describe the **communist** one-party dictatorships in Russia, Eastern Europe, and China as well, implying that the similarities between communism and fascism were more marked than the differences. Critics argue that this application of the term was a product of Cold War propaganda and ignored the substantial differences between communism and fascism. Key theorists of totalitarianism include Karl Popper*, Hannah Arendt*, and Friedrich and Brzezinski (1963).

Tradition

'Tradition' is the term used to describe the handing down of ideas, values, and practices from one generation to another. **Conservatives** attach positive value to tradition, which they see as embodying the accumulated wisdom of the past (see Burke* and Oakeshott* among key thinkers). Whole communities may venerate traditional practices and derive comfort from them. However, the Enlightenment viewed tradition with suspicion, as embodying out-dated ideas and customs that could no longer be rationally upheld. Utilitarians (e.g. Bentham*) applied the test of utility to all traditional institutions and practices and found many of them wanting. **Liberals**, **socialists**,

and reformers and revolutionaries generally have similarly embraced rationalism and criticised traditionalism for endorsing the *status quo* and existing unjustified privilege and power. **Fascism** in practice often involved a curious marriage of modern technology with many traditional values, which was perhaps part of its appeal to communities facing rapid social change.

Utilitarianism

Utilitarianism is a moral and political theory that suggests that laws, institutions, and policies should be judged by their utility (or usefulness), the test of which was how far they promoted the happiness of the greatest number. Jeremy Bentham* was the leading proponent of classical utilitarianism, although he acknowledged a debt to previous writers, including the Scottish philosopher David Hume*, the French writer Helvetius, and the Italian criminologist Beccaria. Bentham assumed that all humans pursue pleasure and avoid pain and that, the quantity of pleasure being equal, no pleasure should be ranked more worthy than another. The greatest happiness of the greatest number could be assessed by a 'felicific calculus' balancing the total quantity of pleasure against the quantity of pain resulting from any act. Bentham was converted by his friend James Mill to **representative democracy**. This, he thought, was the only system that could ensure that **governments** would pursue the happiness of the greatest number rather than the greatest happiness of themselves.

John Stuart Mill* (James Mill's son) championed Benthamite utilitarianism but departed from Bentham in an important respect, arguing that 'some *kinds* of pleasures are more desirable and more valuable than others' (Mill *Utilitarianism* [1861] 1972, 8). The notion of 'higher pleasures' introduces a complicating factor in Bentham's felicific calculus. However, both Bentham and Mill applied utilitarianism in a radical way, and their ideas were later influential with some British socialists, such as Beatrice and Sidney Webb*.

Utopia and utopianism

Utopia was the name Sir Thomas More [1516] gave to his account of an ideal community on an imaginary island. It has since been applied to any fictional account of an ideal political community, from Plato's* *Republic* through to the modern **socialist** and **anarchist** utopias devised by thinkers such as Fourier, Kropotkin*, and William Morris*. Some, such as the British socialist Robert Owen*, tried to establish such model communities in practice, for example at New Lanark in Scotland and New Harmony in the United States. More generally, the terms 'utopian' and 'utopianism' have been employed to mean any idealistic proposal or scheme deemed unrealistic by others. It was in this spirit that Marx* and Engels* described Saint-Simon, Fourier, and Owen as 'utopian socialists' in *The Communist Manifesto* (1848). While these thinkers had a socialist vision of a future socialist society, their socialism lacked a scientific analysis of social change and consequently a realistic strategy for achieving socialism. However, Marx's own notion of the 'withering away of the state' has been deemed utopian by some critics.

Welfare state

A welfare state is concerned not just with the minimum classical **liberal** functions of the **state** – defence against external threats, the maintenance of internal order, and the protection of property – but with the provision of public welfare services, particularly education, health care, and social security 'from the cradle to the grave'. Many Western states developed such welfare services from the late 19th century onwards, although the pattern of provision, and the means for financing it, differed somewhat from state to state. The proportion of public spending and national income devoted to such welfare services grew rapidly after the Second World War, creating economic and political difficulties. In some respects it could be argued that the welfare state was the victim of its own success, as health and welfare benefits increased life expectancy, and driving up costs of retirement pensions, health care, and social services for the greater numbers of elderly. This has sometimes led to cutbacks in some of these services and increased reliance on family and **community** care. The pressures of **globalisation** have also been sometimes blamed for cuts in welfare provision.

GUIDE TO FURTHER READING

Students may wish to compare the accounts here of key political terms and concepts with those in other sources. You can look terms up in an ordinary dictionary for a lay person's definition, but this may not take you very far, as many terms have a relatively specialised use in the academic study of politics and of course their significance will not be explored. More useful are specialised reference works. The standout recommendation is now Andrew Heywood (2015b) *Key Concepts in Politics and International Relations* (Palgrave Macmillan). Other reliable sources include *The Concise Oxford Dictionary of Politics* (ed. McLean and McMillan, 2009), which has good coverage of both traditional political theory and modern political science, and *The Blackwell Encyclopaedia of Political Thought* (ed. David Miller et al., 1991), which remains useful although, as the title suggests, largely concerned with traditional political theory rather than political science. *The Penguin Dictionary of Politics* (David Robertson, Penguin Reference, 1993) is more weighted towards modern politics and contains many clearly written entries.

Bear in mind that some key concepts are highly contentious. It can be useful to know something of about the ideological assumptions of the author or authors. Sometimes these are obvious, for instance *A Dictionary of Marxist Thought* (ed. Bottomore, 1991), whose analysis might be compared and contrasted with that of the conservative Roger Scruton, whose own rather less sympathetic approach to Marxism is evident in his own *Dictionary of Political Thought* (2007). Read critically, and do not expect dispassionate objectivity. You are studying politics!

Students today are only too familiar with the uses of the internet in searching for information. Entries posted on Wikipedia and other sites can be very helpful, but be warned: there is variable quality control on the internet. Some material can be one-sided or idiosyncratic or even just plain wrong [as we showed in Part III].

PART V

Key Thinkers

Contents

INTRODUCTION

This part concentrates on thinkers, political philosophers or political scientists who have made a significant contribution to political ideas and the analysis of politics. It excludes almost all those who are best known for practising politics, although the distinction is not always clear cut. The thought of some (such as Gandhi* and Stalin*) is remembered substantially because of what they did.

Any list of key thinkers is likely to be contentious for both its inclusions and exclusions. A standard criticism of such lists is that they largely consist of dead white males. This is certainly the case here. They are mostly dead and predominantly white and male. Yet they are substantially representative of the writers cited and studied on politics courses around the Western world and reflect the bias in Western society over the whole period in which politics has been studied systematically. While additional modern political thinkers and political scientists might have been included, that would have made the list far longer and perhaps even more contentious. Reputations rise and fall, and it is far from clear who of those writing today will still be studied by generations to come. Thus this list is very sparing in including those still living, and some of these made their reputations decades ago.

Finding your way around this section – and seeking more information

While some of the more important thinkers are given extended entries, the ideas of others are discussed more briefly, and in some cases there is little more than the briefest of biographical details with key publications (usually because their work has already been discussed, in some cases at length, in earlier sections). The same cross-referencing system is employed as elsewhere in the book. Thus there other thinkers who have their own separate entries in this section are asterisked, with bold text for key terms listed and discussed in Part IV. In some cases there are also specific references to analysis in earlier sections of the book. Use the index to follow up other references. If you want to learn still more you will need to look at other sources. [See guidance on further reading, here and earlier in the book.]

KEY THINKERS

Adorno

Theodor W. Adorno (1903–1969) was a leading social philosopher who was part of the Frankfurt school, and was associated with Critical Theory. Born in Frankfurt with a father of Jewish descent, with Hitler's rise to power he quit Germany for first England and then the United States, returning to a professorship at Frankfurt after the war. He is still most best known for *The Authoritarian Personality* (1950), a study of **fascist** psychology based on research he directed. He also wrote on the negative influence on contemporary society of the **mass media** and mass **culture**, which he considered rendered people docile and passive.

Almond

Gabriel Almond (1911–2002) was an outstanding American political scientist with a long career extending from the 1930s right up to his death. He played a key role in the **behavioural revolution** that moved the study of **politics** away from **constitutions** and governmental institutions towards such areas as political **culture** and socialisation. He also was influential in shifting the study of **comparative politics** away from a narrow focus on a few Western systems of government to include the non-Western world. His most celebrated work *The Civic Culture* (with Sidney Verba, 1963) involved a cross-national survey of political cultures in five states (the USA, the United Kingdom, Germany, Italy, Mexico). Almond and Verba suggested that what they called a civic culture was most compatible with political stability and **democracy**.

Althusser

Louis Pierre Althusser (1918–1990) was an influential French **Marxist** philosopher and member of the French **Communist Party**. Suffering from mental instability, he strangled his wife in 1980. Diagnosed as having diminished responsibility, he was committed to a psychiatric hospital and after his release lived quietly in retirement until his death. In his key work *For Marx* (1965) Althusser criticised rival interpretations of Marx's* thought, particularly those involving crude economic determinism and others that drew particularly on Marx's 'humanist' early writings. Althusser argued that there was an 'epistemological break' between Marx's early and later writings. Only the theory of historical **materialism** tentatively outlined in *The German Ideology* (1845) but more fully developed by the mature Marx in *Capital* had real explanatory power and was truly scientific. Althusser is regarded as the leading exponent of **structural** Marxism. He argued it was necessary to go beyond an **empirical** approach focusing on isolated aspects of observable human behaviour to understand the 'deep structure' underlying the complex relations of social and economic processes in totality. Some of the implications of Althusser's interpretation of Marx were explored further by Nicos Poulantzas*.

Aquinas

St Thomas Aquinas (1225–1274) is still widely regarded as the supreme Catholic theologian and philosopher, and much of the political thinking of the modern Roman Catholic church is based on 'Thomist' principles. ('Thomism', derived from Thomas, is the name commonly used to describe the thought of Aquinas). He was born in southern Italy and joined the Dominican order in 1244. He studied at Naples, Paris, and Cologne before returning to teach in Paris and then various centres of learning in Italy. In the 12th and 13th centuries the main works of Aristotle* had been rediscovered in western Europe, in part via Muslim Spain. Key texts were translated from Greek to Latin, while the interpretation of Aristotle was strongly influenced by Arab scholars such as Avicenna and Averroes*. The church was initially uncertain how to regard this new teaching, linked to infidel sources, and there were attempts to ban it. Aquinas instead sought to reconcile the rediscovered philosophy of Aristotle with Christian theology, or reason and faith. *Summa Theologiae* (also known as *Summa Theologica*) is regarded as his key work. While he agreed with Aristotle that man was by nature a social and political animal, he considered that the earthly state could never be a perfect **community** and that man required God's grace and the Christian virtues to lead a good life. Thus he argued, 'Grace does not do away with nature but perfects it'. Yet the principles of **law** and **government** could be derived from **natural law**, common to all men (see Aquinas *Selected Political Writings*, 1948).

Arendt

Hannah Arendt (1906–1975) was a political thinker known mainly for her exploration of **totalitarianism**. A German Jew, she fled

Nazi Germany and eventually settled in the United States. Her key book *The Origins of Totalitarianism* (1951) argued that both Nazi Germany and Stalinist Russia involved an essentially new totalitarian system of government, in which all institutions and interests were subordinated to the state through ideological indoctrination and **terror**. Some critics objected to the equating of **Stalinism** with **Nazism**. In a later book *Eichmann in Jerusalem* (1963), arising from the capture, trial, and execution of the Nazi Adolf Eichmann for his role in the Holocaust, Arendt used the striking phrase 'the banality of evil' to describe Eichmann's attitude and behaviour. Some Jewish critics thought Arendt diminished Eichmann's personal responsibility for his crimes.

Aristotle

Aristotle (384–322 BCE) was a Greek philosopher and political thinker. He was born at Stagira in Thrace and studied under Plato* in Athens from 367, leaving the city after Plato's death in 347. In 343 he became tutor to the young Alexander, son of Philip of Macedon. Subsequently he returned to Athens, where he opened his own school, the Lyceum. Fears for his own safety following the death of his former pupil, Alexander the Great, and an upsurge of anti-Macedonian feeling led him to flee Athens in 323, to die in Euboea the following year.

'It's all in Aristotle' has long been a familiar saying among modern writers on **politics**. He is widely considered one of the greatest political thinkers of all time (although some, including Thomas Hobbes* in the 17th century and Karl Popper* in the 20th, have been less impressed). Although Plato's pupil, Aristotle came to disagree with much of Plato's philosophy, particularly his theory of knowledge. Aristotle's approach to the study of politics was also markedly different. Although like Plato he had clear ethical assumptions, he was less interested in abstract political ideals, and more concerned with political practice. Thus he was a pioneer in the study of comparative politics. He and his pupils are known to have surveyed 158

constitutions, of which the only account surviving is of Athens. Aristotle's *Politics* draws extensively on his knowledge of the Greek city **states** of his own day, although curiously he did not seem to have recognised the longer-term implications of the empire founded by his former pupil Alexander for the future of these self-governing political communities. In comparing political systems he was rather less critical of **democracy** than Plato, but considered that a mixed system of **government** was the most practicable. He argued that man was naturally a social and political animal. Anyone outside the *polis* (roughly translated as city state) was either a beast or a god. However, he assumed that slavery was natural. Unlike Plato, he held conventional views on **gender** relations and the family, and he defended private **property**.

Aristotle wrote extensively on a range of subjects, but key works relating to politics are the *Politics* and the *Nichomachean Ethics*. Aristotle's writings were translated into Arabic in the Middle Ages and had a significant influence on Islamic thought. Through Aquinas* in particular Aristotle became a major influence on later medieval Christian philosophy and political thought.

Arrow

Kenneth Arrow (1921–2017) was an American economist whose work on social theory has had an influence on the study of **politics** and particularly **democracy**. Arrow's book *Social Choice and Individual Values* (1951) demonstrated that it was impossible for any method of **election** to produce a fair and accurate reflection of the aggregate choice of voters (Arrow's 'impossibility theorem'). William Riker later showed the importance of Arrow's work for political scientists, especially for democratic theory, although Riker considered Arrow's work more damaging for **populist** interpretations of democracy than for **liberal representative** democracy.

Augustine

St Augustine (354–430) was one of the first thinkers to explore the relations between religion and the **state**, a key theme of medieval political thought and one that now appears of increasing significance in the modern world. He was born in north Africa, still then part of the Roman Empire, which under the emperor Constantine had become officially Christian but faced increasing threats from without and within. Some indeed considered that the Christian religion was one of those threats, as the whole-hearted exclusive commitment and loyalty required by some church leaders had damaging implications both for the empire and political **authority** generally. Although his mother was a Christian, Augustine himself was not particularly committed to the faith in his early years. He went through a fairly dissolute period as a student in Rome. In his *Confessions* he records praying 'Give me chastity and continency – but not yet!' After further studies in Milan, where he fell under the influence of St Ambrose, he experienced a dramatic conversion to a Christian religious vocation. He returned to Africa in 388, and served as bishop of Hippo from 395 until his death in 430, when the city was under siege from the Vandals.

In his key work *The City of God,* Augustine contrasted the earthly city or pagan state with the kingdom of Christ and examined the implications of Christian faith for **politics** and **government**. While he agreed with pre-Christian writers such as Plato* and Cicero* that the state and **civil society** were both natural and necessary, he denied that fallen man could aspire to the good life or the good society. True **justice** could not be achieved on earth. Yet while the ultimate commitment of the Christian was to the Christian community on earth and the kingdom of heaven thereafter, Christians should obey earthly rulers and behave as good citizens.

Averroes

Averroes [Ibn Rushd] (1126–1198) was born in Córdoba, then a leading intellectual centre of Muslim Spain. The Islamic world had taken up Greek philosophy with enthusiasm, translating works into Arabic. Averroes was the last and greatest of the Arab philosophers, providing commentaries on Plato* and translation of and commentaries on Aristotle's* *Ethics*. The latter was subsequently translated into Latin and had a significant influence on Aquinas* and late medieval political thought in the West.

Bagehot

Walter Bagehot (1826–1877) was a leading British political commentator of his day, remembered for *The English Constitution* ([1867] 1963), which famously distinguished between the 'dignified' and 'efficient' parts of the largely unwritten British **constitution** (a distinction that can be readily applied to other constitutions). Bagehot rejected received opinion on the **separation of powers** and saw the cabinet as the efficient secret of British **government**, binding the **executive** to the **legislature**. Some later observers in the second half of the 20th century (e.g. John Mackintosh, Richard Crossman) concluded that prime ministerial government had subsequently replaced cabinet government, which had become another dignified rather than efficient part of the constitution. Whether they were right or not is less important than the general point that **power** in government is not necessarily located where constitutional texts suggest, and moreover can change over time.

Bakunin

Michael Bakunin (1814–1876) was a Russian revolutionary **anarchist** who spent periods of his life in prison. Unlike some anarchists who were **pacifists**, Bakunin advocated violent struggle and acts of **terrorism**. He and Marx* competed for control of the First International, from which Bakunin was expelled in 1872. He warned of the likely outcome of Marx's notion of the **dictatorship** of the proletariat.

Barry

Brian Barry (1936–2009) was a British moral and political philosopher who taught in universities in the United Kingdom and the United States. His work straddles the divide between traditional political philosophy and modern analytical political science, notably in an influential early work *Sociologists, Economists and Democracy* (1970), which involved a critical analysis of the work of Downs*, Olson*, Almond*, Easton*, and Lipset*, among others. He is best known for his work on social **justice** and was a champion and interpreter of the work of John Rawls*, who he claimed had relaunched political philosophy. Barry's own work on justice includes consideration of international and intergenerational justice. Key works include *Theories of Justice* (1989), *Justice as Impartiality* (1995), and *Why Social Justice Matters* (2005). He also wrote *Culture and Equality: An Egalitarian Critique of Multiculturalism* (2001a).

Baudrillard

Jean Baudrillard (1929–2007) was a leading French thinker, associated with **postmodernism**. Although he began as a Marxist he was later to reject **Marxism**, becoming increasingly preoccupied with the impact of modern **mass** communication. He described the condition of the present age as one of 'hyperreality' with signs, images, or symbols ('simulacra') obscuring or replacing reality. Some of his pronouncements were both paradoxical and provocative. Thus he claimed in 1991 that the first Gulf War 'did not take place' and suggested that the 9/11 attacks on the twin towers had nothing much to do with religion or a clash of civilisations (see Huntington*) but was a reaction against **globalisation**. His work has attracted considerable controversy. One otherwise respectful obituary began, 'Jean Baudrillard's death did not take place' (*The Guardian*, 8/3/2007).

Beck

Ulrich Beck (1944–2015) was a leading sociologist who was one of the first academics to study globalisation. Born in what is now Poland towards the end of the Second World War, in his first major work (*Risk Society*, 1986) he highlighted that modern society as it becomes globalised creates both opportunities and risks. So the process helps raise standards of living for many people, yet the cost is increased environmental degradation.

The key element is that the risks are now transnational.

Bell

Daniel Bell (1919–2011) was an American political sociologist. He is still perhaps best known for *The End of Ideology* (1960), which argued that political differences in the postwar Western world were increasingly over technical means rather than ideological ends. The contending ideologies, Stalinist **communism** and **fascism** that had divided the world earlier in the 20th century were destroyed or discredited. The very term '**ideology**' and all political 'isms' appeared suspect. Downs* had already argued that two-party systems were likely to promote competition over the political middle ground, and Bell's 'end of ideology' thesis matched perceptions of a growing political **consensus** (or agreement) in the USA, the United Kingdom, and the West generally. Critics objected that the presumed 'end of ideology' actually involved the dominance (or **hegemony**) of a particular liberal **capitalist** ideology in the West. Moreover, the growth of political dissent in the 1960s and 1970s (e.g. the peace movement, radical **feminism**, the **neoliberal** revival, **green** thinking) soon suggested that the obituary for ideology was premature (although Francis Fukuyama* was to suggest a similar thesis following the end of the Cold War).

Bell's influential later work *The Coming of Post-Industrial Society* (1973) argued that the society created by the industrial revolution based on manufacturing industry was being replaced by a **postindustrial society** involving a shift from manufacturing to a service economy, in which information and communication would be key resources. He later coined the term 'information society' to describe the postindustrial economy. Others used the term 'knowledge economy'. Bell has been credited for predicting important developments, then in their infancy, that had considerable implications for politics.

Bentham

Jeremy Bentham (1748–1832) was a British legal and social reformer and political theorist who founded **utilitarianism**.

A scathing critic of the doctrine of **natural rights**, which he called 'nonsense on stilts', he championed instead the principle of utility. He asked of any social institution or **law** the question, 'What use is it?' Any such institution or law, however venerable and sanctified by **tradition** and long usage, that failed the utility test should be abolished or radically reformed. Utility was measured by the pain and pleasure produced for **individuals**, counted as equals. The principle on which society should be managed (and the aim of **government**) should be to achieve 'the greatest happiness of the greatest number'. One of Bentham's passions was penal reform, and he designed, on paper, a massive model prison, the Panopticon, in which prisoners would be comprehensively supervised in all their activities. Although proposals to build the prison were approved by parliament, implementation of the scheme was obstructed.

Bentham added parliamentary reform to his other causes after James Mill, the father of John Stuart Mill*, converted him to the principle of **representative democracy**, as the means to ensure that government would in practice be forced to consider the interests of the majority. Although he was also associated with classical economists who advocated the principle of *laissez-faire* and a minimal **state**, Bentham became convinced of the need for increased state intervention in a variety of fields and for a reformed state **bureaucracy** that would be fit for purpose. Thus Bentham's **liberalism** did not take the form of pure classical **free market** liberalism but pointed forward to the interventionist New Liberalism of the late 19th and 20th centuries. In the second half of the 20th century **neoliberals** such as Hayek* were severely critical of Bentham's '**constructivist rationalism**', which they felt was responsible for the growth of the state bureaucracy and **welfare** provision they deplored. The later career of Bentham's secretary, Edwin Chadwick, personified the tensions in mid-19th-century liberalism. Chadwick was the architect of the New Poor Law (1834), which embodied market principles on the one hand but led to the creation of a new state bureaucracy on the other, and Chadwick himself went on to become the leader figure of the interventionist Public Health movement. Bentham died in 1832; in accordance with his wishes his body was preserved, dressed in his own clothes, and kept in a glass case in University College, London.

Bentley

Arthur Bentley (1870–1957) was a pioneering American political scientist in the first part of the 20th century. He may be considered one of the founders of modern **pluralist** theory. As a precursor of the **behavioural** approach, he was sceptical towards formal political institutions and drew attention to the crucial importance of pressure groups in his key work *The Process of Government* (1908).

Berlin

Isaiah Berlin (1909–1997) was an influential British **liberal** thinker. He was born in Riga, Latvia, from which his family fled to Russia in 1915 and then England in 1920. He secured a double first at Oxford University in Greats (Greek and Latin language and literature) and in Philosophy, Politics and Economics. After graduating, he continued to teach and work at Oxford until his retirement in 1971. His writings were wide-ranging, but he is particularly remembered for his essay 'Two Concepts of Liberty' (1958). Here he distinguished between 'negative' **liberty**, essentially the freedom of the **individual** *from* external interference and from oppression of various kinds, and 'positive' liberty, the **freedom** of the individual *to* develop and realise his or her true potential. While the latter might appear to some (e.g. New Liberal thinkers such as Green*) to involve a fuller, richer freedom, Berlin considered the notion of positive liberty to have damaging and even **totalitarian** implications. It could be used (and had been used) to justify interference with the freedom of individuals to further their 'real' higher self-interest as opposed to their own immediate wishes and desires. Thus their 'real will' (what they would want if they were sufficiently enlightened), could be used to over-ride their own actual preferences. Even more dangerously, their 'real will' might be identified with the wider will of the **community** of which they were a part. Berlin acknowledged that sometimes people might be coerced for their own good, but he argued that it was a 'monstrous impersonation' to argue that they really wanted what they were forced to do.

Bernstein

Eduard Bernstein (1850–1932) was a leading German revisionist **socialist**. He sought to update Marx* in the light of subsequent history and the failure of some of Marx's predictions (e.g. the disappearance of intermediate classes and the impoverishment of the industrial working class). He argued that parliamentary **democracy** and a modified **capitalism** could be transformed gradually into socialism. He was denounced by other Marxists (e.g. Karl Kautsky, Lenin*, Rosa Luxemburg*), and his influence declined in his own lifetime, although most Western socialist parties subsequently followed the route he recommended.

Beveridge

William Beveridge (1879–1963) was an influential British liberal social reformer and economist. He worked with Beatrice and Sidney Webb* on their report on the Poor Law (1909) and advised Lloyd George on pensions and national insurance, contributing to the ideas of the New Liberals before the First World War. He was Director of the London School of Economics (LSE) from 1919 to 1937. In the Second World War he worked for the government, delivering the landmark report on *Social Insurance and Allied Services* (1942), known as the Beveridge report, that provided the basis for the postwar **welfare state**. His work and that of Keynes helped to establish the postwar **consensus**, often described as the 'Keynes-Beveridge consensus'. Although his ideas contributed significantly to the postwar Labour government, he remained a **liberal**, and after receiving a peerage in 1946 he later led the Liberal Party in the House of Lords.

Bodin

Jean Bodin (1530–1596) was a French political theorist who argued that only unconditional obedience to a single absolute **sovereign power** could provide internal security and order within a **state**. His key work was *Six livres de la république* (1576), often referred to simply as the *Republic.*

Buchanan

James M. Buchanan (1919–2013) was an American economist largely responsible, with Gordon Tullock*, for the establishment of the **public choice** school (also known as the **rational choice** or the Virginia school – both Buchanan and Tullock taught at university there). Public choice theory has had a massive impact on the study of **politics**, particularly in the United States but also more generally. Buchanan and Tullock argued that the rational choice assumptions made by economists for the behaviour of producers and consumers in the **market** should also be applied to the behaviour of those in the public sector. This had critical implications for the role of **government** and the **state** generally. Their key work was *The Calculus of Consent* (1962).

Bull

Hedley Bull (1932–1985) was the leading figure in the 'English' school of **international relations**, although he originated from Australia. In his key work *The Anarchical Society* (1977) he argued that **nation-states** remained the main actors in an international society characterised by **anarchy** in the absence of any effective international **authority**. Yet anarchy did not necessarily mean the pursuit of state interests at all costs, leading to international disorder and war, as states recognised some **obligations** to each other, and from prudence and fear states sought to preserve a **balance of power**.

Burke

Edmund Burke (1729–1797) is now regarded as a founder of modern **conservatism**. Yet this is a rather surprising verdict on a Whig politician and writer who for most of his life was a scathing critic of King George III and British government policy towards America and India. He parted company with the Whig leader Charles James Fox and much of his party over the French **Revolution**, which they initially welcomed but he condemned from the outset. His essay *Reflections on the Revolution in France* (1790), which was vigorously attacked by radical critics such as Tom Paine*, has become a key text for conservatives everywhere but particularly in the English-speaking world.

The problem with the French Revolution for Burke was that it involved an attempt to build a new system of government and a new society on first principles without reference to the past. Burke thought that the French revolution differed markedly from the United Kingdoms' own revolution a century earlier, the so-called Glorious Revolution of 1688 that Whigs celebrated, as this drew on the past. Burke explicitly compared the **state** with a living organism like a plant, that may be pruned or grafted but not torn up by the roots. Instead, reform should be more limited and cautious, and it should grow out of the past and be based on precedent and **tradition**.

While the 18th century has been called the 'Age of Enlightenment' or 'Age of Reason', Burke challenged prevailing rationalist assumptions. He argued that most people are not ruled by reason but guided by emotions and feelings. Individuals would be better advised to rely on the wisdom inherent in tradition and custom rather than attempt to pursue their own **rational self-interest**. Provocatively, Burke championed what he calls 'prejudice' against 'naked reason'.

Burke, like all conservatives, defended private **property** and justified its unequal distribution. He argued that 'the characteristic essence of property, formed out of the combined principles of its acquisition and conservation, is to be unequal.' Great concentrations of property 'form a natural rampart about the lesser properties in all their gradations'. Thus any threat against the property of the very rich threatens property rights in general. Burke also strongly upheld rights of inheritance.

Burke's old associates accused him of betraying his past principles. Yet while he had been a critic of particular government policies and of abuses of power he had never been a radical nor committed to notions of popular **sovereignty**. Burke as a member of parliament sternly declined to be instructed by the electors of Bristol in 1774. 'Your representative owes you, not his industry only, but his judgement; and he betrays instead of serving you, if he sacrifices it to your opinion' (Burke [1790] 1975, 157). This has become the classic justification for the independence of elected **representatives**, as against the **populist** principle that, as delegates, they should faithfully reflect the interests and views of their electors.

Carr

E. H. (Edward Hallett) Carr (1892–1982) is perhaps best known as a British **Marxist** historian, particularly for his massive *History of Soviet Russia*. However, he made his name as an **international relations** theorist with his *Twenty Years' Crisis* (1939). This book trenchantly advanced Carr's own **realist** position against the then dominant liberal internationalism that he described as **utopianism**. He argued there was no harmony of interests in international relations. States cloaked the pursuit of their own interests in the language of morality. The failure of liberal internationalism to check aggression and preserve peace and stability in the period between the two world wars (the 'twenty years' crisis' of Carr's title) undermined faith in liberal idealist theories of international relations. It led to the dominance of realist and neorealist theories in the study of international relations in the postwar decades.

Cicero

Marcus Tullius Cicero (106–43 BCE) was a Roman lawyer, statesman, and political theorist. He made his name in the law courts, studied oratory in Greece, and served as consul, the highest position in the Roman Republic, in 63 BCE. Subsequently he fell from favour and spent more of his time writing on **law** and **politics**. A keen advocate of the **republican** constitution as well as Roman law, he was killed in the period of political turmoil following the assassination of Julius Caesar and thus did not live to see the emergence of the Roman Empire, which marked the end of the republic.

He popularised key ideas from Greek philosophy, particularly the notion of **natural law**, derived principally from the Stoics. He described the Roman state as *res populi* or *res publica* (the affair of the people). It existed to serve its people, and political **authority** was ultimately derived from the people. Yet although he argued that all men are **equal** in essential respects, he did not favour **democracy** but championed the mixed constitution that he saw embodied in the Roman Republic. Key works are his *Republic* and *Laws*.

Comte

August Comte (1798–1857) was a wide-ranging French philosopher who coined the term 'sociology' to describe the 'new science' of society. He was the champion of **positivism**, of positive rather than normative social science, arguing that it was important to understand actual human behaviour, *how* things were as they were, rather than asking metaphysical questions about *why* they existed. As such he was the fore-runner of the 20th-century **behavioural revolution** in the social sciences, including politics. He foresaw a society organised on scientific and technocratic lines in which decisions would be taken by qualified experts in the interests of the **community** as a whole, but not by the people themselves. He was thus hostile to **democracy**. To help overcome divisive conflict in modern society Comte advocated what was to be in effect a new religion, the religion of humanity, to replace Christianity. Although his scheme for a new religion provoked considerable ridicule, Comte's influence on the subsequent development of the social sciences and the practice of **government** was considerable, particularly in his native France.

Cox

Robert Cox (1926–) is a leading figure in the field of critical theory of International Relations. In particular, he has been influential in the field of International Political Economy. He is a leading critic of the realist perspective that dominates much of the discipline. His key works such as *Production, Power and World Order* (1987) introduce the Gramscian* notion of **hegemony** into the study of International Relations.

Crosland

Anthony Crosland (1918–1977) was the leading **social democrat** (or revisionist) thinker in the British Labour Party in the decades after the Second World War. His key work *The Future of Socialism* (1956) argued that **nationalisation** of industry was irrelevant in an era when effective control of business was increasingly divorced from its ownership. He believed Keynes* had shown that a **capitalist** economy could be effectively managed without resort to nationalisation. Crosland defined socialism in terms of increasing **equality**, and this was being achieved, he thought, through increased **welfare** provision on the one hand and progressive taxation on the other, thus redistributing the fruits of economic growth without necessarily making anyone worse off in absolute terms. He subsequently held various cabinet posts in the Labour governments of Wilson and Callaghan. In government, his expectation of continuing substantial economic growth proved overoptimistic, but he remained committed to public spending and his interpretation of **socialism**.

Dahl

Robert Dahl (1915–2014) is widely considered an outstanding modern American political scientist and political theorist. He was particularly associated with the study of **power**, which he interpreted in terms of the simple formula that A has power over B if he can get B to do something that B would not otherwise do. Some criticised this as involving too narrow a view of power, focusing on observable decisions. Dahl was a key figure in the community power debate between **pluralists**, who argue that power is dispersed, and **elitists**, who claim it is heavily concentrated in the hands of the few, a governing elite or elites. *Who Governs?* Dahl's study of decision-making in New Haven, Connecticut, concluded that there was no single elite guiding decision-making in the town but, rather, that power was relatively widely dispersed through the effective influence of many **pressure groups** on the decision-making process in various policy arenas. His theory of **democracy** (he preferred the term 'polyarchy') rested heavily on the ability of ordinary people to influence governmental decision-making though participation in such pressure group activity. His writings on democracy include *A Preface to Democratic Theory* (1956), *Polyarchy: Participation and Opposition* (1971), and *Democracy and Its Critics* (1989).

De Beauvoir

Simone de Beauvoir (1908–1986) was an influential French **feminist** thinker. Her key work *The Second Sex* (1949) anticipated most of the analysis of the 'second wave' of feminism by American, Australian, and British feminists some 20 years later. Drawing on history, biology, psychology, sociology, literature, and the existentialist philosophy of her long-term partner Jean-Paul Sartre*, she sought to explain why women constituted a 'second' or inferior sex in society, with less freedom to shape their own destinies. She argued that contemporary images of femininity were learned rather than natural and advocated full **equality** for women and a balanced relationship between the sexes, in which both men and women enjoyed **freedom**.

Derrida

Jacques Derrida (1930–2004) was perhaps the most widely respected of the French **postmodernist** thinkers (although he dissociated himself from the label), holding prestigious posts in a number of French and American universities and receiving prizes and honorary doctorates around the Western world. He is particularly associated with the term 'deconstruction', involving deep analysis of a text to uncover multiple interpretations with the implication that none of these interpretations should be privileged over the others. Critics have accused Derrida of obscurity, relativism, and nihilism. Supporters have claimed his ideas have political relevance. While he was not notably active in politics, he supported progressive causes.

Deutsch

Karl Deutsch (1912–1992) was born in Prague where he studied at the German University and Charles University before emigrating to the United States in 1938 where he subsequently taught at Yale and Harvard. He is regarded as one of the pioneers of modern political analysis, particularly the application of quantitative methods and cybernetics to social science, and he contributed notably to the study of **nationalism** and **political communication**. A key work is *The Nerves of Government* (1963).

Downs

Anthony Downs (1930–), made his name as an American political scientist with the publication of *An Economic Theory of Democracy* (1957). This applied the theory and methods of economics to the analysis of the competition between **political parties** for votes and support. A key assumption in economics is that **individuals** both as consumers and producers pursue their own rational self-interest. This compares with approaches to the study of **politics** derived from sociology or psychology that suggest that much political behaviour (for example, voting behaviour) is not particularly rational. Downs assumed that parties, like entrepreneurs in the marketplace, sought to maximise their support and increase their share of the political market by finding out what the majority consumers or voters wanted and promising to supply it. Ideas and policies found to be unpopular are jettisoned. In a two-party system (e.g. the USA and until recently the United Kingdom) the competing parties would seek to maximise their vote by competing for the political centre ground. Downs's book was a key inspiration for the growth of **rational choice** (or **public choice**) theory that now dominates US political science and has a strong influence on the study of politics in the United Kingdom and elsewhere. Downs himself contributed significantly to public choice theory with his later book *Inside Bureaucracy* (1967). This applied the assumption of the pursuit of rational self-interest to those working inside bureaucratic organisations, particularly in the private sector. William Niskanen* has developed further the application of public choice theory to the behaviour of **bureaucrats**.

Duverger

Maurice Duverger (1917–2014) was perhaps the outstanding French political scientist of the second half of the 20th century. His work was founded on extensive **empirical** research. He was perhaps best known for his study of **political parties** published in 1951. His typology of parties is still extensively applied, particularly the distinction between **elite** and mass parties, although the latter have recently suffered a substantial decline both in formal membership and activism almost everywhere. What came to be called 'Duverger's law' suggested a strong correlation between the 'first-past-the-post' electoral system and a two-party system (for example in the United Kingdom, although here this correlation seems weaker today than from 1945 to 1970). Duverger's approach to the subject of **politics** (first published as *Sociologie Politique* in France in 1966 and translated into English as *The Study of Politics* in 1972) was also influential. He likened politics to the two faces of Janus, one involving conflict and power, the other unification and integration. Politics is about both conflict and compromise, the resolution of conflict. Duverger was an academic, who more recently played an active political role as a member of the European Parliament from 1989 to 1994, sitting with the European **Socialist** Party.

Dworkin, Andrea

Andrea Dworkin (1946–2005) was an extremely controversial American radical **feminist**. She was active in left-wing causes before her experience of an abusive marriage in the Netherlands turned her also into a radical feminist, inspired by the writings of Kate Millett* and others. She became a leading figure in campaigns against violence against women, which she linked with pornography, arguing that it involved the domination, humiliation, and dehumanisation of women (*Pornography: Men Possessing Women,* 1979). With Catharine MacKinnon* she campaigned to use civil **rights** legislation to combat pornography. However, her controversial and provocative style led even some feminists to conclude that her influence was counterproductive for the women's movement. Some criticised what they saw as her repressive attitude to sexuality.

Dworkin, Ronald

Ronald Dworkin (1931–2013) was an American legal and political theorist who taught at Yale, Oxford, and London universities. As a legal theorist he disagreed with the English legal theorist H. L. A. Hart whose legal positivism involved a separation of **law** and morality. As a political theorist he made a significant contribution to the modern debate on **equality**, **liberty**, and **rights**. A key work is *Taking Rights Seriously* (1977).

Easton

David Easton (1917–2014) was a Canadian political scientist, known principally for applying systems theory (derived from cybernetics) to **politics** (Easton 1953, 1965). Thus the political system responded to *inputs* or influences (*demands* and *supports*) from its *environment*, converting these into policy *outputs* (or decisions), which in turn affect the environment and lead to new inputs. The systems approach was particularly fashionable in the 1950s and 1960s and fitted **pluralist** assumptions. Critics argued that the systems approach only offered another description of the political system using different terminology. The systems approach also appears to ignore or downgrade the **state** and its institutions and personnel, implying that these involve little more than a mechanism to convert inputs into outputs, without any autonomous power of its own.

Engels

Friedrich Engels (1820–1895) is known largely as the junior partner in his celebrated intellectual collaboration with Marx*. Born in Westphalia, the eldest son of a wealthy textile manufacturer, he was drawn into radical Young Hegelian and **communist** circles as a student in Berlin. Nevertheless he went on in 1842 to work in the family business in Manchester, combining his own employment in the services of **capitalism** with research that exposed the consequences of capitalism in *The Condition of the Working Class in England* (1845). His close collaboration with Marx dated from their meeting in Paris in 1844. They worked together on *The Holy Family*, the unfinished *German Ideology*, and most notably *The Communist Manifesto* (1848). After the failure of the 1848 **revolutions** Engels rejoined the family firm in Manchester, where he also enjoyed riding to hounds with the Cheshire hunt. Yet he remained a committed communist revolutionary, whose own comfortable circumstances allowed him to subsidise the impoverished Marx while he worked on *Das Kapital*. After Marx's death in 1883, Engels edited the second and third volumes of *Kapital* and continued to popularise his partner's ideas. How far he protected Marx's legacy is contentious. Thus his interpretation of dialectical materialism (e.g. in *Anti-Dühring*) was perhaps less subtle than Marx's own. Engels also lived to witness the rise in the electoral fortunes of the German SPD, the **social democrats**, and came to envisage the possibility of **socialism** through the ballot box. Undoubtedly, however, Engels considerably assisted the growth of **Marxism**, widening its appeal, not least to women. *The Origin of the Family, Private Property and the State* (1884) explored **gender** relations and the subordination of women, an issue relatively neglected by Marx.

Enloe

Cynthia Enloe (1938–) is one of the leading **feminist** thinkers, especially in the field of **International Relations**. Her work on gender and militarism as set out in *Bananas, Beaches and Bases* (1989) has been influential in highlighting the link between masculine identities and a particular perspective on peacekeeping in post-conflict zones. She argues that the gendered nature of international relations, especially security, means that women's concerns and perspectives are not considered. These issues are explored in *Nimo's War, Emma's War: Making Feminist Sense of the Iraq War* (2010) and *Does Khaki Become You? The Militarization of Women's Lives (*1988).

Finnemore

Martha Finnemore (1959–) is a prominent constructivist scholar of international relations and University Professor at the Elliott School of International Affairs at George Washington University. Her best-known work, *National Interests in International Society*, was part of the initial constructivist turn in International Relations.

Foucault

Michel Foucault (1926–1984) was an influential French philosopher regarded as a leading influence on structuralism and **postmodernism**, although Foucault himself rejected categorisation. In *Madness and Civilisation* (1965) and *Discipline and Punish* (1977) he argued that our changing perceptions and techniques for dealing with both lunatics and criminals involved not progress and a more scientific and humane approach to the treatment of deviants but institutionalisation and social control that were dehumanising. A particular target was Jeremy Bentham* and his proposed model prison, the 'Panopticon'. Foucault saw the asylum and the prison as metaphors for modern institutions generally and the social control of whole peoples. In *The Archaeology of Knowledge* (1972) and other works on language he connected the 'discourses' or 'discursive formations' used to legitimate modern 'scientific' approaches with **power**. Narrative and discourse reflected power. This connection of power with language is particularly suggestive for students of politics.

Friedan

Betty Friedan (1921–2006) remains the most well-known modern American **feminist** writer. Her best-selling book *The Feminine Mystique* (1965) argued that women had been manipulated into believing that their fulfilment lay in marriage and passive domesticity by women's magazines and the advertising industry. She spoke for millions of American women who felt imprisoned in the home and family, and precipitated the formation of a mass movement in 1966, the National Organisation of Women (NOW) of which she became the first president. This did succeed in achieving some legal changes and more important changes in attitude, not only in the USA, but elsewhere in the West. Radical critics however pointed out that women had manifestly failed to secure equality with men, suggesting that Friedan's **liberal** feminist analysis and strategy did not go far enough. Friedan responded to her critics by placing more emphasis on childcare provision and maternity leave in her later book *The Second Stage*, although she also argued that the shock tactics of the radicals had sometimes been counterproductive and had alienated some women.

Fukuyama

Francis Fukuyama (1952–) sprang to fame with an article entitled 'The End of History?' originally published in 1989, the year of the fall of the Berlin Wall, and reproduced in expanded book form as *The End of History and the Last Man* (1992). Essentially it argued that history, in the sense of a conflict between rival **ideologies** and rival economic and political systems, was at an end. The Cold War between **communism** and **capitalism** was over and **liberal** capitalism had won. Inevitably, Fukuyama's thesis provoked comparisons with the earlier *End of Ideology* (1960) by Daniel Bell*. As with Bell's book, Fukuyama's bold thesis was rapidly overtaken by events. Other forms of ideological and **cultural** conflict soon replaced the now redundant competition between a liberal capitalist West and **Marxist-Leninist** East, and history seemed far from over. Fukuyama has

since produced further controversial books on social trust (1995) and the biotechnology revolution (2002), incidentally acknowledging in the latter that history is not at an end. Although he was until recently regarded as a neo-conservative, initially strongly advocating armed intervention in Iraq, he has since distanced himself from neo-conservatism, criticising the conduct of the Iraq war and American foreign policy generally. He now favours US support for international institutions, with military force only employed as a last resort.

Galbraith

John Kenneth Galbraith (1908–2006) was a celebrated Canadian economist and political thinker who advised several US presidents from F. D. Roosevelt to Kennedy and was professor of economics at Harvard. Some of his many books became best sellers, particularly *The Affluent Society* (1958) and *The New Industrial State* (1967). He was a **pluralist** who coined the phrase 'countervailing power' to describe US political economy in *American Capitalism* (1952). In his later work he advocated increased spending on education and social **welfare** and criticised the neglect of the public sector and the growth of inequality and poverty in the USA, helping to inspire the 'War on Poverty' of Presidents Kennedy and Johnson. Galbraith's influence on government waned subsequently and, as a progressive **liberal** who favoured government spending and redistribution, he incurred the hostility of **neoliberals** such as Milton Friedman.

Gandhi

Mohandas Karamchand (more commonly known as Mahatma) Gandhi (1869–1948) led the ultimately successful campaign for Indian independence but was perhaps more remarkable for his beliefs and methods than for his political achievements. Born and brought up in Porbandar, Kathiawar, in India, with the support of his family he went to London to study law, where he also became active in the vegetarian movement. He returned to India and a lucrative legal practice in Bombay, which he gave up in 1893 to live in poverty and practise law in South Africa on behalf of the Indian community who routinely experienced racial discrimination and injustice. Thoroughly radicalised, in 1914 he returned to India, where he soon became the acknowledged leader of the Home Rule movement. Totally committed to nonviolence, he led campaigns of **civil disobedience** involving passive resistance to forward the cause of independence. It may be questionable how far his **pacifism** would have been successful against a more determined enemy, but it achieved a moral authority that for a time united Indians across barriers of caste, language, and religion. The British government negotiated with Gandhi to secure the independence of India after the Second World War. However, religious divisions between Hindus and Muslims prevented the emergence of a single state for the whole Indian subcontinent. Gandhi was appalled by the sectarian violence in the period leading up to independence and tried to check it. He was assassinated by a Hindu fanatic in 1948.

Giddens

Anthony Giddens (1938–) is a British sociologist whose prolific output has had a significant impact on the study of politics. His theory of structuration, an approach to the problem of **structure** and **agency**, has been particularly influential. He insisted that neither social structure nor individual human agency had primacy but were 'flip sides' of the same coin. We should recognise the duality of structure. Human agents make social structures but are in turn constrained by them. Key works include *Central Problems in Social Theory* (1979) and *The Constitution of Society* (1984). More recently Giddens has focused on the concepts of modernity (incidentally dismissing the notion of **postmodernity)** and **globalisation** and has contributed to the debate on the development of political ideas, particularly the **third way** in *Beyond Left and Right* (1994), *The Third Way* (1998), *The Third Way and Its Critics* (2000), and *The Global Third Way Debate* (2001). He received a life peerage in 2004.

Godwin

William Godwin (1756–1836) was an English **anarchist** who was against all forms of government but was also a **pacifist** opposed to violent **revolution**. His most celebrated work *An Enquiry Concerning Political Justice* (1793) involved an extremely optimistic view of **human nature**. Humans were **rational**, naturally benevolent towards each other, and co-operative. **State government** should be replaced by self-government, and people should live together in small self-governing local **communities**. Issues would be resolved by rational debate. Reason, he thought, would lead people to a voluntary system of **communism**. Godwin was briefly married to the feminist writer Mary Wollstonecraft*. Their daughter, also called Mary, married the radical poet Shelley, who later expressed some of Godwin's political ideas in verse.

Gramsci

Antonio Gramsci (1891–1937), was perhaps the most influential 20th-century Western **Marxist**. Born in Sardinia, he won a scholarship to the University of Turin and was active as a young man in the Italian Socialist Party before the First World War. He enthusiastically welcomed the Russian **Revolution** of 1917 and in postwar Italy supported the factory council movement. He helped form the new Italian Communist Party (PCI) in 1921 and went to Moscow as the party's delegate to the Third International in 1922. Returning to Italy in 1924, he was elected to parliament, two years after Mussolini had become prime minister following the **fascist** 'March on Rome'. In 1926 he was arrested and imprisoned for the rest of his life. It was while he was in captivity that he wrote *The Prison Notebooks*. Gramsci sought to explain the survival of **capitalism** in the Western industrialised world and the failure of the working class to develop a revolutionary consciousness. His answer was linked to his key concept, **hegemony**. Although the ruling class could ultimately resort to coercion, most of the time they could rely on the consent of the ruled because of their effective dominance (or hegemony) over ideas and thought generally, resulting from their control of the economy, the state, culture, and education. The **state,** Gramsci argued, involved force plus **consent**. The role of a revolutionary party was to develop working-class self-consciousness to create an alternative counter-ideology to challenge and ultimately overcome the dominant bourgeois ideology. Gramsci urged a strategy of working with other progressive forces in society to this end, arguably supporting the kind of approach the PCI was later to take in Italy after the end of the war and the fascist dictatorship. However, the relationship between Gramsci's ideas and the subsequent Eurocommunism of the Italian Communist Party is contentious.

Green

Thomas Hill Green (1836–1882) was an Oxford philosopher who was a key influence, along with Leonard Hobhouse* (1864–1929) and John Hobson (1858–1940), on the development of British **liberalism** towards the New Liberalism of the late 19th and early 20th centuries. Green's key work *Lectures on the Principles of Political Obligation* was published after his early death. Influenced by ancient Greek philosophy and German **idealism** (particularly Kant* and Hegel*), Green criticised aspects of earlier schools of liberalism, including both classical laissez-faire liberalism and Benthamite **utilitarianism**. He rejected what he saw as an artificial antithesis between the **individual** and society. A political **community** was a partnership for the common good. Each individual had **obligations** as well as **freedoms**. True freedom does not involve simply the satisfaction of appetites but self-development in common with others. This justified state intervention, particularly in education and health, both for the common good and to allow individuals to make the best of themselves. This positive liberty (freedom *to*) might be contrasted with the negative liberty (freedom *from*) associated with classical **free market** liberalism. (Isaiah Berlin* later famously explored the implications of these two concepts of liberty).

Greer

Germaine Greer (1939–) is a particularly controversial **feminist** writer and broadcaster, who was born and brought up in Australia but has since lived and worked mainly in England. Her best-selling book *The Female Eunuch* (1970) brought feminist ideas to a much wider audience. While critical of the role of the Western nuclear family in the subordination of women, in her later work *Sex and Destiny* (1984) Greer argued in favour of the extended family, familiar in Asian, African, and Mediterranean cultures. She remains the most well-known feminist in the United Kingdom, but her undoubted 'star quality' and her enjoyment of controversy have not always endeared her to other feminists and the women's movement generally.

Grotius

Hugo Grotius (1583–1645) was a Dutch lawyer who is widely considered to have laid the foundations of modern **international law**. Like many classical and medieval thinkers before him he considered **natural law** as the foundation of the law of **states** but argued that it should also govern relations among states in his key work *De Jure Belli ac Pacis* (Concerning the Law of War and Peace, 1625). He asserted, as a central principle of international law, that states and their governments should uphold treaties freely entered into. Only a defensive war, he argued, could be a just war. His ideas are still widely cited in modern theories of **international relations**, particularly by the English school.

Habermas

Jürgen Habermas (1929–) is a wide-ranging German social and political theorist, who is generally considered the leading thinker of the second generation of the Frankfurt School of Critical Theory. Unlike many fashionable modern thinkers, Habermas defends the Enlightenment as a still unfinished project to create a modern, **free**, and **rational** society. This has brought him into conflict with **postmodernists** such as Derrida* and Lyotard* who have reacted against the Enlightenment and its trust in human reason, science, and progress. In *The Structural Transformation of the Public Sphere* (1962) Habermas deplores the decline of what he saw as a once vigorous public sphere of political debate with the growth of a commercialised **mass media**. In *Knowledge and Human Interests* (1971) he argues that people are effectively manipulated in modern capitalist society where everything is treated as a commodity. In his *Legitimation Crisis* (1975) Habermas claims that the modern capitalist **state** is facing a combination of crises. State intervention to deal with or avoid economic crisis risks creating crises of rationality, **legitimacy**, and motivation. However, his key work is *The Theory of Communicative Action* (volume 1 1984, volume 2 1986), where he displays his confidence in the potential for rational communication based on mutual trust and **consensus**. In his more recent work he has apparently modified his earlier hostility to **capitalism**, which he now sees as compatible with a **democratic** society.

Hayek

Friedrich August von Hayek (1899–1992) was the outstanding **neoliberal** thinker of the 20th century. Born and educated in Austria, where he worked as an economist, he moved to the London School of Economics in 1931, becoming a British citizen in 1938. He left the LSE for the University of Chicago in 1950, and moved from there to the University of Freiburg in Germany in 1962, where he remained until his retirement in 1968. He was awarded the Nobel Prize for economics in 1974, was made a Companion of Honour in the United Kingdom in 1984, and received the US Presidential Medal of Freedom in 1991. His ideas have been influential throughout the Western world but have had most impact in his native Austria, the United Kingdom, the United States, and finally Germany, where he died in 1992.

Hayek's *Road to Serfdom* (1944) involved an attack on all forms of **state** economic planning, not just the **collectivist** planning advocated by **communists**, left-wing **socialists**, and **fascists** but the modest state intervention practised by **social democrats**, many **conservatives**, and 'social' or 'new'

liberals. Hayek argued that state economic planning was not only less efficient than resource allocation through the **free market**, it also involved, inevitably, an oppressive interference with **individual liberty**, or in his words, a 'road to serfdom'. Hayek opposed any attempt by **government** to promote social (or distributive) **justice**. He argued that it would lead to constant and extensive control of individuals that was inconsistent with a free society, in pursuit of an unobtainable ideal. The legitimate role of government, according to Hayek, was to provide a framework of law and order within which the free market could flourish, and this he outlined in his later major work *The Constitution of Liberty* (1960). Here he did however allow that governments might provide a minimal safety net for particularly needy individuals.

Hayek's uncompromising free market convictions brought him into conflict not only with socialists but with Keynesians, who believed in government management of the macroeconomy, and all those governments and politicians across the political spectrum who favoured the development of a **welfare** state in the postwar period. For much of this time Hayek's classical liberalism (or neoliberalism) was at odds with prevailing economic and political orthodoxy. However, the problems encountered by governments attempting to manage the economy on Keynesian lines brought Hayek's free market ideas back into fashion. In the United Kingdom, the Conservative leader Margaret Thatcher (Prime Minister 1979–1990) was a self-proclaimed admirer, and there was further support from US President Reagan's Republican administration (1980–1988).

Yet Hayek himself always denied that he was a conservative. Conservatism had not in the past been wedded to free markets. Perhaps Hayek also bore in mind the interventionist record of past Conservative governments in the United Kingdom as well as the continuing emphasis of continental European conservatives and **Christian democrats** on planning and social welfare. Instead, Hayek called himself a classical **liberal** or old Whig. In the United States he is generally described as a 'libertarian'.

Hegel

George Wilhelm Friedrich Hegel (1770–1831) was a German philosopher and political thinker. Born in Stuttgart, he later taught at the universities of Jena, Heidelberg, and Berlin. His key political work is *The Philosophy of Right* (1821), but his writings on logic also had important implications for political theory. He argued that classical formal logic is static and intellectually limited. Instead, he suggested that human knowledge commonly progresses through a dynamic process of argument that he called *dialectic*, involving the statement of a *thesis*, its opposite or *antithesis*, and a *synthesis* incorporating elements of the original thesis and its antithesis. This becomes a new thesis, initiating a new antithesis and synthesis, and so on.

In *The Philosophy of Right* Hegel applies his dialectical analysis to three levels of human social interaction: the family, **civil society**, and the **state**. Within the family people may pursue 'particular altruism', putting the interests of other family members before their own, but the family is a natural rather than a rational form of association and inherently unstable. Civil society involves 'universal egoism', the general pursuit of individual self-interest in the wider community, although people honour their contractual obligations in the marketplace. The state, however, is an ethical community that involves a synthesis of the values of the family and civil society and is characterised by universal altruism, the whole community acting for the common good rather than individual self-interest. Thus for Hegel it is only within the modern state that human beings can realise their true rational freedom in company with their fellows; humans are naturally social animals and can only fulfil themselves through society and political community. Thus he holds an organic theory of society and the state.

Hegel has been variously interpreted. Although he has been accused of being a political reactionary, celebrating the Prussian state that he served, he supported the constitutional and legal reforms undertaken in Prussia and thus advocated limited rather than absolute **monarchy**. The 'Young Hegelians' (including especially Marx*) applied his ideas in a radical or even **revolutionary** way. While Hegel applied his dialectical method to the development of ideas, Marx later applied it to material circumstances, particularly class interests (hence *dialectical materialism*). In the later 19th century Hegel's thought particularly influenced the English idealists, including T. H. Green*, and Bosanquet, notably in their emphasis on positive rather than negative liberty and their general commitment to state action to enlarge **freedom**. More recently some Western thinkers (e.g. Popper*) have detected dangerous **authoritarian** and even **totalitarian** tendencies in Hegel's thought, but his ideas have been more sympathetically re-examined by others.

Hirschman

Albert O. Hirschman (1915–2012) was an American economist who has been described as inhabiting a grey zone between economic and political theory. He was born in Berlin and educated in Paris, London, and Trieste. He helped many European intellectuals escape from the Nazis and emigrated to the United States himself in 1941. After the war he held economics posts at Yale, Columbia, and Harvard, where he worked on the political economy of development. To students of **politics** he is best known for his influential book *Exit, Voice, and Loyalty* (1970), the title of which lists the three main responses open to dissatisfied consumers, employees, or **citizens**. They can leave (exit), they can oppose (voice), or they can keep quiet (loyalty). As Stoker (2017, 74) has pointed out, exit is the classic economic mechanism. In a **free market**, if consumers are dissatisfied, the answer is easy – they can go elsewhere. They do not have to make a fuss. Voice is the classic political mechanism, exercised, for example through such means of political participation as voting, joining **pressure groups**, protesting, taking direct action. 'Voice' requires more effort and carries more costs for the individual than 'exit'. Moreover, 'voice' may not be successful. (This is one reason why Stoker concludes that political decision-making involves 'designed-in disappointment'.)

Hobbes

Thomas Hobbes (1588–1679) is perhaps the most celebrated English political philosopher. Born in the year of the Spanish Armada, Hobbes later claimed that his mother, fleeing the threatened invasion, gave birth to twins, himself and fear. Later fear was to form a significant element in his political thought. Educated at Oxford he was unimpressed by the philosophy of Aristotle*. His political ideas were shaped by the conflict between King Charles I and Parliament that led to the English Civil War, the execution of the king, and the 'Commonwealth' of Oliver Cromwell. Already by 1640 Hobbes had become an advocate of absolute **monarchy** and fled to France with the summoning of the Long Parliament. His thoughts on **government** were set out in *De Cive* (1642). From 1646 he briefly became tutor to the young exiled Prince Charles. In 1651 he published his great work *Leviathan*.

As in his early works, in *Leviathan* Hobbes advocated virtually total obedience to an absolute government as the only alternative to **anarchy**. He argued that humans were competitive, selfish, and acquisitive. Their life without a supreme government to keep them in order would be 'solitary, poor, nasty, brutish, and short' and would involve a war of every man against every man. To avoid this nightmare, men rationally agreed to surrender their right to govern themselves to a common sovereign in a contract or promise. Some political thinkers used the notion of a social contract to suggest a two-way bargain between sovereign and subjects, arguing that if the sovereign failed to maintain his side of the bargain, his subjects were no longer bound to obey him. For Hobbes the surrender of power by subjects was unconditional and permanent. If **sovereignty** was limited or divided, anarchy would result.

Yet his justification of **absolutism** did not involve the conventional royalist argument based on the Divine Right of Kings, but was essentially **utilitarian**. The sovereign should be obeyed because of the peace and security the sovereign provided. For Hobbes the identity of the sovereign was less important. Indeed, he argued that the sovereign power could be either a single person or an assembly (but not both). Hobbes message could be interpreted to mean simply 'Obey the powers that be.' If a former ruler had effectively lost sovereign authority and could no longer provide the peace and security associated with sovereignty, the rational solution was for subjects to transfer their allegiance to the new sovereign. The argument was not spelled out in *Leviathan*, but in 1652 Hobbes returned to England and made his peace with Oliver Cromwell. Subsequently, after the Restoration, he was recognised by his former pupil, by then King Charles II, and brought back to court for a time, until his alleged atheism scandalised the courtiers. He continued to work and write until his death in 1679.

Hobhouse

Leonard Trelawney Hobhouse (1864–1929) was a British **liberal** political philosopher who was an influential figure in the emergence of the New Liberalism that favoured increased state intervention in the early 20th century. In *Liberalism* (1911) he was prepared to justify extensive interference with the **free market** to secure 'the right to work' and 'the right to a living wage'. Although Hobhouse was influenced by the **idealism** of T. H. Green*, he became critical of the influence of Hegel* in particular on the New Liberalism. Hobhouse's book *The Metaphysical Theory of the State* (1918) vigorously attacked *The Philosophical Theory of the State* (1899) by Green's disciple Bernard Bosanquet.

Hooker

Richard Hooker (1554–1600) was an English theologian and philosopher who provided theoretical support for the Elizabethan church and **state**. In his key work *Of the Laws of Ecclesiastical Polity* (1592) he upheld the Church of England as an acceptable middle way between Roman Catholicism and Puritanism and justified the royal supremacy over the church. Like some other thinkers of the early modern period he assumed that legitimate government originated from a contract and thus ultimately rested on the **consent** of the governed. However, he did not draw radical conclusions from this assumption but praised, and preached loyalty to, the English **constitution**. He is thus regarded as part of the English **conservative** tradition of political thought.

Hume

David Hume (1711–76), a hugely influential Scottish thinker, was celebrated in his own time as a historian (for his five-volume *History of England*, 1754–1762) but is today viewed chiefly as a major philosopher (*A Treatise of Human Nature*, 1739–1740). His contributions to political thought are also important, although not easy to summarise. As a philosopher he was both an **empiricist** and a sceptic. Reason is limited and 'the slave of the passions'. Our ideas are derived from the experience of our senses. An association or correlation of events cannot prove a cause and effect. This emphasis on the limitations of reason and human intelligence is compatible with a form of **conservatism**, and Hume's own political sympathies were Tory. In a brief essay, *Of the Original Contract* (1748), he robustly demolishes the argument of Hobbes* and Locke* that our obligation to obey **government** depends on some (implicit or explicit) contract or promise. Instead, Hume argues that we obey government 'because society could not otherwise subsist'. This might be described as a **utilitarian** argument. Indeed, Hume was claimed as a forerunner by the utilitarian thinker Jeremy Bentham*, although he did not share Bentham's **rationalist** and reformist convictions.

Huntington

Samuel P. Huntington (1927–2008) was an American political scientist and a professor at Harvard University. An influential but controversial book was *Political Order in Changing Societies* which appeared in the year, 1968, that saw radical political protest by students in both the United States and western Europe. He subsequently turned his attention to the comparative study of the process of **democratisation** that he saw as developing in the course of the 20th century in three 'waves', with intervening reverse waves (*The Third Wave: Democratization in the Late Twentieth Century*, 1991). More controversial still was 'The Clash of Civilizations', published as an article in 1993 and later expanded for publication in book form as *The Clash of Civilizations and the Remaking of World Order* (1996). This argued that **cultural** (and religious) divisions transcending state boundaries had replaced **ideological** conflict between sovereign **states** in the post–Cold War world. Huntington's thesis was widely seen as prophetic of the apparently growing threat to the West from radical Islam, as represented by the attack on the Twin Towers of 9/11. Some critics accused Huntington of legitimising the subsequent 'war on terror' and the Western invasion of Afghanistan and Iraq, although he was not an enthusiast for extensive 'humanitarian intervention'. Others argued that his analysis was oversimplified, taking insufficient account of the extensive internal differences within civilisations and cultures.

Inglehart

Ronald Inglehart (1934–) is an American political scientist whose work has focused on changes in **political culture**, particularly in advanced Western industrial **states**. He argued in a seminal article ('The Silent Revolution in Europe: Intergenerational Change in Post-Industrial Societies', 1971) that increased affluence and security had led to changes in political attitudes among the younger generation towards **post-material** values that emphasised quality of life rather than economic achievement. This theme was further explored in later works, such as *Culture Shift in Advanced Industrial Society* (1990) and *Modernization and Post-Modernization: Cultural, Economic and Social Change in 43 Societies* (1997). More recently he has (with Pippa Norris) in *Sacred* and Secular: Religion and Politics Worldwide (2004) explored the contrast between the growth of secularisation in the Western industrial societies and the strong maintenance of **traditional** religious convictions elsewhere, particularly among those living in poorer societies and failed states.

Jefferson

Thomas Jefferson (1743–1826), among his many other wide-ranging interests, furnished some of the key ideas behind the American Revolution. As an active politician and statesman he helped shape the United States of America in its early years. Born and brought up in Virginia, where his education introduced him to the ideas of the Scottish Enlightenment, he was elected as delegate from his state to the Continental Congress of 1776 and drafted the *Declaration of Independence*, with its celebrated preamble.

> We hold these truths to be self-evident, that all men are created equal, that they are endowed by their Creator with certain inalienable rights, that among these are life, liberty and the pursuit of happiness. That to secure these rights, governments are instituted among men, deriving their just powers from the consent of the governed.

Jefferson's ideals have remained an inspiration, and not only to Americans. If Jefferson's passionate commitment to **equality**, **liberty**, and universal human **rights** was incompatible with his own position as a slave owner, it was a contradiction widely shared in the new political state and society he helped to create in America.

Jefferson subsequently served as American Minister in Paris (1784–9) where he witnessed the beginning of the French **Revolution** and advised Lafayette on the *Declaration of the Rights of Man* (1789). Thus he provides a crucial link between the American and French revolutions. Back in America he served in Washington's government from 1789 to 1793 and became the third president of the United States (1801–1809). He played a key role in the early US **party** system,

standing for the rural interests of the majority of American voters against the business interests of the Federalist Party.

Kaldor

Mary Kaldor (1946–) has been influential in characterising post–Cold War conflicts as 'new wars' (see *New and Old Wars: Organized Violence in a Global Era*). Her work has also highlighted ways in which the **global** community can come together to propose alternative forms of cosmopolitan **democracy**. Other key works include *Global Civil Society: An Answer to War* (2003) and *Human Security: Reflections on Globalization and Intervention* (2007).

Kant

Immanuel Kant (1724–1804) was an outstanding German philosopher, who was born in Königsberg (then in East Prussia) where he later taught at the university and spent the rest of his life. He is widely considered to be the last great thinker of the enlightenment. His key works include *Critique of Pure Reason* (1781), *Critique of Practical Reason* (1788) ,and *Critique of Judgement* (1790). Although he was not primarily a political thinker, his writings on ethics in particular have made a significant influence on political thought. For Kant morality springs from the exercise of human reason by free individuals. It does not rest on religion or other forms of **authority**. Kant's main moral principle (or 'categorical imperative') was: act only on the maxim through which you can at the same time will that it should become a universal law. In other words, we should act only as we would be happy for others to act in the same circumstances. Kant's best-known moral principle is that we should treat other people as ends, never as means. Thus we should do good for its own sake, not for any benefit it might bring.

Kant also anticipated elements of later liberal **international relations** theory in his essay *Perpetual Peace* (1795), where he argues that **nations**, for the sake of their own security, should seek a 'federation of peoples' to prevent war. This would not involve a global state but would rest on an 'equilibrium of forces' (or **balance of power**). Peace would be aided by the mutual interest of nations in trade and commerce, which cannot coexist with war, so that wherever a threat of war emerged, nations would seek to avoid it by mediation. Kant also argued that **republics** were much less likely to go to war, as the **citizens** who decided the issue would suffer the consequences. (It is often argued today that in practice **democracies** do not make war on other democracies.)

Kautsky

Karl Kautsky (1854–1938) was a leading German **socialist** thinker, responsible, with Bernstein*, for the 1891 Erfurt Programme of the **Social Democratic** Party that committed it to a **Marxist** programme. Subsequently he rejected Bernstein's revisionism, insisting on the inevitability of **class** conflict. Yet he was committed to the **democratic** route to power, and after he criticised the Bolshevik **Revolution** he was in turn attacked by Lenin* as a renegade. After the First World War he played a leading role in the Second International.

Keohane

Robert Keohane (1941–) is a leading American writer on **international relations**. In a volume he coedited with Joseph Nye, *Transnational Relations and World Politics* (1971), much greater importance was attached to the role and influence of non-state actors in international relations, in contrast to the **state**-centred approach of orthodox **realist** theory. In 1977 Keohane and Nye published *Power and Interdependence* (2000), their own theory of international relations, based on the notion of complex interdependence, involving both state and non-state actors.

Key

V. O. Key (1908–1963) was a leading American political scientist who played a significant role in the **behavioural revolution** in the study of **politics**. He was particularly

associated with the statistical analysis of voting and public opinion data. His publications include *Politics, Parties and Pressure Groups* (1942) and *Southern Politics in State and Nation* (1950).

Keynes

John Maynard Keynes (1883–1946) was a celebrated British economist whose work had major implications for politics. He worked in the British Treasury during the First World War and attended the postwar treaty negotiations, writing a celebrated critique of the outcome, *The Economic Consequences of the Peace* (1919). In the 1920s he advised the Liberal Party on economic policy. In 1936 he published the *General Theory of Employment, Interest and Money*, the 'bible' of what came to be known as Keynesianism and provided the theoretical underpinning for government management of the economy in the postwar decades. Briefly, Keynes advocated leaving the micro-economy to market forces but recommended government management of aggregate demand in the macroeconomy through fiscal and monetary policy to stimulate or depress demand (depending on circumstances) to maintain steady economic growth and full employment without inflation. His ideas became official orthodoxy during the Second World War (which saw Keynes back at the Treasury). They were later endorsed with enthusiasm by both progressive **conservatives** and **Christian Democrats**, anxious to avoid the economic difficulties of the interwar years (particularly high unemployment), as well as by **social democrats** searching for some form of state planning and managed **capitalism**. With social **welfare** reforms (in the United Kingdom associated with William Beveridge*), Keynesian economic policy provided the basis for the postwar political **consensus**. Keynes died soon after the war ended, so he did not live to see the use (or sometimes misuse) of his ideas in the postwar period. While Keynes saw his theory as an equilibrium theory, designed to tackle both inflation and depression, governments predominantly sought to maintain full employment by boosting demand, mainly through increasing government spending. This caused inflationary pressures, culminating in an inflationary crisis in the 1970s that partially discredited Keynesian ideas and led to the increased influence of neoliberal thinkers such as Hayek*, Friedman, and the **public choice** school.

King

Martin Luther King (1929–1968) was a Baptist minister who became leader of the civil **rights** movement in the United States. He sought to end various practices that discriminated against American blacks, successfully campaigning in the southern states against segregation on the buses and in schools, and to ensure that the right to vote was conceded and exercised. Inspired by the example of Gandhi*, he was committed to 'active non-violence', although his moderation did not please some black leaders (such as Stokely Carmichael) who advocated less **pacifist** and more assertive tactics. However, many found King's oratory inspiring. In 1963 he led a march of 200,000 to Washington, where he delivered his celebrated speech with the reiterated phrase, 'I have a dream.' In 1964 he was awarded the Nobel Prize for Peace. In 1968 he was assassinated. His life and work helped transform **race** relations in the United States.

Kropotkin

Prince Peter Kropotkin (1842–1921), born a Russian nobleman and educated in a military academy, was converted to **anarchism** in 1872 and became involved in the Russian **populist** movement. Imprisoned for his revolutionary activities he escaped in 1876 and spent most of the rest of his life in exile. He returned to Russia after the **revolution** in 1917 but soon became disillusioned with the new Bolshevik regime. His funeral provoked a mass anarchist demonstration in 1921, which surprisingly was approved by Lenin*. His key work was *Mutual Aid* (1902). Here he argued for co-operation rather than competition and conflict. He claimed that co-operation and mutual aid were in accordance

with nature generally and **human nature**, strongly disagreeing with the views of Hobbes* on the subject. While personally opposed to violence, he considered a popular uprising a pre-condition of an anarchist society. The repressive state would be replaced by a loose federation of small self-governing local **communities**.

Kymlicka

Will Kymlicka (1962–) is a Canadian political philosopher who has particularly explored **multiculturalism** and the issue of group **rights** of minority **cultures**. While he argued the need to respect all minority cultures, he particularly focused on what he called national minorities that were present at the founding of states, such as the Québecois and Inuit Indians in Canada, the aborigines in Australia, and the Maori in New Zealand. These 'minority nations' deserved special rights and freedoms beyond those granted to immigrant minorities, who entered the state subsequently and voluntarily and had some obligation to integrate with the majority culture. Although Kymlika is prepared to argue for group rights rather than purely individual rights, he acknowledges that group rights should not permit interference with fundamental **individual freedoms**, including the rights of women and homosexuals. Key works that tackle some of the philosophical issues involved include *Liberalism, Community and Culture* (1989) and *Multicultural Citizenship* (1995). In *Contemporary Political Philosophy* (1990), he examines major schools in modern philosophy and critically analyses the work of some leading modern thinkers, including John Rawls*, Robert Nozick*, and Ronald Dworkin*.

Lasswell

Harold Lasswell (1902–1978) was a pioneering American political scientist, who emphasised that **politics** was about **power**. His book *Politics: Who Gets What, When, How?* (1936) is regarded as a classic text. He also contributed notably to the study of political communication and wrote provocatively on the subject of propaganda.

Lazarsfeld

Paul Lazarsfeld (1901–1976) was a leading American sociologist. Born in Vienna, he received a doctorate in mathematics and soon applied his quantitative skills to the study of sociology. He moved to the United States in 1933, where he worked at Newark, Princeton, and Columbia, undertaking mass market surveys, and his approach to the collection and statistical analysis of data had a major impact on social science methodology. He was the lead author of the first substantial US survey of voting behaviour, *The People's Choice* (Lazarsfeld, Berelson, and Gaudet 1944).

Lenin

Vladimir Ilich Ulyanov (1870–1924), who later took the name Lenin, was born in Russia to a middle-class family. After his elder brother was hanged for his part in a plot to assassinate Tsar Alexander III in 1887, Lenin himself became a committed **revolutionary**. He joined a small group of **Marxist** intellectuals in St Petersburg, where he was arrested and imprisoned in 1895. He was then exiled to Siberia in 1897, before moving to Switzerland where he joined other Marxist émigrés in 1900. There he edited and contributed to the Marxist paper *Iskra* and published *What Is to Be Done?* (1902). In 1903 Lenin split the Russian Marxist party, the **Social Democrats**. His supporters, briefly the majority, were dubbed Bolsheviks, and his opponents Mensheviks (after the Russian terms for majority and minority groups).

In 1914 Lenin realised that war could lead to the downfall of the Russian tsarist state and seized the opportunity provided by the February revolution of 1917 to return to Russia and eventually seize power for the Bolsheviks in October. He proclaimed 'all power to the soviets' (workers' councils) and dissolved the elected Russian parliament, consolidating the Bolshevik hold on power by abolishing other parties, making peace with Germany, and winning the subsequent civil war between the 'red' and 'white' forces in Russia. In 1921 he exchanged his early 'war communism', which had damaged the Russian economy, for the more moderate New Economic Policy. His death in 1924 provoked a power struggle among the leading Bolsheviks, which eventually resulted in the **dictatorship** of Stalin* and the elimination of Lenin's leading associates.

Lenin, as a successful Marxist revolutionary, effectively created **Marxism-Leninism**, the dominant interpretation of Marxism in the 20th century. Although he was widely seen as a rigidly orthodox Marxist, he adapted and reinterpreted Marx's* thought to meet conditions in Tsarist Russia, where **capitalism** was relatively undeveloped and both the **bourgeoisie** and the industrial proletariat relatively weak. This meant the need to win support from the peasants. Yet Russian Marxists could not hope to build a mass party, as the German **social democrats** had done, as in Tsarist Russia political opposition was necessarily underground and clandestine.

In *What Is to Be Done?* Lenin argued for a small party of dedicated revolutionaries to act as the intellectual 'vanguard' of the working class. He advocated what came to be called 'democratic centralism', involving ruthless party discipline once policy had been decided upon. Thus Marx's notion of a temporary dictatorship of the proletariat evolved under Lenin to mean a more lasting dictatorship of the Communist Party, acting on behalf of the working class. After the Bolshevik revolution Lenin created a one-party state but argued that what he called soviet **democracy** or proletarian democracy was far more democratic than bourgeois democracy, which in practice excluded the working class from active involvement. Lenin's interpretation of democracy was to become the orthodoxy not only in the Soviet Union but also in the so-called people's democracies of Eastern Europe and elsewhere.

Lenin's most important contribution to Marxist theory was perhaps *Imperialism, the Highest Stage of Capitalism* (1916). Here he argued that the apparent failure of Marx's prediction of the increasing exploitation and 'immiseration' of the working class in the most advanced capitalist countries was due to the acquisition and exploitation of colonial empires, which enabled leading capitalist states to postpone the impoverishment of their own working classes. His analysis not only provided a plausible explanation of the apparent decline of working-class militancy in the West but also increased the appeal of Marxism-Leninism to anticolonial movements.

Lijphart

Arend Lijphart (1936–) is a political scientist who was born in the Netherlands but has worked mainly in the United States and holds dual American and Dutch citizenship. The contrast between 'consensus' democracies (such as his native Netherlands) and majoritarian democracies (such as the United States) has informed much of his work. His first major book involved a study of Dutch politics, *The Politics of Accommodation* (1967), where he developed the concept of consociation, which he later applied to other societies divided on ethnic, religious, or linguistic lines.

Lindblom

Charles E. Lindblom (1917–) is a leading American political scientist. He remains best known for his advocacy of incremental decision-making, which he provocatively described as 'The science of muddling through' (1959), rather than the rational decision-making model put forward by Herbert Simon*. For Lindblom, incrementalism (or policy-making by a series of small incremental steps) is a better description of how policy is generally made in practice. However he also argued that it is a better prescriptive model of how policy should be made, as it is less risky and generally reflects a degree of consensus among affected interests (arising from what Lindblom described as 'partisan mutual adjustment'). Lindblom was also influenced by the pluralism of his colleague Robert Dahl* at Yale University, although in his book *Politics and Markets* (1977) he noted the privileged position of business and the limits on effective competition both in the marketplace and politics. Because of these departures from classical pluralism he is sometimes described as a 'neo-pluralist'.

Lipset

Seymour Martin Lipset (1922–2006) was an American political sociologist. He is still best known for *Political Man: The Social Bases of Politics* (1960). However, his interests roamed widely over the whole field of politics, including the relationship between economic development and democracy, US right-wing extremism, the failure of socialism to make political headway in the USA, and the reasons for American exceptionalism.

Locke

John Locke (1632–1704) was an extremely influential English political thinker. He was personal physician and adviser to the Earl of Shaftesbury, who served briefly as a minister under the restored monarchy of King Charles II but subsequently led the parliamentary opposition to the court. Locke left England for Holland following Shaftesbury's fall and death in 1683. He only returned after the 'Glorious Revolution' of 1688, in which the Catholic James II (brother and successor to Charles II) was replaced by the Protestant Dutch prince, William of Orange and his wife Mary (Protestant daughter of James). Although Locke's two *Treatises on Civil Government* (1690) seem to have been largely written before 1688, they provided a theoretical justification for the revolution of that year.

Locke, like Hobbes*, envisaged an original state of nature in which there was no government, followed by a contract to establish a society and government. Yet Locke's state of nature was less fearful than that of Hobbes. It is 'a state of liberty, yet it is not a state of licence.' Men enjoyed natural rights in the state of nature, including, crucially, a right to property, which individuals acquired initially through mixing their own labour with natural resources, although government was necessary to increase the security of property. Locke's contract involved a conditional rather than total surrender of power to the sovereign. Government depended on the consent of the governed. The authority of government was limited rather than absolute, and the powers of government should be separate rather than concentrated. If the sovereign infringed the rights of his (or her) subjects, they were entitled to resist.

All these ideas, natural and inalienable human rights, **government** by **consent**, limited government, the **separation of powers**, and a right of resistance to, and ultimately rebellion against, an arbitrary or tyrannical government became key concepts in **liberal** thought. They seemed to underpin the British system of government as it evolved after 1688 and they helped inspire the American **Revolution** and the **constitution** of the United States, as well as subsequent political developments both in Europe and the wider world.

Whether Locke would have approved these developments is questionable. Although for Locke government depended ultimately on the consent of the governed, he was certainly no **democrat**. While all men were **free** and **equal** in the state of nature, the right to property was entirely consistent with considerable inequality in possessions and power. Indeed, Locke's political theory has been held to justify not only the effective **oligarchy** of rich landowners in 18th-century Britain but also emerging **capitalism** both in Britain and the Western world. Thus C. B. Macpherson described the ideas of both Hobbes and Locke as *The Political Theory of Possessive Individualism* (1962). There were also limits to Locke's liberalism. Even his eloquent defence of religious **toleration** (in his *Letter Concerning Toleration*, 1689) did not extend to Catholics or atheists. Yet, irrespective of his limitations, John Locke remains a crucial figure in the liberal tradition.

Lovelock

James Lovelock (1919–) is a British scientist and **environmentalist**. He is best known for the Gaia hypothesis. Gaia was the name of a Greek goddess of the earth, and Lovelock adopted the name to personify the notion of the earth and the earth's atmosphere as a living organism, in danger from environmental pollution, and specifically global warming. Unlike other environmentalists, he has become a keen advocate of nuclear power,

which he argues is the only feasible way of halting global warming. A recent book expounding his ideas is *The Revenge of Gaia* (2007).

Luxemburg

Rosa Luxemburg (1871–1919) was a Polish revolutionary **socialist**, committed to the international working class and influential in German and Russian socialist circles. She vigorously attacked Bernstein's* revisionism but also criticised Lenin's* views on **party** organisation. She favoured mass strikes and demonstrations as a means to **revolution**. She was imprisoned for her antiwar views in the First World War and brutally murdered by counterrevolutionary solders in the abortive German revolution at the end of the war. She subsequently became an iconic figure in Western **Marxist** circles, rivalling Trotsky* as a source of inspiration.

Lyotard

Jean-Francois Lyotard (1924–1998) was a leading French **postmodernist** philosopher. His book *The Postmodern Condition* (1979, English translation 1984), has become a key text for understanding postmodernism. Lyotard argued that the modern industrial age was over and with it the Enlightenment faith in human reason, science, and progress. The modern age had brought some benefits but also destructive wars and other man-made disasters, leading to disillusion with the Enlightenment project. Modernism had thus been superseded by postmodernism, characterised by an 'incredulity towards meta-narratives', a famous phrase of Lyotard's. By 'meta-narratives' (or grand narratives) he meant any theory, religion, philosophy, or **ideology** purporting to explain the world or its history. Postmodernism instead emphasised difference and diversity. This opposition to 'grand narratives' appealed to some radical alternative perspectives, such as radical **feminism**, critical of mainstream (or 'malestream') interpretations of the world. Yet critics have pointed out that the postmodernist rejection of *all* meta-narratives included radical alternatives such as feminism (and, some argue, even postmodernism itself).

Machiavelli

Niccolo Machiavelli (1469–1527) lived in Florence through a turbulent period of its history as an independent state. After the expulsion of the Medici rulers of the city, he served the Republic of Florence as a diplomat until the Medicis were returned to power. He wrote his best-known work *The Prince* as a kind of unsolicited job application to the restored Medici rulers, an application that proved unsuccessful – perhaps unsurprisingly in view of his **republican** sympathies, evident in his previous employment and in his later books the *Discourses* and *The History of Florence*.

Machiavelli's thought has been very variously interpreted. For many his cynical political **realism** was profoundly shocking and immoral. Thus, in *The Prince* he advised rulers to break their word when the occasion demanded. 'Since men are a sorry lot and will not keep their promises to you, you need not keep your promises to them. A prince never lacks legitimate reasons to break his promises.' Yet while it was not necessary for a prince to have all the virtues, 'it is very necessary for him to appear to have them'. In a similar vein he advises that it is better for a ruler to be feared than loved, as men are 'ungrateful, fickle, simulators and deceivers, avoiders of danger, and greedy for gain' and not to be relied upon. 'Thus fear will more effectively compel their obedience than love.' To his outraged critics, Machiavelli was 'old Nick', the devil, shamelessly advocating immoral conduct. To others, Machiavelli might rather be considered the first modern political scientist, describing and analysing politics as it is rather than as it ought to be. For others again, Machiavelli's real political convictions are not to be found in *The Prince* but in his other writings, where his **republican** ideals are manifest. Thus Machiavelli belongs in the great republican tradition of thought. Yet although the *Discourses* suggest where his real political sympathies lay, it has been argued that both books display a similar pessimistic view of **human nature** and a similar political realism.

MacIntyre

Alasdair MacIntyre (1929–) is an influential Scottish-born moral and political philosopher who has taught at a wide range of universities in Britain and the United States. His key work is *After Virtue* (1981). In the early 1980s he was converted to Roman Catholicism. He is regarded as an important modern **communitarian** theorist, although he is difficult to classify as he draws on ideas from a wide range of thinkers, including Aristotle*, Aquinas*, and Marx*.

MacKinnon

Catharine McKinnon (1946–) is an extremely influential American **feminist** lawyer and theorist. As a lawyer she played a key role in using anti–sex discrimination legislation to help women sue against sexual harassment at work. Her book *Sexual Harassment of Working Women* (1978) became the standard authority on the subject. Her work in this field has changed the law, opinion, and practice. She represented the actress who, under the name Linda Lovelace, had appeared in the pornographic film *Deep Throat* but who later accused her husband of abusing her and forcing her to make the film. With Andrea Dworkin* MacKinnon campaigned to use civil **rights legislation** against pornography. MacKinnon has contributed notably to feminist theory with her books *Towards a Feminist Theory of the State* (1989) and *Sex Equality* (2001). She insists that feminist theory is derived from the specific experiences of women, hitherto ignored. She argues that knowledge is **power**. Power means that your view of how things are is generally accepted. Powerlessness means your view of how things are is marginalised or ignored. Feminism is about giving a voice to women's own experience of how things are.

McLuhan

Marshall McLuhan (1911–1980) was a provocative exponent of media theory. He argued that 'the medium is the message'. Any specific medium of communication, such as the print media, film, radio and televisions, is not neutral but shapes and constrains the message transmitted and effectively 'massages' it. Each medium has its own characteristics. Print allows the reader to assimilate the message in his or her own time, rereading, and reconsidering, if needed, to understand and reflect. Radio and television are both instant, but with radio the listener has to supply any pictures in his or her head, and the sound has to be virtually continuous, as radio abhors silence. There is no time for reflection in answer to questions on radio. Television is essentially a visual medium – the pictures tell the story. while any spoken commentary underlines the pictures, to the extent that any attempt to convey a contrary message in spoken words is likely to fail. A politician on television may be speaking to millions, but this number is made up by countless ones, twos, and threes in specific domestic locations. Thus the politician must adopt a relaxed, low-key intimate style, not address the audience as if it were a public meeting.

Madison

James Madison (1751–1836) was a major American thinker and statesman, the 'Father of the Constitution'. A critic of the Articles of Confederation, the first **constitution** of the United States of America, which had newly won independence from Britain, he led the struggle to revise them in the Constitutional Convention of 1787, helping to devise what was in effect a new system of **government**. He then (with Alexander Hamilton and John Jay) coauthored *The Federalist Papers* (1787–1788), a series of essays that defended the new constitution against its critics. Subsequently he helped promote and defend the Bill of Rights (1791), comprising the first ten amendments to the American Constitution. From 1801 to 1809 he served as secretary of state under Thomas Jefferson* and succeeded Jefferson as America's fourth president (1809–1817).

While Madison thought that political **authority** was ultimately derived from the people, he feared strong popular influence on government. He distinguished between a **republic**, by which he meant a representative system of government, and a pure democracy, which he argued was 'incompatible with personal security or the rights of property'. In a **representative** system, he argued, 'the public voice, pronounced by the representatives of the people, will be more consonant to the public good than if pronounced by the people themselves' (*Federalist Paper* No 10). The American Constitution, defended by Madison, did place some limits on direct popular control of government, although not all the checks and balances built into the constitution operated as intended (thus the president was effectively directly elected by the people rather than freely chosen by members of the Electoral College). However, the main elements of the **federal** system of government, as advocated and defended by Madison, remain in place, and the federal principle has since been adopted in many other countries.

Maistre

Joseph de Maistre (1753–1821) was a French-speaking Savoyard of French descent who initially welcomed the French **Revolution**. However, after the French invasion of Savoy he denounced it and became a leading spokesman for Catholic **authoritarian** counterrevolution from his exile, initially in Switzerland and later in Russia, where he served as the ambassador for the King of Savoy until 1817. Like Burke* he is regarded as an important **conservative** thinker, but while Burke was prepared to accept moderate pragmatic reform, Maistre became an uncompromising advocate of papal and royal authority and reactionary **conservatism**.

Malthus

Thomas Malthus (1766–1834) was an English clergyman and economist, whose main claim to fame was his *Essay on the Principle of Population* (1798) in which he argued there was a natural tendency for population to rise faster than the means of subsistence – thus undermining hopes of raising living standards. It was this work that substantially contributed to the reputation of economics as the 'dismal science'. Economic growth and increased prosperity in the West subsequently suggested that Malthus had been too pessimistic. More recently, **green** thinkers have rediscovered the messages of Malthus about the limits to growth and the dangers of a continued rise in population.

Mandela

Nelson Mandela (1918–2013) is perhaps remembered more for what he did than what he said or wrote, but his political activities were extensively justified in his speeches and writings and he thus became one of the most influential political thinkers of his time. Born and brought up in apartheid South Africa, he trained and worked as a lawyer and witnessed the extensive impact of the political and legal discrimination against non-whites. As a young man he joined the African National Congress (ANC) to campaign against apartheid. He became disillusioned with the lack of impact of nonviolent action and advocated sabotage (directed against **property** rather than people). With others he was arrested, convicted of treason, and sentenced to life imprisonment in 1962. He was to spend 27 years in prison, first on Robben Island and then in Pollsmoor and Victor Verster prisons. Despite an international campaign for his release, those inside white South Africa, and many outside, still regarded him as a terrorist. Yet ultimately, faced with continuing internal and external pressures, the white South African government of F.W. de Klerk negotiated with Mandela, who was released in 1990 and co-operated on the ending of apartheid and the introduction of multiracial **elections** in 1994, in which Mandela was elected as South Africa's first black president. He showed generosity to the white minority and guided South Africa towards a new multiracial polity. His funeral in 2013 was attended by political leaders across the world. He remains an iconic figure for all who oppose **racism** and advocate a **pluralist multicultural** society.

Mao Zedong

Mao Zedong (or Tse-tung) (1893–1976) was born to a farming family in Hunan. He discovered **Marxism** in Beijing and was among the founders of the Chinese **Communist** Party in 1921, influenced by the recent success of the Bolsheviks in Russia. Just as Lenin* had adapted Marx* to Russian circumstances, Mao similarly reinterpreted Marxism for a predominantly agricultural society, emphasising the revolutionary potential of the peasantry. The communists initially supported the Kuomintang, founded by the nationalist leader Sun Yatsen in 1924 to combat the chaos of rival warlords into which China had slipped after the abdication of the last emperor in 1912, but Sun Yatsen's successor Chiang Kai-shek turned ruthlessly against the communists. Mao led a break-out of the remains of communist forces and a 'Long March' to the relative safety of northwest China. Following this feat Mao was the unchallenged leader of the Chinese communists. Subsequently, the communists worked with the Kuomintang in guerrilla campaigns against the Japanese occupation, but after the defeat of Japan the Red Army fought against Chiang Kai-shek's nationalist forces in a civil war from which the communists under Mao emerged victorious in 1949. Their victory owed little to Soviet communism or Stalin*, who had earlier advised working with the Kuomintang, and Mao in power developed his own distinctive and more populist version of communism, which led ultimately to a Sino-Soviet split that was never entirely healed.

Yet although Maoism appeared to be a more **populist**, less **authoritarian**, version of Marxism, it was arguably as damaging to China as Stalinism had been to Russia. Mao periodically sought to revitalise his party through encouraging the active participation of ordinary members against the party **elite**. Yet his Great Leap Forward, an attempt at rapid industrialisation through grassroots enterprise, proved an economic disaster, while his **cultural** revolution, in which young Red Guards denounced party officials, academics, and professionals (including sometimes their own parents) for **bourgeois** behaviour and revisionism, was deeply divisive and damaging. It was in the latter period that *The Thoughts of Chairman Mao* (known more familiarly as *The Little*

Red Book) received a worldwide circulation. After his death his successors continued to pay lip-service to Mao and Maoism but have not protected his legacy. While they maintained the political control of the Communist Party and ruthlessly suppressed demands for political freedoms, they introduced extensive economic reforms, encouraging private enterprise and **free market** forces. In a period of rapid industrialisation and rising living standards, it appears that it is the peasantry who were championed by Mao who have been largely left behind.

Marcuse

Herbert Marcuse (1898–1979) was a German thinker and member of the Frankfurt School who escaped Nazi Germany to live and work in the United States. His writings, particularly *One Dimensional Man* (1964), became particularly influential among **left**-wing student circles in the 1960s, and he was briefly regarded as an iconic figure in the abortive 1968 **revolutions** in France and elsewhere. Like other members of the Frankfurt School Marcuse sought to combine a broadly **Marxist** approach, minus its economic determinism, with insights from other strands of thought, particularly Freudian psychology. He retained his revolutionary enthusiasm until the end of his life.

Marx

Karl Marx (1818–1883) was born in Trier in the German Rhineland to a Jewish family who had converted to Protestantism. Neither faith meant much to Marx, who later declared that religion was the opium of the people. He studied at the University of Berlin, and there became one of the circle of 'Young Hegelians' who interpreted Hegel's* thought in a radical direction. Marx then devoted himself to radical journalism, but after his paper was suppressed by the government he moved to Paris. There he associated with French **socialists** and other German exiles, including notably Friedrich Engels* with whom he formed a lifelong intellectual partnership. In 1848, a year of revolutions in Europe, Marx and Engels wrote *The Communist Manifesto,* still the

most succinct and accessible introduction to Marx's ideas. Following the failure of **revolution** they settled in England, the Marx family in London, Engels in Manchester where he managed a branch of his family's textile business and subsidised the impoverished Marx, who devoted himself to studying in the British Museum and writing *Capital*. From 1864 until 1872 Marx and Engels were actively involved in the International Working Men's Association in which Marx clashed with followers of the anarchist Bakunin*, leading to the collapse of what was subsequently known as the First International.

Marx's thought involved an adaptation and synthesis of German philosophy, French revolutionary socialism, and British political economy. From Hegel Marx derived the philosophy of history and specifically the dialectic, the notion of progression through thesis, antithesis, and synthesis. Yet while Hegel used the dialectic to describe the development of ideas, Marx applied it to the material world, to productive forces, interests, and **classes**, hence 'dialectal materialism'. Hegel's political views have been various interpreted as **liberal**, **conservative**, or reactionary. Marx was a revolutionary. He observed that 'Philosophers have only interpreted the world, in various ways; the point is to change it.' However, he differed from leading contemporary socialists such as Fourier or Owen* in being comparatively uninterested in designing model socialist societies. Instead he devoted his energies to analysing **capitalism** and its internal contradictions that would eventually (he thought) lead to revolution and socialism.

To do this he studied British political economy (Adam Smith* and particularly David Ricardo). He argued that while capitalism was promoting the growth of income and wealth on an unprecedented scale, it was increasingly polarising society between two key classes with conflicting interests: the **bourgeoisie** (or capitalists) who owned the means of production and the industrial working class (or proletariat) who owned only their own labour. Competition between capitalists would intensify the exploitation of the workers. Their 'immiseration' (increased poverty) would lead to revolution and the establishment of socialism, requiring a brief **dictatorship** of the proletariat to prevent counterrevolution, and ultimately a **communist** society, organised on the principle 'from each according to his abilities, to each according to his needs'. Class conflict would be at an end. The **state**, which Marx saw substantially as the instrument of the dominant economic class, would ultimately 'wither away'.

After his death, Marx's influence rapidly grew among socialists the world over, inspiring revolutions in Russia, China, and elsewhere and a **collectivist** economic system that appeared for a time a viable alternative to Western capitalism. **Marxism** thus became the state-sponsored orthodoxy over a large part of the globe. Marx himself might not have approved. In the various avowedly Marxist regimes established long after Marx's death, the temporary 'dictatorship of the proletariat' proved both lasting and highly centralised. The state, far from 'withering away', became omnipresent. From 1989 onwards, most of these regimes have been overthrown or transformed. In many countries where Marx was formerly revered he has since been repudiated.

Even so, Marx remains a towering figure in the history of political thought and in the practice of political science. Many key concepts integral to the modern study of politics derive from Marx. He demonstrated the importance of economic interests in the distribution of political power. He may perhaps have exaggerated economic factors, coming close to economic determinism and underestimating the importance of social divisions that are not primarily economic – those based on **nation**, **ethnicity**, religion, or **gender**, for example. Yet his analysis of capitalism was penetrating and (on the development of monopoly capitalism) prophetic, even if his central prediction of its eventual inevitable collapse now seems further off than ever.

Mazzini

Guiseppe Mazzini (1805–1872) was an Italian **nationalist** writer and political activist. He founded Young Italy in 1831, to work for a united Italian **republic**, and Young Europe in 1834, to encourage nationalism elsewhere in Europe. He argued that in a Europe of **nation-states**, peoples free from foreign domination would live in peace with each other. He headed the short-lived Roman Republic established after the 1848 revolutions. Although he lived to see a united Italy, he was disillusioned by the manner in which it was achieved (diplomacy and war rather than a popular uprising) and by the form the new Italy took (a **monarchy** rather than a **democratic** republic).

Michels

Robert Michels (1875–1936) was a German sociologist who was initially a **Marxist** but after teaching in Italian universities became, like Pareto* and Mosca*, a key exponent of **elitism**. Elite theorists argued that despite the apparent growing acceptance of **democracy**, **power** in society was inevitably concentrated in the hands of minorities – small elite groups. Michels argued this was not only true of society as a whole but of all organisations within society, 'Who says organisation, says oligarchy' (or rule of the few). This was what he described as 'the iron law of **oligarchy**'. In his best-known book *Political Parties* (1911) he tried to show that this was true even of **political parties**, such as **social democratic** parties, that had a mass membership and were explicitly committed to democratic principles and procedures. He argued that any large organisation required permanent leadership and specialised officers, who take key decisions, and that ordinary members lack the time and skill to exert effective accountability and control. Rank-and-file members are relatively disorganised and want and respect strong leadership. Internal party democracy is in practice impossible. Michels concluded: 'The socialists might conquer, but not socialism, which would perish in the moment of its adherents' triumph.' The analysis of Michels is persuasive, even, and perhaps especially, for those who find his conclusions distasteful. For many ordinary members of socialist parties it is unhappily confirmed by the periodic 'betrayal' of socialist objectives by the party leadership.

Miliband

Ralph Miliband (1924–1994) was a leading British **Marxist** historian and political thinker. Born in Brussels in a Jewish family as Adolphe Miliband, he escaped with his father to England in 1940 following the German invasion of Belgium. In England he changed his first name to Ralph and studied politics at the London School of Economics under the socialist Harold Laski. He later lectured at the LSE until 1972 when he became professor of politics at Leeds University. His book *Parliamentary Socialism* (1963) argued that the British Labour Party had consistently, over time, given priority to parliamentary institutions, procedures, and values over **socialism**, implying that the parliamentary route to socialism was inherently flawed. He and his friend, the historian John Saville, employed the term 'labourism' rather than socialism to describe the ideas of the Labour Party.

In *The State in Capitalist Society* (1969) Miliband argued that power in the United Kingdom was effectively concentrated in the hands of interconnected **elites**. This provoked a celebrated debate with Nicos Poulantzas* in the *New Left Review* (1969, 1970). At the end of his life, following the collapse of the USSR, Miliband reaffirmed his own socialist convictions in *Socialism for a Sceptical Age* (1994). Ironically, his sons David and Edward, who helped to see this last book through to publication, were both to become Labour MPs and subsequently ministers in the United Kingdom's New Labour government, with Ed becoming Labour leader from 2010 to 2015.

Mill

John Stuart Mill (1806–1873) was a leading English political philosopher. His father James Mill was credited with converting his friend the utilitarian philosopher Jeremy Bentham* to **representative democracy**. Another close associate was the economist David Ricardo. These three were the dominant early influences on John Stuart Mill's own thought. Indeed, it appears he was educated to champion their cause. He was taught Greek from the age of three, Latin from eight, and began the study of logic and political economy at ten. On top of this rigorous cramming, he was also expected to instruct his younger siblings and work as his father's secretary and research assistant. In 1826 he suffered a mental crisis, widely interpreted as a reaction against his somewhat unnatural upbringing. He read romantic poetry and came to question the limitations of the Benthamite **utilitarian** philosophy in which he had been brought up. He began to study a wider range of ideas, including those of Coleridge, Carlyle, Saint-Simon, Comte*, and Tocqueville*.

In 1843 Mill published *A System of Logic* and in 1848 the first edition of *Principles of Political Economy*. These two substantial works made his reputation, although his fame today rests more on his later essays. In 1851 he married Harriet Taylor (whom he had first met in 1830) after the death of her husband in 1849. Her influence on his writing survived her death in 1858. Mill's key works included *On Liberty* (1859) and *Considerations on Representative Government* and *Utilitarianism* (both published in 1861). *The Subjection of Women*, completed the same year, was not to be published until 1869. In the interim Mill served as an MP for Westminster from 1865 until 1868, in which brief period he unsuccessfully advocated women's suffrage and proportional representation. His step-daughter, Helen Taylor, set up a Women's Suffrage Society with Mill's enthusiastic support. She subsequently prepared Mill's *Autobiography* for publication after his death in 1873.

Of all Mill's works, the essay *On Liberty* is perhaps best known and most widely quoted. It is a passionate plea for full **freedom** of thought and expression. He argued that the only grounds for interfering with the liberty of any **individual** was to prevent harm to others. This individual freedom should include 'liberty of expressing and publishing opinions', full 'liberty of tastes and pursuits', and freedom to unite with others 'for any purpose not involving harm to others'. Mill argued vehemently the benefits to society of these freedoms and the advantages to be derived from the encouragement of individuality. He was worried that social pressures would produce too much conformity of opinion and conduct, fearing what Tocqueville had called the 'tyranny of the majority'.

For this reason Mill, though a consistent advocate of representative democracy, was concerned by 'its natural tendency…towards collective mediocrity'. In *Considerations on Representative Government* he argued that those who were illiterate or in receipt of poor relief should be excluded from the franchise and suggested extra votes for those with superior education. However, he also demanded votes for women on the same terms as men. He urged active citizen participation, anticipating that this would promote the political education of the electorate.

In *Utilitarianism* Mill defended a significantly modified version of Jeremy Bentham's creed. Bentham had assumed that all humans pursue pleasure and avoid pain but had been indifferent to their choice of pleasures. To Mill some pleasures were higher than others. 'It is better to be a human being dissatisfied than a pig satisfied; better to be Socrates dissatisfied than a fool satisfied.' In rejecting Bentham's simple hedonism, however, Mill created additional problems in measuring happiness.

Mill's last major work to be published in his lifetime *The Subjection of Women* (1869) was actually completed in 1861, the year of the start of the American Civil War on which Mill sided decisively with the North on the slavery issue. Mill provocatively compared the position of women in Britain with that of slaves in the American southern states. Critics at the time were outraged particularly by Mill's 'indelicate' references to the physical and sexual abuse of women. While most male commentators since have not given this work as much serious consideration as his other writings, modern radical **feminists**, by contrast, have generally focused on the limitations of Mill's 'liberal feminism'.

Millett

Kate Millett (1934–), a leading American radical **feminist**, adapted the term '**patriarchy**' (literally 'rule of the father') to mean substantially the universal **power** that men have over women. In her ground-breaking book *Sexual Politics* (1970) she drew on examples from modern literature to demonstrate the routine physical and more specifically sexual power, and abuse of power, of men over women that transcends **class** and **culture**. In focusing on domestic and sexual relations between men and women she purposely enlarged the scope of politics beyond the explicitly public arena to the private sphere of home and bedroom, illustrating the radical feminist slogan, 'The personal is political.'

Mills

C. (Charles) Wright Mills (1916–1962) was an American sociologist who taught at Columbia University from 1946 until his death. He is remembered particularly for his key work *The Power Elite* (1956), which became a crucial text in the debate between **elitists** and **pluralists** over the nature and reality of contemporary political **power**. In this book he explored the emergence in the United States of a military elite with close links with the industrial elite (hence a 'military-industrial complex') and also with the political elite. Although C. Wright Mills himself was never wholly convinced by the ideas of Marx*, he strongly influenced some contemporary Western Marxists, particularly the British socialist Ralph Miliband*, who dedicated *The State in Capitalist Society* (1969) to his memory.

Montesquieu

Charles-Louis, Baron de Montesquieu (1689–1755), was a French political thinker who satirised French society and institutions in his *Lettres persanes* (1721). He studied Hobbes*, whose pessimistic view of **human nature** he criticised, and the political writings of John Locke*. His key work *The Spirit of the Laws* (1748) included a flattering analysis of the English **constitution**. He thought this involved a separation of **executive**, **legislative**, and **judicial** powers, in contrast with the concentration of authority in the hands of **absolutist monarchs** common at the time elsewhere in Europe. Ultimately, it was to become clear that there was no clear **separation of powers** in the United Kingdom, but it was an understandable interpretation of the evolving British system of government in the early 18th century.

Morgenthau

Hans J. Morgenthau (1904–1980) was the most influential writer on **international relations** in the 1940s and 1950s. His '**realism**' can be seen in part as a reaction against the '**idealism**' in international relations in the interwar period, which optimistically assumed that international co-operation and collective security could avoid the carnage of another world war. Morgenthau himself escaped from Hitler's Germany and found refuge in the United States, where he was a professor in the University of Chicago. His key work *Politics among Nations* (1948) argues that, despite the growth of international institutions and cross-national interests, **states** remain by far the most significant actors in international relations. States pursue their own national interests defined in terms of **power**.

Morris

William Morris (1834–1896) was an English **socialist** thinker who founded the arts and crafts movement and subsequently, in 1884, the Socialist League. His rejection of modern industrial production and enthusiasm for hand-crafted work by individuals and small co-operatives appeared **utopian** and even reactionary to critics, but his romantic and idiosyncratic interpretation of socialism was influential in the English-speaking world.

Mosca

Gaetano Mosca (1858–1941) was an Italian sociologist and political thinker, one of the classical **elitists** who argued that minority rule was inevitable, even in a **democracy**. His key work was *The Ruling Class* (1896). Yet unlike fellow elite theorists Pareto* and Michels*, he later became more sympathetic towards **representative government**, becoming an elected deputy in 1908 and serving briefly in the government before

becoming a senator in 1919. The introduction of a universal franchise had not led to the excesses that he, as a **conservative**, had feared, and seemed compatible with the limited government that he favoured. Thus he did not support Mussolini and in 1924 spoke in the Senate to 'almost lament' the downfall of the parliamentary government that he admitted he had always sharply criticised. It was a muted dissent, but he declined to embrace **fascism** for the remainder of his life.

Naess

Arne Naess (1912–2009) was a Norwegian philosopher whose academic interests included Spinoza*, Gandhi*, and Buddhism. His most widely known work was done after he retired from his university chair at Oslo in 1970. It was then that he developed his deep **green** or deep **ecology** ideas, expressed in key articles in 1973 and 1985 and in his later book *Ecology, Community and Lifestyle* (1989). He personally engaged in direct action to further his deep green agenda, chaining himself with other protestors to rocks to oppose plans to build a dam in a Norwegian fiord in 1970.

Nietzsche

Friedrich Wilhelm Nietzsche (1844–1900) was and remains a very controversial German philosopher, partly because some of his ideas were later used (or misused) by the **Nazis**. Nietzsche was mad for the last 11 years of his life, looked after by his mother and sister. His sister later became an enthusiastic Nazi and interpreted her brother's thought to anticipate elements of Nazi ideology, particularly *The Will to Power* (1901), put together from discarded scattered notes of Nietzsche after his death. While Nietzsche was opposed to the **racism** and **nationalism** that later became key features of Nazism, his notion of a 'superman' above conventional morality in his best-known work *Thus Spake Zarathustra* (1883–1884) has been seen as the template for charismatic leaders such as Hitler or Mussolini. In his other writings, for example *Beyond Good and Evil* (1886), Nietzsche famously proclaimed not only the death of God but the end of any prospects of establishing universal objective truth. Thus Nietzsche can be seen as a precursor of **postmodernist** thinking.

Niskanen

William Niskanen (1933–2011) was an American economist whose work on **bureaucracy** transformed the study of public sector organisations and officials. In his key work *Bureaucracy and Representative Government* (1971) he argued that, in the absence of market competition and considerations of profit, public sector bureaucrats, in the interest of increasing their own status, income, and job satisfaction, would pursue bureau maximisation (increasing the size of their organisation's work, employment, and expenditure) rather than profit maximisation. His analysis provided a rationale for the steady growth of public sector employment and expenditure and was seized on by the **New Right** in the USA and the United Kingdom. The British political scientist Patrick Dunleavy has used **rational choice** assumptions to argue that public sector bureaucrats pursue bureau *shaping* rather than bureau *maximising* (e.g. because senior bureaucrats may benefit from contracting out some activities).

Nozick

Robert Nozick (1938–2002) was an American political philosopher, best known for his book *Anarchy, State and Utopia* (1974). Nozick himself was more of an old-fashioned laissez-faire **liberal** than an **anarchist**. He resembles anarchists in his extreme mistrust of **government**, particularly government intervention in the interests of redistribution and **social justice**. While the French anarchist Proudhon* had famously declared **property** to be theft and many anarchists have favoured the abolition of private property, Nozick asserted the inviolability of property rights. Like John Locke* he connected the individual's **right** to **liberty** with the right to property, which he derived (also like Locke) from labour. But however it was initially secured, individuals had an absolute inalienable right to acquire, own,

and transfer property. Nozick opposed any attempts by the **state** to take property from the rich to give to the poor in the interests of social (or distributive) **justice**, a concept that Nozick did not recognise. Thus he objected to redistributive taxation, which he regarded as the extraction of enforced labour from those required to pay such taxes. His book can be seen as a reply to John Rawls's* *Theory of Justice*, published three years earlier, and a continuation of an argument between two strands of liberalism: classical or 'new' liberalism. (It was also an argument within the philosophy department of the University of Harvard, where both men taught.)

Nye

Joseph Nye (1937–) is an American political scientist, specialising in **international relations** and foreign policy. With Robert Keohane*, he was responsible for the international relations theory of **neoliberalism** (*Power and Interdependene*, 1977). In 1990 he expounded the influential concept of **soft power** and, later, smart power. He influenced both the Clinton and Obama administrations.

Oakeshott

Michael Joseph Oakeshott (1901–1990) was an influential English **conservative** thinker who was professor of political science at the London School of Economics from 1951 to 1968. *Rationalism in Politics and Other Essays* (1962) is the best introduction to his thought. The title essay involves a wide-ranging attack on what he calls '**rationalism** in politics'. His targets included the French and American **revolutions**, **liberalism**, **socialism** and, effectively, all modern political doctrines or **ideologies**, including some apparently close to his own ideas, such as the **neoliberalism** of Hayek*. Thus Oakeshott observed tersely of Hayek's *Road to Serfdom*, 'A plan to resist all planning may be better than its opposite, but it belongs to the same style of politics.' Significantly, while Hayek rejected the conservative label, describing himself as a liberal, Oakeshott identified with conservatism, though for him this is not a doctrine but an attitude of mind. 'To be conservative is to prefer the familiar to the unknown, to prefer the tried to the untried, fact to mystery, the actual to the possible, the limited to the unbounded.' His preference for limited gradual reform is reminiscent of Edmund Burke*. Thus, according to Oakeshott, the conservative accepts that innovation may sometimes be necessary, but 'he will find small and slow changes more tolerable than large and sudden: and he will value highly every appearance of continuity.'

Olson

Mancur Olson (1932–1998) was an American economist and social scientist whose work had a significant impact on the study of politics. His reputation still rests largely on his first book *The Logic of Collective Action* (1965). This uses economic analysis to explain why small special interest groups often seem to have a bigger impact on public policy than larger, more numerous interests, such as taxpayers and consumers. **Pluralists** had argued that the cumulative impact of countless competing groups would serve the interests of the majority in an essentially **democratic** process. Countervailing power would prevent any small interest group unrepresentative of wider opinion from obtaining too much influence. Olson showed why this is not necessarily true. Individual taxpayers and consumers have little motivation for expending their energies on organising and lobbying to protect their interests, because the costs in time and energy outweigh the potentially small benefits, and they can 'free ride' on the lobbying of others. By contrast, members of small trade associations and producer groups are strongly motivated to organise and push policies with potentially large benefits for themselves, for example involving protection or public subsidies. The costs are spread among the generality of taxpayers and consumers who will have little incentives to organise against them. Subsequently, Olson applied his economic analysis to explain political change, particularly in *The Rise and Decline of Nations* (1982) and his last book *Power and Prosperity* (2000).

O'Neill

Onora O'Neill (2002) is a leading British moral and political philosopher. John Rawls* supervised her doctorate at Harvard, and she subsequently taught in New York, Essex, and Cambridge. A specialist in Kant*, she has written widely on ethics and politics, particularly on trust, the focus of the BBC Reith Lectures that she delivered in 2002. She has also contributed to public life, serving as a cross-bench peer in the UK House of Lords and chairing the Equality and Human Rights Commission.

Ostrogorski

Mosei Ostrogorski (1854–1919) was a pioneering Russian political scientist. His celebrated work *Democracy and the Organisation of Political Parties* (two volumes, the first on the United Kingdom, the second on the United States, 1902) argued that political **parties** were increasingly dominated by their unrepresentative mass membership – the membership may be large but not large enough to be representative of voters (e.g. there is a widespread assumption that Labour Party members are more 'left wing' than Labour voters; Conservative Party members may not share the interests and views of most Conservative voters) – with damaging implications for **representative democracy**. Robert Michels*, by contrast, later argued that power in mass parties was in practice wielded by the parliamentary **leadership** and the party **bureaucracy**. Subsequent research on parties has tended to confirm the analysis of Michels rather than Ostrogorski.

Owen

Robert Owen (1771–1858) contributed to a distinctive British version of **socialism** in various ways in his writing and political activities. He first established his reputation by demonstrating that it was possible to make money as an enlightened employer at the model factory and **community** he established at New Lanark in Scotland, although his more socialist community New Harmony, which he later tried to establish in America, proved less successful. In *A New View of Society* (1813) he argued that man's character was shaped by his social environment. He later became closely involved in early British trade unionism and the co-operative movement. His socialism emphasised peaceful, gradual reform and working-class self-help. Marx* and Engels* in the *Communist Manifesto* regarded Owen as a **utopian socialist**, with a socialist vision of the future but no practical strategy to achieve it. Engels later gave Owen a more generous tribute. 'Every social movement, every real advance in England on behalf of the workers links itself to the name of Robert Owen' (Marx and Engels 1962, vol. 2, 127).

Paine

Thomas Paine (1737–1809) was a radical thinker who was closely involved in the politics of three countries, his native Britain, America, and France. In 1774 Benjamin Franklin helped him to emigrate to Pennsylvania. After war broke out between the American colonies and Britain, Paine wrote *Common Sense* (1776), which urged a declaration of independence. He served as a soldier in the rebel cause, and his writings continued to influence the debate on American politics. In 1781 he was sent on a mission to France, and he returned to England in 1787. There he published *The Rights of Man* (1791–1792) which supported the French Revolution against the criticism of Edmund Burke* (*Reflections on the Revolution in France*). Accused of treason, and burned in effigy by a patriotic mob, Paine escaped to France in 1792, became a French citizen, and was elected to the revolutionary Convention, arousing the anger of the Jacobins by opposing the execution of Louis XVI. Imprisoned and fortunate not to lose his head in the Terror, he wrote *The Age of Reason* (1794, 1796). Here he attacked organised religion and alienated many of his old friends in America, so that when he returned there in 1802, he was ignored and died uncelebrated in 1809. William Cobbett, the former Tory and once fierce critic of Paine who became a convert to radicalism, sailed to America in 1819 to bring the bones of his old enemy

back home. Paine's writings continued to win support for his brand of radical **liberalism**, **republicanism**, and **democracy**.

Pareto

Vilfredo Pareto (1848–1923) was an important Italian economist as well as a political sociologist. In this latter capacity he was an **elite** theorist. He argued that all societies are divided into a minority or elite that rules and a majority that is ruled. Rule is exercised by a combination of cunning and persuasion on the one hand and physical force on the other, through types of leaders Pareto describes as 'foxes' and 'lions' respectively. Elites may be periodically overthrown – for history is 'a graveyard of elites' – but they will be replaced not by **democracy** and the rule of the masses but by a new elite, in accordance with Pareto's notion of the circulation of elites. Pareto was scornful over the prospects for real democracy, despite the introduction of universal suffrage, as he maintained it was always an **oligarchy** that governs. He was equally contemptuous of **socialism**. Italian fascists admired and honoured Pareto, but he did not live long enough after Mussolini took power in Italy, in 1922, to discover the reality of **fascism** in action.

Parsons

Talcott Parsons (1902–1979) was an important American sociologist, whose theory of structural-functionalism and understanding of the social system strongly influenced the study of politics in the 1950s and 1960s, particularly the systems approach of David Easton*. A 'system' is a complex whole of which the parts are interdependent. 'Functions' fulfil societal needs, and operate within broader social structures and social norms to contribute to the smooth operation of the social system as a whole. The social system is in equilibrium when its different parts are operating together smoothly. Any disturbance to equilibrium normally triggers adjustments elsewhere in the system and a return to equilibrium. The systems approach thus emphasises stability and consensus and downplays radical change and conflict. This was a problem for radical sociologists and also for political scientists. Some perceived an in-built **conservatism** in the model; existing features of the social and political system were assumed to be functional or necessary for system maintenance. Critics suggested that the theory involved description rather than critical analysis. Consequently, Parsons's approach rather fell from favour from the 1970s. However, the development of modern political science in the middle of the 20th century cannot be understood without reference to Parsons and structural-functionalism. Key works include *The Structure of Social Action* (1937), *The Social System* (1951), *Economy and Society* (1956), and *Structure and Process in Modern Societies* (1960).

Pateman

Carole Pateman (1940–) is a British political theorist and **feminist** who studied at Oxford and went on to teach at universities in Australia and the USA. She is perhaps best known still for her first book, *Participation and Democratic Theory* (1970), in which she argued for an extension of effective participation, including participation in the workplace, to complement **representative democracy**. Participatory democracy, she argued, would promote a sense of political efficacy, reduce alienation and apathy, encourage a concern with the wider public interest, and assist the political education of **citizens**. Later books have included *The Problem of Political Obligation* (1979) and *The Sexual Contract* (1988), the latter focusing particularly on the marriage contract and the institution of marriage and their continuing implications for the subordination of women.

Pericles

Pericles (c. 495–429 BCE) was the leading Athenian general and statesman of his age. In 431 BCE he led Athens into the long Peloponnesian War with Sparta, chronicled by the historian Thucydides* who put into the mouth of Pericles a great funeral oration over the first who died in battle in that war. How far this speech reported by Thucydides, many years after the event, reflects the real ideas of Pericles is uncertain. However, it

eloquently celebrated Athenian **democracy** and the values of **freedom**, **toleration**, and active **citizenship** linked with it, while ignoring its flaws, most notably the acceptance of slavery. The speech remains a source of inspiration for those who favour participatory democracy.

Plato

Plato (427–347 BCE) is widely regarded as one of the greatest philosophers and political theorists who have ever lived. His extensive surviving writings are still studied and argued over in universities across the world. Born in an aristocratic family in Athens after the death of Pericles* and the great period of its democracy, he grew up during the long war with Sparta, culminating in Athens' defeat and the brief tyranny of the Thirty. The subsequent restoration of democracy led to the trial and execution of his great teacher, Socrates* in 399, an event that profoundly influenced his own political outlook. Later he founded and directed the Academy (c. 385 BCE), where one of his pupils was Aristotle*, who was to criticise some of Plato's ideas.

Plato's surviving writings take the form of dialogues in which his teacher Socrates plays the leading role. Those generally considered early works may represent the arguments of Socrates himself, while in middle and later dialogues (e.g. *Republic, Statesman, Laws*) 'Socrates' is reckoned to be the mouthpiece of Plato's own views. Some of the presumed earlier and shorter dialogues are perhaps the best introduction to Plato's work. These include the *Apology, Crito, Gorgias*, and *Protagoras*. They also involve genuine debates, illustrating what is reckoned to be the Socratic method of question and answer to arrive at a greater understanding of specific ethical and political questions. In the early dialogues these questions included how far one should obey the state (even to the extent of acquiescing in one's own unjust death sentence) or how far political skills can be taught.

The *Republic*, the most celebrated and widely read of all Plato's writings, is a much more complex work covering aspects of philosophy, ethics, psychology, education, economics, aesthetics, and even medicine, as well as **politics**. It begins as a genuine dialogue in which Plato and his companions discuss the meaning of **justice**. One speaker, Thrasymachus, defines justice as the interest of the stronger party. All people seeks their own selfish advantage and pleasure and are only deterred by the fear of punishment. The successful tyrant who is powerful enough to satisfy his own desires is the happiest of men. The rest of the *Republic* (which involves less genuine debate and more of a monologue by 'Socrates' with supportive interjections by his pupils) can be seen as Plato's refutation of this cynical position. It outlines an ideal **state**, in which the 'guardians' or rulers (who can be male or female) emerge from a long and rigorous educational regime, culminating in the study of philosophy, because only philosophers have real knowledge rather than mere beliefs or opinions. Philosophers, Plato argues, should be rulers and rulers should be philosophers, because only the true philosopher knows justice and the other virtues and can be trusted to pursue the interests of the whole community rather than his or her own selfish interests. Indeed, the true philosopher would prefer a life of intellectual contemplation and must be persuaded to accept the burden of **government** in the wider public interest. If the idea of the philosopher king appears bizarre today, the notion that only those who do not want to rule should be entrusted with political power is attractive.

While some of Plato's prescriptions may appear alien in the modern world, much of his political analysis remains acutely relevant. Thus his account of political change in the *Republic* remains penetrating. Particularly memorable is his portrait of the apparently successful tyrant, who is 'really the most abject slave, a parasite of the vilest scoundrels. Never able to satisfy his desires, he is always in need.... His condition is like that of the country he governs, haunted throughout life by terrors and convulsed with anguish.' The tyrant's lot is thus far from enviable. The description might be aptly applied to some modern **dictators**.

If Plato roundly condemns tyranny, his approach to politics in the *Republic* and in other works such as the *Laws* is also profoundly hostile to **democracy**. Partly this perhaps reflects his own experience of Athenian democracy in decline and in particular the trial and execution of his teacher Socrates (referred to in the questionably authentic *Seventh Letter*). Yet essentially it derives logically from Plato's theory of knowledge, which is to be sharply distinguished from the mere beliefs or opinions of the multitude. Only the select few can attain real knowledge, after a long and rigorous system of education (outlined in the *Republic*). It follows (from this premise) that government is a matter for the expert, not for the ordinary man. It involves doing what is right rather than what pleases the public (compared by Plato to a great beast). Some modern commentators (such as Popper*) have attacked Plato for his hostility to the values and practices of democracy. Others argue that it is ahistorical to seek to apply Plato's interpretation of the very different society and political systems of Greece in the 4th century BCE to those of the modern world. However, it is clear that Plato was profoundly unsympathetic to the democratic values of **freedom**, participation, and **toleration** emphasised in the speech that Thucydides puts into the mouth of Pericles.

Popper

Karl Popper (1902–1994), born an Austrian Jew, escaped from Vienna in 1937 shortly before Austria was absorbed into Hitler's Third Reich and taught in New Zealand and then from 1945 to 1969 at the London School of Economics. Popper was best known in the period immediately after the Second World War for his two-volume work *The Open Society and Its Enemies* (1945). Popper's 'open society' was the **free**, **liberal**, **democratic** Western tradition. Its 'enemies' included some of the great names of political thought, including Plato*, Aristotle*, Hegel*, and Marx*. Popper advocated piecemeal social reform rather than sweeping **utopian** reform. In *The Poverty of Historicism* (1957) Popper criticised those who claimed to have discovered laws of historical development.

However, Popper is perhaps most remembered today for his earlier work on scientific method. *The Logic of Scientific Discovery* (1934, English translation 1959) argues that nothing can be definitely proved by induction, generalising from repeated observations. Instead, scientific method proceeds on the basis of 'conjectures and refutations', seeking to falsify (or refute) provisional hypotheses (or 'conjectures'). A hypothesis expressed in such broad or imprecise terms that it cannot be tested and (potentially) falsified is unscientific. It follows that all scientific knowledge (including the social sciences) is provisional rather than certain. This notion of 'falsifiability' as the basis of scientific method remains influential. [See also Part II, Section 2 on Popper and falsifiability.]

Poulantzas

Nicos Poulantzas (1936–1979) was a Greek-born **Marxist** thinker who spent most of his working life in Paris, where he held various university posts. He was strongly influenced by the writings of Gramsci* and various French Marxist thinkers, particularly the structural Marxism of Louis Althusser*. He committed suicide in Paris in 1979.

Poulantzas was involved in a celebrated dispute with Miliband* in the pages of *New Left Review* (1969, 1970). Miliband had sought to demonstrate the close connections between the **elite** who govern the state and the business elite. To Poulantzas this was irrelevant. He argued that the **state** is bound by its structural role within a capitalist society to further the interests of **capitalism**, regardless of whether the state's personnel come from the capitalist class or have social links with capitalism. Yet he also maintained that the state enjoys relative autonomy and does not necessarily act at the behest of capitalists or specific capitalist interests. Rather, the state seeks to manage **class** forces so as to unite sometimes conflicting interests within capital and subtly divide and control other classes. His theory is elaborated in *Political Power and Social Classes* (1968) and *Classes in Contemporary Capitalism* (1973). He also explored contemporary political developments, such as the collapse of military **dictatorships** in his native Greece and in Spain and Portugal. His last book *State, Power and Socialism* (1978) recognised the importance of **new social movements** and explored the problems of transition to democratic **socialism.**

Proudhon

Pierre-Joseph Proudhon (1809–1865) was a **revolutionary** French **socialist** and **anarchist**. In an early publication he famously asked the question 'What is property?' supplying his own answer 'Property is theft!' Following the failure of the 1848 revolution, in which he played a conspicuous role, he devoted most of the rest of his life to political theory, rejecting government and advocating mutualism.

Putnam

Robert D. Putnam (1941–) is an American political scientist, mainly known today for his work on civic engagement and **social capital**. He first came to prominence for his comparative study of the attitudes of political representatives and activists in the United Kingdom and Italy, *The Beliefs of Politicians* (1973). He followed this with broader comparative surveys of political **elites** (1976) and bureaucrats and politicians (1981). In a comparative study of regional governments in Italy, *Making Democracy Work: Civic Traditions in Modern Italy* (1993), Putnam first identified the importance of what he called 'social capital' (the extent of face-to-face social interaction and community engagement) for a healthy functioning **democratic** system. This echoed a key theme of a celebrated earlier study, *The Civic Culture* (1963) by Almond* and Verba, (which specifically involved a study of Italian political culture, as one of five national political cultures).

In a seminal article published in 1995 Putnam went on to suggest that social capital was declining in modern America, and he followed this up with extensive research into levels of social and communal interaction in the United States, documented in *Bowling Alone: The Collapse and Revival of American Community* (2000). 'Bowling alone' was a metaphor for the solitary private leisure pursuits of Americans, which were apparently growing at the expense of more social, interactive pursuits. Putnam argued that the decline of even such apparently apolitical activities as social dining and bridge clubs had damaging implications for civic engagement and democracy. His work on social capital has provoked an extensive debate. Some have questioned whether the apparent decline in social capital in the USA is replicated in other Western societies, pointing to increased participation in some forms of pressure group activity. Others have criticised some of Putnam's assumptions. Thus some 'solitary' activities that do not involve face-to-face interaction, such as communication via the internet, may not be damaging for democracy but may even assist more direct participation in politics.

Rawls

John Rawls (1921–2002) has been credited with reviving political philosophy almost single-handedely, after it had been declared dead in the 1950s, with his *Theory of Justice* (1971). Here he is concerned with the issue of distributive or social **justice** (basically how resources and goods should be shared out fairly between people), a preoccupation of political philosophers since the earliest times. He criticised the **utilitarian** conception of justice as 'the greatest happiness of the greatest number', because it potentially entails sacrificing the interests of individuals or minorities to the greater good.

Rawls postulates a purely hypothetical 'Original Position' (with some similarity to the 'state of nature' in the work of Hobbes* and Locke*) in which people are placed behind 'a veil of ignorance'. They know nothing of the society to which they are to belong and their position within it, nor do they know what talents and abilities they have themselves. It is however assumed that they know that certain 'primary goods' – **rights**, **liberties**, opportunities, income and wealth, respect – will be useful to them, and that they will want as much of these as possible. What moral principles would be agreed on by people who are ignorant as to whether they will be advantageously or disadvantageously placed? Rawls suggests two principles (or effectively three, as his second principle is subdivided). Firstly, each person should have an equal right to the most extensive liberty, as long as this does not infringe on the liberty of others (sometimes called the 'liberty principle'). Secondly, social and economic inequalities should be arranged so as to be of the greatest benefit to the least advantaged (referred to as the 'difference principle') and attached to positions and offices open to all under fair **equality** of opportunity (the 'equal opportunity principle').

What Rawls called 'the difference principle' is perhaps most important and contentious. He assumes people in a hypothetical state of ignorance about their own prospects would opt for a society and system of justice in which even the worst off would have sufficient resources to enjoy a reasonable life. Rawls's concept of 'justice as fairness' was seized on by progressive **liberals** and **social democrats** as justifying some state intervention to secure a measure of redistribution so as to assist the least well-off, through the tax and welfare system. Critics such as Robert Nozick* argued that the 'difference principle' in practice interfered with the 'liberty principle', which Nozick claimed should be paramount.

In his later work *Political Liberalism* (1993) Rawls substantially maintained the principles outlined in his *Theory of Justice* (with minor modifications). He further argued that these principles could be agreed on by rational persons with very different world views. They did not depend on a political consensus. In *The Law of Peoples* (1999) Rawls considered the application of the principle of 'justice as fairness' to **international relations**. He argued that, in the interests of international stability, liberal societies should tolerate 'decent hierarchical' societies that discriminated against minorities. He also denied that the 'difference principle' could be used to justify massive redistribution of global resources between states. Here Rawls disappointed some of his liberal allies and supporters. He is still, however, considered a massive figure in modern political philosophy.

Rokkan

Stein Rokkan (1921–1979) was a Norwegian political scientist, and a professor in comparative politics at Bergen University. He worked with Seymour Lipset* with whom he coedited the influential text *Party Systems and Voter Alignments* (1967). He also studied and wrote about state and nation building in Europe. Key works included another coedited book *Building States and Nations* (with Samuel Eisenstadt, 1973) and *Economy, Territory and Identity* (1983) coauthored with Derek Urwin.

Rousseau

Jean-Jacques Rousseau (1712–1778), controversial in his own lifetime, remains a contentious figure. Although he never advocated **revolution**, his writings inspired some of those who, after his death, were to lead the French Revolution. The first modern thinker to champion **democracy,** he raised doubts over its feasibility while scornfully rejecting the **representative** democracy that was to become its characteristic modern form. Some critics have even argued that his ideas anticipate aspects of 20th-century **totalitarianism**, although others insist that he belongs in the great **republican** tradition.

Although Rousseau wrote in French and spent most of his working life in France, he was not French by birth or upbringing. He was born and brought up in the French-speaking Swiss city state of Geneva, and this shaped his political sympathies. In a note at the beginning of his key work *The Social Contract* (1762) he writes of Geneva: 'I was born into a free state and am a member of a sovereign body.' His political theory reflects experience of his native city and the knowledge he had acquired of the political thought and practice of the small city states of ancient Greece and the early Roman Republic, rather than the powerful and geographically extensive states and empires of his own day.

Rousseau opens *The Social Contract* with the famous declaration: 'Man is born free but everywhere he is in chains.' Before the establishment of government and civilisation, man enjoyed natural **liberty**. In Rousseau's earlier work, *Discourse on the Origins and Basis of Inequality* (1755), there is an element of nostalgia for the loss innocence and freedom of primitive man in his natural state. He is a 'noble savage', free to make his own choices, driven by the instinct of self-preservation, but capable of pity and sympathy for his fellow creatures. Yet while Rousseau's imagined state of **nature** was not, like that of Hobbes*, a nightmare world of brutality and fear, it limited human capacities. These could only be realised in a civil community. Thus man is prepared to join with others in a 'social contract' and surrender his natural liberty in exchange for civil liberty. 'To be subject to appetite', Rousseau argues, 'is to be a slave, while to obey the laws laid down by society is to be free.' His assumption here is that those who obey the laws have had a part in making them. Rousseau's social contract is not, like that of Hobbes, an unconditional surrender of power to a sovereign, nor even, like Locke's*, a conditional surrender that can be revoked if the sovereign fails to maintain his terms of the contract. Rousseau argues that **sovereignty** can never be alienated. In other words supreme **power** remains with the people. Only in such a political society could man still retain (or regain) freedom.

Popular sovereignty was a revolutionary doctrine. It committed Rousseau to a form of democracy. Yet he remained sceptical whether democracy was really practical. He explicitly rejected **representation** as a means of realising democracy. The general will of the people, he argued, can not be represented. The English, he thought, were mistaken in believing they were free. 'They are free only when electing members of parliament, and then revert to slavery.' Thus Rousseau favoured **direct** rather than representative democracy. Such a system could only work, he thought, in a small state where everyone could be gathered together and knew each other and where there was considerable equality of wealth. These were conditions that ruled out most of the states of Rousseau's own day. Thus he pessimistically noted, 'Were there such a thing as a nation of Gods, it would be a democracy. So perfect a form of government is not suited to mere men.'

Rousseau assumed not only active **citizen** participation in making the **laws** that all must obey but virtual unanimity. Laws must reflect not the will of the majority but the 'general will', the will of all, considering not their own particular interest but the general interest. Yet Rousseau acknowledges this may be difficult. 'Left to themselves, the People always desire the good' but 'they do not always know where that good lies. The general will is always right, but the judgement guiding it is not always well informed.' Thus, Rousseau concludes, a legislator is necessary. Rousseau had in mind the example of great lawgivers in ancient Greece – he cites Lycurgus of Sparta. Yet, to some critics Rousseau's notion of a general will interpreted by a charismatic individual sinisterly foreshadows the popular **dictatorships** and totalitarian pseudo-democracies of the 20th century.

Said

Edward Said (1935–2003) was a controversial Palestinian intellectual whose ideas have some continuing relevance for students of politics. He was born in Jerusalem to wealthy Christian Palestinian parents during the period of British rule after the territory had been given to Britain to administer following a League of Nations mandate. He was educated in what he described as 'elite colonial schools' in Jerusalem and Cairo. He completed his education in the United States at Princeton and Harvard, eventually becoming Professor of English and Comparative Literature at Columbia University. His key work *Orientalism* (1978) had implications far beyond the study of literature. In it he argued that both Western academic studies of Eastern culture as well as Western popular conceptions of 'the Orient' were inevitably conditioned and warped by Western power and colonial dominance over the East. (The argument owed something to the work of Michel Foucault* who had argued that prevailing interpretations of reality necessarily reflected **power** relations.) Western

conceptions of the Orient in turn influenced political attitudes and judgements. *Orientalism* was hailed as a masterpiece by some and sharply criticised by others. Said remained to his death a prominent champion of the Palestinian cause and Palestinian refugees. Although he initially supported the two-state solution to the Palestinian question, he later advocated a single state in which Jews and Arabs would have equal rights.

Sandel

Michael Sandel (1953–) is a modern political philosopher who made his name with his criticism of John Rawls's* *Theory of Justice* in his own book *Liberalism and the Limits of Justice* (1982). Along with his own tutor Charles Taylor* and Alasdair MacIntyre* and Michael Walzer*, Sandel is regarded as one of the leading **communitarian** thinkers, emphasising the reciprocal ties between persons and the **community** of which they are a part, in opposition to **liberal individualism**.

Sartori

Giovanni Sartori (1924–2017) was an Italian political scientist who has held chairs in his native Italy and in the United States. He worked extensively in the field of comparative politics. Key works include *Parties and Party Systems* (1976) and *The Theory of Democracy Revisited* (1987).

Sartre

Jean-Paul Sartre (1905–1980) was the most celebrated left-wing French intellectual in the decades following the Second World War. His existentialist philosophy was expressed in his novels and plays as well as his key philosophical work *Being and Nothingness* (1943) which emphasised the need for **individuals** to assert their own **freedom**, unconstrained by conventions and expectations. However, while critical of its determinist strand, he was increasingly drawn to **Marxism**, which he sought to reconcile with existentialism. A committed political activist, he subsequently gave largely uncritical support to the French Communist Party and the Soviet Union. His influence on the young was already declining before his death, replaced by a younger generation of Marxist intellectuals and **postmodernist** thinkers. The work of his long-time partner Simone de Beauvoir* has perhaps lasted better.

Schumacher

Ernst Fritz Schumacher (1911–1977) was a German-born economist who had been initially interned in the United Kingdom in the Second World War, to be rescued by Keynes*. He was to write Keynes's obituary for *The Times,* although he was already beginning to question aspects of Keynesian economics. Much later, his book *Small Is Beautiful* (1976) challenged the then fashionable presumption in favour of large-scale enterprises and economies of scale. It made a significant contribution to **green** thinking, which favours decentralisation and more local production of goods and services.

Schumpeter

Joseph Schumpeter (1883–1950) was born and educated in Vienna, and was briefly finance minister in the new Austrian Republic in 1919, but subsequently emigrated to the USA where he became a professor of economics at Harvard. In his most celebrated work *Capitalism, Socialism and Democracy* (1943) he argued that modern **representative democracy** did not (and should not) involve **government** by the people in the sense of their active participation in political decision-making. The real initiative came not from the people themselves but from political leaders and their parties, rival **elites** periodically competing for public support. The majority were simple not capable of **rational choice** on political issues, and could only be expected to choose, like consumers in the marketplace, between rival teams and programmes at periodic elections. Thus 'the democratic method is that institutional arrangement for arriving at political decisions in which individuals acquire the power to decide by a competitive struggle for the people's vote.' Schumpeter's modified theory of **democracy**, with its restricted and passive role for ordinary people, is sometimes termed 'democratic elitism'.

Simon

Herbert Simon (1916–2001) was an American thinker with expertise in a number of fields. His work on decision-making, the subject of his first book *Administrative Behaviour* (1947), is of particular relevance to politics and **public administration**. Here he put forward an ideal model of **rational** decision-making, according to which the administrator should not start with aims and objectives because these might close down possible options. Instead he or she should start with the situation, consider all the options, all the consequences arising from each option, and select the option with the greatest net benefits. This, Simon recognised, was an ideal that could rarely be attained in practice, because of lack of perfect information, lack of time, and perhaps lack of skills. Administrators thus normally have to operate with 'bounded rationality'. In practice they may not be able to optimise (find the one best solution) but 'satisfice' (continue to search until a tolerably satisfactory solution is found). Simon's work on decision-making influenced much subsequent theory and practice. Charles Lindblom* designed his own rival model of policy-making, **incrementalism**, in direct response.

Singer

Peter Singer (1946–) is a controversial Australian moral philosopher, who is best known for *Animal Liberation* (1975), a book that has had a major influence on the animal rights movement. He argues that all creatures capable of suffering are entitled to equal consideration. Treating animals differently from humans he describes as a form of discrimination, 'speciesism' (analogous to **racism** or sexism). Using animals for food causes unnecessary suffering, thus Singer advocates vegetarianism and a vegan diet. His general moral philosophy is **utilitarian**, set out in his book *Practical Ethics* (1979). Some of his applications of his moral theory have aroused controversy, such as his justification of euthanasia, abortion and even infanticide in certain circumstance. In a celebrated essay 'Famine, Affluence and Morality' (1972) he argued that it is morally indefensible for people to enjoy luxury goods and an affluent lifestyle while others starve. Giving money to avoid famine is not 'charity'. 'We ought to give the money away, and it is wrong not to do so.'

Skocpol

Theda Skocpol (1947–) is a leading American political scientist at Harvard University. She published *States and Social Revolutions: A Comparative Analysis of France, Russia and China* in 1979 and continued her exploration of **revolution** in *Social Revolutions in the Modern World* (1994). She coedited the influential study *Bringing the State Back In* (1985). She has also written extensively on American **democracy**, **government** and public policy.

Smith

Adam Smith (1723–1790) is remembered today as the founding father of classical economics, but he was also an important moral philosopher, holding a chair in the subject at the University of Glasgow from 1752 to 1764. Both his economics and his ethics had important implications for politics. He was a close friend and associate of the philosopher and historian David Hume*; both men were Scots, with closer intellectual ties to France than to England. They are key figures in what is described as the Scottish Enlightenment, which was an important element of the wider European Enlightenment of the 18th century.

In *The Theory of Moral Sentiments* (1759) Smith argued that mutual sympathy was the basis of human co-operation, but he introduced the notion of the 'invisible hand' of market forces as a key to increasing prosperity. In *The Wealth of Nations* (1776) he developed further the role of **individual** self-interest in promoting general wellbeing through the invisible hand of the **free market**. It followed that attempts to interfere with or restrain the operation of free market forces, either by the **state** or by other interests, were generally detrimental to the 'wealth of nations'. Smith also demonstrated the impact of specialisation and the division of labour on productivity and national prosperity.

Smith was both the prophet and champion of industrial **capitalism** and the free market. Yet he also recognised that the provision of some goods and services, for example defence, public works, and education, could not or should not be left to the market. Much of the continuing debate over the legitimate role of the state in economic activities originated with Adam Smith. Although he is most commonly cited by modern **neoliberals** to support their anti-state free market convictions, parts of his writing can also be used to justify the moderate state intervention advocated today by **social liberals** and **social democrats**.

Socrates

Socrates (c. 469–399 BCE) was a celebrated Athenian philosopher who lived through the great days of the city under Pericles* and the ensuing long war between Athens and Sparta. This war ended with the defeat of Athens in 404 and the brief replacement of the Athenian system of **democracy** by the tyranny of the thirty. After democracy was restored, Socrates was put on trial for corrupting the young. He conducted his own defence provocatively and was condemned to death by drinking hemlock. His death sentence has long been regarded as a serious stain on Athenian democracy. The attitude towards democracy of Socrates himself is unclear, although some of his associates were certainly its enemies and his pupil Plato* was very hostile.

The teaching of Socrates himself was oral, so that we rely on his contemporaries and pupils, principally Plato but also, among others, the historian Xenophon and the playwright Aristophanes, for our knowledge of his ideas and methods. Their testimony is somewhat contradictory. However, particularly in his so-called earlier dialogues, Plato may have provided a tolerably accurate portrait of Socrates himself and the 'Socratic method'. This involved rigorous cross-examination of the ideas expressed by others, exposing weaknesses and inconsistencies in their thinking. In Plato's *Apology* Socrates, in the course of his defence at his trial, describes how the oracle at Delphi had declared there was no one wiser than himself. Aware that he had no claim to wisdom, Socrates cross-examined many men considered wise in an attempt to disprove the oracle's verdict. He concluded from his enquiries that the reputation of these men for wisdom was unjustified and that they, like himself, knew nothing of importance. However, he was conscious of his own ignorance and they were not, and to that extent he was wiser than they were.

Sorel

Georges Sorel (1847–1922) was a French thinker associated with syndicalism and anarcho-syndicalism, involving **revolutionary** industrial action and direct workers' control, rather than seeking power through **parliamentary democracy**. Sorel emphasised the importance of myths in sustaining revolutionary consciousness and workers' solidarity, particularly the myth of the general strike, as a means to bring **capitalism** down. His ideas were influential in radical trade union circles before and after the First World War.

Spencer

Herbert Spencer (1820–1903) was a British philosopher whose strong laissez-faire **free market liberalism** was reinforced by Darwin's theory of evolution and the notion of the survival of the fittest. He was strongly opposed to the interventionist New Liberalism that became influential towards the end of his life. His extensive writings include *Social Statics* (1850) and *The Man versus the State* (1884). While his reputation has declined in the United Kingdom, he is still rated highly by some American **neoliberals**.

Spinoza

Baruch (Benedict) Spinoza (1632–1677) was a Dutch Jewish philosopher who vigorously defended free speech and religious **toleration**. His political thought was influenced by Hobbes*, but unlike Hobbes he believed in limited **government**, and favoured **democracy**. Key works include the *Tractatus Theologico-Philosophicus* (1670) and his posthumously published *Ethics*.

Stalin

Joseph Stalin (1879–1953) was born Josef Vissarionovich Dzhugashvili but adopted the name Stalin (meaning 'man of steel') when he became an active Bolshevik **revolutionary**. He was not a leading figure in the 1917 revolution but became a member of the ruling politburo and, in 1922, General Secretary of the Communist Party. He used this administrative post to strengthen his own power base in the party, and after Lenin's death in 1924, over time skilfully outmanoeuvred his opponents, such as Trotsky*, to become Lenin's successor, establishing a ruthless **dictatorship**. His contribution to **Marxist-Leninist** theory was relatively thin but includes his writings on the nationalities issue and his support for the idea of 'socialism in one country', in response to Trotsky's doctrine of 'permanent revolution'. It was the practice of his government that added the term 'Stalinism' to political vocabulary. This included the extermination of millions of peasants who resisted the forced collectivisation of agriculture and the show trials and executions of those perceived as traitors to the regime, who included nearly all Lenin's leading Bolshevik colleagues who had survived long enough to become victims of Stalin. The excesses of his rule were denounced, after his death, by his eventual successor as Soviet leader, Nikita Khrushchev.

Strange

Susan Strange (1923–1998) played a key role in defining and developing the study of international political economy in her works *Casino Capitalism* (1986), *States and Markets* (1988), and *Mad Money* (1998). She claimed that most economists had little understanding of **power**, while most political scientists knew little about financial markets. Her call for greater mutual understanding between these two disciplines led to international political economy becoming an important element of the study of politics and **international relations**.

Tawney

Richard Henry Tawney (1880–1962) was a British economic historian and Christian **socialist**. While many socialists around the world have been indifferent or hostile to religion, Christian socialism has been a significant strand in the British labour movement. Some Christian socialists were Roman Catholics (e.g. John Wheatley), but rather more were Protestant nonconformists, particularly Methodists (e.g. Philip Snowden). R. H. Tawney combined socialism with Anglicanism. Key works were *The Acquisitive Society* (1921), *Religion and the Rise of Capitalism* (1926), and *Equality* (1931).

Taylor

Charles Taylor (1931–) is a Canadian political philosopher, who held professorial chairs at Oxford, where he taught Michael Sandel*, among others, and McGill University, Montreal. He tried four times unsuccessfully to secure election to the Canadian House of Commons as a candidate of the New Democratic Party. His key work is generally thought to be *Sources of the Self: The Making of Modern Identity* (1989). He argues that the self can only be understood in terms of the **community** of which it is a part, and not as an isolated **individual**, as suggested by **liberals**.

Thoreau

Henry David Thoreau (1817–1862) was an American radical **individualist** thinker. In *Walden* (1854) he described how he pursued self-sufficiency while living in a cabin at Walden Pond. He asserted, 'That government is best which governs not all.' He justified resistance to **authority** and **civil disobedience** on grounds of conscience, particularly on the issue of slavery. Prison, he argued, was 'the only house in a slave-state in which a free man can reside with honour.'

Thucydides

Thucydides (c. 460–400 BCE) was an Athenian citizen who served as a general in the early stages of the Peloponnesian War and who later wrote a compelling historical account of the conflict (*History of the Peloponnesian War*, modern English translation by Rex Warner, 1972). In the process, he provides a vivid portrait of Athenian democracy and its leading statesman Pericles*, which has provided a source of inspiration to modern democracies, as well as a warning of dangers to be avoided. It is also a challenging account of interstate conflict that has furnished examples that writers on modern international relations still cite.

Tocqueville

Alexis de Tocqueville (1805–1859) was born into a French Catholic aristocratic family that fully supported the restored Bourbon **monarchy** of Louis XVIII and Charles X. This French aristocrat is today chiefly known for his celebrated and generally sympathetic two-volume study *Democracy in America*. (The first volume was published in 1835, the second in 1840). The still relatively new system of **democracy** in the United States was then regarded with considerable curiosity tinged with apprehension in Europe. Tocqueville went to America in 1831 with a commission from the new French government to research the American penal system, but his real interest was in wider American society and its political system. The result of his extensive travel and research has been described as 'the greatest book ever written on America'. It is still regularly cited by American politicians.

While he was well aware of some of the theoretical issues surrounding the development of the American **constitution**, Tocqueville was more interested in the practice of American democracy. He was particularly impressed by the active participation of American citizens in the government of their own localities: 'The strength of free nations resides in the township.' He repeatedly emphasised the importance of **decentralisation** in the American political system. However, he was concerned over what he called 'the tyranny of the majority' in democratic society, a key phrase that has entered the language. Tocqueville also wrote eloquently on the condition of American blacks, roundly condemning slavery but observing pointedly that racial prejudice appeared stronger in those states that had abolished slavery than in those where slavery still existed. While he was assured that freed male slaves had the legal right to vote in America, he noted that they were effectively prevented from exercising these **rights**.

Trotsky

Leon Trotsky (1879–1940) was a leading Russian **Marxist revolutionary** politician and thinker, whose ideas ultimately became more influential on the **socialist left** in the West than in the Communist bloc. He was born Leon Bronstein but assumed the name Trotsky after he became a Marxist revolutionary. An early associate of Lenin*, Trotsky famously predicted that the democratic centralism advocated in Lenin's *What Is to Be Done?* would mean that 'the party organisation substitutes itself for the party, the central committee substitutes itself for the organisation, and, finally, a "dictator" substitutes himself for the central committee.' Yet Trotsky was not definitely aligned with either the Bolsheviks or the Mensheviks after the party split in 1903. He played a leading role in the abortive 1905 revolution and in 1917 joined Lenin. After the Bolshevik revolution he negotiated the Treaty of Brest Litovsk with Germany and then led the Red Army to victory over the Whites in the Russian civil war. At that time he appeared to be Lenin's leading lieutenant and potential successor, but in the struggle for power after Lenin's death Trotsky was distrusted by the old Bolsheviks and was eventually out-manoeuvred by the party secretary Stalin*, who controlled the **bureaucracy**.

While Stalin advocated 'socialism in one country', Trotsky assumed that the **communism** could not triumph in Russia without **revolution** elsewhere and continued to champion 'permanent revolution'. He was exiled in 1929, fiercely denounced the show trials and executions of the 1930s in which Stalin eliminated almost all the surviving old Bolsheviks, and was finally killed in Mexico by a Stalinist agent in 1940. Trotskyism as an alternative to Stalinism continued to attract a following among Western **Marxists** throughout the period of the Cold War. Trotsky was always the most readable of the Russian Marxists, and his own account of the Russian revolution and its subsequent betrayal won admirers, as did the monumental biography by Isaac Deutscher. In the communist world, while some victims of Stalin were subsequently rehabilitated, Trotsky was not, and he remains a marginalised figure following the implosion of communism in Russia and Eastern Europe.

Tullock

Gordon Tullock (1922–2014) was an American economist. Together with James Buchanan he wrote *The Calculus of Consent* (1962), a classic work of the **public choice** school that became massively influential in American political science. Other works include *The Politics of Bureaucracy* (1965), and *On Voting: A Public Choice Approach* (1998).

Voltaire

Francois-Marie Arouet Voltaire (1694–1778) was a celebrated thinker of the French Enlightenment. Voltaire was a noted critic of the nobility and clergy but not of the **monarchy**, favouring a benevolent despotism. He was a supporter of religious **toleration** and **freedom** of thought; although he did not actually say the famous words, 'I disapprove of what you say, but I will defend to the death your right to say it' (attributed to him by S. G. Tallentyre), he did express similar sentiments. Perhaps, He is most remembered today for his satire *Candide* (1759).

Waltz

Kenneth N. Waltz (1924–2013) was the leading modern **realist** or neorealist American **international relations** theorist. In his key work *Theory of International Politics* (1979) he argued that the international system remains one of **anarchy** in which **states** have to look after their own interests in the absence of effective higher authority to which they might defer. In looking after their own security, states have to consider the threats posed by other states. To reduce such threats, state foreign policy seeks to build alliances to secure a **balance of power** and thus create and maintain stability in the international political system. The balance of power between the United States and its allies on the one hand and the USSR and its allies on the other appeared to be an example of such an (apparently stable) international system at the time of writing. Some **liberal-pluralist** critics argued that Waltz's account was unduly state-centred, involved oversimplified assumptions about the making of state foreign policy and the pursuit of national interest, and downplayed the importance of international institutions and **nongovernmental organisations** (NGOs). Other critics considered Waltz underplayed the effects of a **globalised capitalist** economy on international relations. The unanticipated end of the Cold War provided further problems for the neorealists. Yet realist and neorealist assumptions about international relations have remained influential, not least in the foreign policy of the United States.

Walzer

Michael Walzer (1935–) is a modern American moral and political philosopher, associated with **communitarianism** (along with Alasdair MacIntyre*, Michael Sandel*, and Charles Taylor*). He criticised John Rawls* and his theory of **justice**, for example in *Spheres of Justice* (1983). Walzer has also revived the notion of the just war in *Just and Unjust Wars* (2000), upholding the general principle of nonintervention in the internal affairs of independent **sovereign states**, although allowing a case for humanitarian intervention in very rare circumstances.

Webb

Sidney Webb (1859–1947) and his wife Beatrice Webb (1858–1943) formed such a close-knit intellectual partnership that they are best treated together. They became leading figures in the Fabian Society, a small but influential **socialist** group, named after the Roman general who had defeated Hannibal by patient delaying tactics (declining to fight him in open battle), and committed to gradual reform through the ballot box rather than **revolution**. The Webbs were active in founding the London School of Economics in 1895, indicative of their own enthusiasm for reform based on social science research. They believed that their practical common sense socialist ideas would, over time, permeate society. Initially they were prepared

to work through any politician (including the young Winston Churchill) who would listen to them but became increasingly committed to the Labour Party. Sidney Webb helped draft the original Clause IV of the party's constitution (1918), with its celebrated commitment to common ownership of the means of production, distribution, and exchange. He later served as Labour minister in MacDonald's governments in 1924 and 1929–1931. Subsequently the Webbs visited Stalin*'s Russia, whose socialist system they endorsed with naïve enthusiasm, ironically, as Stalin's interpretation of socialism was far removed from the gradual parliamentary socialism with which they were identified.

Weber

Max Weber (1864–1920) is now regarded as one of the most important social and political thinkers of the 20th century and a founding father of sociology. He was born in Erfut, the son of a prominent German politician, and the family moved to Berlin in 1869. He studied law, history, economics, and philosophy and later taught economics at Berlin and politics at Heidelberg, but he gave up teaching after he quarrelled with his father and his health broke down. In 1904 his celebrated essay *The Protestant Ethic and the Spirit of Capitalism* was published. At the end of the First World War he was involved in peace negotiations at Versailles and was a member of the commission that drafted the Weimar constitution. He returned to teaching at Vienna and then Munich, where he died of pneumonia in 1920. Much of the writing for which he is now most well known was published after his death.

In contrast to Marx*, who believed that economic interests ultimately determined political and social change, Weber thought that historical development was the consequence of a more complex interplay of social, cultural, and religious forces. Thus he famously argued that the rise of **capitalism** in the West was assisted by the emergence of Protestantism, more specifically Calvinism. Calvinism aided capitalist accumulation as this was interpreted as a sign of divine favour. Puritanism also encouraged ploughing back income and wealth into new enterprise rather than wasting it in conspicuous consumption.

To cope with studying the complexity of society and social change, Weber made use of what he described as 'ideal types', involving abstract exaggerations of features of real life. Thus ideal types are simplified explanatory tools or **models** providing insights into complex social reality. '**Capitalism**', '**authority**', '**bureaucracy**', '**class**', and 'status' are among the key concepts that Weber analysed in this way.

Weber's analysis of **power**, authority, **legitimacy**, the **state**, and bureaucracy are particularly important for students of politics. Power he saw as the ability to gain one's ends despite the resistance of others. Ultimately power relies on the threat of physical force. Weber famously defined the state as a human community that (successfully) claims the monopoly of the legitimate use of physical force within a given territory. Yet a key word here is 'legitimate'. Weber recognised that power is often widely accepted as legitimate and used the term authority to describe legitimate power. He argued that legitimate power or authority could be derived from three main sources. It may be traditional, arising from age-old custom and practice, such as the authority of a hereditary ruler. It may stem from the personal qualities or charisma of a particular leader. Weber believed the characteristic modern form of authority was legal-rational, based on clear written rules and procedures. Here, obedience is essentially to the position rather than the person who occupies the position, as long as that person has been appointed or elected according to recognised rules and procedures. Both representative democracy and bureaucracy involved legal-rational authority.

Weber saw bureaucracy as the predominant form of organisation in the modern world in both the public and private sectors. His ideal type of bureaucracy involved a number of features, including a hierarchical structure, with a clear chain of command, adherence to impersonal written rules, recruitment and promotion by merit and recognised professional qualifications, along with the separation of work from private life. Yet while Weber thought bureaucracy was a **rational** and efficient form of organisation, he had some concerns that it might effectively supplant **democracy**.

Wendt

Alexander Wendt (1958–) is a German-born scholar who completed his education in the United States, where he is now a leading **constructivist** theorist of **international relations**. He published two key articles 'The Agent/Structure Problem in International Relations' (1987) and 'Anarchy Is What States Make of It: The Social Construction of Power Politics' (1992), both of which questioned the **realist** and neorealist assumption that international relations were shaped by enduring material objective factors. He argued instead that key concepts (such as **anarchy**) were not immutable but socially constructed (or interpreted) by key actors, such as **states**, thus capable of evolving over time. His book *Social Theory of International Politics* (1999) outlined his own approach to the study of international relations, the title suggesting it was conceived as a direct response to the key work of Kenneth Waltz* (1979).

Wildavsky

Aaron Wildavksy (1930–1993) was an American political scientist who taught at the University of California, Berkeley, and published prolifically on a wide variety of topics. He is perhaps best known among political scientists for his work on policy analysis, including *Implementation* (with J. Pressman, 1973), *The Politics of the Budgetary Process* (1974), and *The Art and Craft of Policy Analysis* (1980). His book (with Hugh Heclo) *The Private Government of Public Money* (1974) is widely regarded as a classic study of British public administration. He has also written on the American Presidency, **cultural** theory, and **environmentalism**. He coauthored *Risk and Culture* with the anthropologist Mary Douglas.

Wilson

Woodrow Wilson (1859– 1924) was a rare example of an eminent American political scientist who went on to become a leading politician and world statesman, as US President from 1913 to 1921. As an academic he wrote articles for the *Political Science Quarterly* and several widely read books, becoming president of Princeton University from 1902 to 1910 and president of the American Political Science Association in 1910. He engaged in politics as a Democrat and was elected governor of New Jersey in 1910. He then successfully ran for the US presidency in 1912 and was re-elected in 1916. As president he took an active interventionist role, reducing tariffs, pursuing anti-trust legislation, and reforming the banking system. However, he is chiefly remembered for his foreign policy and liberal approach to **international relations**.

He had initially pursued a policy of neutrality when war broke out in Europe in 1914, but unrestricted German submarine warfare turned Wilson, and US public opinion, in favour of intervention on the allied side in 1917. Wilson saw it as a war to end war and to make the world safe for democracy. His fourteen points enshrined the principles he thought should govern international diplomacy, including national self-determination. He was a leading figure in the postwar settlement and establishment of the League of Nations (although Keynes* was an influential critic of his diplomacy). The postwar treaties were not ratified by Congress, and the United States never joined the League that he as president had championed. (Ironically, as an academic he had criticised the division of powers and checks and balances in the US **constitution** and advocated a parliamentary system on British lines.) His last years were plagued by illness and strokes.

The subsequent failure of the League and the postwar settlement generally later tended to discredit the **liberal** approach to international relations that Wilson had advocated (see Carr* and Morgenthau*), although it has enjoyed a partial revival more recently.

Wollstonecraft

Mary Wollstonecraft (1759–1797) was a pioneer English **feminist** who sought to apply **liberal** values to the position of women. She associated with radical nonconformists and enthusiastically supported the French **Revolution**. Her book *A Vindication of the Rights of Man* (1790) followed the publication of the revolutionary 'Declaration of the Rights of Man and Citizen' of 1789 and was written in direct response to the *Reflections on the Revolution in France* of Edmund Burke*. Her key work, *A Vindication of the Rights of Women* (1792), followed two years later. In it she argued that women were as **rational** as men and as rational creature should be entitled to the same **rights** as men. Rousseau* had argued in *Emile* that women were different in **nature** to man and 'woman is made to please and to be in subjection to man'. Wollstonecraft vehemently disagreed. If women's nature appeared different, this was because of social conditioning. Women should not be dependent on men for their subsistence and made, by this dependence, into virtual slaves. She placed strong emphasis on women's education as the key to their emancipation. Wollstonecraft's book has remained an inspiration to modern feminists.

In 1797 Mary Wollstonecraft married the **anarchist** thinker William Godwin*, who was later to write her biography. She died soon after the birth of their daughter Mary, who later married the poet Shelley and as Mary Shelley wrote the horror story *Frankenstein*.

GUIDE TO FURTHER READING

Some of the specialist politics dictionaries and other sources recommended for Key Terms and Concepts at the end of Part IV are also useful for Key Thinkers, especially Miller (1991), Robertson (1993), McLean and McMillan (2009), and Scruton (2007).

We also recommend Adams and Dyson, *Fifty Major Political Thinkers* (2007). More detail on some of the leading political theorists is provided in Boucher and Kelly *Political Thinkers: From Socrates to the Present* (2017).

There is ultimately no substitute for reading the key works of the leading thinkers themselves. Fairly readable classics of political theory include: Plato's early dialogues (e.g. in the 1993 Penguin collection *The Last Days of Socrates*) and *The Republic*; Machiavelli, *The Prince*; Rousseau's *Social Contract*; Burke's *Reflections on the Revolution in France*; Tocqueville's *Democracy in America*: Marx and Engels, *The Communist Manifesto*; Mill's *On Liberty*; and de Beauvoir's *The Second Sex*. On modern political science and international relations, follow some of the references to key works in this section and earlier in the book.

REFERENCES

Acharya, A. and Buzan, B. (2007) 'Why Is There No Non-western International Relations Theory?' *International Relations of the Asia-Pacific* 7 (3). pp. 287–312

Adams, I. and Dyson, R. W. (2007 *Fifty Major Political Thinkers*, London: Routledge.

Adorno, T. W. et al. (1950) *The Authoritarian Personality*, New York: Harper and Row.

Ake, C. (1999) 'Globalization, Multilateralism and the Shrinking Democratic Space', in Schechter (ed.), *Future Multilateralism: The Political and Social Framework*, Tokyo: United Nations University Press.

Albrow, M. (1970) *Bureaucracy*, London: Macmillan.

Allison, G. T. (1969) 'Conceptual Models and the Cuban Missile Crisis', *American Political Science Review* 63 (3): 689–718.

Allison, G. T. (1971) *The Essence of Decision: Explaining the Cuban Missile Crisis*, Glenview: Scott and Foresman.

Almond, G. A. (1988) 'The Return of the State', *American Political Science Review* 82: 853–874.

Almond, G. A. and Verba, S. (1963) *The Civic Culture: Political Attitudes and Democracy in Five Nations*, Princeton: Princeton University Press.

Almond, G. A. and Verba, S. (eds) (1980) *The Civic Culture Revisited*, Boston: Little, Brown.

Alter, P. (1994) *Nationalism*, 2nd ed., London: Arnold.

Althusser, L. (1970) *For Marx*, London and New York:

Amin, S. (2010) *Eurocentrism*, New York: Monthly Review Press.

Anderson, B. (1983) *Imagined Communities: Reflections on the Origins and Spread of Nationalism*, London: Verso.

Anderson, P. (2015) 'Imitation Democracy', *London Review of Books* 37 (16): 19–27.

Aquinas, T. (ed. D'Entrèves, A. P., 1948) *Aquinas: Selected Political Writings*, Oxford: Blackwell.

Arblaster, A. (1984) *The Rise and Fall of Western Liberalism*, Oxford: Blackwell.

Ardagh, J. (1982) *France in the 1980s*, Harmondsworth: Penguin Books.

Arendt, H. (1951) *The Origins of Totalitarianism*, New York: Harcourt Brace.

Arendt, H. (1963) *Eichmann in Jerusalem*, New York: Viking.

Aristotle ([c. 335–323 BCE] tr. Sinclair, T. A., 1992) *The Politics*, London: Penguin.

Aristotle ([c. 335–323 BCE] tr. Thomson, J. A. K., 1953) *Ethics (The Nichomachean Ethics)*, Harmondsworth: Penguin.

Arrow, K. (1951) *Social Choice and Individual Values*, New York: John Wiley and Sons.

Ashley, R. (1988) 'Untying the Sovereign State: A Double Reading of the Anarchy Problematic', *Millennium* 17 (2): 227–262.

Augustine ([413–425] ed. Knowles, tr. Bettenson, 1972) *City of God*, Harmondsworth: Penguin.

Bachrach, P. and Baratz, M. S. (1962) 'Two Faces of Power', *American Political Science Review* 56: 947–952.

Bagehot, W. ([1867] 1963) *The English Constitution*, London: Fontana.

Barry, B. (1970) *Sociologists, Economists and Democracy*, London: Collier Macmillan Ltd.

Barry, B. (1977) 'Justice Between Generations' in Hacker, P. and Raz, J. (eds), *Law, Society and Morality: Essays in Honour of H. L. A. Hart*, Oxford: Clarendon Press.

Barry, B. (1989) *Theories of Justice*, London: Harvester Wheatsheaf.

Barry, B. (1995) *Justice as Impartiality*, Oxford: Clarendon Press.

Barry, B. (2001a) *Culture and Equality: An Egalitarian Critique of Multiculturalism*, Cambridge: Polity Press.

Barry, B. (2001b) 'The Muddles of Multiculturalism', *New Left Review* 8 (March/April).

Barry, B. (2005) *Why Social Justice Matters*, Cambridge: Polity.

Baylis, J. and Smith, S. (2005) *The Globalization of World Politics: An Introduction to International Relations*, Oxford and New York: Oxford University Press.

Baylis, J, Owens, P. and Smith, S. (2016) *The Globalization of World Politics: An Introduction to International Relations*, Oxford and New York: Oxford University Press.

Bealey, F., Chapman, R. A. and Sheehan, M. (1999) *Elements in Political Science*, Edinburgh: Edinburgh University Press.

Beck, U. (1986) *Risk Society: Towards a New Modernity*, London: Sage.

Beck, U. (1999) *What Is Globalization?* Cambridge, Polity Press.

Beer, S. H. (1982) *Modern British Politics*, 2nd ed., London: Faber and Faber.

Beetham, D. (1985) *Max Weber and the Theory of Modern Politics*, 2nd ed., Cambridge: Polity.

Beetham, D. (1987) *Bureaucracy*, Milton Keynes: Open University Press.

Bell, D. (1960) *The End of Ideology*, Glencoe: The Free Press.

Bell, D. (1973) *The Coming of Post-Industrial Society*, Harmondsworth: Penguin.

Bell, J. (1993) *Doing Your Research Project*, Buckingham: Open University Press.

Bellamy, A. (2009) *Responsibility to Protect: The Global Effort to End Mass Atrocities*, Cambridge: Polity Press.

Bentham, J. ([1789] ed. Burns and Hart, 1970) *An Introduction to the Principles of Morals and Legislation*, London: Athlone Press.

Bentham, J. ([1776] ed. Burns and Hart, 1977) *A Fragment on Government*, London: Athlone Press.

Bentley, A. ([1908] 1967) *The Process of Government*, Chicago: University of Chicago Press.

Berlin, I. (1969) *Four Essays on Liberty*, Oxford: Oxford University Press.

Beveridge, W. H. (1942) *Social Insurance and Allied Services*, Cmnd 6404, London: HMSO.

Booth, K. (1991) 'Security in Anarchy: Utopian Realism in Theory and Practice', *International Affairs* 67 (3): 527–545.

Booth, K. and Dunne, T. (eds) (2002) *Worlds in Collision: Terror and the Future of Global Order*, Basingstoke: Palgrave Macmillan.

Bottomore, T. (1966) *Elites and Society*, Harmondsworth: Penguin.

Bottomore, T. (ed.) (1991) *A Dictionary of Marxist Thought*, Oxford: Blackwell.

Boucher, D. and Kelly, P. (2017) *Political Thinkers: From Socrates to the Present*, 3rd ed., Oxford: Oxford University Press.

Brautigam, D. (2009) *The Dragon's Gift*, Oxford: Oxford University Press.

Breuilly, J. (1993) *Nationalism and the State*, 2nd ed., Manchester: Manchester University Press.

Brown, C. and Ainley, K. (2009) *Understanding International Relations*, 4th ed., Basingstoke: Palgrave Macmillan.

Brownmiller, S. (1977) *Against Our Will*, Harmondsworth: Penguin.

Brummer, K. and Hudson, V. (2015) *Foreign Policy Analysis beyond North America*, Boulder: Lynne Rienner.

Bryson, V. (2016) *Feminist Political Theory: An Introduction*, 3rd ed., Basingstoke: Palgrave Macmillan.

Buchanan, J. M. and Tullock, G. (1962) *The Calculus of Consent*, Ann Arbor: University of Michigan Press.

Bull, H. ([1977] 2002) *The Anarchical Society*, Basingstoke: Palgrave Macmillan.

Burchill, S. et al. (2013) *Theories of International Relations*, 5th ed., Basingstoke: Palgrave Macmillan.

Burke, E. ([1790] ed. Hill, 1975) *Reflections on the Revolution in France*, London: Fontana, Harvester.

Butler, C. (2002) *Postmodernism: A Very Short Introduction*, Oxford: Oxford University Press.

Butler, D. and Stokes, D. (1969) *Political Change in Britain*, 2nd ed., London: Macmillan.

Buzan, B. (1991) 'New Patterns of Global Security in the Twenty-First Century', *International Affairs* 67 (3): 431–451.

Buzan, B., Wæver, O. and Wilde, J. (1998) *Security: A New Framework for Analysis*, London: Lynne Rienner.

Byrne, P. (1997) *Social Movements in Britain*, London: Routledge.

Calvert, P. (2002) *Comparative Politics: An Introduction*, Harlow: Longman.

Campbell, A., Converse, P. E., Miller, W. E. and Stokes, D. E. (1960) *The American Voter*, New York: Wiley.

Carver, T. F., Cochran, M. M. and Squires, J. A. (1998) 'Gendering Jones: Feminisms, IRs, Masculinities', *Review of International Studies* 24: 283–297.

Carr, E. H. ([1939] ed. Cox, 2001) *The Twenty Years' Crisis, 1919–1939*, Basingstoke: Palgrave Macmillan.

Castells, M. (1996) *The Rise of the Network Society*, Oxford: Blackwell.

Chadwick, A. (2006) *Internet Politics: States, Citizens and New Communication Technologies*, Oxford and New York: Oxford University Press.

Checkel, J. (1998) 'The Constructive Turn in International Relations Theory', *World Politics* 50 (2): 324–348.

Collier, P. (2007) *The Bottom Billion*, Oxford: Oxford University Press.

Cottrell, S. (2011) *Critical Thinking Skills*, Basingstoke: Palgrave Macmillan.

Cottrell, S. (2012) *The Exam Skills Handbook*, Basingstoke: Palgrave Macmillan.

Cottrell, S. (2013) *The Study Skills Handbook*, Basingstoke: Palgrave Macmillan.

Cottrell, S. (2014) Dissertations and Project Reports: A Step by Step Guide, Basingstoke: Palgrave Macmillan.

Cox, R. (1987) *Production, Power and World Order*, New York: Columbia University Press.

Cox, R. (1994) 'The Crisis in World Order and the Challenge to International Organization', *Cooperation and Conflict* 29 (9): 113.

Crenson, M. A. (1971) *The Unpolitics of Air Pollution*, Baltimore: The Johns Hopkins Press.

Crick, B. (1959) *The American Science of Politics*, London: Routledge.

Crick, B. ([1962] 2000) *In Defence of Politics,* 5th ed., London: Continuum.

Crosland, C. A. R. (1956) *The Future of Socialism*, London: Jonathan Cape.

Crossman, R. H. S. (1963) 'Introduction to W. Bagehot, The English Constitution' London, Fontana.

Crozier, M. (1964) *The Bureaucratic Phenomenon*, London: Tavistock Press.

Curran, J. and Gurevitch, M. (1996) *Mass Media and Society*, 2nd ed., London: Arnold.

Daddow, O. (2013) *International Relations Theory: The Essentials*, London: Sage.

Dahl, R. A. (1956) *A Preface to Democratic Theory*, Chicago: Chicago University Press.

Dahl, R. A. (1958) 'A Critique of the Ruling Elite Model', *American Political Science Review* 52.

Dahl, R. A. (1961) *Who Governs? Democracy and Power in an American City*, Newhaven: Yale University Press.

Dahl, R. A. (1971) *Polyarchy: Participation and Opposition*, New Haven: Yale University Press.

Dahl, R. A. (1989) *Democracy and Its Critics*, New Haven: Yale University Press.

Dahl, R. A. and Lindblom, C. (1953) *Politics, Economics and Welfare*, New York: Harper and Row.

Dahrendorf, R. (1990) *Reflections on the Revolution in Europe*, London: Chatto and Windus.

Davies, S., Elbe, S., Howell, A. and McInnes, C. (2014) 'Global Health in International Relations: Editors' Introduction', *Review of International Studies* 40.

Dearlove, J. (1973) *The Politics of Policy in Local Government*, Cambridge: Cambridge University Press.

De Beauvoir, S. ([1949] 1972) *The Second Sex*, Harmondsworth: Penguin.

Denscombe, M. (1998) *A Good Research Guide for Small-Scale Social Research Projects*, Buckingham: Open University Press.

Denver, D. et al. (2012) *Elections and Voters in Britain*, Basingstoke: Palgrave Macmillan.

Deutsch, K. W. (1963) *The Nerves of Government*, Glencoe: Free Press.

Deutsch, K. W. (1966) *Nationalism and Social Communication*, New York: MIT Press.

Diez, T., Bode, I. and Da Costa, A. (2011) *Key Concepts in International Relations,* London: Sage.

Dobson, A. (1990) *Green Political Thought,* London: Harper Collins.

Dornan, M. (2011) 'Realist and Constructivist Approaches to Anarchy', *E-IR*, http://www.e-ir.info/2011/08/29/realist-and-constructivist-approaches-to-anarchy/.

Downs, A. (1957) *An Economic Theory of Democracy*, New York: Harper and Row.

Downs A (1967) *Inside Bureaucracy*, Boston: Little, Brown.

Drake, H. (2014) 'Learning from Peers: The Role of the Student Advisor in Internationalising the European Studies Curriculum', *European Political Science* 13 (1).

Drezner, D. (2011) *Theories of International Politics and Zombies*, Princeton: Princeton University Press.

Dunleavy, P. (1979) 'The Urban Basis of Political Alignment: Social Class, Domestic Property Ownership and State Intervention in Consumption Processes', *British Journal of Political Science* 9: 409–443.

Dunleavy, P. (1980) 'The Political Implications of Sectoral Cleavages and the Growth of State Employment', *Political Studies* 28: 364–383 and 527–549.

Dunleavy, P. (1986) *Studying for a Degree in the Humanities and Social Sciences*, Basingstoke: Palgrave Macmillan.

Dunleavy, P. (1991) *Democracy, Bureaucracy and Public Choice,* Hemel Hempstead: Harvester Wheatsheaf.

Dunleavy, P. and O'Leary, B. (1987) *Theories of the State,* London: Macmillan.

Dunsire, A. (1973) *Public Administration: The Word and the Science*, London: Martin Robertson.

Duverger, M. ([1954] 1970) *Political Parties*, London: Methuen.

Duverger, M. (tr. Wagoner, R., 1972) *The Study of Politics*, Sunbury on Thames: Nelson.

Dworkin, A. (1979) *Pornography: Men Possessing Women,* London: Women's Press.

Dworkin, R. (1977) *Taking Rights Seriously*, London: Duckworth.

Easton, D. (1965) *A Systems Analysis of Political Life*, New York: Wiley.

Eccleshall, R. (1986) British Liberalism: Liberal Thought from the 1640s to the 1980s, Harlow: Longman.

Eccleshall, R., Geoghegan, v. Jay, R., Kenny, M., Mackenzie, I, and Wilford, R. (1994) *Political Ideologies: an introduction*, 2nd ed., London: New York: Routledge.

Eckstein, H. (1960) *Pressure Group Politics: The Case of the British Medical Association*, London: Allen and Unwin.

Engels, Friedrich (1845) The Condition of the Working Class in England, Leipzig: Otto Wigand.

Engels, Friedrich (1878) Anti-Duhring, Leipzig.

Engels, Friedrich (1884) Origins of the Family, Private Property and the State, Stuttgart, Dietz.

Etzioni, A. (1967) 'Mixed-Scanning: A "Third" Approach to Decision-Making', *Public Administration Review* 27.

Enloe, C. (1988) Does Khaki Become You? The Militarization of Women's Lives, London, Pandora Press; San Francisco, Harper Collins.

Enloe, C. (1989) *Bananas, Beaches and Bases: Making Feminist Sense of International Politics*, Berkeley: University of California Press.

Enloe, C. (2010) Nimo's War, Emma's War: Making Feminist Sense of the Iraq War Berkeley: University of California Press.

Evans, P. B., Rueschemeyer, D. and Skocpol, T. (eds) (1985) *Bringing the State Back In*, Cambridge: Cambridge University Press.

Eysenck, H. J. (1957) *Sense and Nonsense in Psychology*, Harmondsworth: Penguin.

Farrell, D. (2001) *Electoral Systems: A Comparative Introduction*, London and New York: Palgrave, Macmillan.

Feuer, L. S. (1959) *Marx and Engels: Basic Writings on Politics and Philosophy*, New York: Anchor Books.

Figes, E. ([1970] 1978) *Patriarchal Attitudes*, London: Virago.

Finer, H. (1932) *The Theory and Practice of Modern Government*, 2 vols., London: Methuen.

Finer, S. E. ([1962] 1988) *The Man on Horseback: The Role of the Military in Politics*, Boulder: Westview.

Finley, M. I. (1963) *The Ancient Greeks*, Harmondsworth: Penguin.

Finley, M. I. (1972) *Aspects of Antiquity*, Harmondsworth: Penguin.

Finnemore, M. (1996) *National Interests in International Society*, Ithaca: Cornell University Press.

Finnemore, M. and Sikkink, K. (1998) 'International Organization at Fifty: Exploration and Contestation in the Study of World Politics', *International Organization* 52 (4): 887–917.

Firestone, S. ([1970] 1979) *The Dialectic of Sex*, London: Women's Press.

Foucault, M. (tr. Howard, 1965) *Madness and Civilisation*, New York: Pantheon.

Foucault, M. (tr. Sheridan, 1972) *The Archaeology of Knowledge*, London: Tavistock.

Foucault, M. (tr. Sheridan, 1977) *Discipline and Punish*, London: Allen Lane.

Fox, R. L. (2006) *The Classical World: An Epic History of Greece and Rome*, London: Penguin.

Frankopan, P. (2015) *The Silk Roads: A New History of the World*, London: Bloomsbury.

Freeden, M. (1996) *Ideologies and Political Theory*, Oxford: Clarendon Press.

Friedan, B. (1965) *The Feminine Mystique*, Harmondsworth: Penguin.

Friedan, B. (1982) *The Second Stage*, London: Michael Joseph.

Friedman, T. (2005) *The World Is Flat: A Brief History of the Twenty-first Century*, New York: Farrar, Straus and Giroux.

Friedrich, C. J. and Brzezinski, Z. (1963). *Totalitarian Dictatorships and Autocracy*, New York: Praeger.

Friedrichs, J. (2004), *European Approaches to International Relations Theory*, Routledge: London.

Fukuyama, F. (1992) *The End of History and the Last Man*, Harmondsworth: Penguin.

Fukuyama, F. (2014) *Political Order and Political Decay: From the Industrial Revolution to the Globalisation of Democracy*, London: Profile Books.

Galbraith, J. K. (1952) *American Capitalism*, Boston: Houghton Mifflin.

Galbraith, J. K. ([1955] 1992) *The Great Crash*, Harmondsworth: Penguin.

Galbraith, J. K. ([1958] 1999) *The Affluent Society*, London: Penguin.

Galbraith, J. K. ([1967]) *The New Industrial State*, London: Hamish Hamilton.

Galbraith, J. K. ([1973]) *Economics and the Public Purpose*, Boston: Houghton Mifflin.

Gellner, E. (1983) *Nations and Nationalism*, Oxford: Basil Blackwell.

Giddens, A. (1979) *Central Problems in Social Theory*, London: Macmillan.

Giddens, A. (1984) *The Constitution of Society*, Cambridge: Polity Press.

Giddens, A. (1994) *Beyond Left and Right*, Cambridge: Polity Press.

Giddens, A. (1998) *The Third Way*, Cambridge: Polity Press.

Giddens, A. (2000) *The Third Way and Its Critics*, Cambridge: Polity Press.

Giddens, A. (ed.) (2001) *The Global Third Way Debate* Cambridge: Polity Press.

Godwin, W. ([1793] ed. Kramnick, 1976) *An Enquiry Concerning Political Justice*, Harmondsworth: Penguin.

Goodin, R. E. and Klingemann, H. (eds) (1996) *A New Handbook of Political Science*, Oxford: Oxford University Press.

Gramsci, A. ([1929–1935] tr. Hoare and Nowell Smith, 1971) *Selections from the Prison Notebooks*, London: Lawrence and Wishart.

Grant, W. (2000) *Pressure Groups and British Politics*, Basingstoke: Palgrave Macmillan.

Grant, W. (2010) *The Development of a Discipline: The History of the Political Studies Association*, Chichester: Wiley-Blackwell.

Green, T. H. ([1882 ed. Harris and Morrow, 1986) *Lectures on the Principles of Political Obligation*, Cambridge: Cambridge University Press.

Greenfeld, L. (1992) *Nationalism: Five Roads to Modernity*, Cambridge: Harvard University Press.

Greer, G. (1970) *The Female Eunuch*, St Albans: Paladin.

Greer, G. (1984) *Sex and Destiny. The Politics of Human Fertility*, London: Secker and Warburg.

Greetham, B. (2013) *How to Write Better Essays*, 2nd ed., Basingstoke: Palgrave Macmillan.

Gunder-Frank, A. (1967). *Capitalism and Underdevelopment in Latin America: Historical Studies*. New York: Monthly Review Press.

Habermas, J. (1971) *Knowledge and Human Interests*, Boston: Beacon.

Habermas J. (1975) *Legitimation Crisis*, Boston: Beacon.

Habermas, J. (1984, 1986) *The Theory of Communicative Action*, 2 vols., Boston: Beacon.

Hague, R., Harrop, M. and McCormick, J. (2016) *Political Science: A Comparative Introduction*, 8th ed., London: Palgrave Macmillan.

Hall, P. A. (1999) 'Social Capital in Britain', *British Journal of Political Science* 29 (3): 417–461.

Hames, T. and Rae, N. (1996) *Governing America*, Manchester: Manchester University Press.

Hampsher-Monk, I. (1992) *A History of Modern Political Thought*, Oxford: Blackwell.

Hampton, W. (1970) *Democracy and Community*, London: Oxford University Press.

Harrop, M. and Miller, W. L. (1987) *Elections and Voters: A Comparative Introduction*, Basingstoke: Palgrave Macmillan.

Hardin, G. (1968) 'Tragedy of the Commons', *Science* 162 (3859): 1243–1248.

Hart Research Associates (2013), 'It takes more than a major: Employer Priorities for College Learning and Student Success. An Online Survey Among Employers', available at https://www.aacu.org/leap/presidentstrust/compact/2013SurveySummary.cfm (accessed 22/11/17).

Hathaway, T. (2015) 'Study Skills for Dissertations, Essays and Exams', in Kennedy-Pipe, C., Clubb, G. and Mabon, S. (eds), *Terrorism and Political Violence*, London: Sage.

Hay, C. (2002) *Political Analysis: A Critical Introduction,* Basingstoke: Palgrave Macmillan.

Hay, C., Lister, M. and Marsh, D. (eds) (2006) *The State: Theories and Issues,* Basingstoke: Palgrave Macmillan.

Hayek, F. A. von ([1944] 1976) *The Road to Serfdom*, London: Routledge and Kegan Paul.

Hayek, F. A. von (1960) *The Constitution of Liberty*, London: Routledge and Kegan Paul.

Heclo, H. and Wildavsky, A. ([1974] 1981) *The Private Government of Public Money*, 2nd ed., London: Macmillan.

Hegel, G. W. F. ([1821] ed. Wood, tr. Nisbet, 1991) *The Philosophy of Right*, Cambridge: Cambridge University Press.

Held, D. (1995) *Democracy and the Global Order: From the Modern State to Cosmopolitan Governance*, Cambridge: Polity Press.

Held, D. (2006) *Models of Democracy*, 3rd ed., Oxford: Polity Press.

Held, D. and McGrew, A. (2003) *The Global Transformations Reader: An Introduction to the Globalization Debate*, Oxford: Blackwell.

Hennessy, P. (2000) *The Prime Minister: The Office and Its Holders since 1945*, London: Allen Lane.

Hermon, E. and Chomsky, N. (1988) *Manufacturing Consent*, New York: Pantheon.

Heywood, A. (2013) *Politics*, 4th ed., London: Palgrave Macmillan.

Heywood, A. (2015a) *Political Theory: An Introduction*, 4th ed., London: Palgrave Macmillan.

Heywood, A. (2015b) *Key Concepts in Politics and International Relations*, 2nd ed., London: Palgrave Macmillan.

Hill, M (ed.) (1993) *The Policy Process: A Reader*, Hemel Hempstead: Harvester Wheatsheaf.

Hindmoor, A. and Taylor, B. (2015) *Rational Choice*, 2nd ed., London: Palgrave Macmillan.

Hirschman, A. (1970) *Exit, Voice, and Loyalty*, Cambridge: Harvard University Press.

Hirst, P. and Thompson, G. (1999) *Globalization in Question: The International Economy and the Possibilities of Governance*, 2nd ed., Cambridge: Polity.

Hobbes, T. ([1651] ed. Macpherson, 1968) *Leviathan,* Harmondsworth: Penguin.

Hobhouse, L. T. ([1911] 1964) *Liberalism*, New York: Oxford University Press.

Hobhouse, L. T. ([1918] 1960) *The Metaphysical Theory of the State*, London: Allen and Unwin.

Hobsbawm, E. (1990) *Nations and Nationalism since 1780*, Cambridge: Cambridge University Press.

Hobsbawm, E. (1994) *Age of Extremes: The Short Twentieth Century*, London: Michael Joseph.

Hobsbawm, E. (1996) 'The Cult of Identity Politics' *New Left Review* 217 (May/June).

Hobson, J. (2012). *The Eurocentric Conception of World Politics: Western International Theory, 1760–2010*, New York: Cambridge University Press.

Hogwood, B. W. and Gunn, L. A. (1984) *Policy Analysis for the Real World*, Oxford: Oxford University Press.

Howard, K. and Sharp, J. A. (1993) *The Management of a Student Research Project*, Aldershot: Gower.

Hrebenar, R. (1997) *Interest Group Politics in America*, 3rd ed., Englewood Cliffs: Prentice Hall.

Hu, A. (2015) 'Embracing China's "New Normal": Why the Economy Is Still on Track', *Foreign Affairs* 94 (3): 8–12.

Hudson, V. (2013) *Foreign Policy Analysis: Classic and Contemporary Theory*, 2nd ed., London: Rowman and Littlefield.

Hughes, O. E. (2003) *Public Management and Administration*, 3rd ed., Basingstoke: Palgrave Macmillan.

Hume, D. ([1739–40] ed. Selby, 1978) *A Treatise of Human Nature*, Oxford: Clarendon Press.

Hume, D. ([1748] ed. Barker, 1947) *Of the Original Contract*, London: Oxford University Press.

Hunter, F. (1953) *Community Power Structure*, Chapel Hill: University of North Carolina Press.

Huntington, S. P. (1991) *Third Wave: Democratization in the Late Twentieth Century*, Cambridge: Harvard University Press.

Huntington, S. P. ([1996] 2002) *The Clash of Civilisations and the Remaking of World Order*, London: Free Press.

Inglehart, R. (1971) 'The Silent Revolution in Europe: Intergenerational Change in Post-Industrial Societies', *American Political Science Review* 65: 991–1017.

Inglehart, R. (1977) *The Silent Revolution: Changing Values and Political Styles Amongst Western Publics*, Princeton: Princeton University Press.

Inglehart, R. (1990) *Culture Shift in Advanced Industrial Societies*, Princeton: Princeton University Press.

Inglehart, R. and Norris, P. (2004) *Sacred and Secular: Religion and Politics Worldwide*, Cambridge: Cambridge University Press.

Jackson, R. (2000) *The Global Covenant*, Oxford: Oxford University Press.

John, P. (2017) 'Quantitative Methods' in Lowndes, V., Marsh, D. and Stoker, G. (eds) *Theory and Methods in Political Science* 3rd Ed. Basingstoke: Palgrave.

Jones, G. W. (1965) 'The Prime Minister's Power', *Parliamentary Affairs* 18 (Spring): 167–185.

Jones, G. W. (1965) 'The Prime Minister's Power, Parliamentary Affairs, vol 18, No 2, pp. 167–185.

Jordan, A. G. and Richardson, J. J. (1987) *British Politics and the Policy Process*, London: Allen and Unwin.

Kaarbo, J. (2015) 'The Domestic Politics and Decision-Making Turn in IR Theory: An FPA Perspective', *International Studies Review* 17 (2): 189–216.

Kaldor, M. (2012) *New and Old Wars: Organized Violence in a Global Era*, Oxford: Polity Press.

Kaldor, Mary (2003) Global civil society : an answer to war Polity Press, Cambridge, USA.

Kaldor, Mary (2007) Human security: reflections on globalization and intervention Polity Press, Cambridge.

Kaltwasser, C. et al. (2017) *The Oxford Handbook of Populism*, Oxford: Oxford University Press.

Kant, I. (ed. Reiss, tr. Nisbet, 1970) *Kant's Political Writings*, Cambridge: Cambridge University Press.

Katz, R. and Mair, P. (1995) 'Changing Models of Party Organization and Party Democracy: The Emergence of the Cartel Party' *Party Politics* (1): 5–28.

Kavanagh, D. (1990) *Thatcherism and British Politics: The End of Consensus?* Oxford: Oxford University Press.

Kavanagh, D. (2007) "The Emergence of an Embryonic Discipline: British Politics without Political Scientists," in Robert Adcock, Mark Bevir and Shannon C. Stimson, eds., Modern Political Science: Anglo-American Exchanges since 1880 (Princeton and Oxford: Princeton University Press), 97–117.

Kedourie, E. (1993) *Nationalism*, 4th ed. Oxford: Blackwell.

Kennedy, S. (2015) 'What's changed in European (Union) Studies?' *Journal of Contemporary European Research* 11 (2): 156–161.

Keohane, R. and Nye, J. (eds) (1971) *Transnational Relations and World Politics*, Cambridge: Harvard University Press.

Keohane, R. and Nye, J. ([1977] 3rd ed. 2000) *Power and Interdependence*, Boston: Little, Brown.

Keohane, R. (1989) 'International Relations Theory: Contributions of a Feminist Standpoint', *Millennium: Journal of International Studies* 18 (2): 245–253.

Kesselman, M. and Krieger, J. (2002) *European Politics in Transition*, Boston: Houghton Mifflin.

Kesselman, M., Krieger, J. and Joseph, W. A. (2000) *Introduction to Comparative Politics*, Boston: Houghton Mifflin.

Key, V. O. (1942) *Politics, Parties and Pressure Groups*, New York: Crowell.

Key, V. O. (1950) *Southern Politics in State and Nation*, New York: Knopf.

Key, V. O. ([1949] 1961) *Public Opinion and American Democracy*, New York: Knopf.

Key, V. O. (1966) *The Responsible Electorate: Rationality in Presidential Voting*, Cambridge: Harvard University Press.

Keynes, J. M. ([1936] 1964) *The General Theory of Employment, Interest and Money*, New York: Harcourt Brace and World.

King, A. (ed.) (1985) *The British Prime Minister*, London: Macmillan.

Kircheimer, O. (1966) 'The Transformation of the Western European Party Systems', in La Palombara, J. and Weiner, M., *Political Parties and Political Development*, Princeton: Princeton University Press.

Krasner, S. (ed.). (1983) *International Regimes*, Ithaca: Cornell University Press.

Kropotkin, P. (1902) *Mutual Aid*, London: Heinemann.

Kymlicka, W. (1990) *Contemporary Political Philosophy*, Oxford: Clarendon Press.

Kymlica, W. (1995) *Multicultural Citizenship*, Oxford: Oxford University Press.

Lamont, C. (2015) *Research Methods in International Relations*, London: Sage.

Lane, J.-E. and Ersson (1999) *Politics and Society in Western Europe*, 4th ed., London: Sage Publications.

Laslett, P. (ed.) (1956) *Philosophy, Politics and Society*, Oxford: Blackwell.

Lasswell, H. ([1936] 1958) *Politics: Who Gets What, When, How?* New York: Meridian.

Lazarsfeld, P.F. Berelson, B. and Gaudet, H. (1944) *The People's Choice*, New York: Columbia University Press.

Leach, R. (2015) *Political Ideology in Britain*, 3rd ed., London: Palgrave Macmillan.

Leff, G. (1958) *Medieval Political Thought*, Harmondsworth: Penguin.

Leftwich, A. (ed.) (2004) *What is Politics?* Cambridge: Polity Press.

Lenin, V. I. ([1902] ed. Service, 1988) *What Is To Be Done?* London: Penguin.

Lenin, V. I. ([1916] 1970) *Imperialism: The Highest Stage of Capitalism*, Moscow: Progress.

Lightfoot, S. (2015) 'Promoting Employability and Jobs Skills via the Political Science Curriculum' in Ishiyama, J., Miller, W. and Simon, E. (eds), *Handbook on Teaching and Learning in Political Science and International Relations*, Cheltenham: Edward Elgar.

Lijphart, A. (1967) *The Politics of Accommodation: Pluralism and Democracy in the Netherlands*, Berkeley: University of California Press.

Lijphart, A. (1977) *The Politics of Plural Societies: A Comparative Exploration*, Berkeley: University of California Press.

Lijphart, A. (1984) *Democracies: Patterns of Majoritarian and Consensual Government in Twenty-One Countries*, London: Yale University Press.

Lijphart, A. (1994) *Electoral Systems and Party Systems*, New Haven: Yale University Press.

Lijphart, A. (1999) *Patterns of Democracy: Government Forms and Performance in Thirty-Six Countries*, New Haven: Yale University Press.

Lindblom, C. (1959) 'The Science of Muddling Through', *Public Administration* 19 (2): 79–88.

Lindblom, C. (1977) *Politics and Markets*, New York: Basic Books.

Lindblom, C. (1979) 'Still Muddling, Not Yet Through', *Public Administration Review* 39 (6): 517–526.

Lindblom, C. (1980) *The Policy-Making Process*, 2nd ed., Englewood Cliffs: Prentice Hall.

Linklater, A. (2007) *Critical Theory and World Politics: Citizenship, Sovereignty and Humanity*, London: Routledge.

Lipset, S. ([1960] 1983) *Political Man: The Social Bases of Politics*, London and New York: Routledge.

Lipset, S. and Rokkan, S. (eds) (1967) *Party Systems and Voter Alignments*, New York and London: Free Press.

Lloyd, J. (2004) *What the Media Are Doing to Our Democracy*, London: Constable.

Lloyd-Jones, H. (ed.) (1965) *The Greek World*, Harmondsworth: Penguin.

Locke, J. ([1689] ed. Montuori, 1963) *A Letter Concerning Toleration*, The Hague: Martinus Nijhoff.

Locke, J. ([1690] ed. Barker, 1948) *The Second Treatise on Civil Government* (in *Social Contract*, ed. Barker), London: Oxford University Press.

Lovelock, J. (2007) *The Revenge of Gaia*, London: Penguin Books.

Lowndes, V., Marsh, D. and Stoker, G. (eds) (2018) *Theory and Methods in Political Science*, 4th ed., London: Palgrave.

Lukes, S. (1974) *Power: A Radical View*, Macmillan: London.

Lyotard, J.-F. ([1979] 1984) *The Postmodern Condition: A Report on Knowledge*, Manchester: Manchester University Press.

Machiavelli, N. ([1513ff] ed. and tr. Bondanella and Musa, 1979) *The Portable Machiavelli*, London: Penguin Books.

MacIntyre, A. (1981) *After Virtue*, London: Duckworth.

McKenzie, R. T. (1958) 'Parties, Pressure Groups and the British Political Process', *Political Quarterly* 29 (1).

McKenzie, R. T. (1963) *British Political Parties*, 2nd ed., London: Mercury Books.

MacKinnon, C. (1989) *Towards a Feminist Theory of the State*, London: Harvard University Press.

Mackintosh, J. (1962) *The British Cabinet*, London: Stevens.

McLean, I. and McMillan, A. (2009) *The Concise Oxford Dictionary of Politics*, 3rd ed., Oxford: Oxford University Press.

McLellan, D. (1979) *Karl Marx*, 2nd ed., London: Paladin.

McLellan, D. (1980) *Marxism after Marx*, London and Basingstoke: Macmillan.

McLellan, D. (1995) *Ideology*, 2nd ed., Buckingham: Open University Press.

McNair, B. (2003) *An Introduction to Political Communication*, London: Routledge.

Macpherson, C. B. (1962) *The Political Theory of Possessive Individualism*, Oxford: Oxford University Press.

McQuail, D. (1992) *Media Performance*, London: Sage.

Madison, J., Hamilton, A. and Jay, J. ([1787–1788] ed. Kramnick, 1987) *The Federalist Papers*, London: Penguin Books.

Mair, P. (1990) *The West European Party System*, Oxford: Oxford University Press.

Maloney, W. (2006) 'Political Participation beyond the Electoral Arena' in Dunleavy et al. (eds), *Developments in British Politics* 8, 98–116, Basingstoke: Palgrave Macmillan.

Mandela, N. (1995) *Long Walk to Freedom*, London: Abacus.

March, J. G. and Olsen, J. P. (1984) 'The new institutionalism: organisational factors in political life', *American Political Science Review* 78: 734–749.

March, J. G. and Olsen, J. P. (1989) *Rediscovering Institutions: The Organizational Basis of Politics*, New York: The Free Press.

Marcuse, H. (1964)) *One Dimensional Man*, London: Routledge and Kegan Paul.

Margetts, H. (2002) 'Political Participation and Protest', in Dunleavy et al. *Developments in British Politics*, 6A, Basingstoke: Palgrave Macmillan.

Marx, K. ([1840s] ed. Coletti, 1975) *Early Writings*, Harmondsworth: Penguin.

Marx, K. and Engels, F. (ed. Feuer, 1959) *Basic Writings on Politics and Philosophy*, New York: Anchor Books, Doubleday.

Michels, R. ([1911] 1962) *Political Parties*, New York: Free Press.

Miliband, R. (1969) *The State in Capitalist Society*, London: Weidenfeld and Nicolson.

Miliband, R. ([1963] 1972) *Parliamentary Socialism*, 2nd ed., London: Merlin Press.

Miliband, R. ([1969] 1973) *The State in Capitalist Society*, London: Quartet Books.

Mill, J. S. ([1859–1861] ed. Acton, 1972) *Utilitarianism, On Liberty, Considerations on Representative Government*, London: Dent.

Mill, J. S. ([1869] ed. Okin, 1988) *The Subjection of Women*, Indianapolis: Hackett Publishing Company.

Mill, J. S. ([1873] ed. Robson, 1989) *An Autobiography*, Harmondsworth: Penguin.

Mill, J. S. and Bentham, J. (ed. Ryan, 1987) *Utilitarianism and Other Essays*, Harmondsworth: Penguin.

Miller, D. et al. (eds) (1991, revised edition) *The Blackwell Encyclopaedia of Political Thought*, Oxford: Blackwell.

Millett, K. ([1970] 1985) *Sexual Politics*, London: Virago.

Mills, C. Wright (1956) *The Power Elite*, Oxford: Oxford University Press.

Milner, H. and Tingley, D. (2015) *Sailing the Water's Edge: The Domestic Politics of American Foreign Policy*, Princeton: Princeton University Press.

Mintz, A. and DeRouen, K. (2010) *Understanding Foreign Policy Decision-Making*, Cambridge: Cambridge University Press.

Mishra, R. (1999) *Globalization and the Welfare State*, Cheltenham: Elgar.

Montesquieu, C.-L. de S. ([1748] ed. Neuman, tr. Nugent, 1949) *The Spirit of the Laws*, New York: Hafner.

Morgenthau, H. J. ([1948] 1978) *Politics among Nations: The Struggle for Power and Peace*, 5th ed., New York: Alfred P. Knopf.

Morrow, J. (2005) *History of Western Political Thought: A Thematic Introduction*, Basingstoke: Palgrave Macmillan.

Mosca, G. ([1896] tr. Livingston, 1939) *The Ruling Class*, New York: McGraw Hill.

Moses, J. and Knutsen, T. (2012) *Ways of Knowing: Competing Methodologies in Social and Political Research*, 2nd ed. Basingstoke: Palgrave Macmillan.

Naess, A. (1989) *Ecology, Community and Lifestyle*, Cambridge: Cambridge University Press.

Neustadt, R. (1960) *Presidential Power*, New York: Wiley and Sons.

Neustadt, R. (1991) *Presidential Power and the Modern Presidents*, New York: Free Press.

Nietzsche, F. W. ([1883–1889] ed. and tr. Kaufmann, 1968) *The Portable Nietzsche*, New York: Viking.

Niskanen, W. A. (1971) *Bureaucracy and Representative Government*, Chicago: Aldine-Atherton.

Nozick, R. (1974) *Anarchy, State and Utopia*, Oxford: Blackwell.

Nye, J. (1990) 'Soft Power', *Foreign Policy* 80.

Oakeshott, M. (1962) *Rationalism in Politics and Other Essays*, London: Methuen.

O'Brien, R. and Williams, M. (2004) *Global Political Economy: Evolution and Dynamics*, Basingstoke: Palgrave Macmillan.

Ohmae, K. (1990) *The Borderless World: Power and Strategy in the Interlinked Economy*, New York: Harper Collins.

Ohmae, K. (1996) *The End of the Nation State*, London: Harper Collins.

Olson, M. ([1965] 1971) *The Logic of Collective Action: Public Goods and the Theory of Groups*, New York: Shocken Books.

Onora O'Neill, (2002) 'A Question of Trust. The BBC Reith Lectures 2002' Cambridge University Press.

Osborne, D. and Gaebler, T. (1992) *Reinventing Government*, Reading: Addison-Wesley.

Ostrogorski, M. I. ([1902] ed. Lipset 1964) *Democracy and the Organisation of Political Parties*, New York: Doubleday.

Paine, T. ([1772–1805] ed. Foot and Kramnick, 1987) *The Thomas Paine Reader*, Harmondsworth: Penguin.

Panebianco, A. (1988) *Political Parties: Organization and Power*, Cambridge: Cambridge University Press.

Parekh, B. (2000) *Rethinking Multiculturalism: Cultural Diversity and Political Theory*, Basingstoke: Palgrave Macmillan.

Parkin, F. (1971) *Class, Inequality and Political Order*, London: Paladin.

Parsons, T. (1937) *The Structure of Social Action*, Glencoe: Free Press.

Parsons, T. (1951) *The Social System*, New York: Free Press.

Parsons, W. (1995) *Public Policy: Introduction to the Theory and Practice of Policy Analysis*, Aldershot: Edward Elgar.

Pateman, C. (1970) *Participation and Democratic Theory*, Cambridge: Cambridge University Press.

Pateman, C. (1988) *The Sexual Contract*, Cambridge: Polity Press.

Peters, B. G. (1997) 'Shouldn't Row, Can't Steer: What's a Government to Do?' *Public Administration and Policy* 12 (2).

Peters, B. G. (1998) *Comparative Politics: Theory and Methods*, Basingstoke: Palgrave Macmillan.

Piketty, T. (2014) *Capital in the Twenty-First Century*, Cambridge: Cambridge University Press.

Piketty, T. (tr. Goldhamer, 2014) *Capital in the Twenty-First Century*, Belknap: Harvard.

Plant, R. (1991) *Modern Political Thought*, Oxford, Blackwell.

Plato ([c. 404–394 BCE] tr. Tredennick and Tarrant, 1993) *The Last Days of Socrates (Euthyphro, Apology, Crito, Phaedo)*, Harmondsworth: Penguin.

Plato ([c. 388–387 BCE] tr. Hamilton, 1971) *Gorgias*, Harmondsworth: Penguin.

Plato ([c. 390–385 BCE] tr. Guthrie, 1956) *Protagoras and Meno,* Harmondsworth: Penguin.

Plato ([c. 386–380 BCE] tr. Lee, 1955) *The Republic*, Harmondsworth: Penguin.

Plato ([c. 350–347 BCE] tr. Saunders, 1970) *The Laws*, Harmondsworth: Penguin.

Politics (2015) 'The Soft Power of Hard States', Special Issue 35 (3–4).

Polsby, N. (1963) *Community Power and Political Theory*, New Haven: Yale University Press.

Popper, K. R. ([1934] 1959) *The Logic of Scientific Discovery*, London: Hutchinson.

Popper, K. R. ([1945] 1962) *The Open Society and Its Enemies*, 2 vols., London: Routledge and Kegan Paul.

Popper, K. R. (1957) *The Poverty of Historicism*, London: Routledge and Kegan Paul.

Poulantzas, N. (1968) *Political Power and Social Classes,* London: New Left Books.

Poulantzas, N. (1976) 'The Capitalist State: A Reply to Miliband and Laclan', *New Left Review* 95.

Pressman, J. and Wildavsky, A. (1973) *Implementation*, Berkeley: University of California Press.

Przeworski, A. (1991) *Democracy and the Market: Political and Economic Reforms in Eastern Europe and Latin America*, Cambridge: Cambridge University Press.

PSA (nd), *Study Politics: A short guide to studying politics at university in the UK*, available at http://www.psa.ac.uk/sites/default/files/12552_PSA_SP_20pp%20v3.pdf (accessed 22/11/17).

Pulzer, P. (1967) *Representation and Elections in Britain*, London: Allen and Unwin.

Putnam, R. D. (1973) *The Beliefs of Politicians: Ideology, Conflict and Democracy in Britain and Italy*, New Haven: Yale University Press.

Putnam, R. D. (1976) *The Comparative Study of Political Elites*, Englewood Cliffs: Prentice Hall.

Putnam, R. D. (1988) 'Diplomacy and Domestic Politics: The Logic of Two-Level Games', *International Organization* 42 (3): 427–460.

Putnam, R. D. (1993) *Making Democracy Work: Civic Traditions in Modern Italy,* Princeton: Princeton University Press.

Putnam, R. D. (1995) 'Bowling Alone: America's Declining Social Capital', *Journal of Democracy* 6: 65–78.

Putnam, R. D. (2000) *Bowling Alone: The Collapse and Revival of American Community,* New York: Simon and Schuster.

Putnam, R. D. (ed.) (2002) *Democracies in Flux: the Evolution of Social Capital in Contemporary Society,* New York and Oxford: Oxford University Press.

Ralph, J. and Gallagher, A. (2015) 'Legitimacy Faultlines in International Society: The Responsibility to Protect and Prosecute after Libya', *Review of International Studies* 41 (3): 553–573.

Rawls, J. (1971) *A Theory of Justice*, Oxford: Oxford University Press.

Rawls, J. (1993) *Political Liberalism*, New York: Columbia University Press.

Rawls, J. (1999) *The Law of Peoples*, Cambridge: Harvard University Press.

Rhodes, R. A. W. (1997) *Understanding Governance,* Buckingham: Open University Press.

Richardson, J. J. and Jordan, A. G. (1979) *Governing under Pressure: The Policy Process in a Post-Parliamentary Democracy*, Oxford: Martin Robertson.

Robertson, D. (1993) *The Penguin Dictionary of Politics*, London: Penguin Books.

Robson, W.A. (1928) *Justice and Administrative Law*, London: Macmillan.

Robson, W. A. (1948) *The Development of Local Government*, 2nd ed., London: Allen and Unwin.

Robson, W. A. (1960) *Nationalised Industries and Public Ownership*, London: Allen and Unwin.

Rose, J. (2017) 'Brexit, Trump, and Post-Truth Politics', *Public Integrity* 0: 1–4.

Rose, R. (1988) *The Post-Modern President,* Chatham: Chatham House.

Rosen, M. and Wolff, J. (eds) (1999) *Political Thought,* Oxford: Oxford University Press.

Rotberg, R. I. (2002) 'Failed States in a World of Terror', *Foreign Affairs* 81 (4): 127–140.

Rousseau, J.-J. ([1755] tr. Cranston, 1984) *A Discourse on Inequality*, London: Penguin.

Rousseau, J.-J. ([1762] ed. Barker, 1947) *The Social Contract,* London: Oxford University Press.

Rowley, C. and Shepherd, L. J. (2012) 'Contemporary Politics: Using the "F" Word and Teaching Gender in International Relations' in Gormley-Heenan C., and Lightfoot S. (eds), *Teaching Politics and International Relations*, London: Palgrave Macmillan: 146–161.

Ruggie, J. G. (1998) 'What Makes the World Hang Together? Neo-utilitarianism and the Social Constructivist Challenge', *International Organization* 52 (4): 855–885.

Sabine, G. H. (1951) *A History of Political Theory*, 3rd ed., London: Harrap.

Said, E. (1978) *Orientalism: Western Conceptions of the Orient*, New York: Vintage Books.

Said, E. (2001) 'The Clash of Ignorance', *The Nation*, October 22.

Sandel, M. (1982) *Liberalism and the Limits of Justice*, Cambridge: Cambridge University Press.

Sartori, G. (1976) *Parties and Party Systems: A Framework for Analysis*, Cambridge: Cambridge University Press.

Sartori, G. (1987) *The Theory of Democracy Revisited,* Chatham: Chatham House.

Savigny, H. and Marsden, L. (2011) *Doing Political Science and International Relations*, London: Palgrave.

Schattschneider, E. E. (1960) *The Semi-Sovereign People: A Realist's View of Democracy in America*, New York: Holt, Rinehart and Winston.

Schlesinger, A. (1973) *The Imperial Presidency*, Boston: Houghton.

Schmidt, B. (1998) 'Lessons from the Past: Reassessing the Interwar Disciplinary History of International Relations', *International Studies Quarterly* 42 (3).

Schmitter, P. C. (1979) 'Still the Century of Corporatism?' in Schmitter and Lehmbruch (eds), *Trends Towards Corporatist Intermediation,* Sage.

Scholte, J. A. (2005) *Globalization: A Critical Introduction*, 2nd ed., Basingstoke: Palgrave Macmillan.

Schumacher, E. (1976) *Small Is Beautiful*, London: Sphere.

Schumpeter, J. (1943) *Capitalism, Socialism and Democracy*, London: Allen and Unwin.

Scruton, R. (2007) *A Dictionary of Political Thought*, 3rd ed., Basingstoke: Palgrave Macmillan.

Self, P. (1993) *Government by the Market? The Politics of Public Choice*, Basingstoke: Palgrave Macmillan.

Seyd, P. (1987) *The Rise and Fall of the Labour Left*, Basingstoke: Palgrave Macmillan.

Simon, H. A. (1947) *Administrative Behaviour*, Glencoe: Free Press.

Sinclair, T. A. (1967) *A History of Greek Political Thought,* London: Routledge and Kegan Paul.

Singer, P. (1972) 'Famine, Affluence and Morality', *Philosophy and Public Affairs* (1): 229–235.

Singer, P. (1975) *Animal Liberation: A New Ethics for the Treatment of Animals*, New York: Random House.

Singer, P. (1979) *Practical Ethics*, Cambridge: Cambridge University Press.

Skocpol, T. (1979) *States and Social Revolutions*, Cambridge: Cambridge University Press.

Skocpol, T. (1996) 'Unravelling from Above', *The American Prospect* March/April.

Smith, A. ([1759] 1976) *The Theory of Moral Sentiments*, Oxford: Clarendon.

Smith, A. ([1776] ed. Cannan, 1976) *The Wealth of Nations*, Chicago: University of Chicago Press.

Sokal, A. and Bricmont, J. (1998) Intellectual Impostures, London: Profile Books.

Spencer, H. ([1884] ed. Mack, 1981) *The Man versus the State*, Indianapolis: Liberty Classics.

Spender, D. (1985) *Man Made Language*, London: Routledge and Kegan Paul.

Steans, J. (1998) *Gender in International Relations: An Introduction*, Cambridge: Polity Press.

Steans, J. (2003) 'Engaging from the Margins: Feminist Encounters with the Mainstream of International Relations', *British Journal of Politics and International Relations* 5 (3): 428–454.

Stoker, G. (2017) *Why Politics Matters: Making Democracy Work*, 2nd ed., Basingstoke: Palgrave Macmillan.

Stoker, G., Peters, B. G. and Pierre, J. (eds) (2015) *The Relevance of Political Science*, London: Palgrave Macmillan.

Strange, S. (1986) *Casino Capitalism*, Oxford: Basil Blackwell.

Strange, S. (1996) *The Retreat of the State*, Cambridge: Cambridge University Press.

Strange, S. (1998) *Mad Money*, Manchester: Manchester University Press.

Strange, S. (1999). 'The Westfailure system', *Review of International Studies* 25 (3): 345–354.

Street, J. (2001) *Mass Media, Politics and Democracy*, Basingstoke: Palgrave Macmillan.

Suiter, J. (2016) 'Post-truth Politics', *Political Insight* December.

Sumner, A. and Mallet, R. (2013) *The Future of Foreign Aid: Development Cooperation and the New Geography of Global Poverty,* London: Palgrave Macmillan.

Sunstein, C. (2001) *Republic.com*, Princeton: Princeton University Press.

Sylvester, C (2002) *Feminist International Relations Theory: An Unfinished Journey*, Cambridge: Cambridge University Press.

Tansey, S. D. (2004) *Politics: The Basics*, 3rd ed., London: Routledge.

Tarrow, S. (1998) *Power in Movement: Social Movements and Contentious Politics*, Cambridge and New York: Cambridge University Press.

Tawney, R. H. ([1921] 1961) *The Acquisitive Society*, London: Fontana.

Tawney, R. H. ([1926] 1938) *Religion and the Rise of Capitalism*, Harmondsworth: Penguin.

Tawney, R. H. ([1931] 1964) *Equality*, London: Unwin.

Taylor, C. (1990) *Sources of the Self*, Cambridge: Cambridge University Press.

Teeple, G. (1995) *Globalization and the Decline of Social Reform*, Atlantic Highlands: Humanities Press.

Thoreau, H. D. ([1854] 1980) *Walden and On the Duty of Civil Disobedience*, New York: New American Library.

Thucydides ([c. 460–400 BCE] tr. R. Warner, 1972) *History of the Peloponnesian War*, Harmondsworth: Penguin.

Tickner, A. (1997) '"You Just Don't Understand": Troubled Engagements between Feminists and IR Theorists', *International Studies Quarterly* 41.

Tickner, A. and Sjoberg, L. (eds) (2011) *Feminism and International Relations: Conversations about the Past, Present and Future*, London: New York: Routledge.

Tocqueville, A. de ([1835, 1840] tr. Bevan, intro. Kramnick, 2003) *Democracy in America*, London: Penguin Books.

Tocqueville, A. de ([1856] tr. Patterson, 1947) *The Old Regime and the French Revolution*, Oxford: Blackwell.

Trotsky, L. (tr. Eastman, 1937) *The Revolution Betrayed*, London: Faber and Faber.

Truman, D. (1951) *The Governmental Process*, New York: Alfred Knopf.

Tullock, G. (1965) *The Politics of Bureaucracy*, Boston: University Press of America.

Tullock, G. (1998) *On Voting: A Public Choice Approach*, Aldershot: Edward Elgar.

UNDP (2015) *The Millennium Development Goals Report*, New York: United Nations.

Van Belle, D. (2015) *A Novel Approach to Politics; Introducing Political Science through Books, Movies, and Popular Culture*, Washington: CQ Press.

Voltaire, F.-M. A. ([1759] tr. Butt, 1970) *Candide*, Harmondsworth: Penguin.

Wæver, O. (1998) 'The Sociology of a Not So International Discipline: American and European Developments in International Relations' *International Organization* 52 (4).

Wallerstein, I. (2004). *World-Systems Analysis: An Introduction*, Durham: Duke University Press.

Walter, N. (1999) *The New Feminism*, London: Virago.

Waltz, K. (1979) *Theory of International Politics*, Reading: Addison-Wesley.

Walzer, M. (1983) *Spheres of Justice*, New York: Basic Books.

Walzer, M. (2000) *Just and Unjust Wars*, 3rd ed., New York: Perseus.

Waters, M. (2000) *Globalization*, London and New York: Routledge.

Weber, C. (1994), 'Good Girls, Little Girls and Bad Girls: Male Paranoia in Robert Keohane's Critique of Feminist International Relations', *Millennium: Journal of International Relations* 23.

Weber, C. (2014) *International Relations Theory: A Critical Introduction*, 4th ed., London: Routledge.

Weber, M. ([1904] 1930) *The Protestant Ethic and the Spirit of Capitalism*, London: Allen and Unwin.

Weber, M. (tr. Gerth and Mills, 1948) *From Max Weber: Essays in Sociology*, London: Routledge and Kegan Paul.

Weber, M. ([1922] ed. Roth and Wittich, tr. Fischoff, 1978) *Economy and Society*, Berkeley: University of California.

Weber, M. (ed. Runciman, tr. Matthews, 1978) *Selections in Translation*, Cambridge: Cambridge University Press.

Wendt, A. (1987) 'The Agent/Structure Problem in International Relations Theory', *International Organization* 41: 335–370.

Wendt, A. (1992) 'Anarchy Is What States Make of It: The Social Construction of Power Politics', *International Organization* 46: 391–426.

Wendt, A. (1999) *Social Theory of International Politics*, Cambridge: Cambridge University Press.

Wendt, A. (2003) 'Why a World State Is Inevitable', *European Journal of International Relations* 9 (4).

Wheeler, N. (2001) *Saving Strangers: Humanitarian Intervention in International Society*, Oxford: Oxford University Press.

Wildavsky, A. (1980) *The Art and Craft of Policy Analysis*, London: Macmillan.

Williams, R. (1976) *Keywords*, Glasgow: Fontana.

Wolff, J. (2015) *An Introduction to Political Philosophy*, 3rd ed., Oxford: Oxford University Press.

Wollstonecraft, M. ([1790] 2008) *A Vindication of the Rights of Men*, Oxford: Oxford World's Classics.

Wollstonecraft, M. ([1792] 1985) *A Vindication of the Rights of Women*, Harmondsworth: Penguin.

INDEX

Note:
Page numbers shown in **bold** type refer to specific relevant entries in Part IV (key concepts) and Part V (key thinkers).

community   6, 7, 11–13, 33, 56, 65, 67, 70, 80,
   81, 98, 113, **186**, **188–90**, **199**, **206**, **212**, **219**,
   224, **228**, **229**, **236**, **237**, **240**, **244**, **249**, **251**,
   254, **256**, **261**, **262**, **264**, **267**, **282**, **285**, **286**,
   288, **289**, **293**, **296**
community power   **224**, **256**
comparative politics   40, 50, 51, 52, 54–5, 84, 85,
   88, 116, 118, 125, 126, 130–2, **190**, **236**, **249**,
   250, **288**, **289**
Comte, Auguste   **226**, **256**, **278**
Congress Party (India)   58
consensus   12–13, 45, 55, 68–9, 80, 96, **185**,
   190, **193**, **207**, **221**, **238**, **252**, **254**, **263**, **268**,
   271, **283**, **287**
consent   9, 30, 31, 35, 38, 74, 102, **190–1**,
   205, **223**, **240**, **254**, **261**, **262**, **266**, **267**,
   271–2
conservatism   130, **191**, **207**, **209**, **215**, **222**, **242**,
   254, **260**, **263**, **266**, **274**, **281**, **284**
Conservative Party (UK)   **221**, **222**, **282**
consociation   68, **271**
constitution   5, 28, 29, 31, 33, 37, 60, 64, 73,
   166, **191–2**, **200**, **201**, **209**, **211**, **227**, **229**,
   236, **237**, **251**, **255**, **256**, **261**, **263**, **266**, **272**,
   274, **279**, **293**, **295**, **297**
constitutional amendment   **192**
constitutional government   35, **205**
constitutional monarchy   30, 40
constitutional reform   **191**, **192**, **215**
constructivism   97, 100, 164, **192–3**, **226**
consumerism   **218**
convention   5, 14, 27, 38, 77, 78, 80, 82, 114,
   184, **187**, **192**, **207**, **214**, **220**, **221**, **236**, **250**,
   265, **274**, **280**, **283**, **289**
cooperation   **184**
co-operative movement   **283**
Copenhagen School   99
corporatism   66, **193**, **200**, **224**
corruption   125, **193**
Countryside Alliance (UK)
Cox, Robert   102, 165, 166, **205**, **210**, **256**
Crick, Bernard   13, 52, 81
critical thinking   137–8, 139, 141, 144, 149, 155
Crosland, Anthony   **256**
crusades   26
Cuba   97, 99, 105
cultural norms   81
culture
   See political culture
curriculum vitae (CV)   172, 174, 176

D

Dahl, Robert   8, 10, 64–7, 126, **195**, **222**, **224**,
   228, **256–7**, **271**
Dahrendorf, Ralf   **236**, **238**
de Beauvoir, Simone   83, **257**, **290**
decentralisation   73, **194**, **205**, **290**, **293**
Declaration of the Rights of Man (1789)   14, 31–3,
   236, **267**, **297**
decolonisation   48
deconstruction   82, 102, **227**, **257**
delegate/delegation   **196**, **205**, **216**, **234**, **255**,
   261, **267**
democracy
   Asian democracy   91, 117
   Athenian democracy   22–3, **194**, **284**, **285**, **291**,
      293
   'bourgeois' democracy   39, 41, 42, **270**
   consociational (or consensual) democracy   68
   cosmopolitan (or global) democracy   111,
      204, **267**
   direct (or participatory) democracy   36, **194–5**,
      234
   illiberal democracy   52, 58, 117, **195**
   'peoples' (or 'proletarian') democracy   39, 42,
      270
   representative democracy   5, 9, 22, 30, 31,
      36–9, 41, 42, 44, 45, 50, 55, 56, 59, 60, 69,
      71, 94, 117, **184**, **185**, **191**, **194–5**, **215**, **223**,
      225, **234**, **238**, **240**, **243**, **250**, **253**, **278**, **279**,
      282, **284**, **288**, **290**, **296**
democratisation   37, 45, 52, 117, **194**, **195**, **266**
Demosthenes   21
Derrida, Jacques   82, 102, **227**, **257**, **262**
Descartes, René   29
despotism
   See dictators/dictatorship
Deutsch, Karl   33, **257**
devolution   **194**, **196**, **239**
dialectic   **218**, **259**, **264**, **276**
dictators/dictatorship   9, 13, 15, 20, 25, 39, 41,
   42, 45, 52, 54, 58, 117, **189**, **190–3**, **196**, **200**,
   211, **217**, **218**, **219**, **225**, **234**, **243**, **251**, **262**,
   270, **277**, **285**, **286**, **289**, **292**, **294**
dictatorship of the proletariat   41, **196**, **251**, **270**, **277**
dissertation   152, 154, 155, 164, 167
Douglas, Mary   152
Downs, Anthony   62, 74–6, 164, **222**, **252**,
   257–8
Dror, Yehezkal   **209**
Dunleavy, Patrick   66, 75, 76, 136, 153, 161,
   232, **281**